C. Blan
2/4/92

REPRINTS OF ECONOMIC CLASSICS

THE PRESENT STATE OF ENGLAND

THE

PRESENT STATE

OF

ENGLAND

IN REGARD TO

AGRICULTURE, TRADE & FINANCE

BY

JOSEPH LOWE

[1823]

REPRINTS OF ECONOMIC CLASSICS

AUGUSTUS M. KELLEY · PUBLISHERS
NEW YORK · 1967

First Edition 1822
Second Edition 1823

(London: *Printed for* Longman, Hurst, Rees, Orme
& Brown, *Paternoster Row;* J. Richardson, *91,
Royal Exchange;* and Messers Constable & Co.,
Edinburgh, 1823)

Reprinted 1967 by
AUGUSTUS M. KELLEY PUBLISHERS

PRINTED IN THE UNITED STATES OF AMERICA
by SENTRY PRESS, NEW YORK, N. Y. 10019

THE

PRESENT STATE

OF

Englanð

IN REGARD TO

AGRICULTURE, TRADE, AND FINANCE;

WITH

A COMPARISON OF THE PROSPECTS OF

ENGLAND AND FRANCE.

BY JOSEPH LOWE, Esq.

Seconð Eðition,

WITH VARIOUS ADDITIONS AND EMENDATIONS.

LONDON:

PRINTED FOR LONGMAN, HURST, REES, ORME, AND BROWN,
PATERNOSTER-ROW;
J. RICHARDSON, 91. ROYAL EXCHANGE;
AND MESSRS. CONSTABLE AND CO., EDINBURGH.

1823.

TO

WILLIAM MANNING, Esǫ.M.P,

AND A DIRECTOR OF THE BANK OF ENGLAND,

THIS VOLUME,

APPROPRIATED TO

OBJECTS INTIMATELY CONNECTED WITH

THOSE OF HIS PUBLIC LIFE,

IS INSCRIBED,

WITH SENTIMENTS OF THE GREATEST REGARD,

BY

THE AUTHOR.

ADVERTISEMENT

TO

THE SECOND EDITION.

In preparing this Edition, the whole volume has been revised with a care proportioned to the importance of the subjects, and a considerable portion of additional matter has been inserted. The result of this will be apparent in several of the tables, as well as in the reasoning on the following topics : —

The Sources of our Financial Supplies during the War.

The Causes of the general rise of Prices in that Period.

The Question of Depreciation and Over-issue.

The Effect of the War on Property, individual and national.

The Connexion between Increase of Population, and Increase of Wealth ; and

The Views of Finance adapted to our present Situation.

INTRODUCTION.

No subject can present a higher interest than an enquiry into the state and prospects of the productive industry of England. Whatever tends to correct error, or introduce improvement into the operation of that industry, must affect the comfort of so large a population, that no research, bestowed on such a subject, can be accounted too minute, no labour too long.

Fruitful as has been the present age in changes, military and political, there has occurred an almost equal degree of revolution in the value of money and the productive power of labour and capital, departments in general so tranquil as hardly to attract the notice of the historian. Those of our readers who are of an age to recollect the peace of 1783, cannot have forgotten the general discouragement caused by the relinquishment of our American Colonies, followed as it was by a season of great financial difficulty. They will remember with more satisfaction the revival of our commercial activity in the years preceding the French Revolution, and the discussions whether we were indebted for so beneficial a change to the natural course of circumstances or the conduct of Mr. Pitt. This was followed by the war with France — a period subversive of all previous calculation in finance, since, after experiencing pecuniary difficulty during a few years, our resources appeared to expand with our wants, and continued so long abundant, that we had no little difficulty in anticipating the possibility of a recurrence of embarrassment.

That which took place at the close of the war (1815 and 1816) was altogether unexpected, and the public, accounting pecuniary straits incompatible with our brilliant success in the field, clung to the expectation that their distress would disappear as soon as peace should be firmly established. This hope was confirmed by the revival of our commercial activity in 1817 and 1818, but the succeeding years dispelled the illusion, and taught us that the evils of transition were not yet at an end.

During the last and present year circumstances have become more favourable, and our lower orders, in particular, enjoy a larger share of comfort than they have known for a long period. Still it might be going too far, were we to flatter ourselves that ·our embarrassments had reached their close. The unfortunate coincidence between the relief of the consumer and the distress of the producer of corn, joined to the portion of uncertainty always attendant on a commerce of export, convey a warning that a season of difficulty must yet elapse, ere our circumstances become thoroughly adapted to our new and more natural state. There exists in some branches a want of employment; in others, a remarkable disproportion in the rate of wages and salaries to the earnings of the employer;—the whole affording a painful lesson how little either the public or our rulers foresaw the consequence of lavish expenditure, and how few among those who undertook to enlighten them, either in parliament, or through the medium of the press, were acquainted with the circumstances of former periods of transition from war to peace.

To elucidate, by a careful survey of facts and documents, the obscurities of the past, and to offer suggestions which may perhaps tend to facilitate our transition to a more safe and steady state of things, is the object of this volume. We shall begin by endeavouring to account for our financial prosperity during the war, and to explain the causes of the reverse that followed the peace. No one has yet attempted to show how far our increase of wealth during the war was real, and how far nominal—a distinction, which, if subversive of a part of the flattering picture with which we gratified our imagination during our long contest, has the consoling accompaniment, that the decrease of our wealth since the peace will be found, by following up a similar reasoning, to be far less than is commonly apprehended.

This enquiry will be necessarily connected with researches into the intricate topics of Money and Exchange. How far did the substitution of paper for metallic currency prove an addition to our resources? At what period did that hazardous

experiment cease to afford relief, or become productive of loss? And do not the public at present
labour under a general misapprehension in regard
to the effect of the resumption of cash payments,
attributing to the act of 1819, commonly called
Mr. Peel's Bill, that fall of prices, that recovery
of the value of money which ought to be traced to
a more powerful cause?

Our next topic shall be the state of our Agriculture, and the causes of the distress that has
assailed this, the most flourishing during the war
of all the branches of our industry. Here also, the
attentive observer will find much miscalculation to
correct and misapprehension to remove. In attempting this we shall draw a comparison of the
charges attendant on British and Continental agriculture, and venture on the more difficult enquiry
how far our produce is likely to continue at its
present rate; also how far a low price of corn is or
is not conducive to the extension of our productive
industry.

A more cheering theme will be opened to us by
the increase of our population, the adequacy of our
produce to its support, and the refutation of the
discouraging theories circulated on this subject
during the war. An intimate connexion evidently
prevails between increase of numbers and increase
of wealth; particularly in a town population,
among whom labour is subdivided, and the possession of capital gives assurance of profitable employment.

These and similar topics will occupy the greater
part of our volume: the remainder shall be appro-

priated to the discussion of propositions for the relief of our suffering classes, founded on the evident tendency of our resources to increase.

To objects such as these any attachment to party politics would evidently be unsuited. A writer thoroughly impressed with the importance of his subject, and animated by the hope of rendering service to his countrymen, will consider as a secondary object the notice either of men in office or their opponents. While he speaks with commendation of measures, which bear the stamp of good intention or laborious exertion, he will animadvert without reserve on such as are indicative of hasty or imperfect views. It is on this ground, far more than on deficiency of zeal for the general good, that our public men are vulnerable. " In retirement," said an eminent public character, " I became sensible, that, when in place, I had been deficient in almost every thing but diligence." * The functions of our heads of office are often ill distributed: the assistance afforded to them in the higher and more difficult departments is apparently very imperfect; and their minds, engaged from day to day in devising expedients to meet a temporary urgency, become less and less accustomed to long-continued reflection on one subject, and to the conclusions for which such reflection is indispensable. Without an admission of this nature, how can we account for their delaying so long the adoption of a decisive course in regard to Ireland ;

* Huskisson on the Bullion Question, 1810.

or, their postponing in this country, till the eighth year after the war, the financial measures which were called for by a state of peace?

An equal disposition to impartiality will, it is hoped, be traced when we carry our views abroad, and speak either of that nation which hereditary feeling still represents as our rival in Europe, or of that which contests of recent date have brought forward as our opponent on the farther shore of the Atlantic. A personal residence of several years in France has given the author occasion to mark the national character, to study the political resources, to calculate the prospective power of our once-dreaded neighbour. It has satisfied him that though France is still the greatest of continental states, yet that England may soon dismiss the apprehensions entertained by our forefathers, and rest tranquil in the assurance of the more rapid increase of her population, wealth, and power. May we not add, that these views receive confirmation from the conduct of our rulers, who, when France was in a manner at the disposal of this country and of allies ready to join in any project of partition, accounted it impolitic either to weaken her frontiers by the retention of fortresses, or to cripple her trade by the imposition of restrictions? How different then our present situation, from that of former years, when we were obliged to seek security in foreign alliances, and to postpone the correction of domestic abuses from a dread of exciting discontent! The most sincere well-wisher to his country may now speak with freedom of past transactions, viewing them merely as historical facts, — as events which, though not remote in date, may be boldly scrutinized without any prejudicial effect on our present situation.

The disposition of the public is fortunately in coincidence with this state of things. During the war events followed in too quick succession to admit of deliberate reflection, or to afford a basis for instructive conclusions : — all was absorbed in the bustle of action, in an expectation of change. At present the public may be compared to those who, retired from active life, pass their transactions in review with the advantage of leisure and experience, — a situation far more favourable than the ardour of a contest, for appreciating both the extent of our sacrifices, and the results of which they have been productive.

In attempting to elucidate these, we shall proceed with a scrupulous reference to facts and documents : but though such details must necessarily form the body of the book, we shall hope to introduce, occasionally, considerations of a higher kind. Those who, from their time of life, have been enabled to follow the course of occurrences since the early part of the French revolution, have witnessed an age of vicissitude, a succession of events which, whether military or political, were often ill calculated to favour the belief that justice and moderation form the true basis of national prosperity. But time alone was wanting to complete the evidence and assert the truth of that doctrine. The triumph of military usurpation was arrested in the wilds of Russia, and received its overthrow in the plains of Flanders. Since then our southern neighbours have been awakened from their dream of continental dominion. We, without having trespassed equally in point of aggression, had also our exclusive creed; — our system of vigour; our jealousy of neutrals; our notion that war was a source of national wealth. How far these impressions have been corrected by recent events, by our experience during the years that have elapsed since the peace, will remain to be explained in the following pages.

CONTENTS.

CHAPTER I.

Events of the War viewed in Connexion with our National Resources.

CHAPTER II.

Magnitude of our Expenditure and Sources of our Financial Supplies.

CHAPTER III.

General Rise of Prices during the War.

CHAPTER IV.

Our Currency and Exchanges since 1792.

CHAPTER V.

Our Agriculture.

Section I.

Historical Sketch.

Section II.

Situation and Prospects of our Agriculturists.

CHAPTER VII.

Population.

CHAPTER VIII.

On the National Revenue and Capital.

CHAPTER IX.

Effect of the War on Property, Individual and National.

CHAPTER X.

Value of Money.

Section I.

Fluctuations in the Value of Money.

Section II.

Plan for lessening the Injury from Fluctuation, and giving a uniform Value to Money Incomes.

CHAPTER XI.

Our Finances.

SECTION II.

Our Prospects in Commerce and Finance.

SECTION III.

Views of Finance suggested by our Situation and Prospects.

CONTENTS OF THE APPENDIX.

CHAPTER II.

The late Wars.

CHAPTER III.

Rise of Prices during the War.

CHAPTER IV.

Currency and Exchange.

CHAPTER V.

Our Agriculture.

CHAPTER VI.

Our Poor-rate.

CHAPTER VII.

Population.

CHAPTER VIII.

Our National Revenue.

CHAPTER X.

Fluctuations in Money.

CHAPTER XI.

CHAPTER I.

Events of the War viewed in Connection with our National Resources.

In appropriating a portion of our volume to military events, our object is to direct the reader's attention to the effects produced by them on our finances and national industry:—to enlarge on the occurrences of a campaign or on the policy of cabinets, would be, in a great measure, foreign to our purpose. In some respects, however, the two departments of enquiry are connected, the effect of our military operations having been repeatedly felt by our exchequer, and requiring of course frequent notice in the subsequent pages. It seems adviseable, consequently, that our reasoning should be preceded by a brief sketch of the events of the war; an outline to which reference may be made from the subsequent chapters, whenever we shall have occasion to allude to the connexion between the state of our finances and the aspect of a campaign. Such a narrative, however cursory, will necessarily lead us over beaten ground; but we are not without hopes of introducing, particularly in regard to France, occasional remarks that are not altogether familiar to the public.

War of 1793. — Nothing would have induced Mr. Pitt to take part in the coalition against France, except a hope that the contest would have been brought to an early conclusion, and himself left at liberty to pursue those measures of finance which had begun to wear so promising an aspect. His apprehension of France could be only of a political nature; a dread of the example of insubordination gaining ground, and of rank and property becoming endangered. In a military sense, France was far from formidable; her army, in 1792*, did not exceed the usual peace establishment of 130,000 men, and its strength was greatly impaired by the emigration of its principal officers, as well as by the general relaxation attendant on a continental peace of thirty years. Her navy having occupied the attention of government during and after the American war, was in a better state than usual; but its efficiency was impaired by the general disorder of the country, and its aspect was certainly far from offensive.

Under these circumstances our government, though in intimate communication with the powers that had taken up arms against France, delayed for some time joining the coalition. The recall of our ambassador from Paris was postponed till the insurrections of autumn 1792, and the subversion of the royal authority; nor did our preparations for war commence till towards the end of the year. This caution on our part, and the impetuosity of the ruling faction in France, caused the declaration of war to proceed in the first instance from Paris, and created a general belief in this country that the French were the aggressors. A speedy termination in favour of the allied powers was promised as well by general appearances as by the early events of

---

* Jomini sur les grandes Operations Militaires, Vol. V.

the war, the French being soon repulsed from the Dutch frontier, and some time after from the Netherlands, while their intestine divisions rose to a height that threatened the downfall of the republican system. A short time, however, sufficed to show the fallacy of judging from appearances, and of listening to representations so partial as those of the emigrants. The great majority of the nation, without cherishing either personal hostility to the Bourbons or schemes of foreign conquest, were strongly attached to the Revolution. They had long felt the want of a representative assembly, and regarded themselves as checked in the career of honourable ambition by the preference shown to the privileged classes. Without any distinct conception of the checks requisite to good government, they entertained a sanguine hope that the revolution was about to prove a remedy for all their grievances.

In such a state of national feeling, the resistance to invasion would probably have been equal, whatever had been the result of the intestine divisions of France. Had the Jacobin party been kept under by the Girondists, the strength of the country would still have been called forth ; the property of emigrants confiscated ; circulation given to the assignats, and military levies enforced on a large scale. It was in the autumn of 1793, and in the early part of 1794, that these potent levers were made to display all their energy. They sent forth armies, which, without being so numerous in the field as was generally imagined, were assured of an ample supply of recruits ; an assurance that justified the new plan of rendering a campaign a reiteration of attacks, on the calculation, that, whether successful or not, the country which should be able to call the greatest numbers into the field, would eventually triumph. Such, with a few qualifications, were the operations of 1793 and 1794 : operations in which the national impetuosity was called into full display; but the command being frequently placed in unskilful hands, the lives of men were exposed with unexampled rashness. The result of continued sacrifices on the one side, and of feeble generalship, of deficient concert, on the other, was that, in the early part of 1795, a total change took place in the aspect of the war. By that time, France had acquired both the Austrian Netherlands and the Dutch provinces, was on the point of concluding peace with Prussia and Spain, and reckoned only Austria and England as her opponents.

From this time forward, we may believe with confidence, that Mr. Pitt deeply regretted that France had been attacked, and the nation driven to exertions so pernicious to its assailants. He saw that revolutionary contagion was no longer to be dreaded, the credulity of the French, their absurd extremes, their repeated changes, their sacrifice of one party to the other, having brought complete discredit on their politics. His objections to peace, very different from those in 1792, were now of a military character : — to negotiate with France would have been to acknowledge inability to resist her; to leave the Netherlands in her hands, would have been to concede that against which we had contended for a century. He determined, therefore, to continue the war, with the aid of Austria ; and the exertions of France might have been equalled, perhaps surpassed, by the two allied governments, had they possessed the knowledge which they afterwards acquired ; — had England directed her chief resources to continental warfare, and had the Austrians opened their eyes to their errors in tactics. The numbers of the French were now less overwhelming than in the time of the assignats; but their efficiency was greatly increased, their soldiers had become well disciplined, and a number of intelligent officers had been formed. Their system of reiterated attack was continued; the national ardour was kept in full exercise; and to the audacity of the first years of the revolution was added, under the command of such men as Bonaparte, Moreau, Kleber, Hoche, Desaix, the advantage of scientific combination. It is to superiority of generalship more than to superiority of numbers, that we should attribute the reverses of the Austrians in 1796 and 1797, followed by a peace (Campo Formio) of which the preliminaries were signed when three armies were in march to their capital.

What in these early years of the war was our situation in regard to financial supplies? A state of war creates a sudden demand for money, by superadding what may be termed the mercantile operations of government to those of individuals. The call for arms, clothing, and military stores, forms a new demand on the manufacturing industry of the country, while the drain of men for the public service, enhances both wages and salaries. On the part of individuals, there takes place a decrease in certain branches of industry, a relinquishment of undertakings which can be carried on only by cheap labour, or a low interest of money; but the diminution, in one sense, is by no means proportioned to the increase in the other. Hence, a rise in the rate of interest, and a difficulty in borrowing, even at an advanced premium. Of such difficulties, and of the expedients adopted to meet them, we have had repeated examples, in our history, during the last century and a half. It was in the reign of king William that England first took a part in continental war, on a scale of great and continued expence; and that reign was accordingly the æra of the imposition of the land-tax, of the establishment of the bank of England, and of the first currency of its paper.

It unfortunately happened that the demand for money in the early years of the wars of the present age, was coincident with unfavourable seasons, our crops, both in 1794 and 1795, being insufficient for our consumption. Hence, a necessity to export coin for the purchase of subsistence, as well as for military purposes; and hence those embarrassments so severely felt in the mercantile world during 1793, 4, 5, 6, and from which we were not effectually relieved until 1797, when there occurred both a diminution of our continental expenditure, and a general acceptance, at home, of bank paper for coin.

At this time, England stood alone in the conflict, and the state of our finances was far from satisfactory; but our navy had in the course of the year (1797) achieved a double triumph, and the war becoming strictly maritime, our attitude, like that of France in 1794, showed all the advantage possessed by a nation, when combining its resources on its proper element. The confidence thus inspired, and the spirit roused by the extravagant ambition of the French government, enabled Mr. Pitt to meet our pecuniary difficulties, by a recourse to the plan which we shall develope presently, — that of raising supplies within the year; a plan to which, still more than to the substitution of paper for coin, was owing the surprizing increase that took place in our financial receipts.

The year 1798 will long be remembered by those who distinguish particular epochs in a great contest, as one of favourable commerce, of improved exchanges, of an abundant harvest, and of relief from the dread of invasion. The French, discouraged by our naval array, and by the failure of their expedition against Ireland, made a tacit acknowledgment of the hopelessness of an attack on England, by directing their disposable force to Egypt. The absence of this army, and our victory at Aboukir, revived the hopes of the Austrians, who regarded the existing peace as a truce, and who have, throughout the present age, shown themselves so prompt to second our efforts, and to take up arms against France.

The year 1799. — We come now to what is termed the third coalition, or the third time that the allied powers commenced operations by land in the hope of either changing the French government, or recovering a portion of lost territory. In adverting to these remarkable æras in the contest, it is fit to recollect that the aggressions were not on the part of France, and that, with the exception of 1792, England was the author and main-spring of every successive coalition. Had this been openly avowed, it is probable, that in those days of alarm the majority of the public would have approved of an offensive system of war; but it is the well-known rule of cabinets, and, of course, of their supporters, whether in parliament or connected with the press, to avoid such admissions, and to throw, as much as possible, the odium of attack on the enemy. At present, such reserve is needless; the question is to be viewed historically, and the point is merely, whether there existed, on the ground of justice and policy, sufficient reasons for calling the continent to arms, and for encountering the hazards of a conflict by land? As usual in such discussions, we shall find much to advance on either side. The dread of revolutionary infection had by this time disappeared; the French themselves had suffered cruelly from their experiments in government, having felt all the instability, all the division and party violence attached to the republican form. But while the majority of our countrymen had dismissed the apprehension of political contagion, they had, in a military view, urgent motives for hazarding an appeal to arms; they entertained the hope, that, with the co-operation of Austria and Russia, we should succeed in expelling the French from Italy, and in recovering the Netherlands.

These hopes, whether on the whole justified or not, received confirmation from the events of the first part of the campaign of 1799: the Austrians took the field with augmented numbers and an improved system; the repulse of the French in every direction, in Germany, as in Italy, proved the danger of neglecting their military establishment, and of the practice which had begun to show itself for the first time since the revolution, of appointing generals by favour. But in the autumn of the year new levies took the field, and abler chiefs commanded; the war changed its aspect; a few months produced the defection of the fickle cabinet of Russia from the coalition, and consolidated the executive power of France in the hands of Bonaparte. The campaign of 1800, though opened by the Austrians with confidence, soon showed their inability to contend with their antagonists; and on the conclusion of the second continental peace, (Luneville,) England was once more left alone in the conflict.

Few periods of the war presented a more gloomy combination of circumstances than the early part of 1801. — Austria humbled, Russia hostile, Denmark and Sweden following her example, and reviving the menace of the armed neutrality: while at home a double failure of harvest had produced a scarcity and rise of prices, which, in some parts of the country, resembled the privations of our ancestors in the latter years of Elizabeth, or the sufferings of France after the dreadful winter of 1709. On the other hand, the value of our paper currency was but slightly affected, our navy possessed the undisputed command of the sea, while our army had improved equally in strength and numbers: hence, the success of our attack on Copenhagen, and our brilliant exploits in Egypt. Still the expediency of peace was apparent; our financial resources had been stretched to the utmost; there remained no definite object of warfare, and no co-operation could be expected from the continent. These considerations were felt by our leading ministers; and, in concurrence with an apprehended division in the cabinet, or a sense that the same ministry could not suitably negociate with a government so long the object of its invective, led to that retirement of Mr. Pitt from office, which many persons still good-naturedly ascribe to his difference with the king on the Catholic question.

Thus ended the first great contest of our age, a contest, of which the most remarkable feature was, its placing the two leading powers successively in opposition to a confederacy, and baffling, in the case of each, the confident calculation of politicians. France, in 1793, could not, in the opinion of these persons, avoid sinking under the coalition; England, when left alone, in 1797, had, in their view, no alternative but a speedy peace. They were more correct in asserting that no war had afforded an example of such sacrifices; of men on the part of France, of money on the part of England. The losses of each seemed of a nature to produce exhaustion, yet each continued capable of prolonging or renewing the conflict. Each had obtained brilliant success, and added largely to its territorial possessions; but the acquisitions of France, at least in the Netherlands, were more compact, and more calculated to add strength to the state, than our dazzling but insecure conquests in the East and West Indies.

Our Situation at the Peace of Amiens. — What, it may be asked, were the chief differences, in our condition at the peace of 1802 and that of 1814? The financial and commercial evils that have since pressed so heavily on us, existed in 1802, but in a very mitigated form. The interest of our public debt, (18,000,000*l.*) was great, but not enormous; our total expenditure, had peace been confirmed, would not have much exceeded 30,000,000*l.* a year. The value of our currency, though shaken at a particular period, (1800 and 1801,) had been reinstated without much injury to the public; and our customers on the opposite shore of the Atlantic, though affected by the transition of Europe from war to peace, were by no means so disabled from paying for our exports as at the peace of 1814. Still our agriculturists felt the sudden change from high to low prices; our merchants were embarrassed by the surrender of the conquered colonies, and had the reduction of our military establishment been permanent, we should have experienced, in 1802, no small share of the embarrassment of late years: it would have been similar at least to that so faithfully described by Sir W. Temple, as affecting the productive industry of Holland, after the peace of 1648.

These complaints, however, had hardly assumed consistency, when the public were roused to new alarms: in France, a ruler whom no power could satisfy; in England, a ministry who followed, instead of leading the public voice, were respectively the authors of an abrupt renewal of war. Seldom has an appeal to arms been made with less of a direct motive or definite object: Malta was too insignificant to form a ground of war; the real cause was of a general nature, and to be sought in the encroachments of Bonaparte during the interval of peace, in the resentment roused by his aggression on Switzerland, and the obstacles opposed to our trade with France. Our ministers could not consider the moment favourable for attempting to recover the independence of the continent; they acted in concert with none of the great powers, and the experience of the past was altogether adverse to hopes founded on a coalition. They knew, however, that our financial resources were large, that the chances of a naval contest were in our favour, and that we should in any event prevent the increase of the enemy's marine.

War of 1803. — During two years the contest was strictly maritime, and the demand on our circulating medium, for subsidies or the purchase of corn being slight, our paper currency maintained its credit. The public attention was closely fixed on the project or pretended project of invasion. But in 1805, the growing discontent of the Russian cabinet with Bonaparte, and the well-known hostility of Austria, induced our government to form a new coalition. Our allies began the war with sanguine hopes, but found it vain to attack a great military state, conducted by a single head. The result would have been alarming even to this country, had it not, by a remarkable counterpoise of fortune, been coincident with a naval victory, which fairly put at rest the question of invasion.

It was under these circumstances of alternate disappointment and success, that Mr. Fox began at Paris the negociation of 1806, a measure by no means sanctioned by the majority of our countrymen. The offers of Bonaparte, towards the close of the conferences, would perhaps have been satisfactory on the score of territorial cession, had they not, when viewed in concurrence with his other projects, appeared to our ministers little else than a link in the chain of aggression; an expedient to procure not a peace, but a truce.

War was accordingly renewed, and by land, victory continued faithful to France : the events of the campaigns of 1806 and 1807, were subversive of the remaining independence of Germany, and by giving France the co-operation of Russia, seemed to leave her without a rival on the continent. Under these circumstances, our only safety lay in our naval superiority, and the war was proceeding without any definite prospect or favourable opening, when Bonaparte committed his first great political error. Hitherto, in his successes, he had shown more moderation, at least apparent

moderation, than might have been expected from
one so little advanced in years, and so confident in
his general calculations. He now, however, forgot
the dictates of caution, turned his aggression to an
unoffending quarter, and by his manner of inveigling
the royal family of Spain, excited not only the in-
dignation of foreigners, but general surprise and
dissatisfaction among the French, who were heartily
sick of war, and coveted no possessions beyond
the Pyrenees or the Alps. It is a truth, by no
means sufficiently understood in this country, that
the French people at no time participated in the
restless ambition of their ruler : their views in
regard to territory were limited to the Belgic
provinces, and those they desired not on political grounds, not from a wish to overawe Holland or threaten Germany, but from considerations
chiefly commercial, from similarity of language
and habits, vicinity of position, and the non-existence of physical barriers. So far from being
animated by that eagerness for war which so many
on our side of the Channel ascribe to them, the
French regarded themselves as the greatest sufferers by the sanguinary contest, and were taught
to ascribe its prolongation to the ambitious views of
our cabinet.

The war in Spain, varied as was its success
during several years, proved the first great scene
on which the hitherto victorious armies of France
were effectually resisted. That power of combination, that skill in generalship, which, in the present age, has been so little conspicuous in the military opponents of France, which, in the long
struggle of the Austrians, was remarked in only
two campaigns, (1795 and 1799,) was here called
into action, and directed against the enemy both

the discipline of the British, and the national anti-
pathy of the Spaniards.   This war was remarkable
as the first in which Bonaparte did not, on the
appearance of serious resistance, forsake his capital,
and bring the contest to a decisive issue.   In 1810,
the humiliation of Austria and Prussia left him at
liberty to recross the Pyrenees, but to the surprise
of France, as of the continent in general, he allowed
his army to remain long in an indecisive position
before our lines at Torres Vedras, and eventually
to retreat.

This signal repulse was followed by symptoms of
resistance in a new quarter.   Russia, alarmed for
her independence, and taught, by the success of
our Portuguese campaign, the means of baffling by
defensive operations, an enemy hitherto accounted
irresistible, no longer concealed her hostility to
France.   Bonaparte passed a year in forming his
gigantic plan of invasion: it failed, as is well
known, less from direct opposition than from physical causes; and that over-confidence on his part,
which we trace on so many occasions, and at such
different periods of his career—at Arcole, at Acre,
at Aspern, and finally, at Waterloo.

The loss of the Russian campaign and of the
flower of the army, however disastrous in a military sense, did not give so great a shock as the
public in England anticipated to the power of
Bonaparte in the interior of France.   The nation
was in affliction at the extent of the bloodshed; but
this feeling was overborne, at least in the middle
classes, by the dread of a counter-revolution, and
the return of the old abuses—the privileges of the
noblesse, the ascendancy of the clergy.   During
1813, the general wish was, not for a change of
dynasty, but for a change of system under the

existing ruler. No insurrection took place, no resistance was made, or even attempted, to the enormous levies of men and money, during that year; nor was it till renewed disasters, and the loss of all Germany, that the public began to contemplate the possibility of the return of the Bourbons. Even in 1814, the operations continued without any rising in favour of that family, or any defection of the military from their leader, till after the surrender of Paris, the possession of which has, throughout the whole of the French revolution, enabled one party to give law to another.

This unconsciousness of the real character of Bonaparte, this credulity in hoping a pacific system from one so long accustomed to war and usurpation, must appear not a little singular to the untravelled part of our countrymen. But those among them who visited France in 1814, had ample opportunity of observing that the name of the late ruler was seldom mentioned with reprobation, and that when, from the decided royalists, they happened to hear language to that effect, it was unaccompanied by any knowledge of the secret springs of his policy, or, indeed, by any attempt to develope his character.

This was, in fact, a task too complicated for the reasoning habits of our southern neighbours: they knew and lamented his propensity to war; but his diplomatic art, his Machiavelian policy, surpassed their analysing powers, unaided as they were by the light of a free press. Nor was it until his sudden return from Elba, when the peace so long desired and so recently obtained, was wrested from them, that the French (we speak here not of the military nor of the party leaders, but of the bulk of the nation,) gave a loose to resentment, and connected with his name that charge of faithlessness, that suspicion of criminality which we, during so many years, had accounted inseparable from it.

The reverses of the French arms occurred most opportunely for our finances, as shall be shown when we treat of the depreciation of our currency; but before proceeding to that, the proper object of our research, we shall bestow a few sentences on the eventful character of the military history of the period.

Alternations of success. —No contest was ever marked by greater variety of fortune, or more chequered by vicissitudes, the effect of which was, at one time, to check sanguine expectation, at another, to prevent despair. The Netherlands recovered in 1793, were again lost in 1794; the successes of the Austrians in 1795 were more than balanced by their disasters in the two following years. In 1799 the revived strength of that power and the co-operation of Russia, led to a brilliant campaign, producing the recovery of Italy, and inflicting severe losses on the French; but fortune once more forsook the allies, and obliged them to conclude at Lunéville a treaty on conditions which left France the leading power on the continent.

In our second appeal to arms, our hopes were raised in 1805 by the co-operation of the great continental powers; these hopes were blasted at Ulm and Austerlitz, but despondency was prevented by our victory at Trafalgar. Next year, the fatal day of Jena, and the conquest, rapid beyond example, of the Prussian dominions, would have excited great alarm, had not our courage been sustained by a successful resistance at Eylau, and by a confident estimate of the power of Russia. These favourable expectations were shaken by the events of the campaign, the treaty of Tilsit, and more than all, by the increasing connection and community of purpose between the French and Russian cabinets. The close of 1807 was consequently a period of gloom, for the capture of the Danish navy, and the issuing of our Orders in council, could afford satisfaction to those only who were incapable of appreciating the odium inspired by the one, and the disastrous effects likely to result from the other.

A more substantial ground of hope was afforded in the ensuing year by the attack on Spain, the general resistance which it provoked, the still more general hatred which it roused. The repulse of the French from the southern and central parts of Spain, and the success of our troops at Vimeira, the first general action on land that we had fought during the war, confirmed these flattering impressions; but they were unfortunately clouded by the repeated defeats of the Spaniards in the winter, and the retreat of our army to Corunna. Next year opened with the arming of Austria, and with some successful operations in the Peninsula, but the battles of Eckmuhl and Wagram, the failure of our Antwerp expedition, the second retreat of our army from Spain, cast a gloom over the aspect of affairs, which continued during the whole of 1810.

At that time the contest presented no expectation of a favourable issue; the Spaniards were inefficient and divided; the northern courts, if not unfriendly, were unable to hazard co-operation with us; and our bank paper, after having during the preceding seven years maintained its value with almost all the stability of a regular currency, now gave way before the triple pressure of corn imports, foreign subsidies, and a suspension of our accustomed receipts from the Continent of Europe on account of American merchants. Our exports to the United States had been, for the most part, paid by remittances in money from the Continent of Europe, and would, had we allowed their navigation to continue, have formed a fund capable, in a great measure, of balancing our demands, whether for military expenditure in the south of Europe, or for the purchases of corn in the north. But this truth was unfortunately unknown to the public, and imperfectly felt by ministers. We persevered in stopping the American trade, and thus deprived ourselves of a powerful counterpoise to the irregularity of our circulating medium. Our situation thus became replete with anxiety : from invasion we were secured by our fleet, but we dreaded to make peace, lest an interval, turned assiduously to account by our artful enemy, might shake even this last stay of our independence. On other grounds also, peace seemed unadvisable, for by this time Bonaparte had incorporated a farther part of Germany with France, and shown himself equally blind to the lesson given by the resistance of Spain, and to the hazard of alarming Russia.

It was under these disquieting circumstances that we passed the latter months of 1810 and the beginning of 1811. The necessity of abandoning the Peninsula was declared by many, and silently anticipated by more, when the scene was unexpectedly changed by the retreat of the French army from Portugal, and by conflicts, which, if not altogether decisive in our favour, were indicative of great improvement in our army. An intimation of a growing hostility on the part of Russia to France, now raised hopes of a higher kind—hopes which, after an interval, were confirmed by the memorable campaign of 1812. Still the period of vicissitude was not passed; the expectation excited by the advance of the Russians, and the zeal of their Prussian allies, were disappointed at Lutzen, Bautzen, and Hamburgh; while our bank paper had fallen above 20 per cent., a fall involving the certainty of a loss to that amount on all the contributions we might make to the cause of the continent, whether in Spain or Germany. It was, however, no time to pause; circumstances had produced an opportunity, such as had not occurred during the whole war, of restoring the equilibrium of the Continent: Austria had joined the alliance, and the inefficiency of the French levies was shown in their actions with the Prussians in Silesia. Germany was now delivered, and the French territory invaded, yet even then there occurred an interval of suspended hope: the imprudence of Blucher, and the prompt decision of Bonaparte, led to a check and partial retreat, which, to the public, assumed a serious aspect, when viewed in connection with a negotiation at Chatillon; but the apprehension inspired by that real or ostensible negotiation, was soon dispelled by the evident superiority of the allies, and by the result of a movement, remarkable as indicative of the over-confident calculation of Bonaparte even under disaster; we mean his march to gain the rear, and cut off the retreat of his enemies—a manoeuvre that might have been followed by success if at the head of such armies as he commanded at Ulm and Jena, but which, with the feeble means at his disposal in 1814, served only to embolden his opponents and accelerate the loss of his capital.

CHAP. II.

Magnitude of our Expenditure. — The Sources of our Financial Supplies.

AFTER this brief sketch of military events, we proceed to the proper object of our enquiry, the expence incurred by the war, the resources by which it was supported, and the cause of our financial embarrassments since the peace. In this we are aware that we venture on difficult ground, and attempt a question of more than usual complexity. War, accounted in former days a season of embarrassment and poverty, assumed in the present age the appearance of a period of prosperity. It closed, indeed, with a great addition to our permanent burdens, but with an increase of national income, which seemed fully to counterbalance it, and to confine our loss to that of our brave countrymen who had fallen in the struggle. Peace, we thought, was about to bring a consolidation of the advantages earned in battle and sanctioned by treaty, but the result has been widely different: every succeeding year has discovered some financial difficulty, some fresh defalcation in our national resources. The causes have as yet been by no means satisfactorily explained, either in or out of Parliament, and the contradiction between what was expected, and what has actually taken place, implies the prevalence of much popular error, as well as the necessity of an attentive and anxiously-balanced enquiry.

This enquiry we may hope to divest, in some measure, of its complexity, by proceeding step by step, and dividing our subject into separate heads. The first point is to form a distinct idea of our war expences, as well the annual charge as the aggregate for the whole contest; a calculation as yet familiar to few persons on account of the magnitude of the sums, the detached manner in which they are generally brought before the public, and the complexity of our finance accounts, which have hitherto presented, in the sinking fund, an apparent surplus, and, under the head of supply, an apparent deficiency.

In the early years of this memorable contest, ministers were almost as little aware as the public of the extent to which the national contributions could be carried, and the increase of our expenditure was, consequently, gradual. Taking the total money raised by loans and taxes, but deducting from it 18,000,000*l.* annually, as the probable expenditure of Great Britain and Ireland, had peace been preserved, we find the following result: —

Sums annually raised for the War of 1793.

1793.	-	£ 4,000,000	1798.	-	£29,000,000
1794.	-	10,000,000	1799.	-	36,000,000
1795.	-	18,000,000	1800.	-	36,000,000
1796.	-	26,000,000	1801.	-	45,000,000
1797.	-	35,000,000	1802.	-	44,000,000

These sums are properly the amount raised, not the amount expended in each year: still they convey a fair idea of the annual cost of the war. Their great increase, in the latter years, was owing to several causes; the augmentation of our establishments, the depreciation of money, and consequent rise of pay, stores, &c.; and, finally, to the accumulation of interest on the expenditure of all the preceding years.

Such was the war of 1793, a war exhibiting an average expenditure of 27,000,000*l.*, which, though nearly double that of any preceding contest, was destined to be surpassed both soon and in a very great degree.

Sums raised by loans and taxes for the war of 1803, after de- ducting the portion appropriated to Ireland, and allowing 22,000,000l. as the total of our probable expenditure, had peace been preserved in 1793.

1803. - - - - -	£29,000,000
1804. - - - - - -	40,000,000
1805. - - - - -	52,000,000
1806. - - - - - -	50,000,000
1807. - - - - -	56,000,000
1808. - - - - - -	57,000,000
1809. (War in Spain) - - - -	61,000,000
1810. (Ditto) - - - -	62,000,000
1811. (Ditto) - - - - -	66,000,000
1812. (War in Spain and Russia) - -	80,000,000
1813. (War in Spain and Germany) - -	98,000,000
1814. (War on the French territory) - -	89,000,000
1815. - - - - -	86,000,000

Here also the increase was progressive ; so ne- cessary was it, even in our day of enthusiasm, to wait until the machine of circulation became adapted to this new impulse. At last, our expen- diture reached a sum unexampled in the history of any country, ancient or modern. It is fit, however, to keep in mind two very material qualifications ; first, that the sums in the latter years are greatly swelled by the accumulation of interest on the pre- vious expenditure ; next, that after 1810, a large sum, fully 20 per cent. on our foreign disburse, is to be put to the account of the depreciation of our bank paper. With these deductions, the expence of the unparalleled year of 1813 may be stated at

70,000,000*l.*, and the other years reduced in a corresponding proportion. But after every subtraction, the amount of our expenditure was surprising: for the whole contest it may be thus stated.

Total money raised in Great Britain by loans and taxes, during the 23 years that elapsed, between the beginning of 1793 and that of 1816; (see Appendix) about - £1,564,000,000

Deduct for the amount of our peace establishment and charges unconnected with the war, a sum, which, from the increase of our population and the necessity of enforcing the collection of the revenue in Ireland, we reckon at somewhat more than the average expenditure of Great Britain and Ireland previous to 1793; making (see Appendix) an amount of about - - - £464,000,000

Remainder, constituting the charge of } the war - - - - } £1,100,000,000

The next question is, in what manner did government find it practicable to raise these unexampled sums? Loans, the great resource in former wars, were resorted to during the early years of the contest; thus —

Money raised by loans.

| 1794. | - | £11,000,000 | 1796. | - | £25,500,000 |
| 1795. | - | 18,000,000 | 1797. | - | 32,500,000 |

The last of these sums being great beyond example in the history of our loans, had the effect of lowering stocks in an alarming degree, reducing the 3 per cents. in 1797, below 48.* Mr. Pitt now felt the necessity of altering his plan of finance, and was led, as well by his characteristic confidence, as by the general increase of individual income attendant on the war, to adopt the very bold expe-

* Dr. Hamilton on the National Debt, p. 252.

dient of war taxes, or, as it was officially termed,
" raising a large proportion of the supplies within
the year." The success of this plan forms the
grand feature of the financial history of our age:
attempted at first on a limited scale, it was carried
by the imposition of the income tax, to a large
amount, and before the close of the war attained a
magnitude almost incredible.

*Supplies raised within the year, being the net produce of our
taxes, after deducting* 18,000,000*l.,* *as the computed average of
a peace establishment, and excluding all loans.*

War of 1793. — During the first four years
the war taxes were in considerable, and in 1797,

they were carried to only	-	-	-	£	3,000,000
But in 1798. they were carried to			-		12,000,000
1799.	-	-	-	-	17,000,000
1800.	-	-	-	-	16,000,000
1801.	-	-	-	-	17,000,000
1802.	-	-	-	-	19,000,000

War of 1803. — The produce of our annual
supplies computed as above, with the exclusion of loans, but after deduction of a larger
sum (22,000,000*l.,* see Appendix,) as the probable peace establishment:

1803.	-	16,000,000	1810.	-	45,000,000
1804.	-	23,000,000	1811.	-	43,000,000
1805.	-	28,000,000	1812.	-	41,000,000
1806.	-	31,000,000	1813.	-	45,000,000
1807.	-	36,000,000	1814.	-	48,000,000
1808.	-	40,000,000	1815.	-	48,000,000
1809.	-	41,000,000			

Respective Proportion of Loans and Taxes.

Of the total sum of 1,100,000,000*l.* expended
during the war, the amount added to our permanent debt was 460,000,000*l.,* so that the aggregate
of the supplies raised within the year, amounted
for the whole war to 640,000,000*l.* a surprising
sum to be obtained by a mode of taxation almost

unknown in foreign countries, and carried in former wars to a very limited extent among ourselves.

The financial history of the war may be divided into three periods :

First, the four years previous to 1797, in which our treasury was conducted as in former wars, without any innovation in regard to war taxes or paper money.

Secondly, the interval from 1797 to 1805, in which we had both war taxes and non-convertible paper, but without greatly depreciating the one, or carrying the other to an extreme.

Thirdly, the period from 1805 to 1815, in which the amount of the supplies raised within the year became enormous, and the depreciation of our paper, particularly after 1810, formed a very serious addition to our difficulties.

We have thus exhibited a statement of our expenditure, which, though brief, is, we trust, perspicuous, all complexities of redeemed and unredeemed stock, all distinctions of funded and unfunded debt, being excluded from our calculation, and the charge of the war considered only under the two great divisions of debt contracted and expenditure defrayed in the current year. Compared with these sums, how insignificant were the additions made to our public burdens by former wars. That of 1689, under King William, cost annually between 3 and 4,000,000*l.* and added in all 20,000,000*l.* to the national debt. Under Queen Anne, the flattering hopes inspired by repeated victories, led to a longer contest and larger outlay, carrying our annual expenditure to 5 or 6,000,000*l.*; the addition to the public debt during the war to somewhat more than 30,000,000*l.* In the less successful contest of 1740, our expenditure differed from year to year; the addition to our public debt amounted to nearly 30,000,000*l.* In that of 1756, the augmented resources of the country, and the bold system of Lord Chatham, raised our annual expenditure to an average of 16,000,000*l.*, the addition to our debt to fully 60,000,000*l.* The unfortunate contest with our colonies, and the war that ensued after 1778 with European powers, was attended with an average charge of 17,000,000*l.*, and an addition to our debt of somewhat more than 100,000,000*l.* The total of public debt incurred in the course of a century was thus 240,000,000*l.*, a sum which, however large, formed only the half of that which we have contracted in the present age.

The Sources of our Financial Supplies. — The next and by far the most important step in the progress of our enquiry is, by what means and from what sources the nation was enabled to meet such unprecedented demands? In the opinion of many, the means were derived from the extension, or as it is commonly termed, our monopoly of foreign commerce. " The French revolution," said the late Arthur Young*, " burst forth like a volcano, " and laid the industry, manufactures, and com- " merce of France, and eventually those of the " whole Continent, in the dust; Britain became the " emporium of the world, and such a scene of wealth " and prosperity filled every eye in this happy " country, as the sun before had never shone " upon." The belief of such a monopoly has, on the part of a merely practical man, or in the pages of a pamphleteer, nothing surprising, but we were little prepared to find it in a publication of large cir-

* Enquiry into the Value of Money in England, 1812; p. 77.

culation and acknowledged ability.* The fact is, that the amount of our *foreign* commerce was not greater, nor so great at any time during the war as since the peace ; a point which may at once be ascertained by a reference to our custom-house return of exports and imports. These documents, however unfit to represent the balance of mercantile payments from one country to another, form good authorities for ascertaining the comparative extent of our business from year to year.

Our Exports according to the official value.—We shall give the result of our custom-house return of exports in two modes ; first, by the official value, which means (see Appendix,) the value computed by the weight or dimensions of merchandize, and at a uniform rate of price, without reference to the fluctuations of the market.

Total Exports from Great Britain, computed according to the fixed official standard of the Custom-house.

Average of the nine years of the first war, viz. from the beginning of 1793 to that of 1802 - - - £30,760,000

Average of ten years of the second war, from 1803 to 1812, both inclusive, leaving out 1813, the records of which were destroyed by fire, and considering 1802 as a year of peace - - · 42,145,000

But if we compare this with the eight years of peace, of which the returns have been made to Parliament, we shall find a considerable increase since 1814.

Average of the total exports from Great Britain computed officially for the eight years, from 1814 to 1821, both inclusive. (See Appendix.) - - 54,200,000

* Edinburgh Review, No. lxv. p. 170., and again in No. lxxii. p. 458.

These custom-house returns, being made on a uniform plan, and calculated by the weight or dimensions of the package, are conclusive as to the *quantity* of our exports. It may be said, however, that, in other respects, they are less satisfactory; and that although the bulk exported at present be greater, the *value* is less in consequence of the general reduction of prices. That prices were much higher during the war, particularly in the latter years, admits of no doubt, but in whatever way the calculation be made, the advantage is on the side of peace, thus : —

Exports from Great Britain during the war, computed chiefly from the declaration of the exporting merchants ; or, when there was no declaration, by a suitable addition to the official value.

Average of the ten years from 1791 to 1801, both inclusive　-　-　£48,890,000

Average of the ten years from 1801 to 1810　-　-　-　-　52,847,000

In peace, our exports afford an average considerably larger, after making (see Appendix,) an allowance for the reduced value of merchandize.

Average of our annual exports during eight years from 1814 to 1821, both inclusive, computed chiefly from the declaration of the exporting merchants. (See Appendix.)　-　-　-　£63,787,000

In both points of view, therefore, our foreign commerce is found to have been less considerable in war than in peace : it is equally easy to show, that its profits were wholly inadequate to the support of any great share of our expenditure. Mr. Pitt, on proposing the income-tax in 1798, computed our foreign commerce to yield to the various persons, merchants and others, engaged in it, an annual income of 12,000,000*l.*, a sum, probably not under-rated at the time, but which, for the sake of giving those who differ from us, the full benefit of argument, ought, we shall suppose, to have been doubled and taken during the war, at an annual amount of 24,000,000*l.* This, be it observed, is not saving, but income, out of which are to be supported all the persons engaged in the business; and if we compute the clear saving in a proportion, which, in regard to most other branches of industry, would be more than sufficiently liberal, the result will be a clear yearly gain of three millions sterling. But what would be thought of that sum, or of double or triple its amount, as a counterpoise to such expenditure as ours during the late wars?

Of all the branches of our foreign commerce, the greatest extension took place in that with the United States : but that outlet was closed several years before the end of the war; and, however productive of work to our manufacturers, has never been considered a source of pecuniary aid, accompanied as it necessarily is, by long credits and debts difficult of recovery.

Our Colonial Acquisitions. — Our other sources of imagined supply were the occupation of new colonies, the suspension of the navigation of hostile states, and a supposed reduction of their rival manufactures. — Of the conquered colonies, the principal were Trinidad, Demerara, Essequebo, Tobago, each little advanced in cultivation, each requiring a large transfer of capital from this country, and each yielding little present revenue. Similar disadvantages characterised, though, in a

less degree, St. Lucia, Guadaloupe, Martinique.
As to the East Indies, our acquisitions, vast in point
of territory, and considerable in regard to internal
revenue, have been as yet of very secondary importance in respect to commerce, though, on the
continent of Europe, there prevails an opinion
that India is the grand source of our national
wealth.

Suspension of Foreign Competition.—We come
next to a very plausible argument, the benefit supposed to arise to us from the suspension that took
place during the war, of the navigation of France,
Holland, and the other states dependent on
France. The fact doubtless was, that the flag of
these countries could not appear on the ocean,
because they had not men of war to protect their
convoys ; but the transfer of navigation was made
less to British vessels than to neutrals, — Americans,
Danes, Swedes, Prussians, and to Dutch shipping,
bearing the flag of the petty ports in the north-west
of Germany. — Lastly, in regard to manufactures,
those of France have undergone no reduction since
the Revolution, and much less fluctuation than is
commonly supposed : during the last thirty years
they have been on the same scale of gradual increase as before ; that is, they have all along kept
pace with the wants of a country, increasing progressively, though not quickly, in population.

Compelled to quit their favourite ground of
foreign commerce, to what do these calculators
resort for the purpose of explaining our prosperity
during the war ? Government loans and contracts,
however profitable in vulgar estimate, are obviously
out of the question as a source of national supply.
The command of money, given by the adoption of

a paper currency, is a theme confidently urged, to use a parliamentary phrase, both " in and out of doors:" it was certainly of great importance, but enough, we trust, will be advanced in a succeeding chapter to show that the extent of supply, derived from that source, has not yet been distinctly comprehended. We dwell, therefore, no longer on delusive suppositions, but proceed to what appears to us the true solution of this financial enigma, seeking it in the increase less of our transactions with foreign countries, than of our productive industry at home.

Increase of Employment during the War.—We begin by requesting those of our readers who are of an age to recollect the period of peace prior to 1793, to recall to mind the circumstances of that time in as far as regarded the employment of individuals, the chance of favourable openings in the different walks of industry. They will not fail to remember, that, though by no means an unprosperous season, it was marked by the symptoms common in an æra of political tranquillity, — complaints of overstock in the genteel professions, and of inadequate payment in almost all of a humbler description. In a season of peace, salaries or wages are adapted with scrupulous nicety to the sum necessary for personal support, and, except in the case of the inheritors of patrimony, the portion of income disposable for purposes of indulgence, is far from large. Such has long been the case in France, and most countries of the Continent; such, at various intervals of the last century, was the case in our own — a state by no means unsound or likely to engender future embarrassment, but leading by very slow degrees to the attainment of professional rank, or the acquisition of property. This tranquil condition, this medium between activity and stagnation, was entirely altered by the war; the army, the navy, the public offices of government opened a career to numbers of every class, and by absorbing a very large proportion of the candidates for employment, created a corresponding briskness in agriculture, trade, and professions; increasing the wages of the lower, and the salaries of the higher ranks.

Capitalists also, a class retired for the most part from active pursuits, partook of the general impulse; the pecuniary demands of government were large, and the rate of interest experienced a general and permanent rise. Occupation was thus afforded to individuals of every age and of almost every degree of capacity; many, who from deficient activity or mediocrity of parts, would, in a state of peace, have necessarily remained unemployed, were brought by the war into situations attended with income; some in the public service, others in private employment, but all in consequence of the extra demand created by government. Several departments of business, such as our fisheries, our trade with the Continent of Europe, and that with our West India colonies, were exposed to heavy losses, and the whole body of fixed annuitants felt severely the increased expence of living. But these classes formed the minority of the public : and even they felt, more or less directly, through the medium of their connections, the benefit of that impulse which for a time improved the income of almost all persons in active life, raising to the monied men the rate of interest ; to the labouring class, the rate of wages; to the manufacturer, the merchant, and, in particular, to the farmer, the profits of stock.

Such was the activity attendant on a state of war, and on the facility with which extended transactions were managed by means of bank paper. If to some our sketch appear too highly coloured, we have merely to refer them to a comparison of the average rate of wages and salaries in particular periods, such as 1792 and 1812; to the increased sales of our manufacturers and merchants; the rise of rent to the landlord; the increase of profit to his tenant.

Consequent Increase of Revenue. — All these circumstances, in particular the increased call for personal labour, had a powerful tendency to augment the relative population of towns, as well by promoting marriage as by drawing to them an extra share of the country population. Now what is the effect of an increase of town population on the productive powers, or, in other words, on the taxable income of a country? To form a due estimate of this, we must point the reader's attention to the passages in our chapter on Population, where, in treating of the comparative revenue of different classes, we contrast the dexterity and dispatch of towns, with the slow, inefficient labour of the country. A transfer of residence from country to town leads to augmented ability in the individual, to the increase of the quantity, the amelioration of the quality, of his work; it raises his wages, and, by enabling him to live better, extends the consumption of articles productive to the exchequer. Of the magnitude of the amount paid by the lower orders, and the increase of public revenue attendant on increase of wages, whether in war or peace, some idea may be formed from the following table.

Abstract of Excise and Custom duties in 1820, affecting the consumption of the labouring classes.

Malt - - - - -	£5,000,000
Beer - - - - - -	2,500,000
British spirits - - - -	3,000,000
Salt - - - - -	1,500,000
Tobacco and Snuff - - -	3,000,000
Soap - - - - -	900,000
Leather - - - -	600,000
Candles - - - - -	300,000
Tea - - - - - -	3,000,000
Hemp - - - - -	200,000
	20,000,000
To which may be added, Timber -	1,000,000
Coals carried coastwise nearly - -	1,000,000
Total	£22,000,000

The progressive increase in the productiveness of our taxes was owing partly to higher wages, partly to augmented population.

Increase of our Population. — We shall have occasion, in a subsequent chapter, to show the close connection that exists between the increase of our numbers and the productiveness of our taxes : at present, our statement shall be brief. Our population returns for the last twenty years indicate an increase of no less than one and a half per cent. annually; but to avoid the hazard of over-rating, we shall suppose that previous to these returns, and to the general introduction of vaccination, the augmentation was less rapid, and shall assume eighteen per cent. on the population of 1792 as the total increase during the fourteen years that followed that date.

After these preliminary remarks, we proceed to state arithmetically, the increase of our resources, beginning by a table of the amount of our excise duties, the operation of which affects, as is well known, a great variety of articles, including as well the wine of the higher orders, as the malt liquor, the spirits, the tobacco, consumed by their humbler countrymen.

Revenue arising from the Excise during the following years of war, being the gross Income, before deducting the charges of collection.

1805.	- - - -	£23,194,000
1806.	- - - - -	24,081,000
1807.	- - - - -	24,681,000
1808.	- - - - -	25,593,000
1809.	(Orders in Council) - - -	23,471,000
1810.	- - - - - -	25,796,000
1811.	- - - - -	26.078,000
1812.	(War with America) - -	23,532,000
1813.	- - - - -	25,272,000
1814.	- - - - -	26,471,000
1815.	- - - - -	27,207,000

Conjectural estimate of the total taxable Income of Great Britain, at different periods, from 1792 to 1814.

Money of the same value as in 1792,

(Great Britain distinct from Ireland.)
In 1792 our taxable income may be computed to have been   -   -   -   -   £125,000,000

In 1806; increase calculated in the ratio of the increase of the population, viz. 18 per cent.,   22,500,000

147,500,000

Probable addition to national income from the higher wages and higher profits of capital in a state of war,   -   -   -   -   22,500,000

Total of taxable income in 1806,   -   170,000,000

We shall now apply this mode of calculation to the last year of the war.

In 1813 or 1814: Increase of national income since 1806, calculated in the ratio of the increase of population, 11 per cent.

National income in 1806 as above, -	£147,500,000
Add 11 per cent. - - - -	16,500,000
	164,000,000
Probable addition to national income, from the higher wages and higher profits of capital in a state of war, - - - -	24,000,000
Total of taxable income in 1813 or 1814, in money of 1792, - - - -	188,000,000

By taxable income, we understand the aggregate
income of the individuals accustomed to consume
taxed articles; and our estimate is founded chiefly
on the returns made under the property tax, with
the addition of the computed amount of wages
and other incomes, which, though exempt from
that charge, are subject to taxes on consumption.

(See the chapter on National Capital and Revenue.)

We shall explain in the next chapter the fluctuation in the value of money since 1792; meantime
by exhibiting our income at different dates in
money of uniform value, we simplify the estimate,
and enable the reader to mark its increase, without
the perplexity attendant on a difference in the value
of our currency.

*A comparative Statement of our Public Burdens, and Taxable
Income.*

*The public burdens include taxes, (with the expence of collec-
tion) poor-rate, and tithe.*

Years.	Annual burdens in the money of the particular year.	The same re-duced to a uniform stan-dard; viz. money of the same value as in 1792.	Our taxable in-come comput-ed by a uni-form standard; viz. money of the value of 1792.
1792. -	£22,000,000	22,000,000	125,000,000
1806. -	60,000,000	46,000,000	170,000,000
1814. -	80,000,000	50,000,000	188,000,000

The advantage of making our computation in money of uniform value is here very apparent. To judge from the numerical amount, our public burdens would seem to have more than tripled in the course of the twenty-three years of war, but when reduced to the money of 1792, the increase is found to be little more than double.

It remains that we bring our reasoning to a point, by ascertaining "the proportion borne at different periods by our burdens to our means." This we accomplish by a calculation founded on the preceding tables, but modified by some considerations which shall be explained in our chapter on National Revenue and Capital. The result is, that our burdens bore to our resources,

(Great Britain distinct from Ireland.)

In 1792. a proportion of nearly	-	18	to	100
1806. - of	- -	27	to	100
1813. or 1814. of	. -	27	to	100

(See Chap. VIII. p. 269.)

Such was the proportion of our burdens to our resources, after including in the latter the increase arising from the augmentation during the war, both of our numbers and our pecuniary means. The additional pressure stated arithmetically, was about nine per cent. on our national income, a charge less great than is commonly attributed to our taxes, but sufficiently large to call for some farther explanation of the remarkable circumstances that enabled us to defray it.

Our War Taxes. — The amount of our loans, though very different in different years, averaged, on the whole of the war, the annual sum of 20,000,000*l*. This bold use of our credit, this free

draught on our future resources, was almost all
expended in the extension of our domestic industry. It may be termed a premium given to the
existing generation at the charge of posterity: it
may be compared to a stream, which, though
proceeding from an unnatural and temporary
source, diffused a fertility approaching to luxu-
riance, so long as it continued to flow. Our
readers have probably little difficulty in conceiving
the operation of borrowed money; — in comprehending how individual, and consequently public
income may be increased by giving activity to the
present age at the expence of the next. The intricacy lies in a different question; in the mode of
accounting for our *taxes,* and for the ease with
which sums of unprecedented magnitude were
raised in that manner during the war. To solve
this difficulty, some writers adopt the convenient
theory, that taxation may be made an engine for increasing national wealth, as if the money expended
on an indecisive campaign were ultimately as profitable as a rate imposed for the improvement of
our streets, roads, and canals. Without becoming
converts to this singular opinion, we have no difficulty in regarding taxation, when *expended at home,*
less as a privation of wealth than as an instrument
of circulation. It is evidently applied to the extension of employment, and, by increasing the incomes of individuals, enables them to find a fund
for answering its own demand, — the subsequent
visits of the collector.

Taxation considered as Circulation. — Imagine
the case of a contractor receiving annually 100,000*l.*
from the Treasury, and distributing it in an addition
to the wages, salaries, and profits of two or three
thousand persons. Without the war, these indivi-

duals might, and probably would, have had employment, but not to an equal extent, receiving perhaps
60*l.* annually instead of the 70*l.* or 80*l.* given them
by the war, an addition which fully enabled them
to pay the extra charge imposed in the shape of
taxes. Or suppose the whole expenditure of the
nation, in other words, the amount disbursed on
articles, which directly or indirectly pay taxes, to
be 200,000,000*l.* a year, and that in addition to
former burdens new taxes are imposed to the extent
of 20,000,000*l.* The effect of this heavy impost
is a correspondent rise in the price of the articles
consumed; but as the amount received by the
Treasury is forthwith circulated among the payers
of the taxes, and applied to remunerate their exertions, the latter are enabled to indemnify themselves
by an addition to the charges constituting their
respective incomes, whether in the shape of wages,
salary, or profit of stock. Possessed of this power,
the higher price paid for articles of consumption
becomes a matter of indifference, particularly when,
in consequence of the government demand for men
and money, the increase of their incomes exceeds
the increase of their expence. The result accordingly is, that they pay 10 per cent. additional on
their consumption, and add as much, or more, to
the charges constituting their incomes.

To what amount, it may be asked, did the circulation in question take place, in consequence of
taxes? To a sum very different in different years,
and increasing largely after 1806, but forming, on
an average of the whole period of war, more than
40,000,000*l.* a year. In what particular mode did
the annual expenditure of that sum, and of the farther 20,000,000*l.* supplied by loans, chiefly take
place? In recruiting, clothing, and victualling our

militia, army, and navy; in the purchase of stores, the building of ships of war, the repair of fortifications; in contracts, pay, salaries, pensions. Even in that which seemed strictly foreign expenditure, our subsidies to the continent, and the maintenance of our garrisons abroad, the remittances took place less in money than in articles of British manufacture.

It remains to add a few remarks on the manner in which these large sums were repaid to the Treasury. Of our taxation, the far greater proportion (40,000,000*l.*) is on articles of consumption, a mode in which the tax, blending itself with the price of the article, escapes, in a great measure, the observation of the consumer. No wonder, therefore, that such imposts were, in a manner, overlooked in the general rise of wages, salaries, and profits. In like manner, the increase of stamps, heavy as it became, was accounted a secondary object after the great augmentation of price obtained, as the war proceeded, by the venders of property. The assessed taxes and poor-rate being undisguised burdens, excited more animadversion, but they were submitted to as well from a conviction of their necessity, as from the general ardour in the contest with France, and her dreaded ruler.

Computed Amount thus repaid to the Treasury. — If we go a step farther, and endeavour to define the amount repaid, during the war, to the public Treasury, the plan is to revert to the estimate we have already made of the proportion of our burdens to our national income. That proportion, (27 per cent. for the country at large,) was greater in towns, on account of the more general consump-

tion of exciseable articles. Now as the expenditure of government for the war, or, to speak more
correctly, the increased expenditure of individuals
consequent on government disburse, took place
almost entirely in towns, we shall probably not
exceed in calculating that it returned into the
Exchequer a proportion approaching to 33 per
cent., or a third of the amount that had issued
from it. This estimate justifies the following inference:

Total of expenditure for the war - £1100,000,000

Of which a third, or 33 per cent., paid back
   in taxes, formed a sum of about - 360,000,000

a sum which goes far towards accounting for the
payment of our war taxes, enormous as they were ;
or, in other words, towards proving that those
pecuniary sacrifices on which the public received
such eloquent compliments from ministerial orators
and newspaper writers, were often little more than
a repayment of money issued from the Treasury.

The power of paying taxes during the late war
is thus to be sought, not in retrenchment on the
part of the public, but in an increase of the general
activity, and still more in that which a writer of
the present age, (as yet little known to the public,
but to whose works we shall frequently have occasion to refer, Mr. S. Gray) terms the power of
" charging and counter-charging ;" the power of
individuals to augment those demands which constitute their respective incomes; and thus to transfer
from one hand to another the burden of a new tax.

Absence of Foreign Competition. — This augmentation of charge, this transfer of burden, was

facilitated during the war by various causes, among which is to be included the existence of similar, though not equal demands from continental governments on their subjects. These demands, in conjunction with the obstructions to intercourse attendant on a state of war, had the effect of preventing the high prices in England from being lowered by foreign competition. Had the war affected only France and England, had the rest of Europe been exempted from the burdens of great military establishments, such a system of increased taxation, or, in other words, such a rapid augmentation of prices would have been impracticable: our countrymen would have emigrated; capital would have been sent abroad; foreign manufactures would have been smuggled among us; the supplies for the United States and other distant markets would have been prepared on the continent. But Holland, the only continental country possessed of disposable capital, was subjected to great oppression; while Germany, and in the latter years of the war, Denmark and Sweden, were burdened with heavy military charges. British capital was prevented from finding its way abroad, as well by dread of Bonaparte's despotism, as by the profitable employment afforded it at home. Smuggling was continued, but only in articles (such as spirits, tea, laces,) in which it had been carried on in peace: the number and activity of our cruisers prevented its extension, notwithstanding the additional temptation arising from our augmented duties.

Our country was thus insulated commercially as well as physically, and an amount of taxation, a rise of prices, which at other times would have been ruinous, were comparatively innoxious when

our neighbours were subjected to heavy burdens.
As soon as this point is clearly comprehended by
the enquirer ; as soon as he becomes satisfied of
the *non-existence of foreign competition ;* he will
find much less difficulty in the solution of our
financial problem.

Substitution of Bank Notes for Coin. — To
all those causes there remains to add the exemption of our banks from cash payments ; the
effect of which, though less great than is vulgarly
supposed, was to make money almost as plenty in
war as in peace ; and to increase the amount of our
circulating medium in proportion as other circumstances led to a rise in prices.

———

Thus was carried on, from year to year, a most
expensive contest, without much pressure on any
part of the public, unless the fixed annuitant, and
without a depreciation of our national capital, except of that portion (such as the funds, or loans on
mortgage,) of which the value is permanently represented by money. To many persons, and in
particular to those interested in the expenditure,
this state of things bore a favourable appearance ;
conveying to some the idea of an accumulation of
national wealth, to others the belief that we defrayed all our burdens from funds arising from
the war. The general enhancement of commodities
was ascribed to an abundance of money, and
deemed a symptom, or rather a proof, of the
increase of our national wealth.

These explanations enable us to account in some
measure for a notion very prevalent on the continent, and which, in the latitude in which it is entertained, strikes every Englishman with surprise,—

That we prolonged the war with a view to our pecuniary advantage — as if a charge, which may be true in regard to particular classes, could, with any degree of justice, be applied to our countrymen at large.

The temporary stimulus afforded to productive industry by the funding system, though never so strikingly exemplified before, might have been traced in various periods of the history of Europe during the last two centuries. Was it not conspicuous in the long contests of the Dutch, first with Spain and subsequently with France, as well as in every war that has been carried on by England since the revolution? In none of these, it is true, did the amount of loans, and still less the amount of war taxes, bear any proportion to those of the present age; but they supplied facts of a nature to suggest serious conclusions, had studies of that description entered into the habits of our legislators. To the more cautious among them, it seemed to occur that our situation was, in some degree, unnatural; that the great expenditure of government was not compensated, on the part of the public, by economy, or by any great share of extra exertion. Hence an apprehension, on the part of some, that the war must entail a burdensome inheritance, but at what time, or to what degree, they did not attempt to calculate. Of the reaction to be expected at a peace, no one appears to have had a distinct conception. To foresee its extent was, we admit, impossible; but few of our public men bestowed a serious thought on its nature, while some of them seemed hardly aware of the possibility of its occurring; so limited had been their study of political economy as a science, so cursory their examination of corresponding periods of our history.

CHAP. III.

Effect of the War on the Price of Commodities.

WE shall now fix our attention on that general rise of prices which took place during the war, and continued almost without interruption from 1793 to 1814. As this formed one of the principal changes in our situation, both individually and nationally, it is fit we should investigate it with minute attention.

Of the causes of rise during the war, the principal were : —

1. The great demand of men for government service, and the consequent increase of wages and salaries.

2. The insufficiency of our agricultural produce, caused partly by bad seasons, partly by the drain of labour and capital for the public service.

3. The increase of taxation.

4. The addition to the cost of imported articles, arising from the greater expence of freight, insurance, and other charges of transport; and still more from,

5. The depreciation of our bank paper after the year 1809.

Of these different causes, the insufficiency of our agricultural produce, and the non-convertibility of our bank paper, are reserved for separate discussion: at present, we proceed to the effect of the demand of men for government service.

Proportion of our Population engaged in the Public Service. — In 1792, and the preceding years of peace, the demand made on our population for military purposes was very limited. In 1793, our levies took place on a large scale, and in 1795, the numbers raised in three successive years were such as to form a very large establishment. Recruiting, however, continued with activity during the whole war, until the signature of the preliminaries of peace, in the autumn of 1801. — In 1803, the renewal of hostilities was attended by a call on our population, which led, in little more than a year, to a more numerous establishment than we had ever had on foot. The decisive victory of Trafalgar removed the dread of invasion; but the continental successes of the French, the aggrandizing projects of Bonaparte, were such as to admit of no reduction on our part; and after 1808, all hearts were united in the cause of Spanish independence. Hence a continued demand for recruits, an increase of levy money, and a progressive addition to the numbers on foot, during the rest of the war.

The proportion of our population under arms was larger in this country than in any other state in Europe. In March 1804, Lord Liverpool, then Lord Hawkesbury, declared in Parliament, that our army and navy, including militia, but exclusive of volunteers, approached to the number of 400,000, being more than one in ten of the able-bodied population (then computed at 3,800,000) of Great Britain and Ireland. France, he added, had at that time in arms about 560,000 men, or one in fourteen of her able-bodied population. Austria had on foot also one man in fourteen; and Russia, if any dependence was to be placed in the loose returns of her population, nearly the same proportion. Prussia was the only power whose military force (about 240,000) bore, like ours, the proportion of one in ten to her able-bodied males : but it was with her a season of peace, and a number of her soldiers were permitted, by furlough, or otherwise, to give a part of the year to productive labour.

It is usual to compute the proportion of able-bodied men in a country at a fourth of the total population. The war of 1793 lasted nine years, and in the middle of that period (the year 1797 or 1798), the population of Great Britain and Ireland was probably about 14,000,000, giving for the able-bodied 3,500,000.

The war of 1803 lasted twelve years, and in 1809, the medium year, our numbers appear to have been somewhat less than 17,000,000, giving for the able-bodied a proportion of 4,200,000. The year 1804 was in the middle of our great contest, and his Lordship's computation may accordingly be taken as a fair average of the numbers under arms during the war.

It would be a task of no great difficulty to compute and place in one column the number of our able-bodied population for each year, and in another the number of soldiers, seamen, and militiamen in the public service. But the demand of war on population goes considerably farther, and extends into a field admitting of less accurate calculation, comprising not only persons in public offices, dock-yards, &c., but a number of individuals unconnected with government, such as manufacturers of arms, clothing, naval stores, builders of barracks, contractors, and others, the list of whom is too diversified and too mixed with the occupations of private life to admit of any other than a general estimate. This estimate we are inclined to make, in the proportion of one half of the military servants of the public, taking the average of the army, navy, and militia, at 400,000 during our twenty-three years of war, and at 200,000 the persons deriving an indirect employment from the war.

The number of men thus withdrawn from the pursuits of private industry appears to have been on an average 600,000, or 15 per cent of our able-bodied population. It is of importance to remark, that they consisted of individuals born chiefly between the years 1770 and 1790, a time when our population was very considerably inferior * to our numbers in 1800. We mention the year 1800, because in the event of any contest occurring at present, our recruits would, in general, consist of individuals born about that period, and the abstraction of an equal number of men from productive industry would, of course, be less felt than during the late war. The magnitude of the change which it at that time produced will be put in a striking light by a reference to our annual expenditure, keeping out of view our payments for interest of debt, or the civil service of government, and fixing our attention on a

Statement

* Rickman's Preliminary Observations on the Population Return of 1821.

Statement of the conjunct expense of our army, navy, and ordnance, from the beginning to the close of the war, taken from the accounts laid before Parliament.

1791.	£ 4,226,000	Brought up	£287,333,000
1792.	- 8,750,000	1804.	- 30,854,000
1793.	- 13,511,000	1805.	- 36,219,000
1794.	- 20,247,000	1806.	- 37,706,000
1795.	- 28,751,000	1807.	- 36,176,000
1796.	- 30,165,000	1808.	- 39,778,000
1797.	- 27,606,000	1809.	- 42,073,000
1798.	- 25,982,000	1810.	- 43,246,000
1799.	- 27,257,000	1811.	- 47,968,000
1800.	- 29,613,000	1812.	- 49,739,000
1801.	- 26,998,000	1813.	- 54,872,000
1802.	- 23,121,000	1814.	- 60,239,000
1803.	- 21,106,000	1815.	- 43,282,000
	£287,333,000		£809,485,000

Total exceeding 800,000,000.

To these sums there remains to add a proportion of our subsidies; we mean the part supplied to our allies, not in money, but in stores, the manufacture of which formed, of course, a farther demand on our national labour. Combining these into one sum, and dividing it by the number of years of military expenditure, (in all twenty-three,) we find the average annual charge for the army, navy, and ordnance, to have been *thirty-six* millions, instead of the four or five millions a year prior to 1792.

Observe next, the difference of effect on prices in a sum raised for a military purpose, and that which is levied for the interest of the national debt. The latter bore, like all taxation, on the prices of commodities; but our military expenditure had a double, or rather triple effect of that nature; first, by a drain of money; next, by a drain of hands; and, thirdly, by obliging other hands to work for those so withdrawn. It is only thus that we find it possible to explain either the extraordinary rise of prices in the war, or their no less extraordinary fall since the peace.

Effect of Taxation on House-keeping. — The result, or, to speak more properly, the avowed tendency of most taxes, is an augmentation of price. Taxes on commodities are always imposed on the calculation of being paid by the consumer; the supply of any article, whether a luxury, such as wine and sugar, or a necessary of life, like corn, salt, leather, being presumed to be in proportion to the effectual demand, and the tax intended not as a burden on the producer or vender, but as an addition to the price paid by the consumer. This was strikingly exemplified in the enhancement during the war of several articles of daily use. The sugar which the planter, on paying a moderate duty, could have afforded to sell in England at 60s. the cwt., was raised by the effect of new taxes and war charges to 70s. or 75s. Tea which, after paying half its original cost to the custom-house, might have been sold at 5s. or 6s. the lb., was raised, in consequence of being taxed 100 per cent., to 7s. or 8s., and the salt which (see Sir T. Bernard's pamphlet on the employment of the labouring classes in 1817) might, if unburdened, have been afforded at 1l. a ton, was made, in consequence of the duty, to cost more than twenty times that price.

Holland was the first country in Europe that afforded a striking example of the enhancement arising from taxation, her long and expensive struggle against Spain having necessitated very heavy imposts so far back as two centuries ago. Sir William Temple, among other interesting particulars with which he has diversified the graver matter of his Memoirs, takes occasion (Vol. I. Chapter VII.) to insert the following remark: " The excise in

Holland is great, and so general, that I have heard it observed at Amsterdam, that when, in a tavern, a certain dish of fish is eaten with the usual sauce, thirty several excises are paid, for what is necessary to that small service." — In England taxation was comparatively light, until we became ardent participators in continental war, at first under King William, afterwards under Queen Anne. A long peace, and the prudent administration of Walpole, lessened for a time the pressure of the burden; but it was very sensibly increased by the wars of 1740, 1756, 1775, and, above all, by those of the present age. This is sufficiently apparent from the following table of taxes which affect house-keeping.

Taxes on the necessaries or comforts of life.		Taxes on Luxuries.	
Assessed taxes (previous to the late reduction)	£6,500,000	Foreign spirits, chiefly brandy -	£2,300,000
Malt and Beer, (since the reduction in 1822)	6,500,000	British spirits -	3,000,000
Sugar -	3,000,000	Wine -	1,600,000
Tea -	3,000,000	Rum -	200,000
Coals carried coastways -	900,000	Coffee and Cocoa	300,000
Soap -	900,000	Raisins and other fruits	400,000
Candles and Tallow	400,000	Silk, raw and thrown	500,000
Cotton, Wool	500,000		
Leather (since the reduction in 1822)	300,000		
Foreign timber	1,000,000		
Bricks, tiles, stone, slate -	400,000		
Glass -	400,000		
Hemp -	200,000		

In all, above 32,000,000*l.*, exclusive of stamp duties and postage; also of taxes on foreign articles,

such as wool, butter, cheese, linens, drugs, all of
which have an effect more or less direct on house-
keeping, and were, like those enumerated above,
considerably increased during the war.

It occasionally happens, that, in consequence of
over supply, the market price of an article does
not rise in proportion to the duty, but continues as
low, or nearly as low, as previous to its imposition ;
the consequence of which is to throw the new burden on the producer. Such was long the case
of our West India sugar planters during the
war ; such is, in a great measure, their case at
present : it is the case, also, of a far more numerous class, our farmers, who, in 1823 as in 1815,
are to be considered as paying a large share of
their taxes out of their capital. In general, however, there is made an addition to the price of an
article, not merely to the amount of the tax, but in a
somewhat increased proportion. Suppose a custom
duty paid on an article which, on importation, is
sold to a wholesale dealer of the first class, next to
one of the second class, and, lastly, to a retailer :
the demand of a profit on, or rather of an indemnity for the tax, is repeated three times; and although these demands are far smaller in degree
than has been asserted by the advocates for the repeal of taxes, they form, eventually and collectively, a serious addition to the national burdens ;
an addition which, joined to the charge of collecting our taxes, constitutes, we believe, a dead loss
of from six to seven millions sterling, on the total
amount paid by the public. This loss will be
effectually lessened only by the introduction of a
double improvement ; a farther simplification, on
the part of government, of the process of collection, and, on the part of the public, the adoption of

the practice of ready money payments, so general in Holland, in its day of prosperity.

Next, as to taxation in a more direct and undisguised form, such as the assessed or the property taxes. In what manner, it may be asked, do individuals in general meet burdens of that description? Is it by self-denial and economy, by increased industry, or by adding the amount of the tax to the charge which, in their respective lines of business, they make on the public? Economy is practised, we may be assured, by those only whose income admits of no increase: augmented exertion is more natural to our countrymen, and was, doubtless, made to bear a considerable part in defraying our war burdens; but the latter, whenever it was at all practicable, were charged by the payer on his customers or connections; and the result, as explained in the last chapter, was a progressive enhancement not only of commodities, but of salaries, professional fees, and labour of every kind.

Collective Effect of the various Causes of Enhancement. — The total rise in prices during the war, appears to have been between 60 and 70 per cent., 160 or 170*l.* being required in 1813 to make the purchases, whether for the necessaries, comforts, or luxuries of life, which were made in 1792 for 100*l.* The degree of rise was, doubtless, different in different situations, but in regard to the public at large, that proportion will, we believe, be found to hold. To facilitate the comprehension of this somewhat intricate enquiry, it may be useful to descend into the details of domestic life, and to refer the reader to the subjoined table of family expenditure.

Comparative expenditure of a Family of the middle class in England in the years 1792 and 1813 ; — discriminating the heads of expence (by Nos. 1, 2, 3, 4.) so as to shew the rise produced respectively by each cause of enhancement.

1. Taxation was evidently the chief cause of rise in the following heads of expence :

	1792.	1813.
Assessed taxes and poor rate -	£18	47
Wine and spirits - -	16	35
Tea, sugar, and other groceries - -	22	38
Beer (partly from taxation, partly from enhancement of corn) - - -	7	11

2. The advance of labour, the occurrence of indifferent seasons, and the difficulty of import (from the rise of freight, and depreciation of our bank paper after 1809,) were the principal causes of enhancing

Bread - - -	25	50
Butcher meat - - -	25	45
Milk, butter, cheese, vegetables -	50	85

3. The advance of labour was chiefly instrumental in raising

Servants' wages - - -	18	22
House rent, the rent of houses in occupancy being determined by the expence of building new houses, and the latter by the price of labour -	60	100
Clothes - - - -	60	85
Fuel - - - -	24	35
Furniture; whether we consider the interest on the money vested in its purchase; which we calculate at -	42	63
Or annual repairs and purchases, estimated at . - -	14	24

4. The rise of the following can hardly be referred to any particular head, but appear the mixed result of taxation, enhanced labour, and depreciated currency.

Articles of leather manufacture, chiefly boots and shoes - - -	9	18
Candles and oil - -	6	10
Washing - - -	16	25
Education - - -	14	22
Medical attendance - -	14	20
Incidents, such as postage, stationery, charity, pocket disburse -	35	55
Expences of a less necessary character, viz. travelling, and temporary residence in the country - -	30	50
Expence of company - -	35	60
Total £540	900

A table of this kind, useful as it in some degree is, will hardly enable us to ascertain with precision the rise proceeding from each of the great causes of enhancement. But as on so interesting a topic no enquiry can be too minute, we shall endeavour, by varying our plan and resorting to other grounds of calculation, to attain the desired result.

Effect of Taxation. — For an estimate of the effect of taxes on house-keeping, we are in some measure prepared, by the tables in our second chapter. These, as well as our subsequent calculations, (see the chapter on National Revenue and Expenditure,) exhibit the proportion borne at different periods (1792, 1806, and 1813), by our burdens to our resources. And the result is, that the increase of our taxes, during the war, amounted to a charge of *nine per cent.* on our national capital. This, the arithmetical result, is greatly below the general estimate of the taxes imposed during the war. It is also below the addition which they will be found to have caused to our prices, when we take into account the obstacles they create to improvement in our agriculture and manufactures. These various impediments, unknown to the public, but severely felt by the persons on whose different lines of occupation they bear, all tend to keep up or augment prices, and their collective effect was, we believe, such as amply to justify our computing the addition to our prices, from our war taxation, at *twelve* instead of nine per cent. Of this we shall treat more fully in our concluding chapter, when we come to urge the expediency of a farther reduction in our public burdens.

Substitution of Bank Paper for Coin. — Here we introduce a cause to which, in the opinion of the great majority of the public, we ought to ascribe the chief part of the rise of prices during the war. This, however, is a very complicated question, and one which will require all the elucidation that a separate discussion can confer on it. At present we shall merely observe, that the addition to our prices, arising from the fall of our currency, from the inferiority in value of our paper to coin, appears to have been about 15 per cent. during the latter years of the war.

Rise in the Price of Labour. — To what are we to attribute the remarkable rise in the rate of labour during the late wars? — To two main causes : the demand of men for the public service, and the increased expence of provisions. In the first years of the war, the rise was caused only by the demand of men for the public service, and provisions had very little share in the enhancement during 1793 and 1794. But after 1795, and still more after 1799, the additional cost of provisions became such as to oblige the labourer and mechanic, in self-defence, to stipulate a higher money payment for his services.

A rise of wages may be either real or nominal. That which was consequent on the demand for the militia, army, and navy, proved a real and *bonâ fide* addition, the mechanic or manufacturer who remained at home being in greater request, and receiving larger pay from his employer, without reference to an increase in his expenditure. But a rise of wages proceeding from a rise of provisions is very different : the addition, in one sense, is merely a balance to the addition in another, and the augmentation is consequently nominal. To such an extent did this hold in the case of our labouring classes during the war, that the 28s. or 30s. paid them weekly in our provincial towns in 1812, were hardly more available in the purchase of the necessaries or comforts of life, than 15s. in 1792.

Effect of a Rise in the Price of Labour on House-keeping Expences. — The direct effect of such a rise is readily seen in the increase of servants' wages ; but its indirect operation, its enhancement of work performed out of doors, is of much more consequence. This will be at once apparent on our analyzing the component parts of the cost of manufactures. In cotton goods, after all the aid derived from machinery, labour still constitutes nearly a third of the price ; while in woollens, leather, hardware, linen, and perhaps in silk, its proportion is more nearly a half. Next, as to a very different head in family expenditure, that of house-rent, the chief constituent of charge is labour, since in a country of increasing population, the rent of houses in occupancy is regulated by the cost of new buildings; and in regard to these, the command of materials being unlimited, the question resolves itself into a calculation of the expence of the requisite labour.   In the case of furniture, a similar remark is applicable; and even in services of a higher class, such as teaching or medical attendance, the influence of this cause (rise of labour) is not excluded.

To the lower orders the rate of labour, in a direct sense, is of little consequence, as they are accustomed to serve themselves; but, in an indirect sense, by enhancing corn, it proves of the greatest importance.

Effect of an Enhancement of Corn on House-keeping.—A return of the ten years of peace preceding 1793, gave as the average of the quarter of wheat in the Windsor market, 2*l.* 10*s.* 9*d.* But thirteen years of war, from 1793 to 1805 (both inclusive), gave for the quarter of wheat an average of 3*l.* 17*s.* 2*d.*; in other words, 152*l.* were required to purchase the same quantity as 100*l.* previous to the war. And the succeeding eight years, from 1806 to 1813, gave the still higher average of 5*l.* 1*s.* 8*d.* for the quarter of wheat, denoting that no less than 200*l.* were, during that period, required to purchase what, previous to the war, had been obtained for 100*l.* Such was the rise in wheat: in butcher meat, and agricultural produce generally, the enhancement appears to have been nearly equal ; but for these and other details, we refer to the Appendix, and proceed to lay before our readers a statement of the general result.

Summary of the Rise in House-keeping at the close of the late Wars, making the Calculation in the most comprehensive Form, so as to be applicable, not to particular classes, but to the public at large.

Proportion of rise proceeding from increase of
         Taxation 12 per cent.
———————————— from rise of wages and
labour generally - - - 20 ditto
——————————— from the enhancement
of provisions, (see Appendix) - - 30 ditto
Of this rise in provisions, we may ascribe perhaps the half (or 15 per cent.) to the rise of labour, and other farming charges consequent on the demand of men for the public service : the other 15 per cent. to the depreciation of our bank paper, enhancement of freight, and other charges attendant on import.
Proportion of rise from extra charges on the purchase and import of other articles than corn ; such as wool, cotton, tobacco - 5 ditto

      Total - 67 per cent.

Such appears to have been the operation of the different causes of enhancement during the war. We proceed to exemplify that rise by a reference to real property.

Land.—The farm which, in 1792, let for 170*l.*; and which, in 1803, (see the tabular return of charges of cultivation in the chapter on Agriculture,) afforded a rental of 240*l.*, let in 1813, for 320*l.*

Houses.—The house which, in 1792, let for 50*l.*, and in 1806, for 65*l.*, might be considered in the latter years of the war, as worth 70*l.*, the rise being less great in houses than in land. Its value, as a purchase, originally 1000*l.*, was raised towards the middle of our long contest to 1300*l.*, and eventually to 1400*l.* or 1500*l.*

To define the amount of the rise of prices in particular commodities, would be a task of great labour and nicety : the only person who attempted it was the late Mr. Arthur Young, of whose calculations we shall treat afterwards. If, for the sake of conferring some degree of precision on an obscure subject, an attempt be made to divide the progress of enhancement into periods, we may consider the war as having produced half its effect towards the year 1806, viz. that the rise of prices taken in the most comprehensive sense, whether of provisions, clothing, labour, or professional charges, was in that year somewhat more than 30 per cent. above the prices of 1792. From 1806 to 1813 the rise was more rapid, in consequence of the double effect of a non-convertible currency, and extended military operations, so that in 1813 and 1814 the enhancement was 30 or 35 per cent. on the prices of 1806, or about 67 per cent. on those of 1792.

How far was this rise of prices nominal ? — It is incumbent on the attentive enquirer, to guard against the error so frequent in former years, and at present by no means exploded, of considering a rise of prices in the light of a *bonâ fide* addition to our public wealth. The reader, on referring to the preceding table of house-keeping expence, and considering how different trades and professions are linked together, will readily perceive the manner in which an individual, on the occurrence of a rise of prices in his particular department, indemnifies himself by a charge on the community. If, for the sake of illustration, we advert to articles of daily consumption, and to the tradesmen who are most familiar to us, we find the baker and butcher raise, of course, their demands on their customers, in proportion as the prices of their articles are raised to them by the farmer or grazier. In a similar, though not equally direct manner, the teacher augments his charge for board and instruction; the upholsterer, the price of his furniture; the landlord, the rent of his houses. — The whole partakes of the nature of circulation; or, to borrow an expression from Mr. S. Gray, of " charge and counter-charge."

But a rise which is common to all can be little else than nominal. The owner of a house or land was hardly able to purchase more commodities with the increased rent, during the war, than with the limited sum paid to him in 1792. He found 130*l.* in 1806, or 160*l.* in 1813, of no greater value than 100*l.* at the beginning of the French Revolution; and the correct mode of speaking is, — that land and houses rose in money rent in proportion as money declined in value, that is, they maintained a nearly uniform value, though the sum paid was very different. The same is applicable, as we shall see presently, to the far greater part of income, whether arising from property or labour; from capital vested in trade, manufacture, or agriculture; from wages, salaries, or professional charges, the sum paid having regularly increased as its value diminished.

Money Property, such as a Loan on Mortgage.— We here advert to a description of property materially different from land or houses, a property which experiences neither rise or fall, whatever be the fluctuations in the value of money. Suppose a sum (3,200*l.*) to have been advanced on mortgage in 1792, and to have remained on that security during the war, it will hardly be denied that in such years as 1811 or 1812, it was considered a property of less value than previous to the war. The 160*l.* which the owner continued to draw as interest, was in these years worth to him little more than 100*l.* in 1792.

Proportion of national Income affected in this Manner.—The reader on referring to our estimate of taxable income, in the chapter on National Revenue, will find the sums paid to annuitants, whether creditors of the public or of individuals, computed at 50,000,000*l.* a year, or one-fifth of the total national income. The receivers of the other four-fifths, whether landholders, farmers, merchants, or manufacturers; whether clerks, mechanics, or country labourers, obtained in their annual income, (in the form of rent, salary, wages, &c.) an addition corresponding, or nearly corresponding to the decline in the value of money. From this benefit were excluded the annuitants, to the extent we have mentioned; and many of them would have felt more severely the diminished value of their receipts, had it not been indirectly counterpoised by the activity arising from the war, and the consequent facility in providing for their connections in the public service.

Since the peace, the relative situation of these great portions of the community has, as is well known, been reversed. Annuitants have found their incomes recover their value; while the other classes, above all, the agriculturists, have experienced the most distressing effects from the fall of prices.

Change in the Value of Money. — Our readers will now be able to form a definite idea of what is meant when we speak of a fall or rise in the value of money. The fall of prices since the peace has been very different in different articles ; for while in the produce in the soil it is above 60, and in several branches of manufacture above 50 per cent., in the case of house-rent, or the wages of mechanics, it probably does not exceed 15 per cent. But the business of the statistical enquirer is with the *average*, which is, doubtless, not less than 30 per cent. on all payments determined by free competition ; in other words, in all articles brought to open market. In payments of a different nature, such as professional fees, salaries, servants' wages, the decrease is as yet inconsiderable ; because in these there exists no ready appeal to competition, no prompt means of overcoming the opposition to reduction. In London, journeymen in various trades are, in consequence of their system of combining, still in the receipt of 5s. or 6s. a day, as in the season of war and expensive living; but such a state of things can hardly be of long duration. The fall of provisions, the example of other countries, the diminished profit of capital, all point to the necessity of a change, and will eventually overcome resistance, whether on the part of the lower orders, or of the receivers of pensions and salaries, in whom, possessing as they do better means of information and comparison, pertinacity in retention would be more reprehensible. As such reduction, therefore, will, in all probability, become general, and the words, "fall of price," are too limited to express a decrease of such incomes as arise from personal exertion, we adopt the more comprehensive phrase of a "rise or fall in the value of money."

Prices on the Continent since 1792.—In how far, in the present age, have the other countries of Europe participated in those fluctuations of money which among us have reached so extraordinary a length? This question is of no easy solution, as well from want of documents in countries which had then no representative assembly, as from a depreciated paper having been current in almost every part of Europe. France, the only state that has equalled us in the duration of her wars, exhibits a remarkable contrast to us in the extent of her financial burdens. Her taxation, amounting in the beginning of the revolution, to about twenty-two millions sterling, (see the Report of Camus to the National Assembly, in July 1790), was never increased by more than the half of that sum; while our sixteen millions of 1792, became forty-five millions in 1804; sixty millions in 1808, and nearly seventy millions in 1814. In fact, in the early part of the revolutionary war, the collection of revenue in France was (see the *Duc de Gaete* on French Finance), considerably under twenty millions; the wants of government having been supplied by the emission of *assignats* during four years of emergency, (1792-3-4-5) and afterwards, in a considerable degree, by contributions from conquered territories. After the fervour of the first years of the revolution, there was in France no legislative body capable of conferring credit on government stock : no exemption from cash payments to facilitate to the payers of taxes, the means of reimbursing themselves by a ready addition to wages, salaries, or professional fees. The amount emitted in the form of assignats admits of no definite calculation, the value of that government paper having fallen rapidly, and having been at last, in 1796, reduced to a nullity. But if we compute at two hundred millions sterling the amount of public sacrifice from the assignats, and if we add for the bankruptcy committed in regard to two-thirds of the public debt, the forced loan of 1797, and the augmented taxation of the latter years of Bonaparte, two hundred millions more; and, finally, if we add a national loss of one hundred millions, consequent on his inauspicious return from Elba, and the invasion of 1815, we make in all, a pecuniary sacrifice on the part of France, of five hundred millions sterling, over and above the twenty-two millions of annual expenditure necessary under a peace establishment.

But the political strength of our southern neighbour lies less in money than in men, and that forced annual levy which would be so indignantly received among us, and so subversive of the resources of a commercial and manufacturing country, proved the most effectual means of drawing forth the power of France. In this respect accordingly, her sacrifices have been very great, the number of men who fell in the long struggle from 1792 to 1815, estimated, on a moderate computation, at a million and a half, being probably more than three times the number lost by our country, after every allowance for the destructive effect of tropical climates. In another respect, also, the neglect of education and postponement of the choice of a profession attendant on the Conscription, as well as the loss of time to those who escaped the sword and resumed a pacific occupation, form an amount of national detriment which may very fairly be put in the balance against the vast loss sustained in this country by the transition from war to peace.

The Netherlands, subjected during twenty years to the sway of France, and during a part of the time to the Conscription, were also exposed to heavy losses from the war. If less great than those of France in men, they were larger in a financial and commercial sense, as well from augmented taxation as from interrupted intercourse, and the many abortive attempts made, during the enforcement of the prohibitory decrees, to produce substitutes for coffee and other articles, the growth of a tropical climate.

Of the other European powers, the chief belligerent was Austria, whose pecuniary sacrifice was lessened by our subsidies, but whose loss in men amounted perhaps to the half of that of France. Next came Prussia, Spain, Russia, Sweden, in whose case the duration of suffering was less, but who were all doomed to feel the destructive ravage of war and invasion. A pressure of a more lasting kind, we mean that which is attendant on the maintenance of a large standing force, extended to every state, great and small, on the Continent, from 1793 to 1814. Their taxation consequently increased, and the general demand for men was followed by a general rise in the price of labour. The impracticability of effecting loans prevented that stimulus to productive industry, that drain on the future in favour of the present which took place among us to so great an extent: nor was there in any part of the Continent a continued inadequacy of agricultural produce. Accordingly, though prices on the Continent became higher in war than they had been in peace, though during the one period the demand for labour was brisk, in the other languid, the degree of difference was much smaller than with us. This topic shall be more fully treated in a subsequent part of our volume, (Appendix to Chap. ix.) but were we, for the sake of arriving at a definite estimate, to hazard a conjecture of the difference between the present prices on the Continent and those of 1792, we should pronounce the former about 15 per cent. higher, being half the enhancement that we find in England, comparing our present prices to those of 1792.

This excess on our part in the *ratio* of enhancement, added to a nearly similar excess in prices previous to 1792, makes a total difference between this country and the Continent of from 20 to 30 per cent. The leading causes of this are our heavy excise duties, the larger size of our towns, and the occasional operation of our corn laws. The balance against us would be still greater, were it not in a considerable degree counteracted by the cheapness of fuel and of several articles of manufacture, in particular hardware, in which our command of capital, our inland navigation, and our machinery, afford us a considerable advantage over the Continent.

Rise of Prices apparently indicative of Prosperity. — An increase in the money value of commodities, of land, houses, and stock in trade, accompanied by a general augmentation of salaries and wages, suggested during the war the idea of a general increase of wealth in correspondence, as was commonly believed, to the increase in our circulating medium.

We have already shown that this was, in a great measure, *nominal:* the augmented price of commodities, of land, houses, merchandise, required, to represent it, a larger sum of money, but that such money was of less value. Or, if we admit

that there was in several respects an increase of
property, that the general briskness caused by the
demands of government led to an actual rise of
prices, a rise over and above that which was requisite to meet the alteration in the value of the currency, it is fit, on the other hand, to recollect that
the fixed money property of the country, such as
the stocks and loans on mortgage, all underwent
depreciation, because in these the same sums represented a reduced value. What then was the *real*
result? That, on the one hand, the national property was lessened by the great additional charge
arising from the war: on the other, it was augmented in proportion, not to the rise of prices, but
to the progress of national improvement and increase of population. No such limitations, however, were admitted in the estimate of the public,
or, as far as we can perceive, in that of ministers:
both confidently inferred prosperity from rise of
prices, and appear never to have suspected that
such a rise was deceptive, and might take its origin,
in great part, from an increase of burden.

What a train of misconception, what a series of
sanguine and fallacious notions would have been
prevented, had the public been earlier aware of
these simple truths! During the war, the rise of
price was so regular, and of such long continuance,
(from 1793 to 1814), that the majority of the present generation took for granted that it would be
permanent, ascribing it less to the war and the demands of government, than to causes likely to be permanent, — such as the unknown gains of our foreign
commerce, or the influx of the precious metals of
America. But in this, as in other points, the return of
peace has undeceived us; it has shown that the
amount of our commercial gains, and the influx of

specie, were both over-rated ; and that the origin of high prices is to be sought in less welcome causes. Of these, the demand for men for the public service, the insufficiency of our growth of corn, and the depreciation of our bank paper, have all, for some time, ceased to operate, but their effects have by no means ceased ; while the fourth cause, we mean taxation, continues to press on us with almost undiminished rigour.

Evil of high Prices when peculiar to a Country.— The pernicious tendency of fluctuation in the value of money is generally admitted, but that of a general rise of prices is less understood : it is even the notion of a number of writers, and of a still greater number of practical men, that taxation, though a great cause of enhancement, is productive of no injury in a public sense, because the money thus collected is almost all expended at home. This idea has induced the writer already mentioned (Mr. S. Gray), whose views, sound and liberal in several respects, are in others greatly impaired by over-confidence, to give our national debt the convenient name of " public service capital." " The payment of the interest is," says Mr. Gray, in the work entitled, ' All Classes productive of National Wealth,' (p. 136.) " no disadvantage : the public is just where it was before : they have had thirty millions charged on them, for the interest of the national debt, and they have charged thirty millions in return." — All this might be true were the British Islands a distinct planet, or were they separated from the rest of the world by a " wall of brass ten thousand cubits high : " but, doomed as we are to intercourse with our continental brethren, does not an excess of taxation place us under a great relative disadvantage in a competition with foreign manufacturers? And, before the fall in our corn market, was it not to be apprehended, that our capitalists might transfer to less burdened countries, that money, that machinery, and, in part, those hands, which have so effectually conduced to make us support our financial pressure?

A writer of great notoriety, without carrying his doctrine so far as Mr. Gray, expresses, in more places than one, an opinion that high taxation imposes on us no disadvantage relatively to our neighbours, or, to use his own words, that " a generally high price of commodities in consequence of taxation would be of no disadvantage to a state." * This opinion Mr. Ricardo repeats in another passage (p. 305.) where he says, that the " amount of taxes and the increased price of labour in a country does not, according to his ideas, place it under any other disadvantage with respect to foreign countries, except the unavoidable one of paying these taxes." But he soon after makes a highly important qualification, by admitting that these charges render it the interest of every contributor to " withdraw his shoulder from the burden, and, in many cases, to remove himself and his capital to another country;" a course replete with the most injurious results.

Were we to suppose, for the sake of illustration, that the whole of the civilized world, the whole of the states who carry on a commercial intercourse with each other, were simultaneously involved in war, and obliged to impose on themselves burdens which bear the same proportion to the taxable income of each : — the consequence would be a

* Ricardo on Political Economy, 2d edition, p. 283.

concurrent and uniform rise of prices; and a contest, after lasting twenty years, might terminate without any relative disadvantage to any of the belligerents, as far as regarded their finances, or the state of their productive labour. But in every war there are certain states, whose rulers have the prudence to avoid participating in the unprofitable struggle, and who secure to their subjects the advantages of neutrality, along with an exemption from the burdens entailed on their neighbours. Such, in the present age, was the case of Denmark until 1807: such also was, for a time, the case of Sweden, Prussia, and, above all, of the United States of America.

Holland, a country particularly inclined to a pacific policy, has, from her geographical position, been unavoidably involved in most of the great contests which have taken place since she became a power, so that, during the last two centuries, her history exhibits hardly any period of exemption from them, except in the war of 1756. We, whether from the necessity or belligerent ardour, have so seldom enjoyed the blessing of neutrality, that to trace it in our history, we are obliged to recur to the reign of James I., who, whatever might be his weakness in other respects, stedfastly maintained peace amidst the convulsions of Germany, the dissensions of France, the prolonged hostilities of Spain and Holland. A striking illustration, not indeed of neutrality, but of that prudent mode of warfare which secures national independence, without aiming at foreign acquisitions, is to be found in the troubled reign of Elizabeth, and the wise administration of Cecil. How different would have been our situation in regard to public burdens, had the reins of government in the present age been held by such experienced hands!

Effect of the Rise of Prices on our Finances. — This rise, like all artificial changes, was productive of little permanent effect: it increased the numerical amount of the revenue, but it was ultimately followed by an equivalent loss in augmented expenditure; enhancing stores, salaries, the pay of the army and navy, in short, almost every object of government disburse. Unluckily, the amount of our loans was greatest at the time that money was of the least value. If we calculate the debt contracted since 1792 at 460,000,000*l.*, and divide the period with reference to the value of money, we shall find that the smaller part of this debt was incurred when money was more valuable than at present, the larger when money was more depreciated. Since the cessation of war, money has risen progressively in value, and the interest of our debt, without augmenting in amount, has increased in pressure to a degree which, coupled with the evils of sudden transition, has unfortunately borne hard on the majority of the public.

CHAP. IV.

Our Currency and Exchanges since 1792.

Having now traced the fluctuation in the price of commodities during the last thirty years, we proceed to a topic closely connected with it, the variations in our continental exchanges. In this, one of our chief objects will be to describe the operation of our subsidies, and of our purchases, occasionally to a great amount, of foreign corn; these being the causes which mainly affect our exchanges, and are productive of great and rapid fluctuation. They are, in general, demands both of large amount, and of sudden occurrence, super-added to our customary disburse, and requiring to be paid before time can be given to our merchants and manufacturers to prepare and send abroad an equivalent amount in commodities. This chapter will accordingly comprise,

A historical sketch of our continental ex-changes;

The effects of the exemption of the Bank from cash payments; and

The questions of depreciation and over-issue.

Historical Sketch of our Exchanges.

From 1792 *to* 1797.—In the first year of the war, our participation in the contest produced little effect on the exchange, in consequence of our aid being furnished less in money than in troops and military stores. Next summer (1794) a sudden depression was produced by the remittances commenced for the Prussian subsidy; but it ceased as soon as it became known that that power, a far less zealous ally in those days than subsequently, was not likely to fulfil its engagements. In 1795, circumstances became very different: our troops had been withdrawn from the Continent, our contribution to the allied cause was made, in a great measure, in money, and an unfortunate deficiency in our harvest, forced us to make large importations of corn. A balance from commercial payments began thus to be added to the remittances of government, and the result was a considerable fall in the exchange; money in England becoming inferior in value by five per cent. to the money of the Continent. This difference was of serious moment to the Bank, and obliged them to limit greatly the discount of mercantile bills, under an apprehension that the notes issued for such discount would be presented at the Bank for specie, and the latter exported to the Continent. Of the distress caused to merchants by this limitation, those only can judge who witnessed the pecuniary difficulties of 1795 and 1796, or who have had access to read in the parliamentary papers the anxious correspondence of that date between Mr. Pitt and the Bank directors. At one time (November, 1795) the price of gold, when purchased with Bank notes, had risen to eight per cent. above its value in coin, and necessitated a farther and most distressing reduction of Bank paper. In the autumn of 1796, a better harvest delivered us from one cause of drain; but towards the end of that year, and the beginning of 1797, distrust and alarm were renewed by a threatened invasion from France. The failure of several country banks having unluckily occurred at that critical moment, the consequence was a run on other country banks, and a great demand for gold from the Bank of England. In vain did the Directors resort to their hitherto unfailing expedient, a reduction of the quantity of their notes: the evil was new and peculiar; the drain continued without a prospect of abatement, when, after bringing down their circulation to nearly 8,600,000*l.* and communicating their situation to ministers, the Directors received, on the 25th February, 1797, the well-known injunction from the Privy Council, to suspend all farther payments in cash.

This order, limited at first to a few weeks, was soon after prolonged to the end of the current session of parliament, and eventually to the opening of the succeeding session. In the interval, circumstances became more favourable, corn was abundant, our continental subsidies drew to a close, our exports of merchandize were large, the exchange rose, and specie flowed into the country from causes very similar to those which had lately made it flow out. The bank was now in a state to resume cash payments; but parliament, finding that no inconvenience had resulted from the suspension, determined to adhere to it, and passed resolutions which made exemption from cash payments be considered our settled policy during the remainder of the war.

From 1797 *to* 1802.—The year 1798 was more than usually prosperous, being marked by a favourable season at home, an exemption from the burden of subsidies abroad, and distinguished success in our naval operations. Confidence being now restored, money became more rapid of circulation and comparatively plentiful, while our exchanges with the Continent experienced no fall, although our bank paper was no longer convertible into cash. The succeeding year, however, presented a very different spectacle: Austria, encouraged by a British subsidy and the co-operation of Russia, took the field against France, and hardly did intelligence arrive of the formation of this second coalition, and of an engagement for a double subsidy, when our exchanges began to bear the mark of rapid declension. The summer of 1799 was wet, and it unfortunately happened, as in 1796, that large purchases of corn were necessary at the time of the greatest pressure of foreign expenditure. Such continued our situation during the summer and autumn of 1800, when the successes of Bonaparte in Italy, and of Moreau in Germany, brought our subsidies to a close. Relief would now have been felt, had not the calamity of a deficient harvest taken place in 1800, and raised the price of corn during that and the following year to an unexampled height. The total value of our corn imports during 1800, 1801, and part of 1802, was declared in evidence before a parliamentary committee to be no less than 15,000,000*l.* sterling.

Of all the trials our money system had yet experienced, this was the most severe; and it was accordingly in 1800, that the effects of the non-convertibility of our bank paper became distinctly visible in the state of our exchanges. The wants of the merchants drove them to the bank for discounts, and their demands were supplied with a confidence which the Directors would not have ventured to exercise, had they been liable to pay in specie. This accommodation, though far from beneficial in its remote consequences, served at the time to lessen to the public the evils arising from the fall of the exchange, and the subsequent depreciation of our paper (between three and five per cent.) was hardly perceived, either by us or by foreigners. The charge most open to observation was in the materials of our currency: our guineas had now, for the most part, gone abroad, and our small-note circulation, insignificant during 1797, 1798, and part of 1799, became augmented in 1800, 1801, and 1802, to four millions, exclusive of the small notes of our provincial banks.

From 1803 *to* 1808. — The peace of Amiens was too short to admit of the repeal of the Restriction Act, and on the renewal of war, all idea of repeal was relinquished, a continuance of the suspension being considered an essential part of our policy. Unattended by continental subsidies, or by the necessity of corn imports, the years 1803, 1804, and part of 1805, passed over without pecuniary pressure; and when, in the latter part of 1805, the formation of a new coalition produced a sudden revolution in the exchange, its duration was momentary, for the day of Austerlitz, so disastrous in other respects, dispelled the cloud that was gathering over our financial horizon, and showed in the distance the suspension of our continental remittances. Next year, war ensued between Prussia and France, but that contest took place at a time when we had a ministry (the Whigs and Grenvilles) sparing in their advances to our continental allies: the exchange was not seriously affected, and after the peace of Tilsit (July 1807) began visibly to recover.

Four years of the war had thus passed without any material inconvenience from the non-convertibility of our bank paper, and its depreciation, still unknown to the public, had been but partially injurious. We are now, however, arrived at a different æra; a period when our hatred of Bonaparte, the confidence inspired by our decisive superiority at sea, and the influence of enthusiastic counsellors at home, made us forget calmer considerations, and join in a general call for a " system of vigour." The sufferings of several great branches of our commerce; the stagnation of our East India trade; the progressive sinking of West India property ; the diminished profit of ship owning; — misfortunes arising chiefly from heavy taxes and increased charges, were ascribed by many of the distressed parties to the competition of the Americans. Commercial jealousies have never been inactive : the American navigators had become in our eyes, what the Dutch had been in those of our ancestors under Cromwell and Charles II. ; and our merchants had no great difficulty in persuading a ministry, elated with our success at Copenhagen, and little versed in the sources of national wealth, that when neutral navigation should be controlled, the Continent must draw its supplies through the medium of England. Hence our Orders in council of November, 1807, orders issued with so much ardour, with such confidence of a favourable result, that our government paid no attention to the singular fact, that the intercourse they were so anxious to control, was, in the opinion of our enemies, highly advantageous to us ; for Bonaparte had, almost at the same moment, intimated to the American ambassador at Paris, his intention to prohibit it, declaring that " all maritime commerce tolerated on the Continent, whether through Americans or others, must turn to the advantage of England." These remarkable measures, joined to an embargo adopted by the American government, produced an almost complete suspension of intercourse between the United States and Europe, during 1808; the first time that such had been the case during twenty-five years.

Our stoppage of the American navigation is, we believe, the greatest error on record in mercantile history. Our trade with that country which, on the acknowledgment of its independence in 1783, we considered as wrested from our grasp, had proceeded in a *ratio* of continued increase, affording both advantage to the parties engaged, and the most gratifying lessons to those who, studying in the closet the sources of national prosperity, are enabled to discover how often the real are at variance with the apparent causes. This increase showed first that political and even national antipathies do not impede commerce between individuals, and that it is perfectly practicable to reap benefit from countries that were once our colonies, without the charge of defending them. It showed further the still more important truth, that "the greater the freedom of the trade of the Americans, the more active their intercourse with France, Holland, and other countries, the greater was the advantage arising to us."

In what manner, it may be asked, did it produce that result; a result so contrary to the tenets of the mercantile theory and of the colonial system, not of this country only, but of all Europe? From a cause of which the explanation, at first somewhat complicated, becomes, when examined, sufficiently easy and convincing — the increase of American capital consequent on unfettered trade, and the direction of a larger share of it to the purchase of our manufactures. Our exports to the United States amounted in 1805, 1806, and 1807, to the very large sum of 11 or 12,000,000*l.* sterling, while our imports from that country (Seybert's Statistical Annals, pp. 137. 155.) did not exceed 7 or 8,000,000*l.* : the remainder (Baring on the Orders in Council, p. 155.) was remitted to us in money, or, what is the same thing, in bills of exchange from the Continent of Europe, being the proceeds of tobacco, cotton, rice, and other American products sold there. The Continent, feeble at that time in its stock of manufacture and means of giving credit, could not supply the Americans with merchandize equal to more than half the articles which it imported from them ; and the result was the transmission of the proceeds to this country, a course which supplied us with funds for our continental expenditure as regularly as the packets crossed the narrow seas. Such was the trade stopped by our Orders in Council; a measure which, persisted in with blind pertinacity from year to year, drove the Americans first to the temporary expedient of an embargo, afterwards to the establishment of manufactures in their own country, and, eventually, to a declaration of war.

From 1808 *to* 1814. — This stoppage, sufficient of itself to produce a rapid fall in the exchange, was unluckily coincident in point of time with a heavy drain of money to Portugal and Spain, in support of the contest with France. From the Appendix to the Report of the Bullion Committee, (p. 232.) it appears that nearly three millions sterling were sent in specie to the Peninsula in 1808.

Next year neutral intercourse was, in a great measure, resumed, and the hazard of pecuniary embarrassment would have been less serious, had we not unfortunately been visited by the other great cause of pressure on our foreign exchanges, a deficient harvest. It became indispensable, therefore, to import corn at an unfortunate moment; at a time when, from other causes, our bank notes were at a depreciation of twelve or fifteen per cent. And the sum paid to foreigners for corn in 1810 being very large, exceeding (see the return to Parliament in the following year) seven millions sterling, our exchanges fell so as to bring our bank paper more than twenty per cent. below bullion. This fall took place some time after the public attention had been drawn to the subject by the Report of the Bullion Committee; and, great as it was, it would have been still greater, had not the abundant harvest of 1810 come most opportunely to our relief.

The autumn of 1810 was the first season in which the decrees of Bonaparte against our intercourse with the Continent were actually carried into effect. He had then brought his war with Austria to a close, secured himself by an alliance with that power, and conceived, from the fall of our bank paper and the multitude of our mercantile failures, the hope that a vigorous enforcement of his decrees would complete the measure of our embarrassment. Hence, in the winter of 1810, the general seizure of British shipping in the Prussian harbours; hence also the ridiculous measure of burning quantities of our merchandize in his sea-ports.

In 1811 our corn imports were inconsiderable; but the operations of neutral commerce were much cramped, our remittances to the Peninsula were large, and our exchanges extremely low. The same causes operated with increased effect in 1812, the year that our discussions with the United States unfortunately terminated in war. Happily, towards the end of that year, the result of the Russian campaign opened a cheering prospect in the political horizon; but the result was remote; a great struggle was still necessary, and the campaign of 1813 required exertions in Spain, and aid to our allies in Germany, on a scale of unparalleled magnitude. By this time our metallic currency was exhausted, and the specie bought up for the cause of the Continent, was paid for by government in bank notes, at the enormous premium of twenty-five or thirty per cent. Such continued to be the difference between paper and coin, until the overthrow of Bonaparte in April, 1814, after which the difference diminished to ten, and even to eight per cent. His return from Elba in 1815, and the vast preparations forthwith made on the Continent by us and our allies, again lowered the exchange to twenty, and even twenty-five per cent. — a fall which, after his second overthrow, disappeared with a rapidity that seemed destined to exemplify the arguments of the anti-bullionists; of those who maintained that the depreciation of our notes arose not from over-issue, but from continental demands.

Tabular Sketch of the principal Demands on our Currency for Continental Subsidies and Purchases of Corn since 1792.

Years.	Events Political and Commercial.	State of our Exchange with the Continent.
1792.	Peace.	A little above par.
1793.	Great mercantile failures: limitation of our paper currency.	A considerable rise in the Exchange.
1794.	Confidence reinstated.	Exchange nearly as in -1792.
1795.	Subsidy to Austria.	A fall at first small, afterwards considerable.
1796.	Subsidy continued, & an importation of corn.	Exchange continues very low.
1797.	Reduction of our paper currency; great scarcity of money.	A considerable rise in the exchange; large imports of specie.

(The Bank was exempted from cash payments in Feb. 1797.)

Years.	Events Political and Commercial.	State of our Exchange with the Continent.
1798.	Neither subsidy nor corn import.	Exchange continues in our favour.
1799.	Renewed subsidies followed by a deficient harvest.	Fall of the exchange after Midsummer.
1800.	Continuation of subsidy to Austria; great importation of corn.	Continued depression.
1801.	Subsidy suspended, but corn import continued.	Continued depression.
1802.	Peace.	Exchange reinstated.
From 1802 to 1808.	No large importation of corn, except in the summer of 1805; nor any subsidy of magnitude, except in the autumn of that year.	The exchange little affected during these six years, except in the autumn and winter of 1805.
From 1808 to 1814.	War in Portugal and Spain throughout the whole period; war in Germany in 1809;	The fall in the exchange great and permanent, beginning at eight or ten per cent. increasing

Years.	Events Political and Commercial.	State of our Exchange with the Continent.
	in Russia in 1812, and in Germany & France in 1813 and 1814. Corn purchases to a great amount in 1810. The Americans excluded from intercourse with the Continent after 1808, but more particularly after 1810.	to twelve, fifteen, twenty-five, and eventually to nearly thirty per cent.
1814.	Peace after 1st April, and a great increase in the export of our merchandize, but a continuance of remittances for subsidies and corn imports.	A considerable reinstatement of the exchange, leaving it from only eight to ten per cent. against England.
1815.	In April, May, June, renewal of war.	Fall of the exchange twenty and twenty-five per cent.
	In August and September, peace; cessation of corn imports; renewal of American intercourse.	The exchange recovered and brought first within twelve per cent., afterwards within five per cent. of par.
1816.	No subsidy or import of corn.	Exchange nearly at par.
1817. 1818.	Large imports of corn.	Exchange again lowered three, four, five, and eventually six per cent.
From 1819 to 1823.	No import of corn or heavy continental charge.	Exchange recovers; rises to par in 1820, and has since continued somewhat above par.

Distribution into Periods during the War. — The years in the preceding table may be classed into periods, each marked by distinct features. The first, from 1793 to 1797, preceded the exemption act : after that act came an interval of two years, during which, from a concurrence of favourable circumstances, the non-convertibility of our bank paper was not productive of depreciation. A very different scene was opened by the transactions of the three years between the summer of 1799 and that of 1802; years of heavy continental demand and of great pressure on the exchange. It was, however, reinstated by the peace; nor did it experience any pressure of magnitude or long continuance during the long interval that elapsed from the autumn of 1802 to that of 1808. This period of six years is perhaps the most remarkable of the whole, exhibiting the possibility of carrying on a war of great expence, without a material derangement of our currency, so long as we left to trade its free course, and abstained from great continental advances. It was, doubtless, this long enjoyment of financial ease, this apparent stability of our money system, that inspired our ministers and bank directors with over confidence, leading the former to their unfortunate measures against the American trade, and impressing the latter (Evidence, Bullion Report, pp. 89. 96. 144.) with the notion that their issues of paper had no effect on the exchange. To the measures founded on these views, and to the events noticed in the preceding table, is to be ascribed the depreciation that prevailed during the last period of the war — the five years from 1809 to 1814.

Total of our Corn Imports and Subsidies. — In computing the former, it is fit to bear in mind that we had become previously to 1793, a corn importing country, and that a certain quantity might be termed our habitual supply; an import not affecting

the exchange, but paid by a corresponding export
of our produce or manufactures; our coals, our tin,
our hardware, our cottons. We dwell, therefore,
only on the years of scarcity and extra import,
which, during the war, were 1796, 1800, 1801,
1802, 1805, 1810. After deducting from our total
supply in these years our average annual import,
there remains, as extra import, a quantity of which
the cost, in the six years collectively, was not short
of 25,000,000*l.*

Next as to the amount of our subsidies:
the total during twenty-one years, from 1793
to 1814, was between 50 and 60,000,000*l.*, forming with the corn purchases, an aggregate of
80,000,000*l.* Of this great sum, what proportion
was sent abroad in the shape of specie? Of the
subsidies, the chief part was supplied in clothing,
arms, stores; of our corn purchases, the larger
share was necessarily paid in money. If, without
attempting nicety of calculation, we assume the
export of specie for these purposes during the
whole war at 30,000,000*l.*, we shall be at no loss
to account for the disappearance of our metallic
currency, and of such supplies of bullion as found
their way to this country.

Our Exchanges since the Peace. — Since the
peace, the different periods, though less marked by extremes, have been equally deserving
of attention, as illustrative of our view of the
causes of fluctuation. In the autumn of 1814
our war charges ceased, our exports had free access to the Continent, and the exchange altered
from twenty-five to ten, and even eight per cent.
only, against us: it would have risen farther, had
not our corn imports been large. But no sooner

did the return of Bonaparte from Elba revive the alarm of war and subsidies, than the exchange fell to eighteen, twenty, and twenty-five per cent. ; a depression from which it recovered as suddenly after the battle of Waterloo, and the prospect of a speedy peace. During 1816 there was neither corn import nor subsidy; the American trade with the Continent was open, and the exchange returned to par, at which it for some time remained ; but the deficient harvest of that year necessitated in 1817 corn imports on a very large scale, reduced the exchange, and would have completely overset it, had not all the counteracting causes of free trade been in operation. By their aid we were enabled, during 1817, 1818, and the early part of 1819, to pay for an unexampled amount of foreign corn, (above 20,000,000*l.* as appears by the Appendix to the Agricultural Report of 1821, p. 396.) without a greater depreciation than four, five, or six per cent. Since 1819, these drains have ceased, and the exchange has been steadily in our favour.

Our Bank Paper :—Contradictory Opinions on the Subject.

We have now brought to a close our historical sketch, and shall proceed to make some remarks on the very opposite doctrines held in regard to our paper currency, by the adherents of ministry and opposition ; or, to speak more correctly, by the adversaries and supporters of the Bullion Committee of 1810. The former are still unwilling to admit the existence of depreciation in our bank paper, even in the latter years of the war : the latter equally unreasonable, refuse to trace such depreciation to the extra demands made

on us for subsidies and corn purchases, and insist
that it originated in over issue on the part of our
banks.   A singular discrepancy this, in a country
of free discussion, after the direction of so much
reasoning to the subject, and the lapse of so many
years replete with commercial and political information.   This discrepancy implies, we apprehend,
more than the absence of impartiality : it gives
cause to suspect in one party, an inadequate knowledge of the principles of productive industry ; in
the other, an insufficient attention to the evidence
of facts.

In attempting to point out the manner in which
both have deviated from impartial inquiry, and
exceeded the limits of fair inference, we shall
proceed as much as possible by a reference to
documents.   We shall have little difficulty in de-
scribing the nature of our currency previous to
1797, and the effect produced on it by sudden
drains for continental disburse: our more intricate
task will be to define the results of the exemption
act, the operation of which, has, from very different views, been considerably over-rated by each
party.   The bullionists attribute to it the whole,
or nearly the whole, of the enhancement of commodities during the war ; while their opponents,
regarding it as no less potent in good, than their
antagonists in evil, are accustomed to speak of it
as almost the sole engine of our financial support.
Both sides forget that these effects are too great
for the cause, and that the exemption act was
coincident in point of time with a change in our
financial system, of still more powerful operation ;
we mean the increase of our war taxes and the
reduction of our loans.

Our Money System previous to 1797.—The nature of our money system will be best understood by a comparison with that of the neighbouring countries. The amount of money circulating in France was computed, or rather guessed by Necker at 80,000,000*l.* sterling ; the amount in England and Scotland, not ascertained with more certainty than that of France, is supposed (Bank Committee Report, May, 1819,) to be between 50 and 60,000,000*l.* The currency of France is almost entirely metallic : there are in that country no banks of circulation, except the bank of Paris, and none of its notes being below 20*l.*, paper forms a very small part of the circulating medium. A foreigner may reside many years in a provincial town in France without seeing a bank note, and may occasionally hear the natives speak of having seen them as of a circumstance somewhat unusual and remarkable. France is consequently prevented from saving interest on 40 or 50,000,000*l.* of metallic currency, the place of which, were the banking system general, might be supplied by paper. The case of France is, in a great measure, that of the Continent at large ; while in this country, on the other hand, the saving arising from bank paper has been enjoyed, in a greater or less degree, for more than a century.

In what manner was this saving accomplished before the exemption from cash payments in 1797? A bank of good character issued notes to an extent of four or five times the amount of the gold kept in its coffers, a circulation of 100,000*l.* being maintained in ordinary times without a greater reserve or dead fund than between 20, and 30,000*l.* leaving above 70,000*l.* to be vested in productive securities, such as short-dated acceptances, exchequer bills, or the public funds, all possessing a characteristic indispensable to a banker, that of speedy convertibility into cash. Hence an income to the banking-house of 2 or 3,000*l.* a-year arising from perfectly fair sources; its credit and the superior convenience of paper to metallic currency. This saving, considered in a general sense, was such as to form a national object, England having, even previous to the exemption act, economised the interest on a sum probably exceeding 20,000,000*l.* of its currency.

Such was the state of our money system in the early years of the revolutionary war, when the confident character of our ministers and the surprising exertions of France led to an unexampled extension of our continental expenditure. It became particularly heavy in 1795, and unfortunately a deficient harvest in that year necessitated in 1796 large purchases of foreign corn, augmenting greatly the demand on the bank for metallic currency: hence a reduction of its discounts to merchants, a reluctance or rather inability to make the advances required by government, and a general embarrassment in the money-market. Under such circumstances, nothing could be more natural to all parties than to look for relief in exempting the bank from the necessity of paying cash for its notes; a measure that would enable it to continue its customary accommodation to trade, while government should meet the wants of our allies with our spare coin and bullion. The experiment, however, was too bold and novel to be adopted as a matter of choice; it was delayed until the continued call for guineas in February 1797 left no other alternative. Its adoption excited both surprise and distrust, but was divested of a part of its alarming character by the known solvency of the bank; and the acknowledged discretion of those to whom the new privilege was to be entrusted. A farther source of confidence was afforded to the few who knew the regulations of the bank, by the fact that the personal interest of a director is very slightly promoted by an increase of the income of the establishment.

Effects of the Restriction Act. — This decisive measure, which ought rather to be called an exemption than a restriction act, was limited at first to a few months, and the exchange being favourable during 1797, the bank made ample provision by the autumn of that year for the resumption of cash payments. But that step being deemed unnecessary by government, the exemption assumed the character of a permanent war measure, and enabled the bank to give a greater latitude to its accommodation both to merchants and the treasury. What were the chief characteristics of our money system in the succeeding years? A relief from such pecuniary difficulties as those of 1796 ; an increase of our paper circulation, at first small, afterwards considerable, and eventually very large. Next, in regard to the value of our notes compared to coin or bullion, there was, after 1799, a fall (about four per cent.) in the value of our notes, which long remained uniform, but was followed, after 1809, by a new and much greater fall. Lastly, the general rise in prices, though it in part *preceded* the exemption act, and originated consequently in other causes, continued during the whole period of the non-convertibility of our bank notes, and became greatest during their greatest depreciation.

These facts are admitted by all parties ; the difficulty is in tracing them to their origin, and in discriminating how far the exemption act was or was not instrumental in producing them.

Opinion of the Bullion Committee. — The writers of the Bullion Report, aware that the amount of bank notes in circulation had been materially increased, as well as that the scale of discounts (Report, p. 26.) had been greatly enlarged, naturally became impressed with the idea of over-issue, and ascribed to it almost exclusively the great rise in our prices during the war. But this opinion, when given in the unqualified terms adopted by them and their supporters, is liable to serious objections. First, the amount of Bank of England notes in circulation affords, as we have more fully shown in the Appendix, no satisfactory criterion for estimating the increase of our whole circulating medium, as part of the bank paper may be a substitute for coin sent abroad. In the next place, the means possessed by the Bullion Committee of appreciating the effect of the various other causes of enhancement were very limited : no evidence was given as to the rise of prices prior to the exemption act ; no reasoning attempted in regard to the effect of war in this augmentation. Neither the framers of the Report, nor those who wrote and spoke most confidently on the subject, possessed an accurate knowledge of the increase of our productive industry consequent on the war, or even of the increase of our population. Had Mr. Horner or Mr. Huskisson been aware of these vital truths, — had they known how materially prices were affected by causes altogether distinct from our paper currency, such as the demand for men for the public service, and the insufficiency of our growth of corn to our consumption, the conclusions of the Report would have been materially different. The various facts and arguments adduced in our preceding chapters, show how large an addition to our currency was indispensable to transact our extended business, to correspond with our augmented prices. And when to this is added a reason, different in its nature, but equal in its operation — the inducement after 1799 to export our metallic currency to the Continent, we shall find ample means of accounting for a fact which we admit to be at first calculated to excite surprise, the increase of our bank paper.

What then were the results distinctly attributable to the exemption act ; and, in the first place, what was its effect on the rules followed by the Bank of England in regard to discounts ? Its effect was highly beneficial to that Corporation : the Directors were relieved by it from the necessity of watching continental exchanges, from the apprehension of a drain of metallic currency on the approach of a subsidy, or a large import of corn ; the rules of discount became greatly simplified, and, after some years, the Directors considered themselves at liberty to issue notes to whoever tendered bills possessing the requisite of solidity, and the less easily ascertained characteristic of being for a *bonâ fide* transaction.

Country Banks. — In regard to these, the provision made by the act, if not properly an exemption, was an accommodation of great importance. They were relieved from the necessity of paying cash if they tendered Bank of England notes, a supply of which was attainable (Evidence of Mr. Baring before the Committees on Cash Payments) without the uncertainty and loss so frequently attendant on the acquisition of coin. A stock of notes could be procured at very short notice in exchange for the mercantile acceptances or other securities in which the funds of country banks are generally vested ; and the latter, thus relieved from much expense and anxiety, were enabled to lessen greatly their reserve fund, and consequently to extend their discounts.

Such were the effects of the act in regard to banks : to the public the principal result was a relief from scarcity of money.

If, for the sake of calculation, we assume that in 1796 the total bank paper in circulation in the kingdom was 25,000,000*l.*, and that 7,000,000*l.* of coin were kept in depôt, we may safely infer that of those 7,000,000*l.* two-thirds became in the course of a few years, disposable for the purpose of discount. Now, if from the rapidity of our transfers, a million of money suffice to circulate merchandize to the value of twenty or thirty millions, the change, arising from the addition of four or five millions to our currency, could not be otherwise than great in its degree, and extensive in its operation. Continental demands arose in 1799, and were carried during three years to an unexampled height : these the exemption act enabled us to meet by sending abroad our coin, exempting us, not indeed from a depreciation of our currency, but from pecuniary straits.

The act had another, though as yet unnoticed result — that of counteracting the tendency of our public loans to raise the rate of interest. What, it may be asked, was the current or average rate of interest previous to 1793 ? If we form our computation, not on the price of stocks, which from artificial causes fluctuated greatly, but on the general transactions of merchants, bankers, and capitalists, we shall find it to have been between four and five per cent.; and if we apply a similar mode of calculation to the war, we shall have reason to fix the average rate of interest between five and six per cent., the charge of commission, and other small additions familiar to persons in business (Evidence to the Bullion Report, p. 124.) accounting for the excess above the statutory limit. The effect of a war, the most expensive ever waged, was therefore to raise interest only one per cent.; an effect evidently disproportioned to the unexampled calls made on our national capital, and the cause of which is, doubtless, in a great measure to be sought in the reduction of the charge of banking consequent on the exemption act.

The Question of Depreciation and Over-issue. — We are now arrived at the most important question in the history of our currency; a question in which the advocates of the Bank and those of the Bullion Committee are directly at variance. The former maintain that the public possessed, after 1797, the same power of limitation as before, both in withholding bills for discount, and in paying over their notes to the Treasury, an absorbent to the extent of 1 or 2,000,000*l.* a week. Their antagonists, without denying this, which in fact cannot be controverted, appeal to the state of the bullion market in the latter years of the war; to the acknowledged inferiority of bank notes; and to the formidable argument, that a contraction of the amount in circulation would, at any time, have raised their value, and, if carried sufficiently far, have brought them on a par with coin.

Such was the substance of the reasoning adduced in the various speeches and publications on this subject in 1810 and 1811 : such are still, in a great measure, the tenets of the adverse parties ; each interpreting, in conformity with their own theory, the fluctuations that have occurred since the peace. No speaker in parliament, no writer on trade or finance has, as far as we are aware, endeavoured to reconcile arguments at present so strongly in contradiction, or sought a solution of the problem, while he admitted the substance of the allegations on either side. This we shall now attempt, and as we enter on the discussion with an advantage unknown to our predecessors, — the evidence supplied by several years of peace, — we are not without hopes of conducting our readers to a satisfactory conclusion, if they will summon patience to accompany us through an enquiry which can hardly fail to be both long and intricate.. If the narrators of military events, when entering on the relation of complicated movements, deem it necessary to make a demand of patient attention on the part of their readers, much more is such a warning required when we venture on a question which has been a source of perplexity to the public for a number of years.

Difference between an Increase of Bank Paper and an Increase of Metallic Currency. — The ease with which bank notes are struck off, and the apparent ease with which they are circulated, impressed the public, long before the late wars, with a notion, that banking operated like mining; and the general rise of prices that took place after 1764, was, by many, ascribed to that cause. Fortunately, Dr. Smith was then alive to combat prejudice in the people, or error in their rulers : he undeceived the public in this important point, and showed (Wealth of Nations, Book II. Chap. II.) that bank notes formed not an addition to the circulating medium of a country, but a substitution for coin sent abroad. An increase of coin and an increase of bank paper have this radical difference ; the former tends to lower the value of money throughout the world at large, by bringing forward gold and silver, commodities of undoubted acceptance and universal circulation, while a bank produces an article current only in a particular country. These countries are, as yet, of very limited extent, paper money being hardly known in France or Holland ; while in the rest of Europe the experience of its effects during the present age is not at all of a nature to extend its circulation.

What, it may be asked, are the causes which limit the supply of gold and silver from the mines ? Is it a monopolizing spirit on the part of any government or association, a deficiency of metallic ore, or a limitation in the demand of the public for either plate or currency ? To this we answer, that the mines are open to undertakers of any nation ; that the demand, whether for plate or currency, is unlimited ; and that as to the quantity of ore, it is not probable that one hundredth part of that which is in existence has yet been explored. The difficulty lies in the expence of mining ; for were the machinery and labour thus employed, to be rendered more effectual or less expensive, we should soon see an increase in the quantity of the precious metals extracted and brought to market. How far does a similar reasoning apply to banks ? They, like mines, are subjected to a limitation arising from expence (in salaries, rent, stamps, and the other charges of an establishment) ; but they have a more formidable limitation in the hazard attendant on over-issue, a hazard which may consist either in the discount of doubtful bills, or in the losses, less sudden, but eventually as serious, which are inseparable from an attempt to force paper on the public. How imperiously these obstacles impede circulation, — how effectually they confine a new establishment within narrow limits, is well known to all who have endeavoured to overcome them.

So far we are likely to have the assent of our readers, whether bullionists or advocates of the bank; nor need we enter on any argument to show that the issue of bank paper adds but slightly to the general stock of currency, *so long as such paper is demandable in cash.* But when exemption prevails, the case appears very different, and requires a close and attentive investigation.

Discounts—Increase of their Amount during the War.—Of the great increase during the war in the issues of bank paper for discounts, there can be no doubt, recorded as it is in the books of the Bank of England, and, we might add, in those of almost every provincial bank in the kingdom. On this the supporters of the Bullion Committee found their grand argument for the charge of over-issue, but in their eagerness to attain a favourite result, they overlook several material considerations.

1. The increase of our population between the years 1797 and 1810 (15 per cent.), was necessarily productive of a certain addition to the quantity of our bank paper ; an addition sufficient to balance the saving arising from economy in the use of notes.

2. A farther and more powerful cause is to be sought in the activity arising out of a state of war, a state which, by holding forth the prospect of large eventual profits, naturally induced individuals to

trade beyond their capital. Hence that multiplication of bills, promissory notes, and other expedients for raising money, so well known to those who have marked the course of mercantile affairs during the present age, and so clearly described in the evidence (p. 124.) appended to the Bullion Report. At that time the great object of a man engaged in business, whether as merchant, manufacturer, or farmer, was to gain time by putting off a payment until he had accomplished a sale, or otherwise realised an advantage in prospect. But in a season of peace, business is comparatively stationary. Our currency is adequate to our transactions; bills are less numerous, and payments in ready money or at short dates far more frequent. *

3. Add, farther, that in a state of war, the rise of price proceeding from the various circumstances enumerated in the preceding chapter, (augmented taxation, enhancement of labour, insufficiency of our growth of corn), made a larger sum requisite to circulate the same commodities.

Yet here we must add a remark which we do not recollect to have seen advanced by any writer or speaker on the subject, viz. that an increase of discounts is likely to tend as much to lower as to raise prices. The advances of that nature during the war were made to classes strictly productive, and were evidently instrumental in increasing the quantity of our farming produce and manufactures. If the dearness of our farming produce was owing to the insufficiency of our growth, what could conduce more to retard the progress of enhancement, than to give our agriculturists the means of increasing their supply?

* Tooke on High and Low Prices. Part I. pp. 87. *et seq.*

All this may be readily admitted, but it will be urged that bankers were led by the exemption act, and by the flattering prospects of their customers during the war, to make advances which, under other circumstances, they would have withheld. They were, we believe, very often persuaded to discount bills which were never paid, and occasionally to depart from their proper province by making advances on such securities as land or houses. The Bank of England, in like manner, dispensed on various occasions with a rule to which they would otherwise have strictly adhered; we mean the conviction that the bills tendered for discount had been drawn for real or *bonâ fide* transactions. Such relaxation probably proceeded from commendable motives : from a wish to prevent the extension of bankruptcies in manufacturing towns, in particular Glasgow or Manchester, at seasons when a fall of prices, or the failure of some eminent house threatened to involve in insolvency hundreds of persons engaged in trade with inadequate capital. We admit, however, that on such occasions the bank directors went beyond their province, and that the results were, in general, either unavailing or unfortunate, consisting in a loss to the Bank, or in a fruitless postponement of bankruptcy to the trader. But these advances could have very little tendency either to overcharge currency, or raise prices. The notes issued, whether in town or country, whether on good or bad security, soon found their way into hands whose interest it was to keep them as little time as possible; and any temporary over-issue was of short continuance.

Effect of the Exemption Act on our Currency. — We must thus dissent from the assertion so often urged since 1810, that the exemption from cash payments gave bankers the power of overcharging the currency, or, in other words, of causing a *direct* rise of prices. But in regard to their power in an *indirect* sense, we mean the power of issuing money to meet a rise of prices proceeding from other causes, such as increase of taxes or insufficiency in the supply of corn, we consider the question as very different, and are ready to make a very ample admission.

So long as the currency of a country consists of coin or of bank notes for which cash may be demanded of the issuer, the export of a large sum, whether for military purposes, for a subsidy, or the purchase of corn, is necessarily productive of a scarcity of money at home. This was strikingly exemplified in 1795 and 1796, and in such a case the money price of commodities, far from rising, is likely to be reduced in correspondence with the reduction of the circulating medium. Had such continued the case, the war, we may be assured, would never have been popular. But under the operation of the exemption act, circumstances were altogether different; the check of scarcity was removed, money was to be obtained, as in peace, by whoever was able to offer good bills payable at short dates, and the amount of these was in a state of progressive increase from the various causes recapitulated in the preceding paragraph.

Having thus admitted the principle, the next point is to estimate the extent of its operation. And here, if we cannot agree with the Bullionists as to the *nature* of the power conferred on bankers by the act of 1797, we shall, we doubt not, give them full satisfaction by our view of its *results*.

All parties admit the fact of an increase of currency during the war, but the bullionists ascribe it to a direct power on the part of bankers to over-issue, while we account that power strictly passive and restricted in its duration to a state of war. We consider it, however, to have been of very comprehensive operation so long as it lasted, and if we are asked in what manner its operation, if temporary, proved so extensive; we answer, because it seems to have enabled bankers to meet a rise of price by an increase of issue, *from whatever cause that rise proceeded.* What then was the result during the war? An increase of currency in proportion to rise of price, whatever was the cause that produced the rise; whether taxes, scarcity of corn, demand of men for government, or the additional cost of articles purchased abroad.

Effect, in a political sense, of the Exemption from Cash Payments. — The exemption act was in part productive of, in part coincident with, a great change in our financial situation — a change from embarrassment to abundance, from a state of disquietude to a state of confidence. The continuance of the war, the subsidizing of foreign powers, was no longer checked by pecuniary difficulties, and our rulers were induced to take several measures less necessary for self-defence, and partaking more of an aggressive character, than our countrymen in general are aware of. Is it likely that, without the confidence thus inspired, we should have formed against France the coalitions of 1799 or 1805, or that we should have commenced our second war so early as 1803 ? If, on the one hand, the possession of the Netherlands by France, and the restless spirit of Bonaparte would, under any circumstances, have prevented the enjoyment of tranquillity, it is fit to add, on the other, that the scale of expence on which the war was conducted, was our own act, and attributable in a great degree, to the exemption of our banks from cash payments.

Distinction between Depreciation of Bank Paper, and Diminution in the Value of Money generally. — It is of importance to make a distinction in regard to the operation of the exemption act before and after 1809. During the twelve years that followed the suspension of cash payments in 1797, our bank paper had given the greatest facilities to government expenditure, without incurring any depreciation of consequence, relatively to coin. The average price of commodities had in this interval experienced a great rise, (not less than 40 per cent.), compared to their average price in 1792. But as the causes of rise, (taxation, insufficiency of provisions of home growth, demand of men for government, &c.) were distinct or nearly distinct from an inferiority of paper to coin, the proper term for such rise of prices is not " depreciation of bank paper," but " a diminution in the value of money." In 1809 began a rise of prices from an altogether different cause ; a rise proceeding from our bank paper not being payable in coin, and from its being exposed to a trial it was unable to bear. This trial consisted in the concurrence of three remarkable circumstances ; the expence of the war in Spain ; the necessity of purchases of corn ; and the privation of remittances consequent on our unfortunate stoppage of the American trade with the continent of Europe.

Mode in which Depreciation was incurred abroad. — If we take, as an example, a campaign in the peninsular war, and suppose that in a year, such as 1811 or 1812, in which our expenditure there exceeded 10,000,000*l.* there was supplied to the extent of nine-tenths in clothing, arms, stores, and specie, exported from England, leaving 1,000,000*l.* to be defrayed by bills in our public offices; in what manner, we ask, could the receivers of these bills in the Peninsula turn them to account? There was not there, as in this country, an excise-office, a custom-house, a receiver for the county, nor, after the stoppage of the American trade, were there merchants, to whom they could be transferred at par or at a slight discount. If remitted to England, those bills could not purchase bullion; and if they procured English merchandize without a perceptible loss, the quantity of such was beyond the demand of the peninsular or any continental market, limited as it was in these years by Bonaparte's anti-commercial decrees. The unavoidable consequence was a fall in the value of our bills, in other words, of the bank notes in which these bills were paid, exemplifying the doctrine of Dr. Smith, or rather the self-evident truth, that " whatever causes delay the payment, or restrict the circulation of a currency, necessarily produce depreciation, the ratio of which must increase with the pressure of these causes."

A similar reasoning was evidently applicable to our continental subsidies as far as paid in money. It held also as to the purchase of foreign corn whenever such purchases were of an amount to surpass our export of merchandize.

The degree of such Depreciation.—Of the degree of inferiority in our paper to the metallic currency of the Continent, the only fit index was the rate of exchange; and on referring to that impartial monitor, we shall find an ample confirmation of the preceding reasoning. The extent of fall during the war differed regularly in different years according to the amount of the demands of the Continent on this country. Slight in years such as 1803 and 1804, when the war was merely maritime, it was more considerable in the case of continental operations, as in 1805 and 1806;—serious, when to these operations was joined, as in 1800, the necessity of corn purchases ; and greatest of all when, as in the years following 1809, there existed the double drain of subsidy and corn import, without either a metallic currency, or a free neutral traffic to interpose their countervailing effects.

Effect of high Prices abroad on Prices at home.— Whatever enhances corn enhances labour, and makes itself felt in almost every department of our productive industry. Now, after 1809 the quarter of wheat rose from 80*s.* to 100*s.* in consequence chiefly of the fall of the exchange, of the necessity of paying in paper a fourth or a fifth more than would have been required had not that paper been depreciated. This rise, unfortunately so great in corn, prevailed in other foreign commodities; in timber, hemp, tallow, to which may be added a few articles insignificant in amount, but illustrative of our proposition, because they were wholly supplied by the Continent, such as cork, antimony, and others, the price of which rose rapidly after 1809.

How far were the effects of this enhancement apparent in our hardware, cotton, and woollens, the cost of which was less directly affected by the price of our imports ? The cost in English money of Spanish wool and American cotton, doubtless, rose in consequence of the fall of our paper ; the wages of our workmen had, likewise, a tendency to rise with the price of corn. The finished

article was consequently enhanced, but as the
charges we have mentioned formed only a part of
the cost, the proportion of rise attributable to our
bank paper was not great in the case of our manufactures.

Extent of such Effect previous to 1809. — Having
now explained the mode in which our bank paper
affected the price of commodities, it remains to
ascertain the *quantum* of the enhancement thus
caused. And here when computing such by the rate
of exchange, it would evidently be unfair to draw
our inferences from a short interval, such as the
latter months of 1805, when our exchanges were
depressed by a sudden continental demand : the
correct and impartial mode is to class the years of
the exemption by periods. If we begin with the
twelve years that elapsed from the early part of
1797 to that of 1809, we shall find that the inferiority of our bank notes to coin (see Mr. Mushet's
Tables and Mr. M'Culloch's article on *Money*, in
Napier's Supplement to the Encyclop. Brit.) may
be reckoned, at an average of the whole period,
between three and five per cent. But as this inferiority refers to continental purposes, and as a
considerable interval elapsed before the depreciation became so great in regard to payments at
home, it will suffice that we assume *three* per cent.
as the average rise in our prices, consequent on the
exemption act, until 1809.

The same after 1809. — After 1809 we enter
on a new æra; our financial horizon became ob-
scured, and the tone of the calculator must be
altered. If after that year twenty-five per cent.
was the average depreciation of our bank notes
abroad, and if at home we make the same al-

lowance as before, an allowance founded on the time which it takes to adjust prices generally to an alteration in the value of a currency, particularly where that alteration is not apparent, we shall probably find *fifteen per cent.* a fair representation of the rise of prices, as far as caused by the non-convertibility of our paper, during the five last years of the war ; in other words, that 115*l.* of our bank paper was required to make those purchases, or transact that business for which 100*l.* of it would have been sufficient, had there been no exemption from cash payments.

Summary of the preceding. — If we proceed to make a summary of the various facts connected with our paper currency, and of the conclusions they suggest, we shall find them nearly as follows :

In regard to Diminution in the Value of Money generally, distinct from the Fall of our Bank Paper.—

1. The exemption from cash payments was productive of a saving to our banks peculiar to this country, and enabled them to make advances at a rate of interest lower than that of any other country during the war. This had, in some measure, a tendency to retard a rise of prices ; but

2. The exemption caused a very different result, in as far as it relieved bankers from the necessity of regulating their issues by the state of the exchange. It may even be said to have given free scope to the various causes of enhancement attendant on a state of war.

Depreciation or Inferiority of our Paper to Coin.

1. Our dependence on the Continent, and the non-convertibility of our bank paper, were productive of its depreciation, particularly after 1809 ; but,

2. The effect of that depreciation on the price of commodities, in other words, the rise of prices consequent on the fall of our bank paper, does not appear to have exceeded 15 per cent.

These conclusions will, we trust, be found to give the question a definite form ; yet moderate as our statement may appear to the reader, we hardly expect it to receive a ready assent from either party, so perplexing is this enquiry, and so much has it been involved with other topics of discussion. We shall accordingly proceed to make a few animadversions on the favourite tenets of each.

Arguments of the Advocates of the Bank. — These gentlemen, with all their ardour in the cause of ministers, will hardly refuse to allow that the command of money, to which the exemption from cash payments was so instrumental, increased our scale of expenditure during the war. In admitting this, they can make no great objection to the inference that the exemption act was a powerful, though indirect, cause of the rise of prices previous to 1809. They will be more reluctant to admit our second position, that which assumes depreciation of our bank paper; for though they allow a great fall to have taken place in the exchange after 1809, they are ill prepared to admit that from the moment we declared our paper not convertible into the currency of the rest of the civilised world, we rendered depreciation possible, and that a postponement of the evil, or a mitigation of its extent, would necessarily depend on the nature of our connection with the Continent, on the degree to which our paper should be put to the test.

But those who still feel a difficulty in believing depreciation to have existed at home, should begin by asking themselves whether, without the non-convertibility of our paper, depreciation would have existed abroad ; or, if it had begun, whether it would have continued. If they refer to the evidence of Mr. Goldsmid, and others, before the Bullion Committee, they will find, that had our currency been of coin, or convertible into coin, 7 or 8 per cent. would have been the greatest difference that could possibly have taken place in the exchange even at the time of the anti-commercial decrees. Let them ask, in the next place, whether a reduction of the quantity of our bank paper would not at any time have raised its value, and, if carried a sufficient length, have brought it to a par with coin ?

Supposing the advocates of the Bank to assent to this reasoning, and to admit the existence of depreciation, our next object is to satisfy them that our estimate of it is not exaggerated. This will best be done by a comparison of the rise of prices in England, and on the Continent. If in this country 160*l.* were necessary towards the close of the war to make the purchases which 100*l.* made in 1792, or if, in other words, our prices experienced a rise of 60 per cent., the rise on the Continent will probably have been found to have been about 30 per cent. This difference was too great to be explained by any difference in the comparative charges of war ; for taxation, the demand of men for the public service, and the enhancement of corn, were all operative in a considerable degree on the Continent. Farther, since the reinstatement of our currency, the decline in prices has been about 15 per cent. greater in England than on the Continent, a coincidence which seems fully to justify our computation, that that proportion of the rise in war was produced by the fall of our bank paper.

The Supporters of the Bullion Committee. — We are next to address ourselves to the adherents of a different doctrine, to men who take a bolder tone, and do not scruple to tax their antagonists with ignorance of the principles of productive industry. Nor need we, in truth, be surprised at the confidence of their language in regard to the question under discussion. The rise of our prices during the war was so progressive, and so coincident in point of time with the increase of bank paper, that the connexion of cause and effect was generally asserted, long before it received a kind of official sanction from the Bullion Report. To ascribe enhancement to over-issue, was easy ; to trace it to other causes and to define the limited operation of the exemption act, would have been a tedious and intricate task. Yet the difference between us and the Bullionists consists less in the extent of enhancement, attributed to our bank paper, than in the mode by which that enhancement was produced. While *they* hardly notice the effect of taxation, demand of men for government, or the insufficient growth of corn, as causes of rise of price, and ascribe almost all to bank paper, *we* consider these as the direct causes, and our paper as operative only in a passive sense, by giving scope to these causes, and consequently facilitating the continuance of the war. We can trace no *direct* power in banks to over-issue ; and those who insist on it, will find themselves involved in all the difficulty attendant on an attack of the strong hold of their opponents, viz. the power possessed by the public of relieving themselves of a surcharge, by paying bank notes into the Treasury.

The Bullionists, being in general political economists, will readily assent to the arguments of Dr. Smith, that banks, while subject to cash payments, possess no power of increasing the amount of currency; a power which many projectors, about the middle of last century, fondly imagined to reside in banks, and the non-existence of which is so clearly explained by Dr. Smith, in his account of the unsuccessful career of the Ayr Bank. When satisfied of this, let them next endeavour to show in what manner it was possible that such power could have been conferred by the exemption act. That act was evidently incapable of giving solidity to bills or other securities, which, without it, would have been bad or doubtful; nor did any of its provisions either oblige or induce the public to pay interest on more currency than they required. During its operation as before, our notes were nothing more than an instrument of circulation, and one which continued to cost the holders fully as much as prior to the war. Obtained by a sacrifice of interest, it was important to every individual, whether a speculative or a regular dealer, to circulate them as quickly as possible, to retain them no longer than was necessary to accomplish a specific purpose. From this reasoning we infer that bank paper, whether payable or not in cash, must await the call of the customer, and that its circulation can be augmented only to meet a rise proceeding from other causes. Farther, this extended circulation can continue only so long as the causes of high prices remain in force; for bank paper has neither the power of raising prices in the first instance, or of maintaining them when the causes of enhancement cease to operate.

If this doctrine appear somewhat bold, we appeal to the evidence of facts, and invite our readers to consider how remarkably our conclusions are supported by the course of circumstances since the peace. During the years 1815 and 1816 no compulsion was exercised in regard to a return to cash payments, nor were the advantages arising to bankers from the exemption act, restricted in a single instance ; yet country bankers were forced greatly to curtail their circulation, a measure which, had they possessed the power commonly attributed to them, would, doubtless, have been postponed till the act had been repealed. Further, had our banks possessed this power, the latitude given to circulation during the war, would, we may be assured, have been much greater. Mr. Huskisson, when writing on this subject in 1810, and viewing the question in the light of the Bullion Committee, acknowledged his surprise that the issues of the Bank had not been far greater. Is it going too far to ask whether this does not justify the suspicion of a latent error in the reasoning of bullionists ; of the existence of circumstances of which their arguments take no account? Without pressing this point in the abstract, we shall adduce a fact entitled to the most attentive consideration of those who invest the exemption act with so formidable an attribute as that of enabling bankers to make a direct increase of their issues. Our growth of corn, inadequate during the whole war, became so, in a high degree, soon after the exemption act : our farmers had then a powerful motive to extend their tillage, and, in fact, did extend it as far as their means admitted. It was a general notion on the part of the public,

and we believe of ministers, that this extension was
limited, not by want of funds, but by the nature of
the soil ; an opinion, however, *wholly disproved by
the experience of the last seven years*, in which the
amount produced from our soil has been so greatly
augmented. To what has this augmentation been
owing, except to the application of additional capital and labour? Observe the importance of the
conclusion to which this leads : our soil having
been, as far as regarded natural fertility, equally
capable of increased production, ten or twelve years
ago, would not our farmers, had our *banks possessed
the power ascribed to them*, have obtained such an
issue of notes as would have enabled them to extend their tillage, and bring our growth of corn on
a level with our consumption ? If want of hands
be alleged as the obstacle, we answer, that in Ireland and in Germany there were many thousand
labourers unemployed, and that a command of capital, such as is vulgarly ascribed to our banks,
would soon have transported them to our shores.

Historical Enquiries.

I. *The Exemption Act, viewed in connection with
the events of the War.* — We shall now bestow a
few paragraphs on an interesting, but hitherto unnoticed topic, in the history of our paper currency;
we mean the question, "whether the exemption
act, had it not taken place when it did, would
have been resorted to at any subsequent æra in
the war?" This enquiry, brief as we shall make
it, requires an attentive notice of our situation
relatively to the Continent at particular periods.

The preliminaries of peace between France
and Austria were signed at Leoben in April 1797,

a few weeks after the exemption act, and though the definitive treaty (that of Campo Formio) was not concluded till the autumn, there existed little doubt of its taking place, and it is a well-known fact, that, in the course of the summer, our pecuniary resources became more abundant. This was also a time of naval success, and though the dread of invasion continued, we have the authority of the Bullion Committee (Report, page 27.) that the Bank ought to have met an alarm of that nature by a liberal issue of their notes. Be this as it may, it seems extremely unlikely that at any time in 1797, after the preliminaries of Leoben, ministers would have adopted a measure so new and questionable as the suspension of cash payments.

The succeeding year was one of peace on the Continent, and of prosperity in this country. But in what manner did the renewal of operations by land in 1799, affect the state of our circulating medium? The effect, for some time inconsiderable, became very different after the failure of the harvest; the long interval of two years that elapsed from that failure, until the certainty of a favourable crop in 1801, would, had cash payments been enforced, have recalled all the difficulties of 1796 ; so that we by no means venture to assert that ministers would have forborne a recourse to the measure in question.

The preliminaries of peace with France were signed in the autumn of 1801, and there ensued a long interval of ease in regard to financial and commercial affairs. Even in 1805, when we again roused the Continent to arms, and subsidized not only Austria, but Russia, the pressure on our exchange was temporary ; for this was no season of indecisive warfare, of protracted operations : our allies had now an antagonist who brought a campaign speedily to issue; and who, at Ulm and Austerlitz, effectually relieved us from the pressure of subsidies. In 1806 and 1807, part of our allies continued in arms, but they were not supported by ministers on a scale productive of pecuniary embarrassment, and our corn imports were fortunately not of a magnitude to press on the exchange.

There thus elapsed a period of not less than *seven years* without any great or continued derangement in our continental exchanges. However, a very different prospect was opened by the events of 1809, by our augmented expenditure in the Peninsula, and the necessity of large purchases of corn. Had our bank-paper been at that time demandable in cash, we should, doubtless, have experienced great difficulties, nor would the public, ardent in the cause of Spain, have hesitated to support ministers in any measure that promised an addition to our pecuniary means. There is, on the other hand, equally little doubt, that without the previous existence of the exemption act, and the confidence inspired by its till then successful operation, we should not have interfered with the freedom of American navigation : we would have studied more carefully the effect of that navigation on our resources, and have cherished it as a fund for our continental expences. Our ship-owners might have clamoured, and individual members of the cabinet might have been rendered converts to their views, but the opinion of the bank directors would have been hostile to such a measure; and the danger pointed out by the solitary voice of Mr. Baring (Inquiry into our Orders in Council) would have been brought before government with all the weight of that powerful body.

II. The next and concluding object of our inquiry is, " to what degree did the exemption from cash payments increase to government the means of exertion on the Continent?" By substituting at home paper for metallic currency, it enabled us to send abroad our gold coin, the amount of which, very differently as it has been computed, (Bank Committee Report, May 1819,) was, probably, not far short of 20,000,000*l.* sterling ; — a most substantial aid, doubtless, but one which was, in a great measure, exhausted in the first three years of trial, 1799, 1800, 1801. From that time forward, the portion of gold coin in the country appears to have been comparatively small : at all events, it was found quite inadequate to the demand in the second period of trial, 1809 and 1810, the exchange having fallen rapidly as soon as the pressure on it became considerable.

The extent of direct aid arising from the exemption act, seems thus to have been limited to the amount of our gold coin ; but we should enter into a much wider field, were we to calculate the augmentation of our financial means by the other results of the act; the increased facility of discount, the comparatively moderate rate of interest, above all, the practicability of increasing our stock of currency in proportion to the rise of our prices. After every deduction for exaggeration, and after ascribing the larger share of our financial abundance to the bold plan of raising the supplies within the year, there still remains a great amount referable to the effects of the exemption from cash-payments. Of the extent of aid arising from a moderate rate of interest, some idea may be formed by those who have visited the Continent, and observed how slowly productive industry advances in a country like France, where, even in peace, 6 or 7 per cent. is the current interest of money.

This benefit we experienced without much alloy, until the five last years of the war, when the depreciation of our paper on the Continent caused a sudden increase of our foreign disburse, and some time after, an increase less sudden, but of greater amount and permanency, in our expenditure at home. The losses hence arising may, we believe, without pressing the point to an extreme, be carried to 100,000,000*l.*, in addition to which we have to charge on the exemption act a large proportion of the distress of our agriculturists, conducive as that act certainly was, to the enormous rise of prices during war, the fall of which has been, and will be productive of great embarrassment, until wages, salaries, and other charges, shall be accommodated to the new scale. It thus becomes a question, whether the amount of benefit derived from the exemption in the period preceding 1809 has not been balanced, perhaps more than balanced, by the loss and pressure of the subsequent years. This point, however, we have no wish to urge, and still less the speculative question already alluded to, whether, without the aid derived from this act, our government would have renewed the war in 1803, or have conducted it on so expensive a scale. Our object is statistical, not political ; and in calculating the advantage or disadvantage of a great financial measure, we confine ourselves to reasoning on events as they actually occurred.

Mr. Peel's Bill. — The majority of the public, yielding to first impressions and unable to follow up an intricate course of reasoning, have ascribed to Mr. Peel's bill that re-action which arose from a far more comprehensive cause. As to the *present* effects of that bill, we can trace none of consequence, except a partial rise in the value of gold throughout Europe, consequent on the large purchases of the Bank of England; while, as to its *permanent* effects, we can perceive, so long as peace lasts, hardly any worth notice, except an obligation on that establishment to keep a large reserve in cash, and consequently to reduce its annual profits by 400,000*l.* or whatever may be the charge of providing and keeping that deposit. Country bankers, on the other hand, are subjected to little additional expence, since by a clause in the act of 1819, recently prolonged, they continue exempt from the necessity of paying in cash, if they tender Bank of England notes.

But innoxious as this law in a great measure was, we consider its enactment matter of great regret, partly as subjecting to undue censure the individuals instrumental in passing it, more as tending to make the public mistake the real cause of the distress that has since taken place. Had no such act been passed, and had the Bank been left to pay in cash or not at its option, the public would, as in 1815 and 1816, have fixed their attention on the transition from peace to war as the real cause of the fall of prices, and have been better prepared to comprehend and second the financial measures which such a transition required.

CHAP. V.

Agriculture.

W<small>E</small> propose dividing this very important branch of our subject into three parts :

I. A historical sketch of our corn-trade, particularly since 1792 ; and the causes of the remarkable fluctuations of price.

II. The present situation and prospects of our agriculturists.

III. The question of a protecting duty.

SECTION I.

Historical Sketch of our Corn Trade.

The interference of our legislature with the export of corn dates from a very remote æra ; but our notice shall not be carried beyond the reign of Elizabeth, a reign which, in its early years, exhibited corn at as low a price as at any period of our history, but became in its progress as remarkable for enhancement as the reign of George III. England was in those days, a corn-exporting country, if the name of export can be said to belong to a surplus produce hardly greater than that of a single county in the present age. In the early part of the reign of Elizabeth (1562), export was permitted by act of Parliament, whenever our prices fell to 10*s.* the quarter for wheat, and 6*s.* 8*d.* for barley and malt ; prices remarkably low, when we consider that our coin was, in point of metallic weight and fineness, the same as at present.   At that rate, however, they did not long continue ; a considerable rise took place before 1570 ; and in 1593 the export limit was extended by act of parliament to 20*s.* for the quarter of wheat, and 12*s.* for barley and malt.

This doubling of price in the course of thirty years, has not a little embarrassed political arithmeticians : it is commonly attributed to the influx of metallic currency from the American mines before an outlet was found for it in India and China, but from our experience of the limited effect of such a cause in subsequent times, particularly since the late peace, we are inclined to lay no little stress on the general prevalence of war throughout Europe, from the middle of the sixteenth to that of the seventeenth century.   Be this as it may, the enhancement continued progressive ; for in 1623 the export limit was raised to 32*s.* the quarter for wheat, and 16*s.* for barley and malt.   In the succeeding age, particularly under Cromwell, our markets were considerably higher, but the rise was in some degree nominal, our coin, though no longer debased by government, being deteriorated by clipping and filing, and brought, at times, no less than 20 per cent. below its legal value, —an abuse not completely remedied till 1717.

Bounty on Export. — In the reign of Charles II. the prices of corn declined, and though several acts were passed (in 1660, 1663, 1670), imposing a duty on foreign corn, their effect in our market was inconsiderable, because our growth equalled, or more than equalled our consumption.   Prices accordingly did not rise, the agriculturists complained, and the epoch of the Revolution was marked by a new refinement of legislation in their favour. The necessity of providing supplies for the formidable contest with Louis XIV., led government to contemplate a land-tax, and to offer as a *douceur* to the landed interest, a premium on export, which, accompanied by a prohibition of the import of foreign corn, implied a certainty of increase of price, and consequently of rent. The chief provisions of the act were the payment of a bounty of 5*s.* for every quarter of wheat exported, so long as our price continued at or below 48*s.*, and 2*s.* 6*d.* for every quarter of barley or malt, so long as our home currency for that grain did not exceed 24*s.*

A deficiency of documents in regard to the extent of our tillage, prevents our tracing the effects of the bounty act: it doubtless stimulated production, and, under ordinary political circumstances, might, after creating a temporary superiority of demand to supply, have in some degree lowered prices; but the market was, during many years, kept up by causes not unlike those which followed in our day the French revolution, — war, and a more than usual prevalence of bad seasons. The proportion of the latter in the twenty years between 1692 and 1712, was not inferior to that of the twenty years between 1792 and 1812; and as our drain of men and capital for the war in these days, made no slight approximation to that of our late contest, there were wanting to complete the analogy of high price only two of the characteristics of our age, — a depreciated currency, and an annual insufficiency of growth.

After the treaty of Utrecht, we enter on a pacific æra, on the age of Fleury and Walpole. The

causes of fluctuation in our corn-market were now
much simplified, and the half-century that succeeded presented the following results :

Average Price of Wheat computed by the Winchester quarter,
from Purchases made at Windsor for Eton College.

	£	s.	d.
For ten years ending with 1725 - - -	1	15	5
Do. - ending with 1735 - - -	1	15	2
Do. - ending with 1745 - - -	1	12	1
Do. - ending with 1755 - - -	1	13	3
Do. - ending with 1765 - - -	1	19	3

In what manner are we to explain so near an
approach to uniformity of price during so long a
period? By the maintenance of peace during
thirty-five years out of fifty, and by an exemption,
in general, from bad seasons. The case was the
same with our neighbours, as appears from the
returns (see Appendix) of the prices of corn in
France. In that country, as in England, the
market during the fifty years in question, presented
an average considerably lower than that of either
the preceding or succeeding half-century.

During the whole of this period, we were exporters of corn; the quantity varied, of course,
from year to year, but was almost always sufficient
to establish the fact, that the market price in England was little higher than throughout the maritime part of the west of Europe; we mean the
Netherlands, Denmark, the North of France, and
the north-west of Germany. The cheapness was
materially greater only in inland districts of the
Continent, where, as at present in Lorraine, the
south of Poland, or south-west of Russia, the want
of water conveyance kept down the market.

During this half-century of stationary price, and

óf scanty agricultural profits,—this period, when inclosure bills were so rare, and lease after lease was signed in long succession, without any idea of increase of rent, it must not be inferred that our tillage was on the decrease : it evidently received an extension, but somewhat more slowly, as appears by the ultimate result, than the increase of our population.

After 1764, began a new æra ; our consumption equalled, and somewhat surpassed our growth, so that our import predominated over export. This change, so unsuitable to a season of peace, so contrary to calculation, at a time when additional labour and capital became applicable to agriculture, was owing to several reasons,—an unusual proportion of bad seasons ; the increase of consumers from the extension of our manufactures, particularly cotton ; and in part, doubtless, to the general disposition to withhold surplus capital from the so long unprofitable investment of agriculture.

Act of 1773.—The rise in our market, whatever may have been its causes, was such in the ten years preceding 1773, as to lead to an act of a new kind ; an act implying that, in regard to corn, England was to be considered rather an importing than an exporting country. It permitted the import of foreign wheat whenever our own reached or exceeded 48*s.* the quarter ; a limit just and moderate, which, while it relieved the consumer from an exorbitant rise on the occurrence of a bad harvest, was productive of no injury to our agriculture, the prices of corn continuing to afford a steady return for the labour and capital employed. Our market now exhibited all the advantages of supply duly proportioned to demand : in some years a partial import was necessary; in others, the nature of our crops enabled us to export; but after 1788, a time of extension and prosperity to most of our manufactures, import decidedly predominated.

In 1791, the landed interest, not satisfied with the advantage secured to them by the act of 1773, carried it a step farther, and obtained a law preventing import, except when our wheat should reach or exceed the price of 54*s.* the quarter. Whether this measure would have operated to raise prices, or by directing an extra share of capital to tillage, would have, in some degree, lowered them, we had no opportunity of ascertaining, so soon was it followed by the war of 1793.

The late Wars. — The wars of the present age, attended by an unparalleled drain of both labourers and capital, could not fail to raise the price of corn. For some time, however, the rise was gradual, the average price of our wheat, during the first seven years of the war, not exceeding 63*s.*; but two bad harvests in succession, (1799 and 1800) altered entirely the state of the market, and carried prices to a rate (6*l.* and upwards) till then unprecedented in our history. · The seasons of 1801, 1802, and 1803, were favourable, and produced a fall to nearly 3*l.*, a fall which, in concurrence with the demands of the Treasury on the land-holders for our renewed contest with France, led to the corn law of 1804, by which the import of foreign wheat was in a manner prohibited, until our own should be at or above 63*s.*, and taxed till our own reached 66*s.* These prices, high as they then seemed, were soon surpassed by the currency of our market, in consequence, partly of an unfavourable season (1804), partly of the continued drain of hands and capital for the war. These causes operated in a greater or less degree over the rest of Europe, and greatly lessened the relief which importation would otherwise have afforded us.

The non-convertibility of our paper currency had existed since 1797, and passed, in vulgar estimate, for the principal cause of this progressive rise; but the degree of enhancement proceeding from it was slight (not exceeding 3 or 4 per cent.) until 1809. In that year it was suddenly accelerated by an unfortunate concurrence of circumstances; expenditure in Spain, the stoppage of neutral traffic, and, above all, a deficient harvest. From this time forward, our purchases of foreign corn were made at a sacrifice of 18, 20, or 25 per cent. a loss incurred on the whole of the very large sum of 7,000,000*l.* expended on the purchase of corn in 1810. The currency of our market was now between 5*l.* and 6*l.*, and though, for one year, a rise was prevented by the abundant harvest of 1810, the case became very different after that of 1811, although only partially deficient. A supply from abroad was now, in a manner, out of the question, partly from the anti-commercial edicts of the time, more from our want of specie and the fall of our bank paper. Accordingly, during 1812 and 1813, our prices averaged above 6*l.*, a rate ill calculated to prepare our farmers for the great and general fall to be expected from the approaching change in the state of Europe.

The Peace of 1814. — Never were the effects of peace more promptly or generally felt, than in 1814. Import co-operated with favourable seasons; the price of corn fell rapidly, and it was in vain that parliament passed, early in 1815, a new act, forbidding import till the home-price of our wheat exceeded 80*s*. : the market continued low, and for a time exposed both the farmers and the public to all the evils of sudden transition. In 1816 a deficiency of crop, more serious both in England and the Continent, than any in the present age, reversed this state of things, raised prices, and led, during 1817 and 1818, to an import of unexampled magnitude. But when in the early part of 1819, the effect of scarcity was past, our market fell, and in the autumn of 1820, an abundant harvest brought it to the state of depression under which it so long remained.

Effect of the Fluctuations in the price of Corn, since 1792. — We are next to examine the state of our market during the last thirty years, with a view to its effect on the situation of farmers. The war commenced at a time when corn was abundant, and prices moderate, wheat averaging about 53*s*. a quarter. The immediate effect of the assumption of a military attitude, was to withdraw from agriculture a portion of labour and capital, to produce a rise in the rate of interest, and to necessitate the abandonment of many projects of improvement, such as drainages, canals, and other undertakings, dependent for success on a low rate of interest. This was productive of very general distress, but had little effect on the corn market, the stock in hand being abundant. In 1794 and 1795, a partial deficiency in the crops, joined to the continued operation of the war, produced a considerable rise, and carried wheat, notwithstanding a large premium on import paid by government, to 4*l*. and upwards. This, however, was of short duration : in 1796, the amount of import, followed by a favourable season, reduced our market; in 1797, wheat did not, on average, exceed 3*l.* 2*s.* and its further fall in 1798 (to 2*l.* 14*s.*), showed how effectually a favourable season could, even in the midst of war, counteract the charges attendant on the culture of corn. These charges without being at all on a par with the burdens of an after-period, were such as to make many of our farmers hold the language of complaint, and consider the increase of expence from the war as materially exceeding the increase of price.

This may be termed the first æra in the war, which had lasted six years without producing a material rise, either in rents or in the average price of corn. The case, however, now underwent a complete change, the occurrence of two bad seasons in succession (1799 and 1800) raising prices to a rate (5*l.* and 6*l.*) wholly unknown in our history. What was the effect of these seasons on the situation of our farmers? At first unfavourable, because a rise in price (Evidence, Agricultural Committee, p. 36.) forms no equivalent to a deficiency of crop; but prospectively, it was advantageous, the stock on hand being so reduced as to open a prospect of high prices for some time to come. Accordingly, in spite of the additional burdens of the period, among others the income tax, farmers and speculators in land were induced to contract for rents at an advanced rate. This spirit showed itself strongly in 1800 and 1801, but received a sudden check from the favourable harvest of the latter year, and the unexpected conclusion of peace with France.

Our wheat now (1802) fell to nearly 3*l.* : the effect of high prices was pronounced not only temporary but fallacious; land was almost every where

declared to be over-let, and the consequent stagnation was on the eve of leading to a general reduction of rents, when the scene was once more changed by war. This was followed by the deficient
harvest of 1804; markets now rose, rents were
maintained and augmented, the import of corn was
subjected to additional restrictions, and at home,
all the causes which swell the cost of production,
rise of labour, taxation, interest of money, operated
in conjunction. The effect of all these, was to
carry wheat during 1805, 6, 7, and 8, to an average
of somewhat more than 4*l.*, although the seasons
were not unfavourable.

This may be termed the middle epoch in the
period of war: agriculture had become profitable,
and the style of living of our farmers was considerably altered, but their charges being greatly augmented, their profits were far from unreasonable.
Of this the best proof is, that all the motives
to extension of culture, did not produce a sufficiency of growth for consumption. There prevailed among farmers a general confidence, an
extension of outlay; but their pecuniary advantage was limited to increase of income, to the
more comfortable support of their families; a
substantial addition to property was, as yet, experienced by very few.

We now come to a new æra, —the five last years
of the war, — a time when farming profit, notwithstanding an increase of charges, materially exceeded the preceding *ratio.* In 1809, a deficient
harvest raised prices, and the imports from the
Continent in 1810, though uncommonly large,
could not bring them below an average of 5*l.* or 6*l.*
because our currency was now greatly depreciated.
No class derived such benefit from the fall of our

Bank paper as our agriculturists, their rent and taxes being paid in it without any addition, while in their sales they received a full allowance for its depreciation, not only in their corn and cattle, but in their butter, poultry and other articles. It was at this time that full execution was given to the anti-commercial decrees of Bonaparte, and to our Orders in Council, measures which, without absolutely stopping neutral navigation, added greatly to its cost, and left us more and more to our own resources. This was the season also of extended military operations in Spain, and of the appropriation, in that country and in Portugal, of supplies of flour from the United States, which might otherwise have found their way to England. In 1811 our crop was not equal to our consumption, and in consequence of the want of import from the Continent, our markets experienced a great advance. Rents were now raised rapidly and generally: poor-rate, tithe, and labour received a great increase, and the collection of the property-tax from farmers became more rigorous; drawbacks which were serious, certainly, but more than outweighed by the benefit of high price. In 1812 and 1813 the harvests were, on the whole, favourable; while the augmented depreciation of our Bank paper (now between 20 and 30 per cent.) discouraged import, and kept our prices of wheat at the exorbitant price of 6*l.* and upwards.

At last came peace, followed by the cessation of so many of the causes that had produced the enormous rise of prices; our Bank paper recovered: corn had fallen on the Continent: the expence of freight was greatly reduced, and considerable imports took place. Our market experienced a rapid fall in the summer and autumn

of 1814 ; a fall confirmed by other causes, — a reduction in the price of labour ; in the interest of
money; in taxation ; — while the whole was necessarily accompanied by a diminution of such charges,
(seed, horses, manure, tithe,) as follow, or rather
are identified with the price of grain. A new
corn-bill was loudly called for ; that of 1815 was
passed and our ports shut to import : but the
amount of the stock on hand, and a crop fully
adequate to our consumption, kept prices at a low
rate, wheat fetching only 55s. or 58s. a quarter. Our
agriculturists now experienced all the evils of a
sudden fall : rents though lowered, remained un-
paid ; farming-stock was sold at a ruinous depreciation ; tithe fell rapidly ; and poor-rate, though
not increased in amount, proved, under such
altered circumstances, a ruinous burden. In this
state of things, the want of warmth and continued
wet of the summer of 1816, were viewed by many
of our agriculturists as benefits, as the means of
clearing the market of the over-stock of corn, of
giving efficiency to the recently-enacted bill, and
of bringing back better prices. Such, in fact,
were its results : the crop, though at one time
promising, never ripened in the colder situations ;
our markets rose, and when, after a time, they
reached the limit that allowed of import, the supplies from the Continent were, in consequence of
an almost equally bad season there, paid for at
such a price that our currency for the year 1817
exceeded 94s. a quarter.

We are now arrived at another epoch in the
fluctuating history of our agriculture. Though
the import of foreign corn continued during 1818,
the average price of wheat in that year exceeded
80s. The steadiness of this price, the revival of

our manufacturing industry, the moderate interest of money, renewed the hopes of our farmers, and created, if not a rise in the amount of rent, a general briskness in making offers. But our imports had been over-done, and our crop in 1819 being an average one, the market experienced a dullness and progressive decline. It was in vain that farther import was suspended; our market continued depressed, and all eyes were fixed on the harvest of 1820, with the singular view of discovering whether its abundance would prove a source of embarrassment to the landed interest. The crop, without being particularly favoured by the season, was found equal to our consumption, which, joined to the magnitude of the stock on hand, produced a great fall of prices; and the crops of 1821 and 1822 being in like manner adequate, our markets continued in a very depressed state.

Tabular Statement of the Nature of the Crops and Average Prices since 1790.

Years.			Average price of wheat.
			£. s. d.
1790, 1, 2.	Peace and favourable seasons - - -	— —	2 13 0
1793.	War, but season favourable - - -	— —	2 15 8
1794, 5.	A deficiency of crop in each year - -	{ Average of 1795 & 1796	4 1 0
1796, 7, 8.	Seasons more favourable	{ Average of 1797, 8, 9.	3 4 0
1799, 1800.	Bad seasons - -	{ Average of 1800 & 1801	6 7 9
1801.	A good crop followed by peace; also by favourable seasons in 1802 and 1803 - - -	{ Average of 1802, 3, 4.	3 5 6

Years.		Average price of wheat.			
			£.	s.	d.
1804.	A deficient crop, followed however by average crops in 1805, 6, 7.	Average of the years 1805, 6,7,8.	4	2	0
1808.	A partial deficiency -	Average of the years 1809&1810.			
1809.	A great deficiency -		5	9	0
1810.	A good crop - -				
1811.	A deficiency - -	Average of the 3 years 1811,12,13.			
1812, 13.	Crops favourable, but currency depreciated -		5	18	8
1814.	A crop not exceeding the average, but a considerable import, and a decrease both of demand and of farming charges consequent on the peace	Average during the years 1814, 15, 16.	3	11	5
1815.	A full average crop -				
1816.	A great and general deficiency - -				
1817.	A crop somewhat below an average - -	Average of the years 1817&1818.	4	9	5
1818.	An average crop -				
1819.	A crop somewhat below the average - -	— —	3	13	0
1820.	A crop exceeding the average - -	— —	3	5	7
1821.	An average crop -	— —	2	14	2
1822.	An average crop -	— —	2	3	3

The deficiency of a particular year is felt little on the average price of that year, but greatly in that of the succeeding year, being seldom ascertained till late in autumn.

The prices in the above table are taken from the Windsor market to 1813 inclusive; afterwards from the average return for England and Wales, which is somewhat lower than the price at Windsor.

Causes of Fluctuation in the Price of Corn.

It is common to ascribe a great share of these fluctuations to the corn laws; but those who have written and spoken on that subject, whether in favour of or against these laws, would have performed a useful service had they been more sparing of argument and more attentive to the facts connected with our corn trade. The result would, we believe, have been a discovery, that the effects attributed to our corn laws, whether by their supporters or opponents, have been greatly over-rated, and that parliament, in attempting to regulate the currency of our markets, might, as was remarked by the late Mr. Whitbread, be compared to the philosopher in Rasselas, who regarded the sun, wind, and rain, as under his control. The bounty act of 1689 had, doubtless, for some time, an operation favourable to landlords, enabling them to let their lands more readily, perhaps on somewhat higher terms ; but after the stimulus of war was removed, the bounty proved altogether unequal to the maintenance of prices, and certainly caused to our country gentlemen, as members of the community at large, a loss greater than the benefit it brought them in the capacity of landlords. Their prosperous day did not arrive until after 1764, when their boasted aids, export and bounty, disappeared together. From that time corn maintained a steady price, or rather experienced a gradual rise, the causes of which, as the bounty was now inoperative, will, we believe, be readily admitted to have been,

First, and principally, an unusual proportion of unfavourable seasons between 1764 and 1773.

Secondly, that the increase of capital and labour applied to our agriculture was not in proportion to the increase of our population. This arose from various causes : the wars of 1756 and 1775 : the extension of certain manufactures, particularly cotton ; and an impression, founded on the experience of the preceding half century, that agriculture was an unprofitable pursuit.

We now come to the act of 1773, the only act

which seems to have had an operation steadily advantageous to landlords; our average price of wheat from 1773 to 1788 being about 49*s.* a quarter, while in France it did not (see Appendix) exceed 38*s.* or 39*s.*, and at Dantzic 41*s.* a quarter. Here was a real and steady superiority of price, the maintenance of which was owing in part to the American war, but in part also to the moderate nature of the act, the price of 48*s.*, pointed out by it as a kind of limit, offering no temptation to capitalists to transfer their funds from trade or manufacture to land. Had the import limit been 54*s.* there seems little doubt, after the proofs we have had of the practicability of extending our tillage, that it would, ere long, have been over-done, and our growth rendered not only equal but superior to our consumption. By asking little the landholders obtained a certainty, and this example of the success of interference, when interference is very slight, has a claim to their serious attention at the present moment.

The late Wars.—In the period from 1793 to 1814, the Corn laws were in general inoperative, the currency of our market being usually above the import limit, and our ports consequently open. No difference appears to have resulted from the restraint on import imposed by the act of 1804; an act which had, we believe, the effect of enabling landlords to make a rise of rent more general and more approaching to uniformity over the kingdom in point of time than would otherwise have been practicable, but which had certainly no effect in raising markets, its tendency to extend tillage balancing, or more than balancing, any tendency to keep up prices by an occasional and short exclusion of foreign Corn.

What then were the causes of the unexampled rise of prices between 1793 and 1814?

The unusual number of bad or indifferent seasons, not less than seven (1794, 1795, 1799, 1800, 1804, 1809, 1811,) in the course of eighteen years.

The great demand of men for military service, in consequence of which the increase of the producers of corn failed to keep pace with the increase of the consumers.

The consequent rise in the price of labour, and in farming charges generally.

The increase of taxation.

The prevalence of similar causes on the Continent, and consequent limitation of import.

The depreciation of our currency, particularly after 1809.

Of all the departments of our national industry, none received so continued a stimulus from the war as agriculture. Our manufactures, particularly those of cotton and hardware, experienced at times a greater impulse; but the nature of manufacture admitting of more speedily increasing supply in proportion to demand, the briskness was often temporary, and followed by seasons of discouragement. Our tillage, on the other hand, was hardly at any time brought on a par with our increasing population, so that the stimulant of a demand, equal to or greater than the internal supply, prevailed throughout almost the whole period.

Causes of the Fall of Prices since the Peace. — These have been partly peculiar to this country, partly common to it with the Continent of Europe. Of the latter description were

The application of additional capital, and, in a

greater degree, of labour, to tillage, since the reduction of military establishments.

A succession of seasons more favourable than
during the war; the Continent, like England,
having had, since the peace, only one bad summer,
1816. Though, from the extent of the failure on
that occasion, we may consider it equivalent to
two seasons of ordinary deficiency, the proportion
of favourable seasons since the peace is still considerably greater than during the war.

Next, as to the causes of decline peculiar to this
country, we have

The re-instatement of our paper currency; and,

The great reduction of freight and other charges
of transport; a principal cause of the magnitude
of the import in 1817 and 1818.

Labour applied to Tillage since the Peace. —
The operation of several of these causes is sufficiently obvious, but the extent of one which to us
appears of considerable importance, may be doubted
by many persons, particularly by those who compute the extension of our growth by the number of
inclosure bills, and who have remarked (see Appendix) the great decrease in such acts since the
peace. To those persons we would submit an
observation which, however plain, is of the highest
importance, viz. that "the most productive husbandry is that which is practised on land already
under cultivation." This truth escaped the attention of the Agricultural Committee of 1821, but is
well known to intelligent farmers and land-survey-
ors. In support of our opinion, we refer our readers
to the evidence of a practical farmer, Mr. Becher,
of Suffolk, given before the Corn Committee of 1810.
When asked whether he considered the import limit
of that time (63*s.*) as too low, Mr. B. answered,
(Evidence, p. 55.)

" I look upon the price at which wheat is now imported not sufficient to encourage the culture of wheat to the extent that is necessary for the kingdom ; but I believe there is not the least doubt, if the import price was at 84*s.* instead of 63*s.,* or even higher, that the effect would be, upon a notice given that that would be the import price after the 30th September in any year, that the consumption of the country would be fully provided for at home, even in the first year after such notice."

Could it be provided for in the first year without cross-cropping ?

" I believe that the lands now sown with wheat are not in the high state generally that they might be ; and this I am aware of, that every additional hoeing of the wheat crop will give, upon an average, at least two bushels an acre. I have tried the experiment more than once in the same fields, by not hoeing, hoeing once, and hoeing twice : the difference has been — with one hoeing two bushels an acre more and upwards, and in that hoed twice four bushels more."

This opinion may be followed up by asking what amount of additional labour is at the disposal of our farmers, since the peace ? A comparison of the population returns of 1811 and 1821, appears at first to operate against our argument, and to imply that the increase of the growers of corn was, in the course of these ten years, considerably below the increase of the consumers, the former being in the *ratio* of only 9, the latter of 19 per cent. of our population. But this comparison is made by a number of families, and the effectual plan is to calculate the able-bodied labourers. Now, of these peace restored a number to agricultural labour, and what was of at least equal importance, suspended the drain of others as recruits for the public service. Is it practicable to reduce the numbers in question to the form of specific calculation ? The proportion of the population of Great Britain and Ireland employed in agriculture in the latter years of the war, could not (see the Population Return of 1811) be less than 7,000,000, of whom the able-bodied exceeded 1,700,000. Of these in war there were withdrawn for the army, navy, and militia (exclusive of local militia) nearly one-tenth, say   -   -   170,000

Whereas in peace the number of the agricultural class so withdrawn is not -   30,000

Leaving a difference of   -   -   140,000
or one-twelfth of the whole.

Now if we calculate the produce of their labour on the most moderate scale, not at a twelfth but at a twenty-fourth of our crop, the result is an addition to our supply of more than a fortnight's consumption of our whole population, a quantity which, small as it may seem, was *considerably larger* than our average import during the war. And as no article is so much influenced as corn, (Evidence, Agricultural Committee, pp. 229—240.) by a slight addition to or subtraction from the usual supply, an increase, such as we have mentioned, is sufficient to cause a material change in the market. Viewed in connexion with the conversion of pasture lands in Ireland to tillage, it will, we believe, be found to afford a more adequate explanation of the low price of corn, than any other cause except the continuance of favourable seasons.*

* See the close of the Appendix to this Chapter; also the close of the Appendix to the Chapter on Population.

SECTION II.

Situation and Prospects of our Agriculturists.

We have now explained the causes of the great change that has taken place since the peace, of the remarkable increase in the quantity and reduction in the price of our produce. Our next object is to exhibit the result of this change, and to convey an idea of the actual situation of our landlords and farmers.

Estimate of our Agricultural Produce and Rental.

Produce.—Annual value of agricultural produce, (not only corn but wool, hemp, flax, timber, &c.) raised in Great Britain and Ireland.

In 1812, our produce, exclusive of seed, was computed by Mr. Colquhoun, in his well-known work on the " Resources of the British Empire," (pp. 66—89.) at - - - £217,000,000

Deduct pasture and all produce used for the food of horses, horned cattle, and the lesser animals, about - - - 100,000,000

Value of annual produce for the food of man, or for the purposes of manufacture - - - £117,000,000

Since 1812, prices have fallen above 60 per cent. ; but as Mr. C.'s estimate was made greatly below the currency of the time, the deduction applicable to his results does not exceed 25 or 30 per cent. This deduction in prices, large as it is, appears to be balanced, or nearly balanced, by the increase in the quantity of our produce. To ascertain the extent of such increase is a matter of great difficulty, but the probability of its being very large is supported by several powerful considerations ; viz.

The diffusion of improvements in husbandry.

The addition to our population, and the cessation of a drain of the able-bodied men for the public service.

The excess of the population and produce of Ireland over Mr. Colquhoun's estimate.

The conjunct effect of these causes may, we believe, safely be computed to form an addition of 25 per cent. to the quantity of our produce, and to leave the value of the whole not far short of Mr. Colquhoun's estimate.

Rental. — In 1814 the rental of England, Wales, and Scotland was carried, as appears by the property-tax returns, to nearly £43,000,000
Add for Ireland, (conjecturally estimated) 10,000,000

Together	£53,000,000
Add for all omissions and allowances on the property-tax returns, a supposed amount of - - - -	5,000,000
The great increase that has of late taken place in our produce having been chiefly on lands already under tillage, we add for new land brought into culture since the peace only -	2,000,000
Making in all -	£60,000,000

Deduct for all abatements of rent since 1814 made, making, or which must, ere long, be made, one-third, or 33 per cent. of the war rents, £20,000,000

Remainder £40,000,000

a sum which will probably form the rental of Great Britain and Ireland, when the price of wheat shall be steadily between 50s. and 60s. a quarter, and when farming charges shall be brought down to the peace standard. Large as is this abatement of rent, it is less great than the fall in the price of produce, but the improved husbandry has of late made considerable progress, and the cheapness of provisions has caused a great decrease of poor rate.

In no class of the community has the effect of transition been either so severe or so long continued as among the agriculturists.

If to the rental of landlords in the latter years of the war, we add the income of our farmers, we shall find, (see Property-tax returns for 1812, printed in 1816,) including Ireland, an aggregate of more than 100,000,000l. This, it must be allowed, exceeded all due bounds, and a reduction to 75 or even to 70,000,000l., for the total of rental and farming income, would have been nothing more than a fair participation in the general abatement attendant on peace; a relinquishment of a monopoly for a fair average profit. But of late years the income of farmers is, in a manner, suspended, and of the rents they at present pay, a large proportion is drawn from their capital.

Of the extent of national injury arising from this state of things, some idea may be formed from

the following estimate of the proportion borne by
agriculture to the productive industry of the
country at large.

Proportions
in 100.

Proportion of the national revenue arising from agriculture at the reduced prices of peace, about   -   -   30
Proportion of our population dependent for employment on agriculture (see the Population Return of
1821) in Great Britain, distinct from Ireland   -   33
Proportion of national property annually created, being
the amount of corn, grass, wool, hemp, flax, timber,
&c. after a suitable deduction from Mr. Colquhoun's
estimate   -   -   -   -   -   -   45
Proportion of national capital affected by the prosperity or decline of agriculture, being the value of
our land, farming stock, and houses on farms and
estates, adopting Mr. Colquhoun's mode of estimating, but making a great abatement on the prices of
1812, (see Appendix to the chapter on National
Revenue and Capital) above   -   -   -   -   60

After this statement, it is needless to expatiate
on the magnitude of the injury arising to our manufacturers, our shop-keepers, or the Treasury,
from the distress of agriculture : nor need we go
farther to account for the chief part of the national
embarrassment in 1816, or of our revived prosperity in 1818. It is almost equally idle to discuss
the question, whether the agriculturists are entitled to our sympathy, or whether their profits,
towards the close of the war, were not such as to
exceed all legitimate proportion. Their case involves a question of policy fully as much as of
justice, — the losses of any great part of the nation
forming the losses of the whole, and any deficiency
in their contributions to the exchequer falling necessarily on the other classes.

Present Situation of our Landlords and Farmers.
— A reduction in the circumstances of farmers
was unavoidable, their profits having consisted less
in acquisition of capital than in additions to income — additions which were great only in the
latter years of the war, and arose chiefly from the
depreciation of our currency. With landlords the
case was somewhat different : their increased
receipts had been less connected with depreciation,
while their possession of capital exempted them
from any immediate necessity of altering their
scale of expence. Time has been afforded them
to make a deliberate distinction between nominal
and real income ; between that decrease which
actually deducts from the power of expenditure,
and that which, in consequence of the rise in the
value of money, does so only in appearance.
During the war they had an opportunity of observing how closely augmented expenditure followed augmented income ; it now remains for
them to try reduction, and to carry it to the length
pointed out by the fall in the price of commodities.
That fall does not, we allow, apply to them so
largely as to the lower and middling classes : it has
taken place chiefly in the necessaries of life, and,
as yet at least, holds much less in regard to the
expence of the higher ranks, such as the bills
of tradesmen, salaries, wages of servants, professional fees, to which we may add education at
our public schools or universities, along with the
cost of articles of luxury, such as wines, plate, and
ornamental furniture. Yet even in these reduction
has commenced, and may be carried much farther
when the upper classes think proper to hold a

decided tone, and retrench abuses engendered in days of abundance.

On comparing the present situation of our landlords with what it was in the latter years of the war, we are led to compute the apparent or nominal decrease of their income at forty per cent., the real decrease at twenty per cent. ; assuming that the remaining twenty per cent. are counterpoised by reduction in their expenditure either already made or perfectly practicable. We go, perhaps, too far in supposing an actual loss to the extent of twenty per cent. : if we make allowance for the repeal of the property-tax, and reduction of the assessed taxes, the loss should, doubtless, be less ; but, without pressing that point, we proceed to ask from what source the extra income arose during the war ? Partly from the general rise of profit at that period, more from an advantage peculiar to agriculturists, the monopoly of the market in consequence of the continued insufficiency of our growth. Advantages such as these are necessarily temporary, and, could the nature of our situation have been foreseen, would have been considered by landlords as at a close, as soon as our political circumstances were changed, and the country became assured of peace.

But rents, even on this reduced scale, are not, it may be said, paid at present, nor are our prices equal to the cost of production, leaving rent wholly out of the question. We answer that no calculation can be founded on the circumstances of this season of transition and over-stock ; but as a great part of the distress arises from temporary causes, such as the tardy reduction of farming charges, the better plan is to calculate probabilities, and to reason on a rate of rent, which though not yet generally established, is rendered likely by a concurrence of circumstances.

What, it may be asked, is this probable rate of rent? Several of our principal landlords, convinced of the inefficacy of corn laws to keep up the market, have given examples of successive reduction, carrying the whole, since 1814, to 30 or 35 per cent. on their war rents. Our hope is, that such examples may be imitated in all their extent. Supposing, for the sake of illustration, that of this deduction 10 or 15 per cent. had been in general made between the year 1814 and the date of the examination of the witnesses, before the Agricultural Committee of 1821 ; there then remained to make a farther abatement of 20 or 25 per cent., an abatement repeatedly alluded to in the evidence as necessary, acceded to by many individuals since that time, and which, as far as we are enabled to judge, is imperiously required by the exigency of the case. We shall suppose, therefore, that what is as yet partial, has become general, and that our landlords, throughout the kingdom, aware, on the one hand, of the increased value of money, on the other, of the necessity of sacrificing a part to save the remainder, have consented to this reduction ; also, that the farmers succeed in the arduous task of accomplishing a corresponding diminution in labour and the other charges of culture. Were these grand points adjusted, the prospect of our agriculturists would be cleared of a part of its gloom ; their horizon would brighten, and it would, we might hope, be no longer doubtful whether ruin or recovery is to be their lot.

Supposing this reduction effected, what price, it may be inquired, would enable the farmer to discharge his engagements, and to earn a fair support? *Sixty shillings* for a quarter of wheat in the counties adjacent to the metropolis, and between *fifty-five and sixty shillings* in those where labour is cheaper. This estimate is supported directly by the opinion of Mr. Rodwell, (Evidence, Report of 1821, p. 86.), and of Mr. Brodie, (p. 335.) while indirectly it is confirmed by all who, when desired to say the cost of raising wheat *without rent*, fixed it at the charges of 1821, between 55*s.* and 60*s.* A deduction of 25 per cent. would bring the cost to 45*s.*, and a market price between 55*s.* and 60*s.* would obviously supply the fund requisite for the payment of the rent, which is in general a fourth or a fifth of the produce.

How far is the probability of 55*s.* or 60*s.*, as a medium price in peace, confirmed by other circumstances, in particular by the average price of other countries? Wheat at Dantzic has averaged, (Evidence, Agricultural Committee, p. 366.) during the last half century about 45*s.* a quarter; while in the parts of the Continent, adjacent to England, we mean the Netherlands, and the north of France, 45*s.* a quarter are generally considered sufficient for the indemnity of the farmer. This difference supposes an advance of 20 per cent. to our farmers in consideration of their higher rents and somewhat heavier burdens in other respects. After the high prices of the war, an average of 55*s.* or 60*s.* appears low : but in the payment of labour, in the power of purchase generally, it at present is, or ought to be equal to 80*s.* in the latter part of the war, and the point is not that which may be expected, but that which it is practicable to attain. Add to this, that under such a price our manufacturers would probably acquiesce without complaint, considering our national superiority in fuel, navigation, and command of capital, such as to admit, without much hazard, of a relative disadvantage in the cost of subsistence.

How far is the probability of such an average confirmed by a retrospect to history, to periods in which our agriculture was prosperous? In 1804, a price varying from 63*s.* to 66*s.* was accounted sufficient by Parliament, under charges heavier than those we have now in prospect. During the thirty years between 1763 and 1793, our farmers made few complaints, though the average price of wheat was 49*s.* a quarter, or about 15 per cent. less than we consider necessary for the present time. And if we compare the farming charges on the reduced scale we have anticipated, with those previous to 1793, we shall find that the excess of the former, is, or ought to continue great in one point only, — taxation.

This leads naturally to the inquiry, "how far "the public burdens, at present defrayed by agri- "culture, exceed those of 1792." In treating this subject in a preceding chapter, we have had occasion (p. 59.) to estimate the increase of burden to the public at large at 12 per cent. on their income : in the case of the farmers, we shall make a liberal allowance, and suppose that from the pressure of poor rate, the additional burden since 1792, is nearly 20 per cent. This, be it observed, is burden on *income*, but the *produce* of a farm being computed by surveyors at three or four times the tenant's income, (see the Property-tax return, 1810), it follows that 20 per cent. on income will be defrayed by an addition of 5 or 6 per cent. to the price of the produce. Now could the farmers obtain the 55*s.* or 60*s.* which we have termed a fair average, the result would be their having a surplus above the prices of 1792 sufficient to serve as a counterpoise to labour and the other charges (distinct from taxation), which are higher at present than in 1792, and which it will be a task of great time and difficulty to reduce.

The reasoning in the preceding pages, fair as it may seem to some, and sanctioned as it is by the example of such men as Earl Fitzwilliam and Mr. Coke, may appear in a very different light to others, who, whether landlords or farmers, are ill prepared to relinquish the hope of high price. Of these persons, some may still cling to the imagined effect of a protecting duty, others, with more plausibility, may build their expectations of an improved market on the progressive increase of population and on the contingency of a deficient harvest. It is of consequence, therefore, to enter at some length into a consideration of these arguments, and to attempt to bring into the form of an estimate, results, which, at present, are vague and undefined.

Effect of increasing Population on the Price of Corn. — The returns in the present age have shown an increase in our population to an extent which we had, for some time, difficulty in considering correct, and which when put beyond doubt, was ascribed by many to the temporary stimulus arising from the war. It bids fair, however, to be progressive, arising, as it apparently does, from causes of a permanent nature; from an improvement in the condition of the lower orders, in diet, clothing, and lodging, as well as from the preservation of the lives of children by vaccination. But those who found on this an expectation of relief to our agriculturists, overlook one very material

point; " that the productive powers of our better
soils, far from having reached their *terminus,* may
be made to yield a far larger produce by additional
labour and the adoption of the improved methods
of husbandry."

In support of this apparently bold assertion, we
refer, as well to the already quoted arguments of
a practical agriculturist, (Mr. Becher,) as to our
experience, as a nation, during the last nine years.
No period was more calculated to suggest the inference of a limitation of the productive powers of
our soil than the twenty years preceding 1814, yet
this opinion (see the preceding section, page 137,)
has been completely disproved by the result of our
agriculture since the peace. If we take a wider
range than the experience of the present age, and
refer to the history of this and other countries,
we find France as capable at present of maintaining a population of 30,000,000, as of supporting
20,000,000 in the beginning of the 18th century,
or 15,000,000 in the beginning of the 17th. And
France may be termed an example altogether in
point of increase of produce from increase of hands,
manual labour forming the basis of her agriculture,
to the exclusion, in a great degree, of machinery.

England furnishes a case apparently stronger
than France, the increase of our population, during
the last century, having been considerably more
rapid, and our soil being still equal to their subsistence. But we forbear dwelling on this, because
it may be argued that the productive power of our
agriculture has, particularly in the present age,
been much promoted by means distinct from increase of population, we mean machinery, and
other aids arising from the command of capital.
We cannot, however, but express a belief, that the

next generation of our countrymen will, in all probability, raise a supply of subsistence as far beyond ours, as ours is beyond that of the last age; and that our descendants, on comparing the two periods, will feel no little surprise at the negative predictions of several of our political economists. Without contesting in the abstract the principles of the latter, we must add that nothing is more likely to mislead than the assertions of those who assign limits to the extension of the productive powers of our soil, imperfectly acquainted as they are with its capabilities, and still more unable to foresee the successive improvements that may, and in all probability will, be made in husbandry. How greatly does our prospect of supply exceed their anticipation : how large, for instance, would be the addition to the produce of the West of England, and of Ireland, were these countries merely to adopt the improved plan now generally followed in our eastern and northern counties. (See Appendix, p. [37].)

Consumers may increase without raising Prices. — Our next argument, similar in its object, is somewhat different in its nature. There exists a perpetual tendency to removal from country to town, and, on comparing our population lists at different periods, we find the inhabitants of towns, in other words, the consumers of corn, gradually augment their proportion relatively to the producers. Both classes increase their numbers, but in towns the *ratio* is larger. We must be cautious, however, of drawing from this fact any conclusion as to rise of price; it merely marks the natural progress of society in an enlightened country ; a progress easily traced in our history for more than two centuries, the agriculturists of England, who now form only 33 per cent. of our population, having, we believe, formed upwards of 50 or 60 per cent. of it in the reigns of Elizabeth and James I. Still the supply of produce has continued equal to our increased numbers, and the cause is obvious, the use of machinery, and the adoption of various improvements, enabling the same number of hands to raise a much larger quantity of subsistence.

Is then no rise of prices to be expected from the increase of our population? It certainly may be expected under circumstances which give a new or different employment to a portion of our numbers —such as appear to have prevailed on the extension of our cotton manufactures after 1780, and such as evidently characterise the present emigration to Upper Canada, and the Western States of America, the larger proportion of the emigrants being agriculturists. To this we add, that the increase of our numbers has in it something encouraging and cheering : *it assures, in a great measure, the continuance of tillage on our inferior soils:* and, taken in a more general view, it keeps alive the expectation of national improvement so fully described by Mr. S. Gray, and which shall be noticed at greater length when we come to treat of the subject of population.

Effects of a bad Season on the Price of Corn. — The rise in our corn market, produced by a bad or even an indifferent season, is *in time of war* very considerable. The difference between the crop of one year and that of another will be found, without resorting to an extreme case, such as 1816, to be frequently (Evidence, Agricultural Committee of 1821, p. 264.) between 10 and 20 per cent. Add to this that on such occasions our purchases abroad are generally enhanced by the causes which produce enhancement in this country. The public, particularly the untravelled part of the public, are hardly aware of the similarity of temperature prevailing throughout what may be called the corn-country of Europe, we mean Great Britain, Ireland, the north of France, the Netherlands, Denmark, the north-west of Germany, and, in some measure, Poland, and the north-east of Germany. All this tract is situated between the 45th and 55th degrees of latitude, and subject, in a considerable degree, to the prevalence of similar winds. Neither the superabundance of rain which we experience in one summer, or its deficiency in another, are by any means confined to Britain and Ireland; while in winter, both the intensity and duration of frost are always greater on the Continent. Exceptions certainly exist in particular tracts, but in support of our general argument, we have merely to recall to those of our readers who are of an age to recollect the early part of the war, or who have attended to registers of temperature, the more remarkable seasons of the present age. Thus, in 1794, the spring was prematurely warm on the Continent as in England: there, as with us, the summer of 1798 was dry, and that of 1799 wet: again, in 1811 the harvest was deficient throughout the north-west of Europe generally, from one and the same cause, blight; while that of 1816 was still more generally deficient from rain and want of warmth. In regard to a more remote period, we mean the 17th and 18th centuries generally, if the temperature has not been so accurately noted, we find, from the coincidence in prices, that it is highly probable that there prevailed a great similarity between our weather and that of the Continent: thus, in France the latter years of the 17th century, the seasons of 1708 and 1709, as well as several of the seasons between 1764 and 1773, were as unpropitious and attended with as great an advance of price as in England.

Another observation as yet little attended to, but which has found a place in the Agricultural Report of 1821, is, that an indifferent season is not always followed by a favourable one, but that two, and even more than two deficiencies of crop occur sometimes in succession. Such was the case in the latter years of Elizabeth, in the reign of William III., and in our own time, in 1799 and 1800. On each of these occasions the consequences were very serious, leading to a distressing rise of price, and showing all the importance of making the plenty of one year conduce to the relief of another.

Less felt in peace than in war. — But while in war, the effect of a bad or indifferent season is thus severe, its pressure is greatly alleviated by the cheap freight and open communication of a state of peace. On referring to the record of our prices during a century and a half prior to 1793, we find that throughout that long period the effect of an unfavourable season was to carry wheat from 40*s.* to 50*s.* or 55*s.*, rarely to 60*s.* Now 55*s.* or 60*s.* in these days were nearly equal to 70*s.* at the present value of money, and the latter would probably be the currency of our market in the event of a partial deficiency like that of 1795, 1804, 1809. To carry our peace prices higher would require a failure as general as that of 1816, or two partial deficiencies in succession as in 1799 and 1800. To those who think otherwise, we submit two considerations; first, that the increase of our numbers does not much increase the difficulty of supplying our consumption at home; and next, that the range of foreign territory from which our corn imports may now be derived is much wider than during last century.

Add to this, that a continuance of peace tends in many ways to an equalization of price between different countries. The obstacles to emigration are then removed: the tempting profit attendant on government contracts and other war speculations no longer detain at home either the individual or his capital: the charges of farming as of productive industry generally, are calculated closely, and a decided preference is given to the country where those charges are most moderate. Another, and a still more substantial cause of equalization of price is the increased command of capital in peace, the augmented means of buying up the superabundance of one year as a supply for the demands of the next. Among other structures of recent date in the vicinity of the Thames, are warehouses in which corn may be preserved during six or seven years without injury: the expence, which in the case of wheat was, till lately, 7s. a quarter, would be materially lessened in purchases made at the present low prices, as a portion of it arises from interest on the purchase-money. (See Appendix, p. [42].)

Re-action of the Market Price of Corn on the Cost of its Production. — If the influence of the seasons has not yet been duly appreciated, much less is that the case in regard to another cause of rise and fall which we admit to be somewhat complicated in its nature, and tardy in its operation; we mean the re-action of the market price of corn on the cost of its production. Our object will be best understood by an analysis of the charges of cultivation, as exhibited in the subjoined table.

Expence of cultivating 100 *acres of Arable Land in England, at three distinct periods, calculated on an average of the returns made to circular letters from the Board of Agriculture to farmers in different parts of the kingdom.*

	1790.			1803.			1813.		
	£	s.	d.	£	s.	d.	£	s.	d.
Rent - -	88	6	3¼	121	2	7¼	161	12	7¾
Tithe - -	20	14	1¾	26	8	0¼	38	17	3¼
Rates - -	17	13	10	31	7	7¾	38	19	2¾
Wear and tear	15	13	5¼	22	11	10¼	31	2	10¾
Labour - -	85	5	4¾	118	0	4	161	12	11¼
Seed - -	46	4	10¼	49	2	7	98	17	10
Manure - -	48	3	0	68	6	2	37	7	0¼
Team - -	67	4	10	80	8	0¼	134	19	8¼
Interest - -	22	11	11½	30	3	8¾	50	5	6
Taxes - -		—			—		18	1	4
Total -	411	15	11¾	547	10	11½	771	16	4¼

NOTE. The article manure is underrated in the last column; were it fully stated, the aggregate of 1813 would have exceeded 800*l.*

This document presents materials for reasoning of equal importance to the agriculturist and political economist, exhibiting all the constituent parts of the cost of corn, and enabling us to explain both the high prices of a state of war, and the fall attendant on peace.

War.—The effects of war are first felt in the price of labour, the interest of money, and the direct taxes. These all operate to enhance corn: the price of seed is necessarily augmented by such a rise: an increase of tithe, as expressed in money, is a consequence almost equally direct: the expence of team and manure cannot, under such circumstances, be long stationary; and an advance of poor-rate has, ever since the days of Queen Elizabeth, followed, at no distant date, an augmented price of bread.

Such was the progress of farming charges during the late wars. The early part of the period was with our farmers a season of complaint, and with the exception of tenants on lease, the partial rise in price, accompanied as it was by high charges, was accounted a disadvantage to agriculturists. After 1804, their situation improved, but it was not till 1809 that the advantage of war to the farmer became great and general.

Peace.—Next, as to the reverse of the picture, —the unweaving of that web which owed its texture to a double war and a depreciated currency. Wages, interest of money, the cost of horses, and, in some degree, direct taxes, have all undergone reduction since the peace, in particular since 1820: a fall in the price of seed is a matter of course, while a diminution of tithe and a reduced charge in the bills of tradesmen, are the eventual though less direct results of a decline in the corn market. The remaining charges are rent and poor-rate, both very difficult of reduction, because in the case of landlords the diminution of expenditure is not equal to the fall of corn, while in that of the poor a decrease in employment retards that reduction of parochial charge, which would otherwise follow the cheapness of the necessaries of life. These, however, are only postponements of an unavoidable result: landlords must resign in peace the monopoly attendant on war, while to our labouring classes the extension of manufactures consequent on the fall of provisions, affords relief, not speedy, perhaps, but eventually certain.

What then ought to be our inference from the

preceding reasoning? That farming charges necessarily rise with the market-price of corn, and as
necessarily become reduced by its decline. Now
as the reduction of charge is as yet by no means
proportioned to the fall of price, we are justified in
anticipating that the former will become general,
and afford, in any event, considerable relief to the
farmers.

Evidence before the Agricultural Committee. —
Our reasoning may be somewhat elucidated by a
reference to the answers of the witnesses examined
by the Agricultural Committee of 1821, about the
cost of raising a quarter of wheat. They declared
55*s.* or 60*s.* (Evidence, pp. 37. 55. 72.) to be indispensable to meet the charges exclusive of rent;
but that price will be found to supply a fund for
rent also, if we suppose a general diminution of
twenty-five per cent. on farming charges. An
abatement of this nature was, as we have already
remarked, evidently in the view of several of the
witnesses. One of them, a landsurveyor, declared,
(p. 191.) that a price of 64*s.*, with a *proportional
reduction of charges*, would afford a fair rent:
while another, a farmer residing in Suffolk, adverted (p. 86.) to the remarkable fact that 2,000*l.*
forms as efficient a capital at present as 3,000*l.* in
1817, and considered that in the event of an abatement of one-fourth of rent, poor-rate, labour, tithe,
and taxes, 60*s.* a quarter would afford a fair profit
in his county. The answer of a third witness
(p. 335.) is still more remarkable, for it declares a
much lower price to be sufficient in a quarter (East
Lothian) where labour is somewhat cheaper, and
tithe happily unknown.

How far do these conclusions appear to be fami-

liar to the majority of those who have written or
given evidence on the state of our agriculture ?
Landsurveyors, accustomed to arithmetical calculation, are aware of these truths in a general sense;
but the majority of them, like the majority of our
farmers, long accustomed to a state of war, have
still difficulty in considering as permanent the low
prices and low charges of peace.   Next as to the
Agricultural Report of 1821 ; — that valuable document seems to have been composed under a conviction similar to that which we entertain, but unfortunately it nowhere exhibits a clear and pointed
affirmation of the connexion between the price of
corn and the cost of raising it.

Are low Prices likely to continue ?

We are now to follow up the arguments on the
very interesting question of a rise or fall in the
market price of corn.   Those in favour of a rise
are —

1st. The expence of bringing into culture new
soils of inferior quality to meet the wants of our
increasing numbers.   This, the chief argument of
theoretical writers, is already in a great measure
answered by the result of the last nine years ; by
the evidence that the largest additional produce is
obtained from soils already under tillage ; and that
the grand means of increase consist in the application of additional labour to such soils.   Our inclosure bills in the six years previous to 1815
averaged 115 annually ; in the six following years,
during which our produce has increased so largely,
they averaged only 48 ; a decisive proof that the
quantity of produce may be kept up and augmented
without bringing much new soil under culture.

2d. The expence of keeping inferior soils in cultivation, and the necessity of abandoning them if low prices continue. This argument carries much more weight than the preceding, and might produce a kind of revolution in prices were it not counteracted by a cause of most powerful operation, — the decrease in farming charges consequent on a decrease in the price of corn. This fact, joined to the increase of our population, will probably prevent the abandonment, to any great extent, of inferior soils. No inference can be drawn from the *present* situation of our agriculturists who labour under all the evils of transition and disproportion; subject at once to heavy charges and low prices. At a time when we are told from so many quarters of over-cropping, of decay of farming stock, and of multiplied bankruptcies, we must necessarily take for granted that the plough will, to some extent, at least, be withdrawn from the less productive lands. In the parts of Scotland where tillage was carried farthest, this painful alternative seems hardly to be avoided: in England, at least in various parts of England, the case is somewhat different: tillage was not so often carried to an extreme, and the solicitude of the landlords (Evidence, p. 43.) to prevent the degradation of their estates by paying for lime and other requisites to the maintenance of good husbandry, will operate to lessen this and other evils. Add to this the remarkable fact, that after all the extension given to our tillage in the present age, the proportion of ground under the plough and spade is (Napier's Supplement to the Encyclopædia, head of France, p. 373.) considerably smaller in England than in France. Add also another fact hardly less important, that the practice of drilling corn, so lately introduced, is particularly suitable to second-rate soils.

But supposing that the tillage of inferior soils were relinquished to a certain extent both in England and Scotland, it does not necessarily follow that the amount of our produce would decrease : our labour must be employed somehow, and would be transferred to the richer soils. A diminution of production is altogether contrary to the disposition of our countrymen : an increase of quantity, even when an article sells for a low price, is more in correspondence with their active and enterprizing habits. No decrease of our agricultural produce took place during the long stagnation of last century ; during the fifty years that elapsed between 1713 and 1763. And if we advert to a parallel case in the present age, that of our West India Sugar planters, we shall find that during a number of years, (1802. 1805, 6, 7,) their produce as little paid the expence of raising it, as corn does at present. A number of estates were abandoned ; in others, the cultivation was reduced ; but this was so effectually balanced by the increased productiveness of the richer soils, that very little, if any, diminution took place in the total quantity raised.

3d. *A protecting Duty on Foreign Corn.* — The efficacy or non-efficacy of such a measure is, in a great degree, matter of opinion. Without assuming a decisive tone on either side, we shall have occasion to show in the next section that a high duty would by no means cause a permanent rise in our corn market, and that the only safe course is to regard the last thirty years as a period peculiar in its circumstances, and altogether different from a season of peace. We ought in the next place, to carry back our view to the period preceding 1793, and ascertain whether the increase of the charge of raising corn arising from taxes or otherwise, exceeds the saving attendant on the improvements adopted in our husbandry. In that proportion only would it be practicable to maintain an increase of price : any attempt to carry it higher would be defeated by the extension of our home growth. Agriculture, like trade, has its projectors ; men ready to transfer to it capital from other pursuits, and who would find, particularly in Ireland, many rich tracts open to their speculations, now that there remains so little inducement to keep them in pasture. The only method, therefore, of giving the established farmer a fair chance is, to be very sparing of bounties, protecting duties, and other stimulants ; the effect of which is unnatural, temporary, and eventually pernicious to those who receive them.

4th. *Contingency of a bad Season.* — On this head we have already attempted a calculation, showing that in former periods of peace the extent of rise varied from 10*s*. to 20*s*. on the quarter of wheat, according to the degree of failure in the harvest. Under present circumstances, this limited advance is much more likely to characterise our markets than the greater fluctuation that took place in the late wars.

That our prices of wheat are not likely to exceed 55 or 60*s*., is confirmed by some arguments of a more consolatory nature; viz.

The increase of our growth from the diffusion of the improved Husbandry. Under this head we are disposed to class the more general introduction of drilling ; the farther consolidation of small farms ;

and the more frequent adoption of leases when the changes in our money system shall have reached their termination. For her pasturage England is deservedly celebrated, but her tillage is only partially good. In no branch of our national industry has improving example been as yet less generally followed : in none has it a wider field to occupy.

The reduced Interest of Money. — The fall of interest on public securities since the peace is about one per cent., and the prospect is in favour of some farther decrease ; or rather, that the reduction, at present partial, will become general, and be communicated to private as well as public securities. No line of business offers at present a tempting return ; nor is any likely to withdraw money investments from agriculture. Add to this, that from the reduced price of all farming stock, the appropriation of 1000*l.* to farming (Evidence, Agricultural Committee, p. 86.) is likely soon to be equivalent to that of 2000*l.* in the time of high prices.

Such are the principal arguments against any material rise in our corn market ; and if their conjunct effect be merely to give us the supply of a three weeks' consumption above the average of our crops in war, the result will be a prevention of high prices, so nearly did our growth approach even in former years to our consumption.

Contingency of War. — In the event of war, all these anticipations would be overturned : our capital would no longer be abundant ; our navigation no longer cheap ; while from no branch of our industry would labourers be more generally withdrawn for government service than from agriculture. At present, however, we leave this formidable contingency out of the question : in France, the only country which immediately affects our foreign politics, there exist the strongest reasons for adhering to a pacific course ; and if that government be induced for a time to deviate from it, the recurrence of a state of war so general as that which followed the French Revolution, is certainly not to be expected in the life-time of the present generation.   Or, if we admit it to be impracticable to reason with confidence on so wide a question, there is at least one point which we may safely take for granted, viz. that our public men, in the event of a new appeal to arms, will abstain from two of the measures, which, more than any other, contributed to raise our corn market, — interference with our currency, and the stoppage of neutral navigation.

" These they will shun through all the dire debate,
And dread those arms whose force they felt so late."

Prospect of Relief to Farmers. — This question, though apparently identified with that of rise of price, will be found on examination to rest on very different grounds, and to present, happily, a less unfavourable prospect.   The reasons for this opinion are,—

1. The interest of all farmers who are not tenants on lease (Evidence, Agricultural Committee, pp. 49. 120.) is to have not a *high, but a steady price.* Taken in a permanent view, that price is most desirable which gives stability to our manufactures, and prevents our continental rivals from having too great a superiority over us in the main point of subsistence.

2. Our growth, if it equal, does not, in ordinary seasons, exceed our consumption ; a situation a good deal different from that of our agriculturists

after the peace of Utrecht. This fact, if it does not justify the expectation of a rise of price, affords, when considered along with our increasing numbers, a kind of guarantee of the past; a security against the abandonment, to any great extent, of the inferior soils.

3. The tendency of agricultural charges to decrease with the market-price of corn, and of the rate of profit in every line to approach to a common standard.

4 *Tithe.*—Since war and high prices can no longer enter into the calculation of our agriculturists, it becomes indispensable for them, as for the equally unfortunate sugar planter, to seek relief in a reduction of expence. In this by far the most effectual step would be a commutation of tithe, an exchange of a crude, unequal, and at present oppressive, mode of providing for the clergy, for a contribution from the public generally; a change which would be facilitated by the growing nature of our financial resources, and for which, as shall be shown in a subsequent passage (p. 185), the landed interest would be able to make an adequate return to the public.

5. *Poor-rate.*—To this subject we shall shortly appropriate a chapter, and take occasion to show how little information is as yet possessed either by government or individuals, in regard to various essential points, such as the different modes of distributing relief, the number of poor in workhouses, the allowance granted for children, and finally, the proportion of disburse for law charges, removals, and other outlay, distinct from the relief of the poor. With such evidence of imperfect information, (acknowledged in the Report on Poor-rate, July 15. 1822,) is it too much to question, whether we act an equitable part in continuing the pre-

sent mode of assessment? Without at all entertain-
ing the proposition of rendering poor-rate national,
we may claim attention to the arguments for a
more limited change, for rendering it an equal
tax on the parish or district, the levy being made
not on rent but on income generally, and extending
to other classes besides the farmer and householder.

These considerations confirm the hope that,
eventually, the situation of our agriculturists will
alter, and our tillage be carried on without the im-
poverishment of a most useful and respectable body
of men. Still their distress must, under any circumstances, continue some time longer, and be shared
by the numerous persons resident in towns whose
livelihood depends on ministering either to the
wants of the farmer or the luxury of the landlord.
Every feeling mind must sympathize with those
industrious classes, whether in town or country,
whose privations, very different from those of their
superiors, too often imply the renunciation of real
comfort. They have, however, already experienced
considerable relief from reduction in their expenditure; and a cheering, though somewhat indirect
prospect, is opened to them from the improved
condition of other classes. All must allow that the
sum withdrawn from agricultural income has been
far too great in its amount and too sudden in its
deduction; but it is a consolation that it does not,
like shipwrecked merchandize, or the expence of
an indecisive campaign, form a total and absolute
loss to the community: it is compensated, as far
as the evil of sudden transition admits of compensation, by the cheaper maintenance of our manufacturers, the prevention of their emigration, and
the ultimate benefit arising to our agriculturists
from their consumption on a more liberal scale.

SECTION III.

A Protecting Duty.

W E come now to the portion of our subject which caused so much discussion in the session of 1822 — the imposition of such a duty on foreign corn as shall afford protection to our agriculturists. Our reasoning on this head will be found materially different from that of the majority of parliamentary speakers, the amount of duty appearing to us a secondary object to the public at large ; while to our agriculturists, it would, if raised to an undue height, be replete with as pernicious consequences as the bounty act of last century. Without further preamble, we proceed to examine the following points : —

The comparative burdens on agriculture in France and England.

How far our manufactures receive protection from our custom duties.

The danger of over-extending our tillage.

The tendency of our commercial legislation to the abolition of all restrictions.

A populous Country not necessarily expensive.

England is, after the Netherlands, the portion of Europe in which population is both most dense as to numbers, and most closely connected by roads and canals. Compared to us, the inhabitants of

France, on an equal surface, are in the proportion of only two to three ; and the degree of separation is very materially increased by another cause — the inferiority of the roads and the want of water communication. Germany is still more inferior to England, both in numbers and in frequency of intercourse ; and it is needless to show how much more the deficiency prevails in the other parts of Europe, in Spain, Sweden, Poland, Russia. The point at issue is, to ascertain whether density of population necessarily tends to raise prices, to render a country dearer than its scantily peopled neighbour?

That it has in an eminent degree that tendency is the general impression and report of those among our travelling countrymen, who found their inferences on a few points most obvious to common observation, such as the moderate price of labour on the Continent, and the no less moderate rate of excise duties ; but they overlook the various considerations on the opposite side of the question, such as the general inferiority of machinery and workmanship, the loss of time caused by distance from towns, and by the necessity of doing personally that which, in a busy, commercial community, is prepared by others, and obtained by purchase. In a subsequent publication, when treating of " Economy and Retrenchment," we shall take occasion to explain the distinction between real and apparent saving, and describe the habitual waste of time in petty occupations by the inhabitants of provincial towns on the Continent : at present our wish is merely to lay down the general rule, that a population dense, improved, affluent, does not *necessarily* render a country more expensive than one that is poor and thinly inhabited. The difference is in the mode of living, not in the price of the articles.

An increase of population, by leading to an abridgment of labour, and to the transaction of business
en masse, brings with it a dispatch and an extent of
accommodation ; the saving from which is equal,
we believe more than equal, to the enhancement
in provisions attendant on augmented numbers.

It is not in towns of moderate size, however near
each other, but only in the case of an overgrown
capital, such as London, Paris, or Constantinople,
that the real and unavoidable difference of expence
becomes considerable.   Holland and England are,
it is true, dearer throughout all their provincial
towns than the rest of Europe ; but that is owing
partly to style of living, partly to high taxation, — to
the price paid by either country for the rank which
it has maintained in the scale of European politics.
Were we to subject individual expenditure to an
analysis, and to keep separate the portion of it
which results from these causes, we should find
that our actual prices, the purchase money of commodities at market, are not, on the whole, much
greater than in other countries.

These remarks are general, and apply to all
classes of society.   We now proceed to the point
more immediately in question, the situation of our
agriculturists.

Comparative Burdens on French and British Agriculture.

That the pressure on our agriculture is greater
than on that of our neighbours is sufficiently known,
or rather, sufficiently believed ; for very few persons have been at pains to analyze the burdens on
either.   On our side, they consist of tithe, poor-
rate, land-tax, along with a participation in the

assessed taxes, the excise duties, and the customs. To begin with the burdens directly applicable to agriculture—tithe and poor-rate—we are inclined, in consequence of the fall of corn, to anticipate that these charges, *as far as paid by the landed interest, and as far poor-rate is distinct from wages,* will, ere long, be reduced to a sum of about 7,000,000*l.* for both. The amount of the land-tax, adding the redeemed to the unredeemed, is about 2,000,000*l.*; making together a sum of somewhat more than 9,000,000*l.* To this formidable burden the French may, with a qualification to be mentioned presently, oppose their *foncier,* or assessment on real property; which, after the partial reduction of late years, still forms a charge of 17 or 18 per cent., not on the rent merely, but on the rent and farmer's profit together. Next come our assessed taxes, which, in their present reduced state, are probably balanced by the *portes et fenêtres* of our southern neighbours, when added to the *mobilier,* or tax on the reputed value of furniture. Our stamps, swelled as they have been during the late wars, are considered by our landlords as a very serious charge, whether on leases, sales, or loans; and a member of Parliament, remarked for his acquaintance with such subjects *, went lately the length of asserting that this charge was the most heavily felt of any by our agriculturists. Heavy, however, as it is, even after the modification granted in 1822, its pressure is equalled, in respect to sales at least, by the French *enregistrement,* a duty of no less than 5 per cent. on the purchase money, which, added to the other departments of the stamps, produces an amount of 5,000,000*l.*; a

* Mr. Frankland Lewis.

surprising sum to collect from a country never
remarkable for its wealth.

So far we may be said to have preserved equality
in our comparisons : we now come to points in
which there necessarily prevails a difference, though
less great than is commonly imagined.   Thus, in
regard to the charges incurred in the course of cultivation, viz. seed, manure, wear and tear, working
cattle, — the difference, very great during the war,
has lost, or is now losing, much of its amount. The
cost, as expressed in money, is still, we admit,
smaller in France ; but in the case of implements,
and, in some measure, in that of working cattle,
the difference means little more than inferiority of
quality ; an inferiority not unlike that which would
be exhibited by a parallel between our agriculture
of the present age and that of the beginning or
middle of the last century.   A similar remark applies to the domestic expences of a farmer.   The
difference lies in the style of living more than in
the price of the articles ; for in two material points,
clothing and fuel, the cost is not higher in England
than on the opposite side of the Channel.   The fuel
of the rural districts of France is generally wood ;
sometimes, though rarely, it consists, as in Ireland,
of turf or peat.

We come next to a highly important part of
agricultural disburse, the price of labour ; a point
in which the balance is greatly in favour of France,
the wages of an able-bodied labourer not exceeding (Chaptal sur l'Industrie Française, vol. i.
p. 245.) six shillings a week without victuals, a
rate considerably below any reduction that we
can reasonably expect from the fall in the price of
provisions.   Nor is this advantage lessened, as
some of our countrymen may imagine, by any

personal inferiority on the part of the French peasantry, who repair to their work at as early hours,
and continue engaged in it with as much steadiness and activity as our own labourers. Add to
this, that the saving we have mentioned is enjoyed by the French farmer equally in the case of
domestic servants, whose diet is plain and whose
habits are sober. In what, then, shall we be able
to find on our side of the Channel a counterpoise
to this essential advantage?—First, our implements, particularly those of iron, being much
superior, enable men of the same bodily power to
do more work, or to do it better. Secondly, the
use of machinery, such as threshing-mills or drill-
ing-implements, is almost totally unknown in
France. Thirdly, our farms are of appropriate
size; while those of our neighbours, limited often
to such petty occupancies as those of our ancestors of the 16th and 17th centuries, afford no
field for the beneficial employment of either capital
or machinery. Lastly, our farmers, in borrowing
money, pay an interest less by one or two per
cent. than is required in France, six or seven per
cent. being still a very common rate in that
country.

A long list of the agricultural disbursements of
the two countries is thus made to balance, and the
remainder of the parallel is brought within a comparatively narrow compass. It may, in fact, be
considered as reduced to two points : on the one
hand, the contingency of benefit to the English
agriculturist from a protecting duty; on the other,
the heavier excise and customs to which he is subjected. A protecting duty is not unknown in
France ; and, under the provisions of the late
acts of 1819 and 1821, the price of 46s. or 47s.

for the Winchester quarter of wheat is apparently secured to the farmer; but, in a country which generally grows its full consumption, regulations affecting import must be of rare and temporary operation.

We pass over, therefore, this frail support, and proceed to the permanent and substantial points of difference in the condition of the British and French farmer. These will be found in the magnitude of our taxes on consumption. Our custom duties, being chiefly on luxuries, do not very greatly affect our agriculturists; but, among our excise duties, the tax on leather, which, after the late reduction, still forms a burden of nearly 150,000*l.* on our peasantry, is unknown in France; while our duties on malt, beer, and corn-spirits, amounting, after the abatement made in 1822, to the surprising sum of 9,000,000*l.* sterling, are feebly met by the French taxes on wine, cider, and malt. In years of over-stock of corn, as since 1820, the whole of the very large sum we have mentioned may be said to form a charge on our agriculturists, exactly as the tax on sugar, in a season of over-growth, falls on the West India planter. These, however, are happily extreme cases; and we shall at present suppose them out of the question, calculating that of such duties no more usually falls on our agriculture than the portion paid for the consumption of the farmers and peasantry. Even then, it will exhibit a sum of 3 or 4,000,000*l.* sterling; a sum which, added to the 1,000,000*l.* by which our tithe and poor-rate exceed the French *foncier*, may be said to represent the greater share of public burdens (4 or 5,000,000) borne by the British agriculturist.

If we bring these charges into the form of a

comparative per centage, we shall find that the
foncier in France may, after making allowance for
all abatements and omissions, be computed at 18
per cent. of the rent and farming profit; while in
England, the amount of land-tax, tithe, poor-rate,
and additional excise-duties, form a tax on rent
and farming income to the extent of 25 per cent.
The result is, a heavier burden on the English agriculturists, to the extent of 7 or 8 per cent., except
in as far as it receives an occasional counterpoise
from the duty on the import of foreign corn. *

What then, it may be asked, has been, during
the present age, the respective situations of the
agriculturists in France and this country? The
war was productive of a rise of rent in both; but
while in France that rise was comparatively slender, in this country it doubled, and in many cases
more than doubled, the payments of 1792; so that
in 1813 the landed rental of Great Britain and Ireland considerably exceeded that of their southern
neighbour. The rental of France, however, was
much more secure : the price of corn in that country is little lower in peace than in war; and the
travellers who passed over her departments did
not, until last year, hear much of those reductions
of rent and wages which among us have been required on so large a scale since the peace.

The price accounted sufficient to enable French
farmers to make a livelihood and pay taxes is
about 45s. the Winchester quarter, in peace.

We shall now suspend our continental parallel,
and bestow a few paragraphs on one of a different

---

* In Scotland the burden is much less, the agriculturists of
that part of the kingdom being comparatively exempt from
tithe, poor-rate, and land-tax.

kind — on the comparative situation of our agriculturists and manufacturers.

Are our manufacturers actually benefited by protecting duties? — That such is the case, and in a very considerable degree too, is the opinion of the majority of our agriculturists. It is true, however, only in a slight degree, as will soon be apparent from the following facts. — The total value of British manufacture annually prepared, whether for home consumption or export, was computed in 1812 by Mr. Colquhoun, at 123,000,000*l.* Since then their quantity has greatly increased; but as their price has experienced a material reduction, we shall probably deviate little from the truth, in assuming that sum as a fair representation of their present aggregate value. But of this very large amount, more than 80,000,000*l.* consist of the three great articles of cotton, woollens, and hardware; none of which receive protection from custom-duties, our manufacturers being enabled, by inherent advantages, to repel foreign competition, and even to meet our rivals in their own markets. Thus our cottons are cheaper than those of France, Germany, or the Netherlands, from various causes — the import of the raw material is somewhat less expensive, our machinery is superior, our supply of fuel more abundant, and the capital employed subject to a less heavy charge of interest. In hardware, we possess a similar advantage in point of fuel and capital, with farther aids in the carriage of the ore by water, and in a subdivision of labour, to which the Continent in no degree approaches. If in woollens our superiority be less decisive, and if the quality of French cloth be more substantial, the fact is, that from our power of giving long credit to Americans and others, we, as yet, retain possession of most of the foreign markets.

We have thus narrowed, very considerably, the extent of manufacture supposed to be benefited by protecting duties. We might go a step farther, and enumerate various articles (such as refined sugar or pottery ware), in which protection is out of the question; while the remainder that are more or less protected by our custom-duties do not, perhaps, surpass the value of the agricultural produce to which favour is extended from the same quar-ter; our duties on foreign timber, flax, hemp, tallow, seeds, madder, butter, cheese, and rice, all operating, or being intended to operate, in favour of our agriculturists.

We add a few words in regard to our taxes on consumption generally. Of these, it does not appear that the agriculturist has greater reason to complain than his mercantile or manufacturing neighbour. Those most severely felt are on leather, soap, candles, and glass; also those on tea and sugar, since they were raised in the course of the last war to an immoderate rate. But these, as well as the farther imposts that form the long list of our excise duties, are paid in common by residents in towns; and if the pressure of the malt-tax be more heavily felt in the country, a kind of balance is afforded by the untaxed substitutes for groceries, which the country supplies to its inhabitants.

If against the payment of land-tax, we place the heavier assessed taxes of towns, we find the amount of public burdens balanced, with the exception of tithe and poor rate. These forming an extra burden on agriculture, and one of great amount, parliament have endeavoured to countervail by our corn-laws : at one time by a bounty on export, at another by a restriction on import.

What, it may be asked, was the real motive on the part of government for these multiform regulations — this long list of duties, drawbacks, bounties? Not to confer on any of the parties, whether agriculturist or manufacturer, an absolute advantage; but to reconcile them to the taxes imposed on the respective articles of their produce, and to prevent foreigners from underselling them in the home market. Under this impression, and considering the amount of tithe and poor-rate at present a dead loss to the landed, interest, we can hardly coincide with the argument in the Agricultural Report of 1821 (pp. 23, 24.), that our landholders have not a *right* to custom-house protection. Our hesitation would arise from a very different cause : first, from a doubt of the efficacy of a protecting duty ; and, next, from a dread that the expectation which it would so generally excite, might, as in the case of the bounty, lead to excess of home growth.

Danger of an over-extension of our Tillage.

This danger, which some years ago would have been treated as chimerical, we now find to have as strong a claim to attention and to precautionary measures, as the hazard of an over-extension of manufacture. Of the truth of this our readers will be satisfied on referring to our arguments in the preceding section ; and, above all, to the fact, that with so small a number of enclosure acts (forty-eight annually), we have found the means of meeting every year, since the peace, the demand of the 200,000 consumers annually added to our population. To what can this be mainly owing, except to the diffusion of improved methods, to the application of additional labour and capital to soils already under tillage ? And who, in this age of agricultural discovery, in this season of abundant supply, both as to labour and capital, can with confidence predict either the limit or the result of such application ?

In prosecuting this inquiry, our readers may, we believe, leave at once out of consideration all arguments against the increase of our growth, founded on the expence of reclaiming poor soils ; not that such expence is over-rated by Mr. Ricardo and others, but because it is unnecessary, a larger produce being obtained by bestowing additional culture on the better soils. If in regard to England and Scotland, our conclusions are called in question, and it is maintained that recourse to inferior soils must ere long follow an increase of our numbers, our reasoning can hardly be contested in respect to the sister island, where such extensive tracts of fertile land await the application of a better system. Under such circumstances, what security have our established farmers against the agricultural speculator, except in a measure at first apparently disadvantageous to them, we mean the removal of a tempting contingency, and an assurance, as far as can be conveyed by legislative regulation, that the prospects of agriculture are not of a nature to justify the transfer of capital from other lines of business ? The true interest of both farmer and landlord is to beware of extending tillage, to adapt our growth, as nearly as they can, to our consumption ; and to keep the former, were it practicable, somewhat below the latter, submitting, as after 1773, to a small but regular import.

It is that course alone which can give assurance of a steady demand, of a generally brisk market.

The Corn committee of 1813. — This Committee, actuated by a mixture of ignorance and selfishness, hardly to be credited in men of their station in society, ventured to recommend the prohibition of import, except when our own wheat should be at or above 105*s.* the quarter. Now, if with the comparatively small encouragement held out by 80*s.* our tillage has so much increased, how much greater would have been the augmentation had the extravagant proposition of the committee been adopted by parliament? What an extent of inferior soil would have been brought under the plough in the course of two years! What an overstock on the market before discovering the inefficiency of a corn-law to keep up prices!—an overstock admitting not of remedy, like excess of import, by shutting our harbours, but remaining in force for years, perhaps requiring the ruinous alternative of abandoning land under tillage.

The weekly Averages. — Among the various expedients suggested by the distress of late years, was that of comprehending in the returns, which form our weekly averages, such Irish wheat as is sold in England : the result of this, in consequence of the inferiority of Irish wheat, is to render a return of 60*s.* equivalent as a representative of price, to 62*s.* or 63*s.* on the former plan of taking the averages. Under present circumstances this has no practical effect; but were our market to rise, we should soon see that all expedients of this nature tended to stimulate production to a hazardous extent.

Objections to a high import duty. — After these arguments, we may venture to hazard an opinion, which would otherwise have appeared not a little paradoxical, viz. that in peace the injury resulting from a high duty on foreign corn would in all probability be greater to the producers than to the consumers of provisions. Were a high duty imposed, the rise of price would be temporary: extremes soon produce their own cure, and consumers might safely trust to the extension of home culture. The evil, however, would not stop there: the agriculturist would be sunk in distress by overproduction, and the merchants and manufacturers would consequently be subjected to an extra share of the public burdens. Hence the importance of maturely weighing, not the demands of a particular class, but the interest of the public in the most comprehensive sense.

Farther, the misfortune of the present day is less the reduction of income than the existence of inequality, the evil of transition ; and the public are entitled to expect such measures as shall set at rest this ruinous fluctuation. If our present *desideratum* be a general reduction of wages, salaries, and other money payments, not yet brought to their level, nothing, it is clear, can so effectually promote that object as a moderate rate of duty on foreign corn ; an assurance, as far as assurance can be given, of our market being kept at a steady price. How satisfactory to merchants, manufacturers, annuitants, and, above all, to farmers, to know on what probable price of corn they are to found their future calculations, to fix wages and salaries, to regulate their domestic expenditure !

In what manner, it may be asked, can a reference to the past be made instrumental in guiding us to a knowledge of the rate which forms a fit protecting duty ? By fixing our attention on the cost of raising wheat, not in a period such as that of the last thirty years, a period as anomalous in productive industry as in politics ; but at a time when Europe enjoyed that tranquillity which she has happily now in prospect. Comparing the present and the former charges on our tillage, we shall find that labour, team, manure, may and ought soon to be brought back to a rate not much exceeding that of 1792 : that tithe is necessarily proportioned to the market price of corn, and must follow its fall ; while poor-rate, though more difficult of reduction, ought to yield to the substantial advantage of cheap provisions, and the opportunity of work afforded by our manufactures.

All those considerations are of a nature to show that the late Corn bill, which admits foreign wheat when our own attains the average of 70*s.* has not brought our import limit too low.

Tendency of our Legislation to ultimate Freedom of Trade.

We shall now suspend, for a few moments, the consideration of temporizing measures, of the ex- pedients devised to meet the pressure of the day, and carry our speculations to a more distant object ; to the probable situation of our agriculturists and manufacturers of the next generation. In their time, our financial circumstances will probably by more favourable ; and parliament, relieved from imme- diate urgency, may legislate with no other view than that of the permanent advantage of the public.

It was long an opinion among our countrymen, that the landed and commercial bodies had opposite interests ; that a tax imposed on the land was of no particular detriment to trade ; and that the

gains of our merchants were of little consequence
to agriculture. In the present age a more ample
experience, a community of suffering on the part
of these great portions of the community, have
taught them a more liberal doctrine. It is no
where more emphatically urged than in the passage
(p. 20.) of the Agricultural Report of 1821, where
the intimate connexion, the strict dependence of
agriculture and trade on each other, are proved by
the evidence of the last hundred years of our history.
Assuming, therefore, that such will be the ultimate
basis of our legislative measures, we are naturally
led to take a view of our productive industry somewhat more comprehensive than in the preceding
paragraphs, and to inquire on what particular advantages our national prosperity has been and is likely
to be established.

Advantages of particular Countries. — Every country possesses its physical characteristics, its peculiar
and distinctive aptitudes. If, adverting to the
early history of civilization, we cast our eyes over
a map of Greece, and observe how much intercourse was there facilitated by maritime inlets,
and by insular positions in a sea of easy navigation,
we shall find it easy to account for the early improvement of that country, without ascribing any
great share of influence to fortunate accidents, to
the exploits of warriors, or the counsels of legislators. If we take a wider range, and inquire by
what features the physical structure of Europe is
discriminated from that of Asia or Africa, we shall
find its advantages consist partly in a climate
exempt from extremes, but more in the ample
means of navigation afforded by the Mediterranean
and the Baltic. Lastly, if, drawing nearer home,

we endeavour to ascertain how it happened that Flanders was flourishing amidst the barbarism of the thirteenth and fourteenth centuries, we shall trace it principally to two causes ; fertility of soil and ease of water communication. The latter, joined to the advantage of a free government, explains the still more remarkable growth of the Dutch provinces in the seventeenth century.

Of England. — By what peculiar advantages has England been distinguished, and enabled to take the lead of France and Germany, countries equally favoured in soil and climate ? In a religious and political sense, our superiority has consisted in the enjoyment of the reformed faith and a representative government ; in a physical sense, in our extent of coast, and in the productiveness of our coal mines. Natural superiority of another kind we can hardly boast : our pasture is, indeed, richer than that of continental countries, and we consequently take the lead in horses, cattle, and, in some degree, in the woollen manufacture ; but whatever comes under the description of agricultural advantages, ought, we believe, to be left out of the question, and to be considered as balanced by the less variable temperature, the greater warmth of the continent. Our farming is, indeed, much more advanced ; but is not that the result of indirect causes, of the reaction of our trade and manufactures, of the application of capital to tillage and pasturage, and of our tenantry being thus enabled to occupy farms of suitable size, instead of the insignificant tenures still' so common among our neighbours ?

In what manner, it may be asked, is this reasoning applicable to the present discussion, the question of a protecting duty on corn ? Our answer is, that we should greatly mistake our national prospects were we to suppose that we have as yet received all the benefit attainable from our superiority in the grand points of fuel and navigation ; — on the contrary, it may safely be asserted, that we are not yet in the midst of our career, not half-advanced in the task of turning these advantages to account. Continental countries are making a very slow progress, either in navigating the ocean, in forming canals, or in working coal mines : in each of these our superiority still offers an ample basis for the superstructure of national wealth. It would probably be such as to enable our manufacturers, though taxed in regard to provisions, to maintain a competition with their continental rivals ; but it is perfectly clear that they never will be able to do *full justice* to our national advantages until placed on a footing of equality in that very essential point. A reference to our custom-house returns would soon show how small our export of articles, such as hardware, glass, and even woollens, is, in comparison with what it might be, were equality in the price of provisions added to our other advantages.

A free Import of Corn. — This opens to our view all the advantage that would arise from a free trade in corn, or from the reduction of the protecting duty to a lower scale than has as yet been contemplated, either by ministers or by the most temperate of their opponents. *   In another place (see Appendix) we have appropriated a few paragraphs to this topic ; and these, under present circumstances, are, perhaps, all that it is advisable to urge in regard to it. The landed interest are as yet but imperfectly apprised of the extent of its ultimate

* Ricardo on Agriculture, pp. 82, 83.

advantage to them; nor can we expect that their attention will, for some time, be weaned from the high prices, the great nominal rents of the years of war. If our ministers are more deeply read in the science of national wealth, more fully convinced of the reaction of the prosperity of trade and manufacture on agriculture, they have objections of another kind; they cannot but regard a fall of prices as a virtual augmentation of the public debt. They are aware, likewise, of the evils of transition; and must, to use the language of the Agricultural Report, be anxious " to spare vested interests, and to deal tenderly even with obstacles to improvement, when long implanted in our system."

To all these difficulties we have to add, that the exemption of our agriculture from its extra share of poor-rate, and from tithe in England as well as Ireland, would be an *indispensable preliminary* to a measure which would bring our corn market almost as low as that of the Continent. Now government, however convinced of the impolicy of these burdens in their present shape, could hardly fail to consider a change in long-established assessments, above all, a new demand on our exchequer, as replete with embarrassment. Several of the late measures of ministers, such as the limitation of the Sinking fund, the remission of the most injurious of our taxes, the extended freedom of navigation, the transfer of the half pay and pension list into Long Annuities, evidently proceed on sound.calculation. They seem to indicate an adequate estimate of our resources on the part of our political guides; but the free import of corn would be so great a departure from our past policy, and would involve so many accompanying changes, that we can contemplate it only as a remote result, as less likely to be the consequence of any arguments that can possibly be urged, than of a continuation of low prices; which, by reducing the cost of production, and replacing our tenantry in nearly the same situation as in 1792, may cause our corn laws to *expire by a natural death.*

———

Such were our views of this interesting subject last year, on sending to press the first edition. Since then, there have occurred several circumstances favourable to an approximation to a system of freedom, and to the hope of that advantage which always arises from the removal of restraints from productive industry. The lapse of time, the reduction of charges, and the prospect of continued peace, have gradually accustomed both landlord and farmer to regard 60s. for a quarter of wheat in the light of a remunerating price : the next step may be to consider it as a kind of standard for the duty on the import of foreign corn. Now, so soon as the landed interest shall be willing to permit import on the average price of our wheat exceeding 60s., they will be entitled to call on the public for decisive concessions in regard to tithe and poor-rate, — in other words, by giving an assurance of a permanently moderate price to the consumer, they will have a right to demand that these burdens (tithe and poor-rate) shall be shared by the public at large.

Are the recent measures of ministers of a nature to promise a concurrence in this plan of mutual concession? To this we are inclined to answer in the affirmative, and, with confidence, whether we look to the personal change in the Chancellorship of the Exchequer; to the reduction so promptly made in the assessed taxes; to the limits which, as far as we can judge, men in office think it fit to affix to the Sinking Fund; and, above all, to the introduction of the too long delayed measure for the commutation of tithe in Ireland.

Of the power of the monied interest to come to the relief of their countrymen engaged in agriculture, we shall treat in our concluding chapter.

CHAP. VI.

Poor-Rate.

THE subject of poor-rate has already engaged so much attention both in parliamentary investigations and published works, that we shall avoid all general discussion, and confine ourselves to what may be termed plain, practical topics, such as the comparative amount of money distributed at different dates to the poor, and the degree of pressure on the contributors. We take up the subject less as a national question, than as an appendage to our observations on agriculture: but our summary, brief as it may be, will, we trust, explain two points, at present little understood ; — the great increase of parochial charge during the war, when labour in general was so liberally paid, and the very considerable reduction that is now taking place, notwithstanding the apparently less favourable state of our productive industry.

We propose to treat successively of the —

Origin and progress of our poor-law system ;

Its degree of pressure considered as a tax ;

Its effect on the condition of the lower orders.

Origin of our Poor Laws. — The origin of the English poor laws, a system so different from that of neighbouring countries, is to be traced to two causes, — the call, at the time of the Reformation, for a provision for the poor, when deprived of charitable aid from monasteries ; and the enhancement, both progressive and rapid, which, as explained in the preceding chapter, took place in provisions during the 16th century. If the former offered a fair plea for the new system, the latter presented the more substantial grounds, since the rise of wages seldom keeps pace with a rise in provisions. The conjunct operation of these causes led to various enactments in favour of the poor, which were definitively consolidated in the act of 1601, — an act prepared with all the care and deliberation characteristic of the ministers of Elizabeth, and which would never have received a pernicious extension had its execution fallen into proper hands. Its provisions were intended at first for the relief of merely the aged and infirm, and led to little beyond the degree of aid afforded at present to the poor in Scotland or in France; but, from unfitness on the part of annually changed overseers, and from the remissness always attendant on the disposal of public property, when unchecked, the act received, in time, a wider construction. It was interpreted into an obligation to find work for the unemployed generally, as well as to make up to those who had children the disproportion which in dear seasons took place between the price of bread and the rate of wages.

Our poor-rate became thus a fund, not merely for charitable purposes, but for the equalization of wages; a counterpoise to the fluctuations arising from inclement seasons, or from any cause productive of a rapid fall in the value of money. This result, certainly well intended, and which at first sight seems of beneficial operation, is found, on trial, to be replete with all that irregularity and abuse which it is so difficult to avoid in any interference with the natural course of productive industry. Of this, a striking proof is given, not only in this country, but in the New England states, and in the state of New York; for even in these, the countries of the world in which the pay of the labourer is most liberal, the number of paupers has become large. They are, happily, the only foreign countries in which our example has been imitated. On the continent of Europe, the public institutions afford protection only against infirmity and extreme penury : even Holland, so long noted for its hospitals and charities, has not a poor-rate on the comprehensive plan of England.

Its Progressive Extension. — Our records of the distribution of relief to the poor during the seventeenth century are very imperfect : its amount, however, must have been considerable in the first half of the century, in consequence of the continued rise of corn during the reign of James I., and part of that of Charles I. But during the thirty years that intervened from 1660 to 1690, the price of corn was on the decline, and the country experienced in no great degree either the visitation of inclement seasons or the burden of military expenditure. In the reigns of William and Anne the case was far different; an enhancement of corn consequent on bad seasons, on war, and interrupted navigation, concurred with the disorder in our currency to render· a state of suffering general among the lower orders, and to give a melancholy corroboration to their claims for parochial relief. The number of persons receiving such aid is said (Clarkson on Pauperism), to have amounted, towards the close of the seventeenth century, to as large a portion of our population as at present, viz. a tenth part of the inhabitants of England and Wales. The amount of money collected for this purpose has not been put on record : it is said, somewhat loosely, but without much appearance of exaggeration *, to have approached at the period in question to a million sterling ; a burden heavily felt in these days of limited rental, and productive consequently of great complaints.

The long peace and reduced price of provisions which followed the treaty of Utrecht, were both conducive to the decrease of poor-rate, and, notwithstanding an increase in our population, we find that, in the middle of the century, viz. in the three years ending with 1750, its amount did not (Reports on the Poor Laws in 1817 and 1821) exceed an average of - - - - 700,000*l.*

After 1760, the charge for the poor participated in the general charge which took place in the state of prices, and amounted in that year to 965,000*l.*, while at a subsequent date, in 1770, it was carried to - - - - - 1,306,000*l.* ; so much did the effect of indifferent seasons and the enhancement of corn counterbalance the otherwise favourable circumstances of the latter period — the enjoyment of peace, the extension of our manufactures. Next came the contest with our colonies, along with the various losses attendant on interrupted export, and the suspension of undertakings dependent on a low interest of money, the result of which, in concurrence with other causes, carried the charge of poor-rate in 1780 to - - - - - - 1,774,000*l.*

The peace of 1783, though favourable in the main, was. not unaccompanied by the evils of transition. Our productive industry partook at first of the discouragement excited by the loss of our colonies ; and though it soon exhibited

* Sir F. Eden on the State of the Poor.

symptoms of vigour, and even of prosperity, the price of bread was kept up by the indifferent harvests of 1788 and 1789. When to this we add the increase of our population, and make allowance for the progressive introduction of abuse into a system subject to so little check or control, we need not be surprised that in 1790, the sum collected for the poor amounted, when joined to the minor rates for highways, church, and county charges, to -   -   -   -   - 2,567,000*l.*

The late Wars. — Such was the state of our poor-rate at the beginning of the French Revolution, the time when we entered on a course of circumstances productive of a continued fall in the value of money. As wages seldom rise in proportion to a rise in provisions, an increase of poor-rate is the necessary consequence. Previously to the war of 1793, the augmentation of our rates had been gradual, a century elapsing before they doubled, a ratio of increase little greater than that of our population. But after 1793, the concurrent effect of war, and indifferent seasons, rendered the price of bread so disproportionate to the wages of country labour, that in 1800, the poor rate, exclusive of the highway, church, and county-rate, amounted to   -   -   - 3,861,000*l.*

In 1810 to   -   -   - 5,407,000*l.*

And in 1812 to -   -   - 6,680,000*l.*

The peace of 1814 opened, in some respects, a new æra. It was followed, as is well known, by a rapid fall in the price of corn, which continued during two years; and had, notwithstanding the many new claims for parish relief arising from want of work, the effect, on the whole, of a partial reduction of the poor-rate. This is apparent from the subjoined table.

RETURNS FOR ENGLAND AND WALES.

	YEAR ending Easter, 1813.	Easter, 1814.	25th March, 1815.
	£.	£.	£.
Total money received by poor-rate, and in a smaller degree by church-rate, highway-rate, county-rate, &c. in England and Wales	8,651,438	8,392,728	7,460,855
To these sums are to be added charitable donations, whether arising from land or money, managed by the clergy, church-wardens, or overseers: Annual average -	238,310	238,310	238,310
EXPENDITURE.			
For the maintenance and relief of the poor	6,679,658	6,297,331	5,421,168
Law-suits, removal of paupers and expences of overseers or other officers - - -	325,107	332,966	324,665
Families of militia-men and other militia charges - - .	246,202	188,576	105,394
Church-rate, county-rate, highway-rate, &c. - - -	1,614,871	1,692,990	1,657,627
£.	8,865,838	8,511,863	7,508,854

The average of the two years 1815 and 1816 was,
Church, county, and highway-rate   - -   £ 1,212,918
Maintenance and relief of the poor, including law-
   suits, removal of paupers, and expence of overseers 5,714,506

In all - - £ 6,937,425

Increase after 1816. — The poor-rate was thus in progress of reduction, both as to the amount levied, and the number relieved, when a general re-action took place, in consequence of the high price of provisions that followed the bad harvest of 1816.

AVERAGE OF TWO YEARS.	Relief and Maintenance of the Poor ; also Law Suits, Removal of Paupers and Expence of Officers.	Church-rates. County-rates, Highway-rates, and Militia-charges.	TOTAL.
	£.	£.	£.
1816 and 1817	6,918,217	1,210,200	8,128,417
1817 and 1818	7,890,148	1,430,292	9,320,440
1818 and 1819	7,531,650	1,300,534	8,932,185
1819 and 1820	7,329,594	1,342,658	8,719,655
Year ending Easter 1821	6,947,660		
Do. 1822	6,335,820		

The amount of our payments was highest during the interval (1817, 1818, 1819,) when a high price of corn unfortunately concurred with the derangement of productive industry arising from our great national transition.

Since 1819 the amount of this formidable charge has experienced a progressive, though very gradual reduction.

The year ending Easter 1819, was less than the
  year ending Easter 1818, by   -   5 per cent.
Do. ending 1820, less than 1819, by   3
Do. ending 1821, less than 1820, by   5
Do. ending 1822, less than 1821, by   9
                                        ——
Total reduction since 1818,   22
                                        ——

For the year ending 25th March, 1823,
the returns as yet received exhibit
a diminution, which, joined to a
further reduction in the year now
in progress, justifies our assuming
the total of our present expenditure
for the poor, at less than £6,000,000

NUMBER OF PERSONS RELIEVED.

	YEAR ending Easter, 1813.	Easter, 1814.	March 25th, 1815.
Poor permanently relieved in workhouses	97,223	94,085	88,115
Ditto, ditto, out of workhouses (without reckoning children)	434,441	430,140	406,887
Parishioners relieved occasionally - -	440,249	429,770	400,971
Total of paupers relieved - -	971,913	953,995	895,973

Workhouses. — The preceding return exhibits in
a separate line the number of poor living in workhouses. This plan is, in a manner, peculiar to
England; the public establishments in other countries being confined to hospitals or houses of correction. The workhouse plan, originally adopted
above a century ago, received a great extension
from an act passed in 1782, commonly called Gil-
bert's Act, from the name of the member of parliament by whom it was framed. This act, aiming
to combine the advantages of an assemblage of a

number of poor on one spot, of a minute division of labour, and a joint management of disburse, empowered all magistrates to consider any large workhouse as a common receptacle for the poor throughout a diameter of twenty miles. Sound as these reasons apparently were, the plan has as yet been by no means successful : proper care has seldom been taken to separate the inmates of the workhouses according to their age or their habits ; nor has the division of employment been at all carried to the necessary length. Their earnings have consequently been insignificant, and the charge to the parish amounts, in general, to 9*l.*, 10*l.*, or even 12*l.* per head, while half the sum would suffice, if paid to the poor at their own habitations. It is thus in some measure fortunate that the limited extent of our workhouses hardly admits above 100,000 individuals.

Scotland and France. — It is a general notion in England, that Scotland has no poor laws, — a notion originating in the very satisfactory circumstance of the lightness of her poor rate. But there are and have long been in that country statutes enacting that certain funds shall be faithfully applied to the relief of the poor. These funds, however, are levied by a very easy process: first, from collections made at the parish church ; next, from the interest of money or rent of land bequeathed by individuals for the use of the poor; and, lastly, from a moderate assessment, paid in general half by the landlords, the other half by the rest of the parish. In 1817, a year of scarcity and distress, the total poor-rate collected in Scotland was 119,000*l.*, of which nearly 70,000*l.* proceeded from charitable collections and donations ; the remainder from assessment. The latter, however, did not extend over the whole of Scotland, being levied only in the low country, particularly in the districts containing manufacturers; while the mountainous counties of the north remained, as they have always been, exempt from assessment.

The paupers in Scotland are in the proportion of only *one in forty*, a proportion which would doubtless have been increased, had the price of corn, and the attendant operation of the English poorlaws, continued as in 1817 and 1818; for it is a remarkable fact, that the distribution of a parish allowance to manufacturers in England operates as a serious comparative disadvantage to their humble brethren in the north. Thus, when in a depressed branch the wages are equal to only 8*s.* or 9*s.* a week, the allowance of poor-rate to the English manufacturer may, and generally does, carry his receipt to 10*s.* or 12*s.*; a difference which has had the effect of inducing a number of the Scottish workmen to forsake their homes.

What, it may be asked, have been the causes of so material a difference in the management of the poor in Scotland and in England? The two countries embracing the Reformation in the same period, and falling under the sway of the same sovereign soon after the enactment of the poorlaw of 1601, the regulations were originally similar; but in Scotland their execution was vested, not in temporary officers, such as churchwardens and overseers, but in the landholders, clergymen, and elders or deacons, whose functions were permanent, and whose personal acquaintance with the poor enabled them to act with discrimination. The good effects of this plan, evinced as they have been by the practice of two centuries, induced the Committee on the Poor Laws in 1817, to recommend, that in England the overseer should be a permanent officer with a salary, and should act, if necessary, for several districts; a practice that has since been adopted with a beneficial result in a number of the parishes and townships of England.

In France, before the Revolution, the poor were supported, as in Spain, Italy, and other Catholic countries, chiefly by the abbeys, priories, and other beneficial establishments. These sources of income being absorbed in the sweeping changes of the Revolution, there took place in the *Assemblée Legislative,* in 1791, a long discussion on the fittest mode of providing for the poor : the result was a decided determination to avoid the English plan, but to provide at the public charge a fund of about 2,000,000*l.* a year, for the relief of the aged and infirm throughout the whole of France. In the disorders of succeeding years, great defalcations took place in regard to this fund; but in the reign of Bonaparte there were imposed, or rather revived, *octrois,* or dues on wines, cider, spirits, and other articles of consumption, paid on the introduction of these articles into towns. The imposition of a tax was in these days a matter of far greater difficulty in France than in this country; and the revival of the *octrois* was for a time attempted only as a fund for charitable purposes; but when the public became accustomed to this mode of contribution, its rate was augmented, and the proceeds rendered available to a variety of local purposes.

In addition to the aid arising to the poor from these dues, collections are made in France by subscription in the depth of winter, or on the occurrence of extraordinary distress; and, finally, in a season of general hardship, such as the winter that followed the bad harvest of 1816, occasional issues are made from the public treasury, on the application of mayors or local magistrates. In Paris there are a number of hospitals : in the large provincial towns there are, in general, two; one for the sick, the other for the aged. These institutions, however, are managed with all the laxity and want of method so common among our southern neighbours: mendicity is unrestricted, and prevails in many places to a reprehensible degree. In fact, the dwellings of the lower orders throughout France generally, whether in the country or in the suburbs of a town, exhibit to an English eye a very bare and denuded appearance. But to account for this general aspect of poverty by the want of parochial aid, would be as erroneous as to ascribe the comfort of the lower orders in Holland, to the aid afforded by charitable contributions. In that country, as in England, the better lodging and better furniture of the poor are the result of long-continued commercial activity; of that ample supply of work, of those habits of care, cleanliness, and order, which, in the course of time, it imparts to the agricultural portion of the community.

Poor Rate considered as a Tax.—Our next, and equally interesting object of inquiry, regards the contributors to the poor-rate, and the comparative degree of pressure imposed on them at different periods. And here our readers must be prepared for our making a large deduction from the increase of burden indicated by the numerical returns of poor-rate during the late wars; a deduction justified on two grounds,—the depreciation of the money in which it was paid, and the increase in the number of the contributors. In what manner, it may be asked, do the latter receive an increase ?

Of those who pay poor-rate it may be safely assumed, that the augmentation, in point of number, is on a par with the general augmentation of their countrymen; and we shall probably not err by assuming, that our national resources increase in proportion to our numbers. This opinion, already advanced in our pages, and about to be more fully developed in the sequel, we shall for the present consider as admitted, and extract from the work of a diligent and benevolent enquirer into such subjects, (Barton on the Labouring Classes, 1817,) a table in which these different considerations are taken into account.

Table of the Annual Expenditure for the Poor, computed with reference to the Price of Corn, and the general Increase of our Population.

Periods.	Average Price of Wheat.		Average of Annual Expenditure on the Poor.	Forming a Charge per Head on the whole Population of the Kingdom.
	s.	d.	£.	
From 1772 to 1776	48	2	1,556,804	44 pints of wheat.
1781 to 1785	49	2	2,004,238	53 Do.
1799 to 1803	84	8	4,267,965	54½ Do.
1811 to 1815	93	2	5,072,028	50 Do.

To judge from this sketch, the burden of the poor-rate, estimated not by the price, but by the quantity of subsistence, had actually begun to decline before the close of the war; but instead of pressing any inference on this head, we point the attention of our readers to the near approach to uniformity in the *real* charge at the time of the greatest apparent variation. This inference is farther confirmed by the following extract from a pamphlet on Pauperism, by Mr. W. Clarkson, published in 1815.

Year.	Population of England and Wales, about	Total of Rates, including Highway, Church, and County-rates.	Number of Paupers relieved.
1688	5,300,000	£.665,362	563,964
1766	7,728,000	1,530,804	695,177
1783 1785	8,016,000	2,004,238	818,851
1792	8,675,000	2,645,520	955,326
1803	9,168,000	4,267,965	1,040,716

In the fifty years that elapsed between 1764 and 1814, the increase of our population was as 7 to 11, and the rise in the price of provisions exceeded the proportion of 7 to 13. Here, accordingly, the two great causes of increase of poor-rate operated in concurrence; and in 1814 it was incumbent on us to be prepared, not only for an augmentation of claimants in the proportion of 11 to 7, but for an increase of expence in their maintenance, in that of 13 to 7 ; the two together forming, when compared to the return of 1764, a sum (24 to 7) more than triple the responsibility of that year. Is it then matter of surprize, that 5,000,000*l.* should go no further in its discharge in 1814, than 1,500,000*l.* in the beginning of the reign of George III.

Wages paid by Poor Rate. — It is a great, though very common error, to account poor-rate a *bonâ fide* tax, an actual sacrifice to its apparent extent. But the leading rule of our system, particularly in the west of England, is, to afford relief to the lower orders on a conjunct calculation of the price of bread, and the number of children in a family. An allowance made on this plan represents less the degree of distress prevalent in the country, than the difference between the market price of provisions, and the existing rate of wages; a rate, perhaps, transmitted with little variation from years of greater cheapness. It is thus that our poor-law system was rendered, during the late wars, an expedient for *preventing a rise of wages*, as far at least as regarded country labour, on the avowed ground, that wages once raised cannot be reduced without the greatest difficulty.

What, it may be asked, was the effect of the war on the price of labour generally? To increase the demand, and to place a number of the lower orders in towns, whether manufacturers or mechanics, in a better situation than before, notwithstanding the rise in provisions. In no department did it render the demand greater than in agriculture, and in none did the wages of the labourer experience a greater rise in Scotland; but in England, at least in most parts of England, from the effects of an artificial system, the case was very different. Wages were subjected to regulation; and their rise, though considerable, being inadequate to the rise of corn, the unavoidable result was a great increase of poor-rate. It is only thus that we find it possible to explain the remarkable anomaly, that in a period when farming was flourishing beyond example, the number of agricultural paupers should increase in a proportion fully equal to that of our trading and manufacturing districts. This was exemplified in Bedfordshire and Herefordshire, the two counties which employ the largest proportion of their inhabitants in agriculture.

	Expended on Paupers in 1776.	Average expenditure of 1783, 84, 85,	In 1803.	In 1815.
Herefordshire	£10,592	£16,728	£48,067	£59,256
Bedfordshire	16,663	20,977	38,070	50,371

There is thus no doubt, that a part of the poor-rate ought to be deducted from our estimate of it as a tax, and considered in the light of an equivalent for wages. If it be asked, what proportion should thus be deducted, we must answer, by admitting, that the enquiry is complicated, involving a reference to the rate of wages in Scotland and the counties in the north of England, where poor-rate is comparatively light. The proportion, besides, must differ materially under different circumstances, in consequence of the greater or less demand for labour. In this uncertainty, and in the absence of the necessary documents, we are confined to a conjectural estimate; but if a third of our poor-rate is to be thus accounted for, we exclude the idea of a tax or sacrifice to the extent of nearly 2,000,000*l.* annually, during the last ten years.

Mode of Assessment. — Amidst the various suggestions entertained during the agricultural distress of 1816, was that of rendering the burden of poor-rate national, instead of parochial; of paying it out of a general, instead of a local fund. This proposition is noticed here, merely to show its absolute inexpediency. Under our present system, it could be accompanied by no adequate checks, — by no satisfactory rule for restricting either the number or the allowance of the pensioners. In Scotland, in France, in short, in all countries with which we are acquainted, the relief of the poor is defrayed by a local contribution. But while we determine to keep up the distinction of parishes and townships, and to oblige each to provide for its poor, there appear to be strong reasons for a change that would be perfectly compatible with the maintenance of local distinction : we mean new-modelling the assessment of property. At present the whole falls on land and houses; but would not, we may ask, the income of the inhabitants of the parish generally, returned on a plan somewhat similar to that of the property tax, form a much more equitable basis of repartition ; particularly since the landed interest appear to have lost their principal stay—the counterpoise afforded by the corn laws.

The yearly rental of the land and houses of England and Wales, on which poor-rate was collected in 1803, was not (Clarkson on Pauperism) returned at more than £24,000,000

The latter years of the war exhibited both a large increase of rental and a more correct return, the amount assessed being (Report on the Poor Laws, 1817) not less than 51,898,000

But increase of demand followed, or rather accompanied, increase of means : the rate, 3s. 7½d. in the pound in 1803, was not below 3s. 4d. on the far larger sum assessed in the years 1812, 1813, 1814. At present, whatever be the official allotment, the burden bears an equal proportion to our resources, because, since the fall of corn, the rental of land and houses in England and Wales can hardly exceed . . . 45,000,000

In 1803, the sum collected for the use of the poor was below 4,000,000*l.* ; and if, in some years hence, it be reduced, as we anticipate, (see **Appen-** dix to the chapter on Agriculture, p. [35]) to a sum (4,500,000*l.*) not greatly exceeding that amount, it would form a charge of from two shillings in the pound on the actual rent of our land and houses, (45,000,000*l.*); but, if levied on the in- come of the parishioners generally, 4,500,000*l.* would form a rate of less than *one shilling* in the pound.

Did Increase of Wages and Poor-rate counter- balance the Enhancement of Provisions? — It would, we believe, be a mistake, to imagine that the in- crease of wages and parochial aid during the war, counterbalanced to the country labourer the en- hancement of produce, and had the effect of ren- dering his situation more comfortable than in the preceding period. A very different conclusion is suggested by the following calculation made by Mr. Barton, who, in his pamphlet on the " State of the Labouring Classes," published in 1817, shows, that whatever may have been the case in towns, wages in the country, estimated by their power of procuring subsistence, experienced a considerable diminution in the sixty years between 1760 and 1820.

Statement showing the Proportion of the Wages of the Country Labourer to the Price of Corn.

Periods.	Weekly Pay.		Wheat per Quarter.		Wages in Pints of Wheat.
	s.	*d.*	*s.*	*d.*	
1742 to 1752	6	0	30	0	102
1761 to 1770	7	6	42	6	90
1780 to 1790	8	0	51	2	80
1795 to 1799	9	0	70	8	65
1800 to 1808	11	0	86	8	60

Happily the other articles of the expenditure of the lower orders, in particular clothing, were enhanced in a far less degree than bread. Without that advantage, their situation, favourable as was the period to our agriculture, would have been deteriorated, as will at once appear by a reference (see Appendix) to the table of the constituents of family expence in the middle and lower classes. We there find, that while provisions of home growth form hardly 30 per cent. of the disburse of the middle classes, they amount to 50 per cent. of the more rigorously calculated out-lay of the lower orders.

A still more serious confirmation of the importance of the price of corn to the poor, will be found in another short extract from Mr. Barton's tables. Inefficacy in point of relief has seldom been urged against our poor-law system, but the following return shows that it is far from being completely successful in preventing an increase of suffering, and even increase of mortality, among the poor and their children, in times of scarcity. The return comprises seven manufacturing districts in England, distinct from each other.

Years.	Average Price of Wheat per Quarter.		Deaths.
	s.	*d.*	
1801.	118	3	55,965
1804.	60	1	44,794
1807.	73	3	48,108
1810.	106	2	54,864

It was thus equally desirable, on grounds of humanity and of policy, that the price of provisions should experience a reduction. It was in 1820

that this took place on a large scale ; and the fall
of wages, though considerable, being still far from
proportioned to it, the condition of the lower
orders, at least of all who can find employment, has
experienced a favourable change. Were we in
possession of returns to a late date, Mr. Barton's
parallel of weekly pay and price of wheat, given in
our preceding page, might be continued to the
present year, and would exhibit an approximation
to the wages of the middle of last century ; in
some measure in the smallness of the money
amount, more in its efficiency in the purchase of
provisions.

But without such a return, enough appears to
establish the important fact, that notwithstanding
the relief afforded by an increase of poor-rate, the
condition of the labouring classes experiences a
very unfavourable change on the enhancement of
corn ; while, in return, it is greatly to their advantage, that the provisions should fall, and rates be
reduced. Need we then wonder, that in 1810 the
framers of the Bullion Report should have considered the situation of the country labourer deteriorated by a continuance of high prices, notwithstanding the increase of parochial aid ; or, that
after 1820, ministers should have accounted the
public tranquillity so firmly secured, as to admit of
a large reduction in our army.

Objections to our Poor Laws. — We come next
to the objections urged against our poor-laws, viz.
that they induce the labouring class to contract
premature marriages, depress their circumstances
by an undue increase of their numbers, and ac-
custom them to a state of humiliating dependance.
Admitting that these charges are considerably ex-

aggerated, (since the poor increase their numbers
almost as quickly in Scotland, where there is so
little parochial aid,) a sufficient proof of the radical
defects or absurd misapplication of our system is
afforded by the fact, that aid, originally restricted
to the aged and infirm, should be extended to more
than a twelfth part of our population ; for the persons receiving parish relief in England and Wales,
amount, without reckoning children, to nearly *a
million*. But, unluckily, we cannot speak with approbation of the course as yet pursued, in regard
to the poor in almost any other country. That
which is followed in Scotland is charged with a degree
of indifference to their sufferings in dear seasons;
a time when (Evidence of P. Milne, Esq. M. P.,
before the Poor Law Committee) necessity prompts
labourers to undertake taskwork at reduced rates,
and frequently to exceed their strength. A similar
feeling must have occurred to most of our countrymen who have lived in France, or other countries
of the Continent, and witnessed the habitual privations of even the sober and industrious, among
those of the lower orders who happen to have families. Hence, a reluctance on the part of many
benevolent minds to relinquish our poor-law system, defective as it is, or to forego the hope of
solving that most interesting problem, the means
of lessening to them the difficulty of rearing a
family.

Reduction of Taxes on the Necessaries of Life. —
To attain this humane object, the better plan, we
believe, is to abandon our attachment to system,
and to relinquish, as soon as in our power, whatever
is artificial in our regulations. No contrivance, however ingenious, no combination, however plausible,

can be so advantageous as the plain rule of enabling the poor to provide for themselves. Much has been lately done to this effect, by the reduction of the duties on salt and leather : let our grand object be, the removal of the remaining obstacles, whether existing in the shape of taxes on the necessaries of life, or of restrictions on employment, such, for example, as arise from our duties on coals carried coastwise or by canal.

A tax on a necessary of life has, in regard to the poor, the same operation as the enhancement of corn : wages do not become proportionally augmented, and a new pressure falls on those who are least able to bear it. The great addition to the tax on leather imposed in 1813, was, doubtless, for a time, an absolute sacrifice on the part of the lower orders. That they are indemnified, or partly indemnified, in the rate of wages, at times when their services are in demand, we do not deny ; but the equivalent is uncertain, the sacrifice immediate and unavoidable.

From this painful consideration, we turn to the consolatory reflection, that " any reduction of the taxes on the necessaries of life, may, with confidence, be considered the forerunner of a reduction of poor-rate." The more the charges on the necessaries of life, in this country, are approximated to those of the Continent, the more we perform towards confirming the superiority of our manufacturers ; resting the support of our lower orders on the *basis of the wide world, instead of England,* and substituting for an eleemosynary grant, the earnings of independent labour. Is it necessary that we should specify the advantages with which our countrymen enter on the field of competition with their continental neighbours ?

They have the aid of productive mines, of extensive water communication, of a minute subdivision of labour, of habits formed during successive ages to industrious pursuits. These grounds of superiority, imperfectly perceived by Englishmen who have remained at home, are amply appreciated by all who have witnessed the slow progress, the deficient resources, the general backwardness of most countries on the Continent.

But while the benefit arising from this reduction is admitted, the practicability of carrying it to any considerable extent may be questioned by those who look to the magnitude of the wants of government. These persons, however, would soon modify their objections, and extend their hopes, were they to give due attention to a few fundamental truths ; such as, " that the proceeds of a tax by no means decrease in proportion to the reduction of its rate ; " and " that new and unforeseen resources are opened by the extended activity consequent on such reduction." Whenever circumstances shall admit of giving a complete latitude to the course we recommend, the public may safely take for granted, that England will have, if not fewer paupers, at least fewer real sufferers from poverty than any country in Europe.

Could this highly desirable result be attained, our upper classes would find their duties towards the poor greatly simplified. They would be justified in confining their interference and aid to cases of urgency ; such as an inclement season, a great and general transition like that from war to peace, or from peace to war ; or, finally, to a time when, as is at present the case of the lace-manufacturers on the Continent, a multitude of persons, habituated to work of a particular kind only, find their earnings suddenly reduced by the introduction of machinery. Assistance thus conferred would be substantial charity; exempt in its consequences from the hazard and mischief attendant on our poor-law system, and, on that account, doubly gratifying to benevolent minds — to those who, eager to bestow, are withheld only by a doubt of their donations producing a beneficial result.

CHAP. VII.

Population.

Few subjects in the range of political science have given rise to more opposite theories than that of Population. It is now fully a century and a half since our venerable countryman, Judge Hale, taking doubtless for granted, like a number of reasoners in a more advanced age, that the quantity of food in a country is limited by physical causes, declared gravely from the bench, that " the more populous we are, the poorer we are." And the present age has witnessed the promulgation of a doctrine of kindred import, though somewhat more elaborately expressed, viz. " that population is imperatively limited by subsistence." This opinion, proceeding from a writer of extensive research and professorial rank, has been very generally received, not only in England, but in the country of Dr. Smith; a quarter where political economy forming more particularly a study, a rigid scrutiny of its merits might naturally have been expected.

Of the various answers to Mr. Malthus, the most substantial in argument, though far from the most attractive in style, is the work entitled the " Happiness of States," published in 1815, by Mr. S. Gray; a work of which the leading principles were, some time after, developed in a more condensed and popular form.* Far from coinciding with the uncomfortable doctrine, that increase of numbers leads to increase of poverty, Mr. G. maintains, that augmented population forms the basis of *individual* as well as of national wealth. He has been, on the whole, fortunate in the events that have followed the publication of his opinion, the present abundance of subsistence being particularly calculated to relieve the alarm of those who considered our numbers likely to outrun our means of support. Still the public mind is far from being completely satisfied in regard to the benefit arising from augmented population : the reasoning in its favour is not yet clear and convincing; while the occasional want of work among our lower orders is attributed by many to a population increasing too rapidly for employment, if not for subsistence. In this view of the subject, we are far from joining, and proceed to investigate it at some length, in the hope of finding not only a confirmation of the consolotary and cheering doctrine of Mr. Gray, but of being enabled to found on it a practical measure ; to discover in the increase of our numbers, the means of lessening our financial pressure.

Our principal topics of enquiry shall be —

The condition of society in an early age ;

The change effected by increase of population ;

How far subsistence is limited by physical causes;

The state of Europe in regard to increase of numbers and wealth.

* In two lesser works, entitled, respectively, " All Classes productive of National Wealth," 8vo. 1817 ; " Gray *v.* Malthus, the Principles of Population and Production Investigated," 8vo. 1818.

SECTION I.

Increase of Population.

Penury of an early Age.—The predilection with which the popular writers of almost every country have contemplated a primitive age, and the colouring cast over it by romantic imaginations, have had the effect of misleading the majority of readers, and rendering them strangers to the privations experienced by their ancestors. These, however, were multiform and grievous; such, in short, as to form a most striking contrast to the comfort of an advanced state of society; and if in England we are happily unable to find an existing likeness to a rude age, the sister island will amply supply it. The Irish peasant, occupying a hovel without furniture, and carrying on his cultivation with wretched implements, may convey to us an idea of the state of England five or six centuries ago, as well as of the present state of a great part of the east of Europe, of Poland, Russia, Hungary, and the inland provinces of Turkey. The improvement of these countries at present, appears to an English traveller extremely slow; but, aided as it is by the introduction of settlers from Germany and other parts, it is, of course, far less tardy than the advancement of Europe in the Gothic ages, when all were equally backward. In those days, a few cottages formed a hamlet, and many centuries elapsed ere the hamlet became a village. In point of property, extremes predominated: on the one side was the lord, on the other his vassals; while the middle class were few in number, and uncomfortable in circumstances.

Effect of increasing Population.—What a different aspect of society is exhibited after a progress in the useful arts, accompanied as it is by the rise of towns and general increase of population! If we compare such countries as Russia, Poland, Hungary, or the Highlands of Scotland, with the more thickly-peopled districts of the Continent, such as the provinces of Holland, Zealand, Flanders, Normandy, or, on our own side of the Channel, with such counties as Lancashire, Warwickshire, the West Riding of York (to say nothing of Middlesex), we find a surprising difference in the number and comfort of the middle class. A return of annual income from the first-mentioned countries, would exhibit a few princely fortunes, with a long succession of names below the limit of taxation: in the other, it would show a number of gradations rising above each other in a manner almost imperceptible. How different is the England of the present age, from the England of feudal times, when we could not (see the Appendix, p. [75].) boast twenty towns of 3,000 inhabitants each, and when the Commons or middle class were too unimportant to hold a share in the representation, until brought forward by the crown as a counterpoise to the aristocracy.

Gradual Transition from Penury to Comfort.—In what manner does the transition from penury to comfort, in general take place? If not altogether caused by density of population, it must be al-

lowed to have very close connexion with it; the conjunction of individuals in villages and towns being
productive of a degree of accommodation, comfort,
and finally, of refinement, which would be altogether beyond their reach in an insulated position.
In these assemblages the acquisition of one comfort
creates a desire for another, until society eventually
attains the high state of polish which we at present
witness in several countries of Europe. All this,
says Mr. Gray, leads the consumer to make fresh
demands on the producer; demands reciprocated
by the latter on the former, in a different line of
business. Hence, the dependence of one class on
another; hence, the prosperity caused to agriculture by the success of trade, and to trade by the
success of agriculture. It is of no great consequence to our argument, whether these wants are
of first or of second necessity, that which is deemed
a superfluity in one country, being often accounted
no more than a comfort, a requisite in another.

What, it may be asked, is the criterion of the
difference in wealth and general improvement between different countries? The relative density,
not of population generally, but of *town population.*
This is apparent in almost every link in the chain
of European civilization, Holland having in the
seventeenth century taken the lead of England,
exactly as England at present takes the lead of
France; France of most parts of Germany, and
Germany of Spain and Poland. The distinction of town population from population generally, is important, for were the same advantage
to belong to districts strictly rural, Ireland would
claim an equal rank with England, and Flanders
take precedence of Holland. It is in towns only
that we reap the advantage of collective over

scattered population; — an advantage consisting in extensive markets; a minute subdivision of employment; the greater dispatch and finish of workmanship, and a supply of occupation to indiduals of every age and every degree of capacity.

New Settlers. — It is but too common among unthinking persons to consider new-comers as unprofitable intruders,— as dealers, not customers,— as sellers, not buyers. This, however, is but a superficial view, a first impression, for there is very little reason to doubt that in one way or another these persons will disburse in proportion to their earnings. When it happens that they or any other part of the community do not make such disburse, the only source of detriment to the public is the practice (now very rare) of hoarding; for money saved and lent at interest becomes of service to the community, increasing the capital of the country, and lowering, or contributing to lower, the premium paid for its use. We may safely take for granted, that much public advantage arises from the arrival of new settlers, whether manufacturers, such as England and Prussia acquired from France on the repeal of the edict of Nantes, or agriculturists, such as Canada and the United States are now receiving from us.

Population, however, is generally augmented less by settlers from a distance, than by a local increase; by an excess of births over deaths : a mode, which, very different from the easy acquisition of foreigners of mature age, implies a long and often a heavy charge, until the youth of either sex acquire the strength or knowledge requisite to their support; requisite, in the language of the economist, to constitute them "producers as well as consumers." Though in such a case the acquisition of new members is much more dearly purchased, the effect in a statistical sense is the same as in the case of arrivals from abroad.

Is the amount of Subsistence limited by Physical Causes ? — We now approach the much-disputed point of the physical limits to increase of population; to the question, whether it is imperiously limited by subsistence, or possesses the power of augmenting subsistence in proportion to its own increase. The well-known argument of Mr. Malthus is, that population, if unchecked, would proceed in a geometrical ratio (1, 2, 4, 8, 16, 32, &c.), while the supply of food cannot, he thinks, be brought, by the greatest efforts of human skill and industry, to increase otherwise than in the arithmetical ratio of 1, 2, 3, 4, 5, 6, &c. This position he illustrates by a reference to the United States of America; a country where the abundance of food is so great as to admit of the inhabitants doubling their number each succeeding generation, the 3,000,000 of 1775 having become 6,000,000 in 1800, with a probability of increasing to 12,000,000 in 1825, and so on progressively.

That, as far as regards physical considerations, there is both an ability and a tendency in mankind to double their numbers in every generation, we readily admit; also, that wherever such reduplication does not take place, the causes are to be sought in checks, such as the poverty that deters from marriage, the occurrence of pestilential disease, or some other preventive of the increase of numbers. So far we agree with Mr. Malthus; but in regard to his second proposition, the causes that limit the increase of food, we must observe that the subject has as yet been by no means satisfactorily illustrated, the attention of the different writers on the subject, whether himself, Mr. Ricardo, or others, having been fixed too much on the necessity of having additional land to afford the produce required, and too little on the increase derived from bestowing additional labour on the same soil. What were the circumstances of the period when Mr. Malthus' book was composed? It was a period of war, of deficient crops, of continued enhancement of agricultural produce; and the author, like the public at large, was necessarily unacquainted with our power of augmenting the supply, a power so remarkably displayed since our seasons have become more favourable, and peace has restored to agriculture a sufficiency of labourers.

Average Increase of Population.—In attempting a computation of the average increase of our numbers, we begin by making an exception of the United States, peculiar as are the advantages possessed by that country. They consist in a territory of vast extent; a river navigation of great importance; a people enjoying unrestricted intercourse with the civilized world, and closely connected in language and habits with the most commercial and colonizing country of Europe. Such an example is necessarily rare, and ought to be considered an extreme case : a more satisfactory result as to the average increase of population would be obtained from a combination of cases, among which, assuming the United States as the example of the most rapid augmentation, we may take, as the second, England, in which, under circumstances more favourable than on the Con-

tinent of Europe, but less so than on the other side
of the Atlantic, population has doubled within the
last century, and bids fair to double again in sixty
or seventy years. As a farther example, we may
take France, where, though the records are far
from accurate, the doubling of the population has
as yet required a term of from 100 to 120 years.
Other countries exhibit a greater or less degree of
slowness in the ratio of increase, and as these
returns apply to them when exempt from the
visitation of war, pestilence, or any violent check
to increase of numbers, Mr. Gray's inference is,
that the average furnished by the whole may be
assumed as indicative of the *natural progress of
population.*

After thus endeavouring to establish the natural
ratio of increase, Mr. Gray proceeds to argue that
such increase is no farther limited by the difficulty
of obtaining food, than by the difficulty of obtaining clothing or lodging, because the supply of food,
though apparently restricted by a physical cause,
is, on a closer examination, found to depend on
the amount of capital and labour applied to raising
it. In arguing this very interesting question, Mr.
Gray and the other opponents of Mr. Malthus,
would do well to guard against the charge of over-
confidence, and to begin by making a distinct admission of the difficulty of raising a family, a task
which to the middle classes is one of labour and
anxiety ; to the lower, of toil, privation, and often
of distress. Of this heavy burden, what portion is
to be ascribed to the charge of food ? In the middle classes, food forms (see Appendix, p. [11].) between 30 and 40 per cent. of the whole expence of
a family ; but in the lower above 50 per cent., constituting thus, the grand article of charge in that

class in which the pressure of a family is most severely felt.

After this precautionary statement, we may safely allow Mr. Gray and his followers to give a latitude to their inferences, comprehensive as they are, viz.: —

That the quantity of subsistence in the world may be augmented in the same manner, and by the same means, as the quantity of our clothing, or the size of our dwellings; and,

That an addition to our numbers implies no diminution of individual income or property.

Such assertions would have appeared not a little extraordinary during the greatest part of the war, when a continued insufficiency in our agricultural produce favoured so strongly the negative doctrine of Mr. Malthus: they would have been received also with no small surprise during 1817 and 1818, when a scarcity of provisions, a general irregularity in the state of our productive industry, concurred to produce apprehension in regard to our increasing numbers. But a different lesson has since been taught us: we have now evidence that numbers, increased greatly beyond anticipation, may draw their subsistence from the same territorial surface; that the amount of produce may be greatly augmented without bringing new soil into cultivation. A similar result from a similar cause is at present exhibited on the Continent of Europe.

Comparison of the present with former Periods. — How far does the preceding opinion appear to be confirmed by a general retrospect to the past? During the twenty years that elapsed between 1692 and 1712, the average price of wheat (about 44s. per quarter,) had been such as to afford, in these days of low rent and cheap labour, an ample inducement to the extension of tillage. It was consequently considered as having reached its *terminus,* and no idea was entertained of the practicability of any considerable addition to our produce. The result, however, proved very different, for though during the half century that followed the treaty of Utrecht, our population received (see Preliminary Observations on the Population Return of 1821, p. 29.) an augmentation, including Ireland, of fully 3,000,000, the increase of our agricultural produce was such as more than counterbalanced that new demand. This was apparent from the average price of wheat, which during that long period did not exceed 35*s.* the quarter. — Were it true that the acquisition of subsistence becomes more difficult as our numbers increase, we should naturally expect to find the greatest abundance in a remote age ; in times when the number of consumers was small, relatively to the extent of territory. But if we look back to the earliest periods of authentic history, to the ages when Greece and Italy were most thinly peopled, we find neighbouring tribes maintaining sanguinary struggles with each other, the motive of which, as far as regarded the lower orders, was the hope of acquiring additional territory, and increased means of subsistence. It is thus that we are to explain the obstinate warfare for small but fertile districts, such as the plain of Thyria, the plain of Tanagra, the Colles Tusculani ; — to say nothing of contests, in a record of higher authority, for the valleys of Palestine, or the banks of the Jordan. Had subsistence been abundant in these days, the inhabitants of the towns of Greece would have shown less eagerness in emigrating to new colonies ; while at Rome, the demand of an Agrarian law would have been a less powerful lever in the hand of demagogues. But to confine our examination to our own country, and to times comparatively recent, how different is the present situation of our lower orders from that of their forefathers under Henry VIII., or under our admired Elizabeth, when, without any disposition to severity on the part of the sovereign or her ministers, the number of capital punishments (Speech of Mr. Fowel Buxton on our criminal code, May, 1821), averaged no less than five hundred annually! Various causes, in particular the want of education, must have contributed to this unfortunate prevalence of offences; but can any be supposed to have operated so largely on the part of the commonalty, as the difficulty of obtaining subsistence, although in that age our population did not exceed a third of its present number?

But what, it may be asked, was the cause of this difficulty, — of the supply of subsistence being so scanty, when the number of consumers was so small? Of this problem the solution is to be sought in the unproductiveness of even the fairest tracts so long as they remain in a state of nature. Whatever be the serenity of the climate or the richness of the soil, they continue unavailing to any useful purpose, until the application of labour. By labour only can over-luxuriance be corrected, the forest cleared, a superabundance of water removed from one spot, a deficiency of it supplied in another. It is to the performance of tasks like these, the most acceptable of any in an early age, that we trace the honours so liberally bestowed in ancient mythology, — the apotheosis of the warrior who drained the Lernæan marsh, and combated the savage occupants of the woods.   But we are under no necessity of dwelling on an age of tradition, on a scene embellished by fiction : if we turn to plain reality, — to the times in which we live, and to a people noted for their adherence to the pursuit of substantial profit ; if, in short, we fix our attention on the western states of America, or on Upper Canada, we shall find an example abundantly convincing of the unproductiveness of the finest tracts until improved by labour and capital.

It would be easy to multiply illustrations from history, but as our limits hardly admit of detail, we extract from one of the works already mentioned (Gray *versus* Malthus), a summary of the leading ideas in the opposite systems of population.

Mr. Malthus's leading Ideas.	*Mr. Gray's leading Ideas.*
The increase of population has a tendency to overstock, and to lessen the average amount of employment to individuals.	The increase of population tends to increase the average amount of employment to individuals.
The increase of population has a natural tendency to promote poverty.	The increase of population has a tendency to increase wealth, not collectively only, but individually.

From the conclusions of Mr. Malthus we dissent almost entirely ; to those of Mr. Gray, we would suggest the following modification :

Increase of population, when *accompanied by improvement in agriculture, manufacture, and the useful arts generally,* has a tendency to augment both the

Average amount of employment ; and
Our wealth, not collectively only, but individually.

Mr. Malthus.	Mr. Gray.
The amount of subsistence regulates the amount of population.	The amount of population regulates the amount of subsistence, in the same way as it regulates the supply of clothing and housing, because with the exception of occasional famines, the quantity of subsistence raised depends on the amount of labour bestowed on it.
Population has a natural tendency to increase faster than subsistence.	Population has a tendency to increase, but this increase carries in itself the power of supplying its wants.

Here, also, we are desirous to introduce a reference to the progress of improvement, since, although the application of labour on the part of an increasing and unimproving society, like the peasantry of Ireland and Brittany, augment the quantity of the mere necessaries of life, the hazard of famine can be prevented only by improvement in agriculture, or in those arts of which the products enable a people to purchase subsistence from their neighbours. The early marriages of the Irish without the certainty of wages, or a stock of implements and furniture, are productive of incalculable suffering.

That the supply of food may be extended, by labour and capital, in the same manner as the supply of manufactures and buildings, we readily admit ; but, as in the case of four-fifths of mankind, food forms by far the greatest article of charge, and is, consequently, the most difficult of acquisition, we are fully prepared to excuse those who, in their writings, have over-rated the labour of procuring it. From the unqualified, and sometimes confident tone of Mr. Gray, an inhabitant of

Canada or the United States might fall into the grievous miscalculation, that to procure food for a family in Europe, was a task of no greater difficulty than in his own country, where a grant of land may be had on such easy terms.

Progressive Increase of Population in Europe.

The arguments in the preceding table are of general application, referring to the state of mankind in every age and country. To give the question a more specific form, we shall now introduce a few statistical results, and explain in what manner are effected those improvements in agriculture and the useful arts, which we consider as conferring the ability to support an augmented population.

Effects of Soil and Climate. — Fertility of soil is too directly conducive to increase of numbers, to require illustration ; but in point of climate, we cannot avoid remarking that the superiority of one part of Europe over another, is, as far at least as regards the productive power of the soil, much less than is commonly imagined. The great art of the husbandman consists in adapting the object of culture to the peculiarity of the temperature. In various parts of Scotland, accounted half a century ago unfit for wheat culture, the progress of improvement has led to raising that grain not only in abundance, but of a quality fit for the London market ; while in the boasted climate of the south of France, the season is often too dry for wheat, and the frequent failure of that crop seems to point out maize as a more appropriate object of tillage. In regard to potatoes, the culture of which is so directly connected with density of population, the warmest and finest climate of the Continent has no superiority over our own. It is thus only, when in extremes, as in the bleak tracts of Russia, Sweden, and Norway, that climate has operated materially to restrict produce and population : the physical superiority of the south of Europe, whatever may be its eventual effect, has not, as yet, been such as to outweigh the political advantages of the north.

Effect of Communication by Sea, Rivers, Canals, Roads. — The effect of prompt communication in promoting commercial intercourse is sufficiently apparent, but its tendency to increase the population of towns may require some explanation. What, in the first place, are the advantages enjoyed by the inhabitants of towns over those of the country; by a collected over a scattered population? They consist in a more ample field for sale or purchase ; a better division of employment; greater dispatch and finish of workmanship ; — a more varied supply of occupation, so as to suit individuals of almost any degree of strength or capacity. Now these advantages, arising, in a large town, from concentration of numbers, may, in a great degree, be enjoyed by places comparatively small and distant from each other, when connected by rivers, canals, or a line of sea-coast. Such was the origin of the prosperity of Greece ; such, at present, is the cause that the maritime part of her population make in their contest with the Turks a figure not unworthy of their ancestors. It is thus that the several towns of Holland, Zealand, and Flanders, have for many centuries maintained an active intercourse with each other ; that Paris is so closely connected with Rouen and Havre de Grâce; that Switzerland maintains by the Rhine an intercourse with Holland; and that in England, particularly since the multiplication of canals within the last seventy years, the conveyance of coal, iron, salt, and other bulky commodities, is so much facilitated. On the other hand, the want of such intercourse is, as we shall see presently, the principal cause of the backwardness of Spain, Poland, the south of Germany, and, in no inconsiderable degree, of France.

Effect of the Protestant Religion. — The adoption of the reformed faith has been found conducive to the increase, not only of individual comfort, but of the population of towns in the countries into which it has been introduced. Among its other effects, are a more general diffusion of education, and an exemption, in the case of the labouring classes, from the loss of time attendant on the endless holydays of the catholic church. In agriculture, the operation of these advantages is less apparent, most countries sufficing wholly, or nearly, to their own consumption, while the insulated position of the husbandman prevents, in a great measure, the benefit arising from competition and frequent personal communication. But in manufactures, particularly in those prepared for foreign sale, the case is very different; the ease of transporting them to a distant market, and of comparing their respective quality and price, opens a wide field of competition, and awards the preference to superior skill and ingenuity. Accordingly, though the catholics of Europe are, collectively, much more numerous than the protestants, the far larger share of exported merchandize proceeds from protestant countries, the labour of the Flemings, the French, and the northern Italians, forming a feeble counterpoise to those of the Silesians, the Saxons, the Prussians, and, above all, of our countrymen. In Ireland, linen weaving, the only great branch of manufacture, is almost wholly in the hands of protestants.

We proceed to apply this reasoning to the progress of population in Europe, availing ourselves of the official returns which have been made in most countries in the course of the present age, and which supply the following abstract : —

	Inhabitants per square Mile.
East Flanders	554
West Flanders	420
Holland (Province of)	362
Ireland	237
England distinct from Wales	232
Austrian Italy, viz. the Milanese and the Venetian States	219
The Netherlands, viz. the Dutch and Belgic Provinces, collectively	214
Italy	179
France	150
The Austrian dominions	112
The Prussian dominions	100
Denmark	73
Poland	60
Spain	58
Turkey in Europe (conjectural)	50
Sweden (distinct from Norway and Lapland)	25
Russia in Europe	23

Here are, indeed, some very remarkable differences in population, and to trace this diversity to its source, is an object of no slight interest.

Flanders possesses, in a high degree, the main causes of dense population, fertility of soil, and ease of communication, having on the north the sea and the Scheldt, while the flatness of its sur-

face admits of easy intersection by canals. According-
ingly, so early as the 12th century, when productive industry was in its infancy in every part of
Europe, except Pisa, Venice, Genoa, and a few
other towns of Italy, Bruges was a place of commercial eminence, a kind of centre for the intercourse of the north-west of Europe. In this it was
succeeded by Antwerp and Amsterdam; but
though Flanders has long ceased to have much
foreign trade, its population and manufacturing
industry have not declined. The great articles of
its produce are, corn, hemp, and flax; of its manufactures, linen, lace, leather, and, in later times,
cotton. Of cities, it contains only two, Ghent and
Bruges, and their conjunct population does not exceed 90,000. But it abounds in towns and villages which are populous, though not noticed in
history, and hardly in geography.

Of the Dutch provinces, the most remarkable
for population, as for other characteristics, are Holland and Zealand. On the ground of fertility they
have little claim to density of numbers, the soil
being, in general, ill adapted to tillage; but in
ease of water communication, they surpass every
other part of Europe. The mouths of the Rhine,
Maese, and Scheldt, afford capacious inlets for
foreign commerce, while the level surface of the
territory admits of easy intersection by canals.
These provinces possessed, consequently, considerable population and trade before the 16th century,
when their prosperity was confirmed by the adoption of the protestant religion, and by the establishment, after a long struggle, of an independent
government.

How far does fertility of soil account for the increase of population in England? Inferior to se-

veral tracts on the Continent, such as Flanders or the Milanese, but more fertile than the mountains of Spain or the sandy levels of the north of Germany, the soil of England may be said to hold a medium, and to have a claim to rank with the average of the French and Austrian territory. This degree of fertility would have determined a population in the present age of perhaps 150 to the square mile : the additional number is, as far as regards *physical causes,* to be attributed to our insular position, and the productiveness of our mines, particularly of coal ; advantages which lead so directly to the increase of our manufacturers, seamen, and traders. In ease of inland navigation, England is second only to the Dutch provinces.

Inland Countries : Austria and Prussia. — From these examples of maritime prosperity, we pass to inland countries, and begin by the dominions of Austria, which, with a slight exception, are at a distance from the sea, traversed by few navigable rivers, and by hardly any canals. Though equal to France or England in fertility, the communication between the different provinces is difficult, the progress of improvement extremely slow, manufactures backward, and the town population very limited. Prussia, in like manner, has few harbours or navigable rivers, indifferent roads, and canals that are only in their infancy : the majority of her subjects enjoy the advantage of the protestant religion, and of an education less imperfect than that of their southern neighbours ; but her population is thin, in consequence of a great part of her territory being sandy or marshy.

A still stronger example of the disadvantage of an inland position is afforded by Poland. That country, without possessing all the fertility vulgarly ascribed to those which export corn, is not naturally below the average productiveness of Europe. Its climate, if in winter it partake of the rigour of Russia, is in summer favourable to corn culture, and the great impediment to the increase of its produce is not a mountainous surface, but a cause more within the remedying power of industry — extensive marshes. Still, its town population is scanty and wretched, the causes of which, in a political sense, are, long continued misgovernment, a bigotted creed, the almost total neglect of education ; in a physical, the difficulty of transporting commodities, the extent of sea-coast being small, the roads proverbially wretched, and the access to the interior by the Vistula, circuitous, and too confined for so large a tract of country.

France. — Between these extremes, our ancient rival forms a medium, possessing a considerable extent of coast, but labouring also under the disadvantage of an inland territory, square in its form, slightly penetrated by navigable rivers, having, as yet, very few canals, and roads good only in particular directions. Compared to the Austrian or Prussian states, France is an improved country, but the case is far otherwise when put in competition with the Netherlands or England. Superior to our island in climate, and equal to it in soil, she is greatly inferior in density of population, and still more in the average income of individuals. Of her population, two-thirds (above twenty millions) live in the country, and her peasantry partake, in many provinces, of the poverty of those of Ireland. In the size of her towns, this great kingdom, so long the dread of our forefathers, and of Europe, has, in the last and present age, been altogether surpassed by

England and Scotland; for though our island boast only half her population, the distribution of it is made, in a manner, far more conducive to efficiency in a commercial and financial sense. This is, at once, apparent from a comparison of the twelve principal towns in each.

Population Return of 1821.

ENGLAND AND SCOTLAND.		FRANCE.				
London, Westminster, Southwark, and the adjoining parishes -	1,225,694	Paris -	-	-	-	720,000
Glasgow with suburbs	147,043	Lyons	-	-	-	115,000
Edinburgh with Leith and their suburbs -	138,235	Marseilles	-	-	102,000
Manchester, with Salford - - -	133,788	Bordeaux	-	-	-	92,000
Liverpool - - -	118,972	Rouen	-	-	-	86,000
Birmingham with Aston	106,722	Nantes	-	-	-	77,000
Bristol and suburbs -	87,779	Lille	-	-	-	60,000
Leeds and suburbs -	83,796	Strasburg	-	-	-	50,000
Plymouth, with Dock and suburbs - -	61,212	Toulouse	-	-	-	50,000
Norwich - - -	50,288	Orleans	-	-	-	42,000
Newcastle on Tyne, with Gateshead - -	46,948	Metz	-	-	-	42,000
Portsmouth with Portsea - - -	45,648	Nîmes	-	-	-	40,000

Ireland.—In our enumeration of towns we have omitted those of Ireland, because the situation of that country is peculiar. Possessing, in point of navigation, maritime and inland, advantages equal to those of England, her towns are comparatively small, her manufactures considerable in one province only. To what, then, is owing the remarkable density of her population? To two causes, fertility of soil, and the habit on the part of the peasantry, of subsisting on a food, the produce of which, on a given spot, is much larger than that of the wheat, the rye, or the oats, which, in other parts of Europe, form the basis of national subsistence.

Italy. — Few countries surpass Italy in natural advantages ; in soil, in climate, extent of sea coast, and, in her northern part, in the means of inland navigation.   But a bigotted creed has confirmed the indolence inspired by the climate, and her unfortunate division into petty states, has prevented measures for the advancement of her productive industry.   Though more populous than France, her inhabitants have a smaller average income : the want of a concentrated government may be considered the cause of lighter financial burdens, but the advantage is balanced or more than balanced by the loss of that rank among the states of Europe, to which this country is entitled by her population and geographical position.

Spain has a climate on the whole, favourable, but in respect to territorial surface, it is, after Switzerland, the most mountainous country in Europe.   Having been all along deprived of the blessings of good government and enlightened religion, the physical obstacles to communication between one district and another, have been very little lessened by exertion on the part of the inhabitants ; the roads are few and indifferent, while of canals there are hardly any.   Her great extent of sea coast, ought, it may be thought, to have remedied these disadvantages, but the small number of her navigable rivers has confined this benefit to the outskirts of her territory, leaving the interior untraversed and almost unopened.   Thus, with the exception of Catalonia, Biscay, and part of Andalusia, Spain exhibits all the backwardness of a country deprived of water communication. Portugal is more favourably circumstanced ; she has two great inlets from the ocean, the Tagus and Douro ; her towns are less thinly scattered, and without surpassing Spain in climate or soil, she is enabled to pay a larger revenue in proportion to her population.

Russia and the north of Sweden, form an example of extreme thinness of population, consequent, partly on rigour of climate, partly also on difficulty of intercourse.

Connection between Increase of Numbers and Increase of Wealth. — Having thus explained the increase of population in Europe, we are, in the next place, to examine the circumstances connected with the *increase of wealth.*

Our experience since the peace, unfortunate as it has been to particular classes of the community, has put beyond doubt one material point, we mean our power of subsisting an increased population. The case of England is that of Europe at large, and even anti-populationists can hardly apprehend that such abundance is temporary, or that the civilized world is at all in hazard from insufficiency of subsistence. Equally little can they deny that increase of national wealth, has, for a long time, accompanied increase of numbers. Such has evidently been the case in France, in Germany, in the countries along the Baltic, and, above all, among ourselves.

But while the facts are undoubted, the inference that the increase of wealth is closely connected with increase of numbers, will not be so readily granted. From the adherents of Mr. Malthus, it is not to be looked for, nor do we expect it for some time from the majority of our public men.

Their objections to it however will, we believe, be lessened by a qualification similar to what we have

already suggested, viz. that our arguments for
" an increase of wealth from increase of numbers
are urged only in regard to a society advancing
in a knowledge of agriculture, manufacture, and
the useful arts generally."

After inserting this important condition, we may
with confidence propose some interesting questions,
such as " whether, when the same portion of public
burdens is distributed over a greater number of per--
sons, the pressure on the individual is not necessarily lightened?" Our revenue arises chiefly from
consumption : each individual bears his part, and
the 50,000,000*l.* at present paid by somewhat less
than 15,000,000 of inhabitants in Great Britain,
will obviously give a smaller average per head
when they shall come to be shared among a population of 16,000,000. Our next question is, "whether the effect of augmented numbers, in adding
to the revenue, has not been remarkably exemplified
in the present age : whether it had not an important share in swelling the product of our taxes
during the war, and in preventing their diminution
since the peace ?" If these preliminary points
are admitted, we may proceed to put the more
general question, whether " when a greater population is maintained in equal comfort on the same
territory, the wealth and power of the community
are not increased ?" This approaches so nearly to
a self-evident proposition, that we shall not hesitate
to take for granted, that as to *national* income and
power, no doubt can be entertained of an increase
attendant on the increase of our numbers. It remains that we investigate its effects in another sense.

Increase of Income to the Individual. — Has an
augmented population a tendency to expand or

contract the separate earnings of its members? The present may be termed the age of statistical returns, the first period in history in which the governments of the civilized part of the world have called periodically for returns of population. It has also been an æra of great fluctuation in the property of individuals; yet amidst all the complaints of losses arising at one time from the expenditure of war, at another from want of employment or superabundance of produce, we have nowhere seen it argued that the circumstances of our population have undergone deterioration from the increase of their numbers. Of this one main cause is, that the necessity of providing for a family is the strongest of all stimulants to the renunciation of indolent habits, to the productive employment of time and capital. What a contrast in the result of the labour of the parent who necessarily adheres to a uniform pursuit, and of him who, exempt from the calls of a family, is at liberty to pass his time in speculation, indecision, and change! In nothing is the advantage of a mercantile community, like England, Holland, or the United States of America, more conspicuous over most countries of the Continent of Europe; where fanciful changes and visionary pursuits are so common, and where the upper classes, or, as they are styled, the *noblesse*, so frequently pass their lives without a definite object, and seek to escape trouble by avoiding the responsibility of a family.

Let us not, however, be understood as asserting that the increase of our population cannot be too rapid, or as making light of the pressure on the parents of a numerous family; a pressure which in general implies the necessity of renouncing the gratifications of leisure, and of almost " sacrificing enjoyment for the means of living." That this is applicable to the middle as well as to the lower classes, we are fully convinced; and if we do not dwell on it more largely, it is because we have already adverted to it, and our present enquiry regards the effect of increasing numbers in a sense strictly statistical.

Mr. Gray, not content with stipulating for an equality of circumstances to the rising generation, goes a step farther, it being one of the fundamental articles of his creed, that an increase in the numbers of a nation or society, tends, not only to keep up, but to improve the income of its members : that the 30*l.* forming the average income of individual workmen in one age, may, and, in fact, is likely to become 31*l.* in the next; or to express it in a comprehensive form, that " the more varied the classes of a community, the more they conduce to the welfare of each other." To this interesting and important conclusion we are ready to assent, provided the increase of income be considered as dependent less on increase of numbers, than on the circumstances under which (see p. 222.) such increase takes place.

How far exemplified in the State of Europe. — We proceed to put this doctrine to the test, by a reference to the returns of taxation and other public burdens, in different countries of Europe. These, we are aware, do not furnish an unexceptionable criterion of national wealth, as the proportion of public burdens may differ from circumstances unconnected with the state of productive industry, such as the greater or less participation of a particular country in war, since the adoption of the funding system. They form, however, the least defective basis, the nearest approximation to the truth in the present imperfect state of public surveys ; for few countries have been the object of an assessment so directly calculated to convey an estimate of national wealth, as the property-tax of England or the *foncier* of France.

	Population per square Mile.	Proportion of Public Burdens paid by each Individual.
		£. s. d.
England distinct from Scotland and Wales	232	3 2 0
England, Scotland, and Wales, collectively	165	2 15 0
The Netherlands *	214	1 10 0
France	150	1 4 0
The Austrian Empire	112	0 12 4
The Prussian Dominions	100	0 13 4
Denmark	73	0 16 3
Spain	58	0 11 6
Sweden	25	0 10 0
Russia in Europe	23	0 9 9

The maritime provinces of Holland and Zealand, are perhaps as heavily taxed as England, the charge of defence against the sea, added to the interest of a heavy debt, contracted during two centuries, rendering the total assessment probably equal to our 3*l.* 2*s.* per head. France exhibits a medium in her taxes as in her population : while in our case, the increase of taxation since 1792 has been more than double the increase of our population, in France the proportion of the former has outstripped that of the latter only by a fourth, or 25 per cent. Still the average payment per head is much greater in France than in the Austrian empire, a country fully equal to France in fertility, but more thinly peopled, because it is devoid of the means of communication afforded to France by a considerable extent of coast.

* The repartition of taxes is here very unequal, the Dutch provinces, particularly those of Holland and Zealand, paying much more than 1*l.* 10*s.* a head, the Belgic considerably less.

The population of Denmark, though more thinly spread than that of Austria or Prussia, pays a larger average contribution, the chief cause of which must be the extent of water-communication.

Rural Population ; its stationary Condition. — Of the poverty of rural population, examples are but too abundant in every part of Europe, with the exception of England and Holland : we confine our notice, however, to those quarters that are populous, and which ought to be comparatively exempt from poverty, did the same rule hold, as in the case of town population. That such is far from being the case is apparent from the following return :

	Population per square Mile.		Payment per Head, only.		
			£	s.	d.
Ireland - - -	237	-	0	11	0
The Milanese and Venetian territory - - }	219	-	0	10	0
The Neapolitan Dominions	154	-	0	8	0

What, it may be asked, are the causes of the stationary condition, we may almost say the hereditary poverty of cottagers? Their insulated position ; their want of ready co-operation with their neighbours, for purposes of labour; and the imperfect subdivision of employment even in their own families. For most kinds of manufacturing and mechanical labour, such a situation is decidedly unfavourable, since it offers neither stimulating example, nor the means of directing the exertion of others. In a state of society like that of the Irish peasantry, the acquisition of food is almost the only consideration; the son subsists himself and his family on the potatoes raised on a patch of land, separated from the occupancy of his father, and regards lodging, clothing, and still more, furniture, as secondary objects. In such a situation, what connection can there be between increase of numbers, and increase of individual income? Mr. Gray could here trace hardly a single feature of the animating picture he has drawn of a country with augmenting numbers: yet it seems to form rather a qualification than a contradiction of his doctrine; and to prove nothing at variance with his creed in regard to a population differently circumstanced; we mean so placed as to be near to, and in a state of co-operation with each other.

Town Population. — What a contrast to this stationary condition is exhibited by the progress of towns, whether we go back to the days of antiquity, or fix our attention on modern history: whether we contemplate Tyre, Carthage, Athens, Syracuse, in the former; or Pisa, Genoa, Venice, Bruges, Antwerp, Amsterdam, in the latter; or, finally, look to the growth of the towns of our own country in the present age. Widely different as is this progress, according to difference of situation, we can hardly trace in any country an example of numbers collected in one spot, without an accompanying increase of wealth. Even such a place as Debreczin, in Hungary, an assemblage of 40,000 souls in a succession of cottages, affords relief from the poverty that reigns throughout the greatest part of that backward and thinly-peopled region.

In what consist the advantages of a concentrated population? In the subdivision of labour; in the power of making the exertions of many concur to one object; in the means of giving employment, of some kind or other, to persons the most different in education and attainments. In proportion as employment becomes subdivided, the efficiency of the individual is increased, and the same labour enables him to furnish commodities, superior, either in quantity or quality, generally in both. Besides, an assemblage of numbers is highly favourable to those discoveries and inventions, the effect of which, whether in agriculture, manufacture, or mechanics, is to increase so remarkably the productive powers of a country, to render the articles produced so much cheaper and better. It admits, we believe, of no doubt that the rate of wages in a capital, such as London or Paris, or in a large town, such as Manchester, Birmingham, or Rouen, exceeds those of a small town in a degree greater than the difference in the expence of living.

The resources of collected population have been exemplified in the Dutch provinces of Holland and Zealand, during two centuries, by the payment of an amount of taxation almost unparalleled in the annals of finance. At a time when in England, the majority of the inhabitants lived, as at present in France, in the open country, Holland had accumulated the larger part of her population in towns; and though their numbers have now experienced a decrease, Amsterdam and the eight cities situated within a circuit smaller than one of our middle sized counties, still contain a population of more than 400,000, a density exceeded only by London and Paris, and which, rapidly as the numbers of our manufacturers increase, will hardly be surpassed in the present age by the population of either our cotton, our woollen, or our hardware districts.

These districts, however, and the parts of our island rendered populous by navigation, already confirm the result exhibited by Holland, the average income of individuals being considerably greater in these than in the less populous parts of our island. This was apparent from the returns made under the Property-tax Act. In like manner in France, the returns made to government under the *foncier*, or tax on the income of landlords, farmers, and house proprietors, show that the revenue not only of the public, but of the individual, is smaller where the numbers are thinly scattered, — smaller in the mountainous departments of the south, than in the more fertile and populous districts of the north. In the main articles of food and fuel, the peasantry are often better provided than the lower orders in towns, but in other respects, there are on the Continent the same reasons as in England for allotting the superiority in property to the latter. It is in a large association only that activity and talent find an adequate field ; that the command of capital, the co-operation of assistants, can be turned to account : there is, hence, no comparison between town and country in the proportion of those who from poverty attain the comfort of a middle station; to say nothing of those who reach a high rank in the scale of property.

Farther, as every country raises food for the far greater part of its consumption, density of town-population implies, in general, an advanced state of agriculture : it is along with such density that we find extensive farms, a general application of machinery, and a variety of improvements which enable cultivators to send to market a much larger proportion of produce than can be spared in a country like the centre and south of France, where all work being done by manual labour, the larger share of the produce is necessarily consumed by those who raise it. In all respects, therefore, a

numerous town-population seems to us a proof of
wealth; an evidence of the tendency of individual
as well as national income, to increase as society
advances in improvement. (See Appendix, p.[75].)

*Subsistence more easy of Acquisition as Society
advances.* — The late wars, remarkable as they were
for the frequent recurrence of bad seasons, exhibited no examples of local suffering equal to
those which marked the latter years of the 16th
and 17th centuries; the scarcities in the reigns of
Elizabeth and William. The cause is to be sought
in the general ease of communication arising from
the improvement of our roads, canals, and maritime
navigation; also in the more ample means of purchase afforded to the lower orders by the diffusion
of employment, chiefly mechanical and manufacturing, throughout almost every corner of the
island. One part of the kingdom is thus enabled
to come to the relief of the other, and prices are
kept nearly on an equality throughout. To this
source of relief at home, is added, particularly since
the peace, a supply from abroad, arising from the
extension of tillage over countries in a manner unknown to our ancestors. In our chapter on Agriculture, (p. 152.) we took occasion to remark that
that which formerly constituted the corn country
of Europe, meaning the country producing corn in
sufficiency for export, is comprised between the
45th and 55th degree of latitude, and has a similarity of climate greater than is supposed by those
of our countrymen who have not travelled or
studied the temperature of the Continent. This
remark applies to the Netherlands, the north of
France, the north of Germany, Denmark, and even
to part of Poland, all too similar to our country in

latitude and vicinity to the sea, to escape a participation in those causes of deficiency, whether
arising from want or excess of rain, which, from
time to time, affect our harvests. But the extension of tillage along the shores of the Euxine, and
the increased cultivation of the United States, afford new sources of supply: these countries are
distant, indeed, and the amount of import from
them, must, from the cost of conveyance, necessarily be limited; but as it will proceed from climates not likely to be affected by the causes which
lead to deficient crops in the north-west of Europe,
it will of course be available in the day of need.

These different inferences, whether deduced
from historical or geographical authority, may be
admitted by the adherents of Mr. Malthus, and
when viewed in connection with our present
abundance of subsistence, may be allowed to be of
a nature to relieve a few generations from the apprehension of scarcity; but the anti-populationists
will still contend that their *principle* is correct,
and that a time must come when the world will
be exposed to the misery of over population. The
argument is thus brought to a kind of *ne plus ultra*,
but even on this final and decisive ground we are
not afraid to meet our antagonists. Without denying that there is in the womb of time, a period
when population will attain its complement, we
contend that such a period is far more distant,
and the intermediate increase of our numbers
likely to be far greater than enters into the conception of either our opponents, or the public at
large. Nor does it follow that when such a period
shall arrive, it must be necessarily a period of
misery: — but to waive all speculation on this
mysterious point, and to confine ourselves to that

which is of nearer interest, we shall briefly give our
reasons for the opinion that our posterity, for many
generations at least, are likely to increase their
numbers with less difficulty than has been experienced by us or our ancestors.

1. Our fundamental doctrine, that increase of
produce depends less on the extent of newly-culti-
vated soil, than on the number of hands employed
on the old, will be found proof against the severest
analysis. It is supported equally by the experience
of the present age, and the general evidence of
history : it supposes besides, a proportion between
demand and supply,—that ability on the part of
labour to obtain its reward, which corresponds so
clearly with the benevolent ordinations of Providence.

2. From the great diversity of soil and climate in
the cultivated portion of the globe, scarcity is never
general : " when famine was in other lands, in the
land of Egypt there was bread."   If this applied to
an age when civilization extended over hardly ten
degrees of latitude, how much more does it hold
at present, and how greatly do the advantages arising from improvements perpetually in progress,
increase the power of mankind to turn to account
the bounty of nature ?   Extended communication
by water enables even distant countries to supply
the deficiency of each other ; while in the same
territory improved methods of preserving corn,
additional granaries, augmented capital, all concur
to enable the inhabitants to keep over the surplus
of one year, as a provision for the possible failure
of the next.

3. The labour employed in raising subsistence,
becomes progressively more effectual, the source of
a larger produce, as society advances.   This is

evinced in two ways; one, the use of improved implements, is obvious to the common observer; the other the supply of the requisite produce by a smaller number of agriculturists compared to other classes, is less obvious and requires the evidence of statistical documents. A census of our ancestors, taken a century and a half ago, would have given, under the head of agriculturists, above 50 persons in 100, instead of the 33 of the present day. The majority of our present population are thus enabled to reside in towns and villages, and are rendered disposable for other purposes: the humbler orders employ themselves in supplying clothing or lodging; a higher class minister to the amusements, the education, or the luxury of the rich; while the highest of all are exempt from the necessity of following any occupation whatever. Confining our view to the topic at present under discussion, in what light may we consider the persons who minister to our luxuries? They may be said to form a reserve of capital and labour applicable to the increase of subsistence, in a case of imperious necessity.

A population return in France, or almost any part of the Continent, exhibits, it is true, a larger number of residents in country than in town, but many of the former are producers of other articles than food: the flax, the hemp, the madder of their fields, the wool of their flocks, the timber of their forests, the hides of their cattle, are all constituents of supply or ingredients of consumption, quite distinct from the raising of provisions.

4. As society advances, and a part of the lower orders participate in the comfort of the middle classes, food forms progressively a less considerable proportion of their expenditure. In a popu-

lation like that of Ireland, the chief part of France, and the poorer counties of England, food constitutes above 60 per cent. of the total family charge; but in our more populous rural districts, in our larger villages, and in our towns generally, the proportion (see the Appendix, p. [11],) is little above 50 per cent. What does this imply, but the enjoyment of greater comfort on the part of our lower orders, the possession of a fund with which to purchase clothes and furniture in years of plenty, and to pay, in years of scarcity, the extra price required for provisions? Hence, the less severe pressure of high prices of food on a population, such as that of Holland and England, than on one devoid, in a manner, of exchangeable commodities, such as the peasantry of Poland, Russia, or the inland districts of the Highlands of Scotland.

Ought Government to take Measures for promoting Population. — " The maxim of the politician," says Mr. Gray, " ought to be to take care of population, as population will take care of subsistence and of every other species of supply." Though convinced that there is much more truth in this than in most political apophthegms, we do not go quite so far as Mr. G., and have no wish to keep in the back ground the case of a population like that of Ireland, Brittany, and Poland, in which increase of numbers is attended by a very slight increase of comfort to the individual, or of strength to the public. Nor do we assert that even in a country the most fortunately constituted, increase of population can bring with it a *speedy* cure to a disordered state of productive industry, such as has existed among us since the peace. In the case, for example, of agriculturists, distressed by a superabundance of home growth, little relief is to be anticipated from increase of consumers, because the producers can hardly fail to augment their numbers in an equal proportion, leaving relief to arise from the extension of home manufacture, the removal of hands from country to town, or other causes uncertain in the time of their occurrence, and distinct, in a great measure, from the general increase of our numbers.

Next, as to men in office, on whom Mr. G. seems to think it incumbent to take measures, more or less direct, to promote population, we confine our exhortation to a passive course, satisfied if they do nothing to obstruct the natural increase of numbers. Let them carefully guard their minds against the notion which so naturally follows the creed of limited subsistence ; viz. that the discouragement of marriage, or the loss of lives in the field, and in unhealthy colonies, are not, in a statistical sense, a great misfortune, because they operate, forsooth, as checks to superabundant numbers. — In regard to population, as to national wealth, the plain rule is to avoid interference, to take no step for the purpose of giving a new direction to the course of events, but to remove obstacles wherever such have been interposed by the mistaken, though well intended intervention of preceding legislators. As to town population, with all our conviction of its advantage, both to the individual and the community, we should infinitely regret the adoption of any measure to increase its relative amount. Let the tide flow in its natural course : the duties of government evidently extend no farther than keeping open the channel.

We shall now turn aside from general reasoning and direct the attention of the reader to *data* of a more specific character, to an estimate of the population and resources of the different states of Europe :

STATISTICAL TABLE OF EUROPE, IN 1823.

	Total Population.	Persons to a square mile.	Taxes and public burdens generally.	Proportion of such burdens per head.
				£. s. d.
Norway, including Finmark - - -	950,000	6		
Sweden, Norway, and Swedish Lapland -	3,600,000	10		
Sweden, distinct from Norway and Swedish Lapland - - -	2,600,000	25	1,300,000	0 10 0
Russia in Europe - -	37,000,000	23	18,000,000	0 9 9
Scotland ; viz. the Highlands distinct from the low country . -		30		
Turkey in Europe, not ascertained, but probably not above -	8,000,000	50	5,000,000	0 12 6
Poland, before the partition - - -	15,000,000	55		
Poland, the present kingdom of, distinct from the provinces incorporated with the Austrian, Russian, and Prussian dominions - -	2,850,000	60	1,200,000	0 8 8
Sardinia, island of -	520,000	57		
Spain - - - -	11,000,000	60	6,000,000	0 11 0
Denmark, exclusive of Faroe and Iceland -	1,600,000	73	1,300,000	0 16 3
Hanover - - -	1,300,000	90	900,000	0 14 0
Portugal - - -	3,700,000	90	3,000,000	0 16 3
Switzerland, the twenty-two cantons - - (The pecuniary burden is very small, but the Swiss are liable to military service.)	1,750,000	91	430,000	0 5 0
Wales - - - -	740,000	96		
The Austrian empire, including Lombardy, and Austrian Poland -	29,000,000	112	18,000,000	0 12 4
The Prussian dominions	10,500,000	100	7,000,000	0 13 4

	Total Population.	Persons to a square mile.	Taxes and public burdens generally.	Proportion of such burdens per head.		
				£.	s.	d.
Bavaria - - -	3,600,000	120	2,500,000	0	14	0
Sicily, island of - -	1,655,000	132				
Dominions of the king of Sardinia, viz. Piedmont, part of the Milanese, the Genoese territory, Savoy, and the island of Sardinia - -	4,000,000	148	2,200,000	0	11	0
States of the Church -	2,450,000	150	900,000	0	7	6
The Neapolitan dominions, including Sicily	6,700,000	154	2,700,000	0	8	0
France, including Corsica	30,700,000	150	37,000,000	1	4	0
Scotland; the low country distinct from the Highlands - -		150		2	0	0
Great Britain exclusive of Ireland (the taxes computed according to the value of money on the Continent	14,500,000	165	40,000,000	2	15	0
Wirtemberg - - -	1,400,000	170	1,000,000	0	14	4
Saxony - - -	1,200,000	170	900,000	0	15	0
Italy, exclusive of Sicily	17,000,000	179				
Great Britain and Ireland collectively - -	21,500,000	182	44,000,000	2	0	0
The Netherlands * -	5,300,000	214	8,000,000	1	10	0
Austrian, Italy, or the Lombardo - Venetian kingdom - -	4,000,000	219	2,000,000	0	10	0
Ionian islands, republic -	250,000	230	100,000	0	8	9
England, distinct from Wales - - -	11,600,000	232	36,000,000	3	2	0
Ireland - - -	7,000,000	237	4,000,000	0	11	0
Holland, province of -	760,000	362				
West Flanders - -	630,000	420				
East Flanders - -	610,000	554				
Europe collectively, about - - -	200,000,000	58	180,000,000	0	18	0

* The repartition of taxation is here very unequal, the Dutch provinces, particularly those of Holland and Zealand, paying much more than 1*l.* 10*s.* a head; the Belgic much less.

These returns, both as to population and public burdens, are, in general, taken from official documents: they require, however, a few explanations; thus,

Extent in square Miles. — The amount assigned to England, Scotland, and Wales is taken from official returns, but in regard to Ireland and most parts of the Continent, the statements are, in some measure, conjectural, and to be considered only as approximations.

Our Public Burdens. — The sum of 44,000,000l. as the aggregate of our public burdens, may appear greatly below the mark, but it is formed by two important deductions from our present payments; first, by taking credit for a farther reduction of our taxes, and, in the next place, by making an abatement (of 20 per cent.) from the numerical amount of our burdens, to bring their value on a par with those of the Continent, with which they are here compared.

Taxation of Rural Districts. — It may be objected to the preceding table, that an estimate founded on taxation does not do justice to the property of a rural population, who, in many parts of the Continent, seem almost to escape the grasp of the exchequer. This exemption, however, is limited chiefly to excise dues, and is, in a great measure, balanced by a heavy land-tax, which, under different names in different countries, forms the basis of continental taxation, and is included in the column of public burdens.

Population per Square Mile. — Mr. S. Gray assumes, (Happiness of States, p. 421.) that an individual for every two acres, or 320 persons for a square mile, would be a fair complement of population for the soil and climate of Europe. From this rate, however, we are still at a great distance, having attained it only in Flanders and Holland: in England and Ireland we are likely, if we proceed as in the present age, to reach it in somewhat less than twenty years.

In Iceland the proportion is little more than one person to a square mile, but the lowest extreme of European population is exhibited in Lapland, where there is not more than one inhabitant to two or three square miles.

Europe taken collectively. — Our estimate is greater in regard to population, and smaller in respect to public burdens than that which is at present current on the authority of German statisticians ; but the latter made their computation in or before the year 1817, since which, population has increased, and taxation has experienced a partial reduction.

If those of our readers who are familiar with history, will compare the present state of Europe in population and revenue, with what it was two or three centuries ago, they will perceive a degree of extension that is hardly credible. How feeble do we find the establishments of France, even when administered by Sully ; of England, when guided by Burleigh ; of Austria, when stimulated by the vigour of Charles V., if we compare them to those of the same powers at the present day ! The army of Henry IV. of France, was, when at the highest, only 40,000 men : the revenue of queen Elizabeth was 600,000*l.* * Even the Spain of Philip II., aided by the mines of America, is found, when her revenue and her army are brought to the test of

* Napier's Supplement to the Encyclop. Brit. under the heads of England and France.

accurate computation, to have been on a par with only the second-rate powers of our age.

What a striking example is here afforded of the tendency to rapid improvement in those communities which have overcome the difficulties of primitive ignorance, and in which safety is afforded to persons and property! More than that the inhabitants of the Continent can hardly be said to have received at the hands of their respective governors, since if some sovereigns have been distinguished by active measures for promoting improvement, the beneficial result of their labours has been balanced or more than balanced by ambition and unnecessary warfare on the part of their brethren. How much more effectually would the latter have consulted, not merely the happiness of their subjects, but the increase of their political power, had they never unsheathed the sword, but been content to allow individual industry to work its way, augmenting the number and wealth of the community by a silent but sure increase!

It would be idle to lament what cannot be recalled; but in regard to the future, we may be allowed to indulge a hope that the sovereigns of the Continent will pursue a more enlightened course! How wide a field of improvement is open to them, if they will merely labour to transfer to their respective territories the degree of agricultural knowledge introduced into this country! No Englishman who has not travelled can form an idea of the general backwardness of the Continent, of the poverty of the farmers, the awkwardness of their implements, the deficiency of their buildings. If we cross the narrow seas and fix our attention on the districts of the Continent said to be farthest advanced, such as Flanders, Normandy, or the *Pays de Beauce,* we shall find their machinery so rude, and their work performed in so great a degree by manual labour, that the productive powers of their soil might be doubled by the mere application of the discoveries and inventions that have taken place in our eastern and northern counties. If we carry our observation farther, and calculate how much remains to be done in the neglected plains of Hungary and Poland, in the half-irrigated provinces of Spain, Italy, and even the south of France, the inference is, that Europe, that boasted seat of cultivation, is not peopled to the extent of a fifth of the numbers it may be rendered capable of supporting.

The prospect of England.—Let us not, however, imagine, that the advancement of the Continent would have the effect of lessening the relative superiority of this country; on the contrary, those advantages which have enabled us to take the lead —extent of water communication, richness of mines, command of capital, superiority of civil institutions, formed habits of business,—are all calculated to confirm our pre-eminence, and even to lead us forward in a quicker *ratio* than our neighbours. To comprehend this fully, the reader ought first to acquire the conviction, that national improvement is likely to be progressive, and has at present no more reached a limit, than it had thirty, fifty, or one hundred years ago. To acquiesce in the notion, that the present mode of tilling the ground, of navigating the ocean, or performing mechanical labour, is the best that can be devised, is the part of the indolent and unthinking; such is the creed of the spiritless Asiatic, of the unenlightened peasant, and the almost equally unenlightened manufacturer in many parts of the Continent of

Europe.　In this country, happily the discoveries that so rapidly succeed each other, afford a proof that we have not yet advanced half way in the extension of our national resources. Of this, a more ample developement shall be given in our concluding chapter, when we shall shew how surprisingly we have gained on our political rivals, in the course of the last century, and how little we have at present to dread at their hands — considerations calculated to confirm the public, in an approval of the pacific system which we have now so fortunately adopted, and to satisfy the apprehensive among our countrymen, that with a steady adherence to such a course, the day of trial in the finances of England will ere long be surmounted.

CHAP. VIII.

National Revenue and Capital.

HAVING appropriated several chapters to an examination of the condition of the country, under the separate heads of Agriculture, Population, and Poor-rate, we are now to make an attempt of a more comprehensive nature, and to bestow a chapter on our National Revenue and Capital generally. This will lead us to discuss
The amount of our taxable income.

The connection between its increase and the increase of our population; and lastly,

The fluctuations it has experienced in the thirty years that have elapsed since the French Revolution.

Estimate, by the late Mr. Colquhoun, of Property created in Great Britain and Ireland, in the Year 1812.

Agriculture in all its branches, (including pasture) - - - - -	£217,000,000
Mines and minerals, including coals - -	9,000,000
Manufactures in every branch - -	114,000,000
Inland trade and banking - - -	35,000,000
Foreign commerce and shipping - -	46,000,000
Coasting trade - - - -	2,000,000
Fisheries, exclusive of the colonial fisheries of Newfoundland - - - -	2,000,000
Foreign income remitted - - -	5,000,000
Total - -	430,000,000

Such was the amount of the property created in Great Britain and Ireland in 1812; since which there have occurred two very material changes, — a great increase in the quantity, and a still greater decrease in the prices. The latter, in the case of agriculture amounts to 60 per cent; in that of manufactures to 40 or 50 per cent.; but as Mr. Colquhoun's estimate was made greatly below the currency of the time, 20, or at the utmost, 25 per cent., will form a sufficient deduction from its amount. To this we find an ample counterpoise in the increase of quantity arising from

The additional produce on the part of the hands restored to labour by the peace;

The increase of our population since 1812; and

The progress of improvement in agriculture and manufactures, by which the same number of hands are enabled to produce a considerably larger quantity.

The result, therefore, is, that even at reduced prices, the value of the produce of the present year, equals or exceeds t...t of 1812; but as Mr. Colquhoun's calculation included, under the head of agriculture, a very large sum for produce, such as oats, hay, grass, &c. appropriated to the food of horses and cattle, and as our object is to confine our table to articles for the consumption of man, or for the purposes of manufacture, we assume the total at 350,000,000*l.* That sum, then, we consider as representing the amount of the property annually created in Great Britain and Ireland; in other words, the amount of our annual production.

Of this large sum, what proportion, in this land of taxes, can be considered as exempt from the visit of the assessor? About 25 per cent., as appears from the calculations in the Appendix, leaving for our taxable income, somewhat more than 260,000,000. Thus,

Estimate of our Taxable Income, in 1823,
(Great Britain distinct from Ireland.)

Rent of land returned in 1814, at 43,000,000*l*., and probably amounting, after allowing for all deductions, omissions, and evasions in the returns, to -	£48,000,000	
Add for land brought into culture since the peace -	2,000,000	
Together -	50,000,000	
Deduct for all abatements of rent since the peace, made, making, or which must ere long be made, one third, or 33 per cent.	17,000,000	
Probable rental in peace -	33,000,000	
Deduct further for temporary deficiencies on the part of farmers, at this time of peculiar pressure	3,000,000	
		£30,000,000
Tithe; amount in 1812 (see Returns of Property Tax) 4,700,000*l*.; at present computed, after making an addition for the increase of produce, and an abatement for the great fall of prices - - - - -		4,000,000
Rental of houses, returned at nearly 16,000,000*l*. in 1814; since which, the houses are augmented in number by 15 per cent., and as rents have fallen only partially, we compute the amount at - -		17,000,000
Farming income, which, during the latter years of the war, was so large as to equal the rental of our land, but which is at present so greatly		
Carried forward -		51,000,000

Brought forward - 51,000,000
reduced, we estimate, with a view to the
future, at the medium rate of 6 per cent. on
200,000,000*l*, the supposed amount of capital
invested in agriculture - - - 12,000,000

Income from trade and professions, comprising not
only manufacturing and mercantile profits, but
income from mines, docks, canals, tolls, iron-
works ; likewise salaries, as far as derived from
the concerns of individuals ; to the exclusion,
however, of all incomes below 50*l.* a year,
This portion of our national revenue, returned
during the war at 30,000,000*l.*, and which,
if augmented in proportion to the increase of
our numbers, should at present be 35,000,000*l.*,
we compute, in consequence of the change in
the value of money, and the decrease of business, at a great reduction, say - - - 22,000,000

Wages and all incomes below 50*l.* a year, computed on a population, which, (exclusive of
Ireland) is now nearly 15,000,000, but from
which somewhat more than a third is deducted
for persons either above or below the station of
those receiving wages. This large deduction
comprizes not merely paupers, but cottagers
and all others whose mode of life is such as to
lead, in a very slight degree, to the consumption of taxed articles. The result, estimated
on a population of 9,000,000 working at the reduced wages of peace, but adding the earnings
of women and children to those of the men, is 90,000,000

Interest of our debt, funded and unfunded, since
the reduction of the 5 per cents. - - 30,000,000

Conjectural amount of interest from other money
securities ; viz. mortgages, private securities
generally ; also public securities, such as bank
stock, East India stock, foreign stock, in short,
all securities distinct from those of our government - - - - - 20,000,000

Income of the army, navy, civil list, and public
offices, after allowing for the late retrenchments,

Carried forward - 225,000,000

Brought forward -	225,000,000
and leaving out the proportion expended in Ireland - - - -	15,000,000
Total of Great Britain	240,000,000
Ireland : taxable income computed during the war at 35,000,000*l.*; at present at - (See Appendix, p. [79].)	- 25,000,000
Total of Great Britain and Ireland	265,000,000
Of which, lost to taxation, being expended abroad by travellers and emigrants	4,000,000
Remainder -	261,000,000

Ireland.—The total produce of land and labour in Ireland cannot, from the magnitude of the population, be below 70,000,000*l.* a year, but the cottagers are so numerous and their mode of living so inferior to that of the inhabitants of towns, that the portion of national income expended on taxed articles can hardly, (particularly since the fall of rents, and the general decline of incomes,) exceed the 25,000,000*l.* which we have introduced into the table.

Increase of National Income since 1792.—The last thirty years have been a period equally remarkable for financial as for political revolutions. Do we, it may be asked, possess the means of forming, with any degree of accuracy, an estimate of the increase of national income since 1792? Such an estimate, whether in peace or war, is a matter of great difficulty: the improvements in our land, our houses, our furniture ; the additions to our towns, our harbours, our manufacturing establishments, in the present age, are obvious, and have been great beyond example ; but as no record can express the amount of expenditure incurred, or the success, necessarily very various, of such investments of capital, it remains with the inquirer to seek a standard of computation. For this we are in some measure prepared by the researches in the preceding chapters; and by following up that course of reasoning we shall probably be enabled to reduce to a systematic form that which seems at present involved in contradiction. The cause of the changes since 1792, we are disposed to seek in —

Fluctuations in the activity of our productive industry ;

Fluctuations in the value of money ;

The increase of population.

Of these different causes the first and second have already been illustrated (Chap. II. and III.) at considerable length ; and whatever may be wanting in regard to them shall be supplied in a subsequent part of our volume. At present, therefore, we confine our attention to the effect of the third cause, — increase of numbers ; — adopting the principles laid down in our chapter on Population, and applying, or endeavouring to apply them, to the circumstances of the present age.

Connexion between the increase of Numbers and increase of National Income. — We have already remarked that no adherent of Mr. Malthus, whatever might be his objection to increase of numbers, has alleged that our lower orders have made a descent in the scale of comfort; nor does the surprising increase of our population in the present age appear (Chapter on Poor Rate, p. 199.) to have carried the proportion of our paupers to our total numbers, much beyond what it was a century ago. We are far from maintaining that marriages in humble life are contracted with the requisite prudence, or that the parents of a numerous family can avoid a long and serious struggle : our argument merely is, that the situation of the lower classes generally, is not altered for the worse. It is the characteristic of a civilized and industrious society, like the inhabitants of Holland, England, or Scotland, to make successive discoveries in the means both of augmenting produce and diminishing expense ; improvements by which, whether effected in agriculture, manufacture, navigation, or trade, a country is enabled to support many more inhabitants in equal comfort. Increase of numbers therefore is, even in the case of the lower orders, conducive to increase of taxable income ; for we have already had occasion to show what large sums are annually brought into the exchequer by the duties on beer, spirits, tobacco, groceries ; all of which enter into the consumption of the classes in question, particularly when resident in towns.

The lowest class of Poor.—How, it may be asked, stands the question of increase of income, in regard to a population of such primitive habits as the cottagers of Ireland, or the mountaineers of Scotland, accustomed to confine their demands to mere subsistence ? In such a case, an increase of numbers implies a correspondent increase, not of taxable income, but of the produce which, like potatoes or bread, constitutes the mere necessaries of life ; and the result is an addition to our population of individuals, who, though able to earn their subsistence, can be said to add to our political strength in hardly any other sense than as recruits for the public service, or as mere manual labourers, being unable to make the sacrifice requisite for learning the business of an artisan.

The connexion between increase of numbers, and increase of wealth, will appear more clearly, if we have recourse to arithmetical statement, and if we subject to an analysis the 250,000,000*l.* constituting the taxable income of the nation. This will exhibit the following proportions:

Great Britain and Ireland.

(Taxable Income, exclusive of the pay of the Army and Navy.)

Arising from wages and salaries, and of course, directly affected by increase of population -	£100,000,000
From capital and labour combined, a portion of national income, which also is much increased by increase of population - -	50,000,000
From rent of land, houses, or interest of money, which are influenced, though indirectly, and in an inferior degree, by the increase of numbers - - - -	100,000,000
Total -	250,000,000

That the increase of taxable income, as far as such arises from wages and salaries, is in correspondence with the increase of our numbers, requires no demonstration: the same holds in regard to professional men, to merchants, to master manufacturers, in short, in respect to every line in which income depends on *personal exertion.* Thus, land in the hands of the farmer, like money in those of the merchant, is productive in proportion to the labour which it is made to put in motion. So far the connexion is clear and undoubted; the case, it may be said, is somewhat different in regard to a *fixed income,* whether derived from real or personal property; but even in that, the effect of increasing numbers is great, producing, as is well known, an increasing demand for both land and money capital. In proof of this, we have merely to take, as an example, the almost daily case of a family becoming numerous; the consequent repartition of the paternal property, and the increase of productive power given to the portion that is put in a state of activity.

Fluctuations of Income since 1792.—These arguments will readily be accounted applicable in a general sense, and for ordinary times; but what shall furnish a rule for computing national income in so fluctuating a period as that through which we have passed since 1792? The question is certainly very complicated, and seems at first to admit of no clear solution; for while a calculator, in forming an estimate twelve or fifteen years ago, could hardly have failed to pronounce the war highly favourable to the increase of our wealth (our debt forming apparently no counterpoise to the increase of our resources), a statement prepared since our years of distress would convey a very different result. In France, the Revolution has been styled, the " queen of all earthly reverses;" but we might almost hazard an opinion that the effect of that convulsion, viewed in regard to change of property and in all the extent of its duration (now above thirty years), has been as great in this country as in that which gave it birth. Among our neighbours, the change was more sudden, directed more against a particular class, and bringing with it, too often, the melancholy consequence of loss of life; but with us it has been more comprehensive, for the alteration in the value of money has come home to every class and condition. If in France, government annuitants suffered during the war a much greater reduction than here, there is no comparison between the two countries in the extent of fluctuation in the circumstances of a far more numerous class—the farmers. Their prosperity during the war and their decline since the peace, have both been much more in extremes among us, than on the Continent.

An Estimate of them attempted.—Amidst all these changes in individual property, is it practicable to discover any rules of general application, any *data* on which to found a comparison of the circumstances of the public of the present day with those of the public of 1806 or 1792? This task may, perhaps, be found less difficult than it appears. In a community so great and so varied as the population of these kingdoms, the ease of one part is often cotemporary with the embarrassment of another; and there prevails, in the general result, a tendency to a balance, an approach to uniformity which would hardly be credited by those who, in drawing their inferences, allow themselves to be forcibly struck by the fluctuation of particular classes. It was thus that our revenue stood its ground during all the trials of the war and the no less trying interval that has followed: it is thus, also, that the amount of our exports and imports has continued to bear a proportion to two regulating circumstances (the value of money and the increase of our population), amid all the anomalies, introduced by restrictions, prohibitions, licences: it is thus that at present, the distress of the producer of corn, is accompanied by a temporary advantage to the consumer. The political arithmetician is, therefore, in some measure, justified in forming a conclusion, which, without this collateral support, might appear vague and untenable; viz. " That though the circumstances of individuals, separately, are so much altered since 1792, those of any given number, whether 100, 1000, or 10,000, are more nearly on a par than is generally supposed."

This reasoning is calculated to lead to the inference, that our national income, (at least that of Great Britain distinct from Ireland), has increased since 1792 in the *ratio* of the increase of our population. We have, however, no wish to press this point, it being of little consequence to our argument, whether the proportion of the one, has been greater or less than that of the other. It is enough that we obtain assent to one leading consideration, viz. that the surprising addition to our numbers, since 1792 (50 per cent.) is, as far as can be ascertained, unaccompanied by any general deterioration of private circumstances. The changes in such circumstances have been almost infinite, but there seems no reason to imagine that the number of families or individuals, who have experienced a decline, exceeds that of those who have improved their circumstances.

But are we, it may be said, authorized to assume an equality in the individual income of this country between 1792, a season of tranquillity, and the present, which is one of general embarrassment? To this argument, unluckily of great weight, we oppose one of equal, or almost equal power; viz. the great comparative increase of our town-population, the extent of which, *as income increases so much more in town than in the country* (Chapter on Population, p. 240.) would have justified us, had our present circumstances been as tranquil and secure as in 1792, in assuming an increase of national property considerably beyond that of the 50 per cent. indicated by our numbers,

Without, therefore, affecting precision in a calculation where it is evidently unattainable, we shall adopt the increase of our numbers, as an approximation to a basis for calculating the increase of our national revenue. Proceeding on this ground, we shall exhibit in the tabular form, the augmentation that has taken place since 1792, premising that our chief materials are the population and property-tax returns, and that for the period of war, we make a considerable addition on the score of extra wages and profits.

Conjectural Amount of our National Revenue or Taxable Income at different Periods, from 1792 *to* 1822.

Great Britain distinct from Ireland.	Money of 1792.	Totals, also in Money of 1792.
In 1792, our taxable income appears to have been as stated in p. 35. about -	£125,000,000	
In 1806 : increase calculated in the *ratio* of the increase of our population, 18 per cent. in 14 years - -	22,500,000	
Together - -	147,500,000	
Probable addition from the higher wages and higher profits of a sate of war -	22,500,000	
Total of taxable income in 1806 - - - --		170,000,000
In 1813 or 1814 : Increase of national income since 1806, calculated in the *ratio* of the increase of population, 11 per cent.; thus : —		
National income in 1806, as above - - - -	147,500,000	
Add 11 per cent. - -	16,500,000	
Together - -	164,000,000	
Probable addition from the higher wages and higher profits of a state of war -	24,000,000	
Total of taxable income in 1813 or 1814 - -		188,000,000
Great Britain and Ireland.		
1823. Increase of taxable income in the *ratio* of the population, 15 per cent. since 1814 ; thus : —		
Amount in 1814 - -	164,000,000	
Add 15 per cent - -	24,000,000	
Add farther the taxable income of Ireland 25,000,000*l.* equal in money of 1792 to - - -	21,000,000	
Total of our taxable income in 1823, (in money of 1792)		209,000,000

These results, which, we repeat, are only approximations, convey a clear idea of the effect of increasing population on national income. The next point is, the difference of numerical amount produced by the rise or fall in the value of money.

Great Britain distinct from Ireland.	Money of 1792.	Money of subsequent years.
1792 : Taxable income as per preceding table - -	£125,000,000	
1806 : Do. per do. - -	170,000,000	
After the general rise of prices that took place between 1792 and 1806, 170,000,000*l.* in money of 1792, was in the transactions of 1806, equivalent to		220,000,000
And an actual return of our national revenue or taxable income in the currency of 1806, would probably have given a sum of 220,000,000*l.*		
1813 or 1814: Taxable income as in last page - -	188,000,000	
The rise of prices, in all 60 per cent. since 1792, rendered this sum equal in all money transactions in 1813 and 1814, to nearly -		300,000,000
Great Britain and Ireland.		
1823. Taxable income as in last page - - - -	209,000,000	
The calculation in regard to the value of money is now reversed, prices having fallen, or, in other words money having risen in value between 1814 and 1823, nearly 30 per cent. Still it is about 30 per cent. lower than in 1792, so that the last mentioned sum 209,000,000*l.* money of 1792), is equal in the currency of 1822, to about		270,000,000
A sum not materially different from the amount of the table of taxable income contained in p. 258.		

Our next object is to introduce our burdens into this comparative table, and to calculate their proportion at different periods to our revenue.

Statement of our Public Burdens and National Revenue, calculated for distinct Periods. The Public Burdens include Taxes (before deducting the Expence of Collection), Poor-rate, and Tithe.

Great Britain distinct from Ireland.

Years.	Public Burdens.	Our National Revenue or Taxable Income.	Proportion of Burden to Revenue.
1792	£22,000,000	£125,000,000	nearly 18 to 100
1806	60,000,000	220,000,000	27 to 100
1814	80,000,000	300,000,000	27 to 100

Great Britain and Ireland, (*see Appendix*, p. [85].)

1823	64,000,000	260,000,000	25 to 100

That we may divest this statement of the intricacies attendant on the difference in the value of money at different periods, we subjoin a table, in which the sums on both sides are reduced to a common standard, viz. the money of 1792.

Great Britain distinct from Ireland.

Years.	Public Burdens, in Money of 1792.	Our National Revenue or Taxable Income in Money of 1792.	Proportion of Burdens to Revenue.
1792	£22,000,000	£125,000,000	nearly 18 to 100
1806	46,000,000	170,000,000	27 to 100
1814	50,000,000	188,000,000	27 to 100

Great Britain and Ireland, (*see Appendix*, p. [85].)

1823	50,000,000	200,000,000	25 to 100

The reduction to a common standard is useful in several respects, particularly in correcting the exaggerated estimate, which, during the war, we were accustomed to make of both our burdens and our resources.

France ; her National Income. — We conclude our chapter by a brief parallel between this country and her most powerful neighbour. The national income, by which we mean the aggregate of individual income, is, in one sense, somewhat greater in France than in this country ; but in regard to the portion of it that is taxable, the advantage will be found on our side, in consequence, chiefly, of our greater town-population : thus,

Comparative Sketch of National Income expended on taxed Articles.

	Great Britain and Ireland.	France, after adding to the actual receipts 20 per cent. for the greater value of money.
	£	£
Rent of land and farmer's profit at peace prices.	50,000,000	60,000,000
Tithe - - - - -	5,000,000	
Rent of houses - - - -	18,000,000	18,000,000
Income arising from commerce, manufactures, and professions, as far as such are of 50*l.* and upwards; also income from mines, docks, canals, tolls, &c.	24,000,000	18,000,000
Small incomes (below 50*l.*) and wages of all accustomed to consume taxed articles, as beer, tea, sugar, tobacco, in England ; or wine, cyder, tobacco, sugar, coffee, in France. - - -	100,000,000	110,000,000
Together -	197,000,000	206,000,000

Such is the amount of income arising from the land and labour of either country. To this we now make an addition of great importance as a source of taxation, what-

	Great Britain and Ireland.	France, after adding to the actual receipts 20 per cent. for the greater value of money.
	£	£
Brought forward - ever may be thought of it as a constituent of national wealth.	197,000,000	206,000,000
Income from money in the public funds, or lent on private securities - - - - -	50,000,000	25,000,000
Received from government, distinct from the interest of the public debt; viz. the pay of the army, the navy, the public offices, the civil list, the miscellaneous services, after allowing for the late reductions - -	18,000,000	19,000,000
Total taxable income * - -	265,000,000	250,000,000

* Any discrepancies between this column and that in page 25, arise from the latter exhibiting the returns of Great Britain distinct from Ireland.

Wages.—To put the two countries so nearly on a par in regard to wages, may seem hardly fair towards France, superior as that country is in population, and reduced as wages in some measure have been, and are likely to be among us. But in a calculation of national revenue, the magnitude of the population of France ought, in a great measure, to be kept in the back ground, many millions being cottagers, who, as in Ireland, do little more than maintain themselves on their petty occupancies, consuming few articles productive to the exchequer, and adding little to the national strength, otherwise than by recruits for the military service. Wages are highest among a town-population, in which England takes greatly the lead. Add to this, that in all Catholic countries there is a considerable loss of wages from holidays.

Rent of Houses.—In this respect, France was formerly entitled to rank before us ; but houses in a rural district yield very little rent ; and while French towns are comparatively stationary, ours have been and continue in a state of rapid increase.

Comparative Prospects of England and France.— This interesting question shall be discussed at considerable length in our chapter on Finance.

CHAP. IX.

Effect of the late Wars on Property, individual and national.

THE researches we have already had occasion to make in regard to our agriculture and national revenue, prepare us, in a considerable degree, for the farther and more comprehensive enquiry to which this chapter is appropriated. In the investigations connected with it, we shall studiously avoid discussing the policy or impolicy of our great contest; the practicability of avoiding it in the outset, or of terminating it in an earlier stage. We shall avoid, in like manner, any parallel between the magnitude of our sacrifices on one hand, and the benefit resulting on the other from restoring the equilibrium of the Continent. Nothing, indeed, would be more hopeless than an attempt to produce any thing like uniformity of opinion on such a subject. The oppositionist, in his review of the events of the last thirty years, takes little account of the danger that arose after 1795, from the aggrandizing spirit of the French government; nor, while urging, and urging justly, the insignificance to us of most causes of continental quarrel, does he make due allowance for the importance of the Netherlands, and the alarming addition which their possession made to the power of France. The ministerialist, on the other hand, is equally confident and indiscriminating, making no admission of the occasions on which (as in 1793 and 1807) our government acted an aggressive part, and justifying the attack on Copenhagen as he would the defence of Spain. From the delusion that the war was a source of permanent wealth, we now begin to be awakened; but, in other respects, we are yet far distant from the time when the public shall be enabled to view the transactions of this eventful age with the calmness of historical enquiry. It will be for a succeeding generation to appreciate, on the one hand, the ferment produced by the French Revolution; on the other, the course by which our political guides, had they been aware of the little dependence to be placed on foreign allies, and of the aid to be derived for the maintenance of order from the upper and middle classes at home, might have endeavoured to conduct our affairs during the period of alarm. The hazardous alternative of an appeal to arms would probably have been avoided, had our councils been guided by a Burleigh or a Walpole; or had he who was placed at our helm in those critical times, been of an age to derive from personal reflection and experience that knowledge in which he was necessarily deficient, and the want of which was so feebly supplied by the coadjutors with whom our system of parliamentary influence obliges a minister to become connected.

Political Economists.—The discrepancy that prevails among politicians is equally remarkable among political economists. To the follower of Smith and Say, all war seems impolitic and unnecessary; in his eyes, the whole of military array, the training, equipping, and maintaining of fleets and armies, is an absolute sacrifice, the loss of the labour of the most valuable part of our population. It is with great difficulty that he can be brought to allow that war brings with it even a temporary aliment to its consuming powers. Mr. Say, the political economist of France, after visiting this country in the first year of peace, published the following remarks.

" Ministers and public men in England are as yet, (he wrote with reference to our ministry of 1807), far from having a just sense of the folly and ruinous tendency of war: their progress has not kept pace with the progress of the nation. The misfortunes of England take their rise in the higher regions, like the hail and the tempest: her blessings spring from beneath, like the fruits of an inexhaustible soil. The taxes have not only doubled, but tripled since 1792; and still the war expenditure greatly exceeded their amount. The consequence is, an enormous enhancement of prices; mercantile men are obliged to do business on very slender profits, and what is still worse, many of the manufactured articles are sadly fallen from their former reputation. My French readers," he adds, " will be surprized to find in my pages an opinion so much at variance with the current notion that England is the land for the easy and rapid attainment of fortune; but the reality is widely different from the appearance."

A very different picture of the effect of war is given by Mr. S. Gray, to whom we have so frequently referred in our chapter on population, and who came several years ago before the public, as the author of a system bearing the emphatic name of " productive." The pages in which that doctrine is recommended to the world, contain a number of arguments on the connexion between government expenditure and the increase of individual income, taxes being considered by Mr. Gray in the light of useful stimulants to our national industry. He has the merit of detecting several imperfections in Dr. Smith's definition of productive and unproductive labour; but in reasoning on our war expenditure, he evidently fails to distinguish between a temporary and a lasting excitement, and assumes, from the circulation of money raised by loans and taxes, as much advantage as if war prices were necessarily permanent, and as if, on concluding peace, we could consider ourselves exempt from the frightful reaction experienced during the last nine years.

To these opposite authorities, each tending in some degree to an extreme, we add the observations of a third writer.

" Notwithstanding the immense expenditure of the English government during the late wars, there can be little doubt but that the increased production on the part of the people has more than compensated for it. The national capital has not merely been unimpaired, it has been greatly increased; and the annual revenue of the people, even after the payment of their taxes, is probably greater at the present time than at any former period of our history. For the proof of this, we might refer to the increase of population,— to the extension of agriculture,—to the increase of shipping and manufactures, —to the building of docks,—to the opening of numerous canals, as well as to many other expensive undertakings ;— all denoting an increase both of capital and of annual production." (*Ricardo on Political Economy, second Edition*, p. 170.)

This passage presents, perhaps, too favourable a a view of our situation; and ought, before we can receive it as a true picture, to be accompanied by two admissions. First, that though our national income has increased, our burdens have augmented in a still greater *ratio* ; and, secondly, that in any estimate of our wealth expressed in money in the present day, a considerable deduction is to be made from an estimate in 1792, on account of the inferior value of money. It is fair, however, to add, that this passage was written at a time (1816) when the fall of prices was only beginning, and when we were unable to calculate the extent of fluctuation and loss arising from the war. Since then, seven eventful years have elapsed, and have disclosed a succession of circumstances beyond the reach of foresight, but replete with instruction when examined in the order of their occurrence. With this advantage, we now follow up the enquiry, and instead of reasoning in general terms, like the writers we have quoted, we shall endeavour to build on a secure foundation, and proceed, as in our preceding chapters, by a series of calculations and specific results. Our arrangement shall be as follows:

Losses incurred during the prosecution of the war.

Losses attendant on the transition from war to peace.

Comparative amount of our national income in war and peace.

Have our public men understood our financial situation?

Losses to our productive Industry on a Transition from Peace to War. — These losses, unknown in a great measure to the younger part of the present generation, will long live in the recollection of those who are of an age to remember the bankruptcies of 1793. These pervaded equally our commercial, manufacturing, and agricultural interests, and affected almost all whose undertakings were not supported by substantial capital. To what was a pressure so general to be ascribed? To the sudden and extensive change that took place; to a demand on the part of government for men and money; and to the consequent necessity of abandoning various undertakings, the profit of which, almost always less than is vulgarly imagined, could be made to answer only by the aid of a low rate of interest and moderate price of labour. In these days, as at present, our countrymen were speculative, eager to embark on new enterprises, and apt to trust to prospective advantages for those means of providing for payments which their limited capital did not afford. This sanguine disposition may be termed the great feature that distinguishes our countrymen and the North Americans from the traders and agriculturists of the continent of Europe, among whom the same occupation is so often followed from father to son, with little idea of change or attempt at extension. But our spirit of enterprise, however favourable to discovery and improvement, is necessarily attended by a revolution in the circumstances of individuals on the occurrence of any political change. The blow first strikes establishments of the most adventurous character, and goes on to involve others injured by the failure of the first, and possessing, like them, few resources against an unforeseen demand. Embarrassments of this description were felt chiefly in the first and second years of the war, during the interval that unavoidably elapsed before the capital and labour disturbed in their employment by the war, could receive a new direction, and be invested anew in a productive form.

From this almost forgotten theme, we proceed to a part of the subject much more familiar to the majority of our readers; to an

Estimate of the Burden arising from Government Expenditure during the War.

Interest of the debt contracted during the war, after allowing for the reduction of the 5 per cents. - - - - - £22,000,000

The annual amount of half-pay and pensions in the army, navy, and civil service, arising from the war, is at present (1823), about 4,500,000*l.*; but consisting almost all of life annuities, may be computed equal to a permanent burden of - 2,000,000

Exclusive of this, the expence of our army and navy is very greatly augmented since 1792, partly from the extension of our foreign possessions, partly from causes unconnected with the war, such as the increase of our population, and the necessity of enforcing the collection of the revenue in Ireland. As yet the charge of our army and navy (distinct from half-pay and pensions), exceeds that of 1792 by 6,000,000*l.*, but from the prospect of continued peace, and the general fall of prices, we may anticipate a farther eventual reduction of 1,000,000*l.* Of the remaining 5,000,000*l.*, we put to the account of the war, somewhat more than half, viz. - - - - - 3,000,000

Add, for increase of the civil list, salaries, pensions in consequence of the war and of the rise caused by it in prices - - - 2,000,000

Other war charges not enumerated - - 1,000,000

Total - - £30,000,000

Such is the amount of burden arising from our war expenditure; happily, however, there are alleviating considerations.

Deductions from our apparent Burdens.

Taxation of other Countries.—It is in some respects a matter of little difficulty to understand
the financial relief which we have in prospect;
such, for example, as the decrease in our half-pay
and pensions, either by the occurrence of deaths,
or a transfer for long annuities; but the case may
not be quite so clear in regard to a deduction of
another kind, we mean that which arises from a
" community of the pressure of taxation on the civilized world at large." Yet, however real our losses
from the war, however inferior our national wealth
to what it would have been, had peace been unin-
terrupted, we cannot be said to have incurred absolute injury, or to labour under any permanent
disadvantage, in as far as *similar burdens* have
been imposed on those who are our competitors
in the career of productive industry. This, we
say, though perfectly aware of the folly of the doctrine that one nation gains by impoverishing another. Our argument, when attentively examined,
will be found to rest on a very different basis:
war, at all times a losing game, would be doubly
so, were our opponents to escape a participation
in the pecuniary pressure; our productive labourers would soon emigrate, and pursue their industry
in untaxed countries. To bring our argument to
a point: if in England the late wars have increased
the proportion of burden to income by twelve
per cent., and if in France, Germany, or the
Netherlands, the comparative increase be five or
six per cent., our loss, serious as it is, can hardly
be considered as exceeding the difference; we

mean that in whatever regards the hazard of rivalship, or the injury from foreign' competition, our
disadvantage is limited to the extra six or seven
per cent.

Our War Taxes.—Our next modification of our
losses is also of a very extensive character, though
it does not happen to form a deduction from the
preceding table. It comprises no less than the
larger portion of the sum raised by war taxes, which,
though (see Chapter II. p. 24.) of very great
amount, we are disposed to consider as defrayed
out of the extra profits of a state of war ; so largely
were the gains of the public, whether in the shape
of interest, salary, wages, or profit of stock, increased by the circulation of the money raised by
our loans. In making this great allowance, we are
perfectly aware that in many cases, particularly after
our unfortunate Orders in Council, our merchants
and manufacturers paid their taxes, as our farmers
at present pay their rent, not from income but from
capital. We are aware, also, that the resources
which supplied our war taxes were, in a great measure, temporary, and of a nature to disappear with
the stimulus that excited them : but our estimate
is confined to the years of war ; and we are probably justified, on considering all circumstances, in
making the preceding deduction, important as it is.

Public Works, such as Canals, Roads, and Bridges.
— These, however commendable in the intention,
are expedient as undertakings only when the
returns are such as to afford a fair interest for the
capital invested. From the high price of labour
and materials in the latter part of the war, most
speculations of the kind, such for example as the
new bridges of the metropolis, were attended with

a far greater charge than if they had been postponed and executed in peace.   The same holds in
regard to our agriculture, in which a large share of
the outlay was incurred on the assumption of high
prices.   Even in the case of our manufacturing
machinery, a part erected when labour was high, is
no longer necessary or profitable, now that labour
is reduced.   Still, a great part of such loss is merely
in appearance, and resolves itself into the different
value of money : the canal share, which, in 1813,
cost 100*l*., may be said to indemnify its owner, if it
at present fetches 75*l*., because that sum is at present equal in the power of purchase to the 100*l*. of
1813.   Such investments of property involve an
absolute loss only, in as far as they fall below that
proportion, a case at present unfortunately too
frequent.

Tithe. — This portion of our burdens is different,
in several respects, from general taxation.   Its
amount, as expressed in money, increased surprisingly during the war, in consequence of two
causes, — the enhancement of produce, and the
extended cultivation attendant on the increase of
our numbers.   How far did the payment of this
increased amount prove of detriment to our resources?   It was defrayed by that portion of the
community, who, so long as the war lasted, were
most able to defray their burdens.   On the public
at large, its pressure was not apparent ; in an indirect sense, however, that pressure was great, for
tithe *operated as an obstacle to cultivation,* and
greatly restricted the amount of our produce, at a
time when it would have been most desirable to
increase it.

Poor-Rate. — In this respect, the estimate of

burden during the late wars is subject to considerable qualification. The increase of the rate having been as great in agricultural as in manufacturing districts, although in the former, work was, all along, abundant, the inference is, that the rise was, in a great measure, *nominal,* and would otherwise have been paid in the shape of wages. Add to this the decrease of rates in the last and present year, with the probability of a progressive diminution, and we shall find that the portion of burden attributable to the war is by no means so great as might be inferred from the numerical statements of the poor-rate.

The National Debt. — After all these allowances, it may be incumbent on us to answer the question, whether we " consider our national debt as forming an actual loss, an absolute addition to our public burdens?" This question, idle in the view of the attentive enquirer, is by no means superfluous in regard to the cursory observer, to those who imagine our debt a property which, without the war, would have had no existence, a responsibility of little importance because due among ourselves. All such notions we entreat our readers to dismiss from their minds, and to consider our debt as not less real for being due to our countrymen. It is the record of money expended, gone for ever; and involving, as far as our burdens exceed those of other countries, a series of disadvantages. Had we had no war, the capital and labour that has led to the formation of our debt would not have been unemployed; it would have been put in activity by other causes, and received its increase in a different form. The product, we allow, would, probably, have been smaller, because the *ratio* of increase, whether from interest, profit of stock, or personal exertion, would, in a state of continued peace, have been much less considerable.

Effect of the War on the Habits of Individuals. — The increase of wealth arising from the war was much more an increase of income than of property.   In the latter sense the war was beneficial to those only who had formed their habits in a season of tranquil occupation, of moderate profit, and who, from their experience and time of life, were capable of reaping the new harvest without abusing it.   The case was very different with those who, entering on business during the war, took for granted that circumstances would continue as they found them, and made no provision for a reverse. The characteristics of this youthful generation may be said to have been a general confidence, a habit of early expence, a repugnance to the cautious perseverance of former days.   The extent of evil arising from such a source can be computed by those only whose observation has embraced a wide range, who have marked throughout the present age the frequent substitution of adventure for industry, and the reiterated loss of capital when entrusted to the young and inexperienced.

Losses on the Transition from War to Peace.

No period of our history affords an example of a change so sudden and so extensive as that which took place in the state of our productive industry after the peace of 1814.   For the relinquishment of foreign colonies, and for an active rivalship in manufacture, on the part of the continent of Europe, the public were prepared ; but they had, in a manner, lost sight of the great difference between government expenditure in peace and war ;

and the few who took this difference into account, imagined that the diminution of demand at home would be balanced by our exports to newly opened markets in America and Asia. These persons were by no means aware either of the magnitude of our circulation at home arising from war expenditure, or of the substantial difference between an assured payment in England, and the hazard attendant on transactions with distant countries. Many anticipated a partial reduction of wages, but not a general want of work ; a diminution of mercantile and manufacturing profit to a certain extent, but in no degree proportioned to that which took place. Yet the years of peace have been marked by no calamity of a general nature ; by no such bankruptcy as the South Sea or Mississippi scheme; by no territorial cessions, like the relinquishment, at the peace of 1783, of our North American provinces; by no insurrection in our colonies ; no successful rivalship on the part of competitors either in manufacture or navigation.

Magnitude of the Change. — What, then, were the causes of our great and unexpected embarrassments? Not a reduction of our means considered physically or intrinsically, but a general change in the mode of rendering them productive; a sudden removal of the stimulus arising from the war. In no former contest had our military establishments been carried to such a height : the number of our militiamen, soldiers, and sailors, discharged, amounted to between two and three hundred thousand, while the individuals employed in the manufacture of clothes, arms, stores, in the supply of provisions, the navigation of transports, amounted, perhaps, to two hundred thousand more. The magnitude of the transition will be best shown

by a brief comparison of the sums expended by
government in the five last years of the war, and
the five first years of peace :

YEARS OF WAR.

1811.	-	£ 92,200,000	1814.	-	£117,000,000
1812.	-	103,400,000	1815.	-	110,000,000
1813.	-	121,000'000	Average -		108,720,000

YEARS OF PEACE.

1816.	-	72,000,000	1819	-	59,000,000
1817.	-	66,300,000	1820	-	61,000,000
1818	-	67,000,000	Average -		64,660,000

Peace thus caused an immediate reduction of
more than forty millions in the amount of the
money distributed by government to pay employment, or, in other words, to stimulate productive
industry.   Add to this that during the war most of
our establishments had been formed on a large
scale, a scale that supposed a power of demand, a
capacity of payment much greater than was found
to exist after the peace.   This was the case in
regard not only to great offices, but private establishments of the most dissimilar character ; manufactures, mercantile houses, seminaries of education,
and a variety of undertakings, almost all of which,
whether in the metropolis or provincial towns, were
adapted to a community increasing not only in its
numbers, but in its power of expenditure.

The means by which we were enabled to pay
such heavy contributions during the war have been
already explained.   Exempt from continental competition, the public, or at least four-fifths of the
public, had at that time the power of indemnifying
themselves for their taxes by an increased rate of
charge.   This was the case of the land-holder, the
farmer, the owner of houses, the receiver of tithe :

it was the case, likewise, of persons exercising professions, of those receiving salaries, and of the very numerous class, whose dependence is on wages. At the peace, all or almost all was reversed : agriculturists, merchants, manufacturers, fell from their 'vantage ground, and prosperity was, during several years, confined to annuitants, to whom, since 1820 or 1821, we are enabled to add the majority of the labouring classes. It must not be inferred from this that our consumption, whether of agricultural or manufactured produce, experienced an absolute diminution ; for our numbers, as was shown at the time by the extent of new buildings, and subsequently by the population returns, were annually on the increase ; but partly from the economy introduced by altered circumstances, more from an augmentation of supply, the increase of buyers did not equal the increase of sellers, and a general fall of prices became unavoidable. Finally, our distress was aggravated in no slight degree by the absence of many of our countrymen of the upper and middling classes, who, whether as travellers or as residents on the Continent, incurred an expenditure of several millions annually abroad, at the time it was most wanted at home.

Distress of Foreign Countries.—Similar causes of embarrassment were unfortunately in operation on the Continent of Europe. In former wars the evils of transition had been felt in few countries, and to a comparatively small extent ; but in 1813 and 1814, almost all Europe had been in military array, and every country felt the sudden change from disembodying of armies, cessation of government purchases, and an overstock of productive labourers. Add to this, that our greatest cus-

tomers, the United States of America, had suffered
so severely, first from the stoppage of their navigation, and afterwards from the return of peace, as
to be far less able to pay for our goods than during
the continuance of the war. The consequence
was that our foreign trade, though not diminished,
and even partially increased in amount, failed,
from irregularity in the payments, to prove an
efficient source of relief.

Temporary Revival of Activity in 1818.—The
extent of our suffering might have been in some
degree lessened, had our real situation been earlier
known, or had it not undergone considerable fluctuation in the years that have elapsed since the
peace. The year 1814 produced two great results; a fall of corn, and a reinstatement of the
value of bank paper. Both continued during 1815
and 1816, but the bad harvest of the latter year
renewed the operation of our corn laws, and being
followed by a revival of trade and manufacture,
accustomed us anew to high prices, gave a temporary increase to the revenue, and suspended the
measures that might otherwise have been taken for
a general adaptation of our burdens to our means;
we mean a reduction of salaries and those other
incomes in regard to which, from the sums being
previously fixed, the course of circumstances has
not had free operation. Our second period of distress (beginning in 1819) thus came on us as unexpectedly as the first, and we are now, in the
ninth year of peace, discussing those points which
it had been of infinite importance to us to have
understood from the moment that the overthrow
of Buonaparte opened the prospect of a general
change.

Our probable Situation had the War been avoided.
—We shall close these remarks by a brief calculation of what would probably have been our finan.
cial situation, supposing political science to have
been as well understood at the time of the French
revolution as at present, and our statesmen equally
convinced of the close connexion between the preservation of peace, and the increase of national
prosperity. Had such been the case, we may
fairly assume that our cabinet would either not
have interfered in the war at all, or would have
made peace in 1793, as soon as the French were
driven within their frontiers. For tranquillity at
home they would probably have trusted to measures of police, to the aid of an armed force, and to
the support of the middle and upper classes of
society. The troubled aspect of the times, and
the necessity of arming the executive branch with
power both to repress sedition, and to effect such
measures as the union with Ireland, and the equal
collection of taxes throughout the kingdom, would
doubtless have obliged us to increase our army and
carry our expenditure considerably beyond that of
1792. The result might have been that our taxes
and poor-rate which in 1792, amounted (including
Ireland) to about 20,000,000*l.*, might by this time
have been carried by a gradual increase to 28 or
30,000,000*l.* In other respects also, our situation
would have been exempt from the extraordinary
fluctuations we have witnessed. Thus the price of
wheat would, even after the double failure of crop
in 1799 and 1800, hardly have exceeded 80*s.* moderate as would have been the charges on import.

In a state of peace the attention of our ministers
might have been bestowed on measures of internal

improvement, such as commutation of tithe, equalization of poor-rate, or the removal of commercial restrictions, all necessarily postponed during a contest, which not only absorbed their time, but obliged them, from their dependence on the support of particular interests, to submit to a tacit continuance of abuses. If we are told that the average rate of profits and wages being smaller in peace than in war, our national income would not in the former alternative have been so large, our answer is, that while we admit the quicker increase of invidual income during war, we have to bring against it a formidable deduction in the losses attendant on the transition to peace. Or if, to avoid argument, we limit our estimate of loss arising from the war to a sum of which the interest is 15 or 18,000,000*l.* a year, we allow even then that we have incurred a burden equal to the revenue of the Austrian or Russian empire.

The late Wars examined by moral Considerations. — We proceed to bestow a few sentences on the events of the late war, considered on higher grounds than those of mere calculation. The apparent triumph of injustice, in national as well as individual transactions, has, as is well known, often embarrassed candid inquirers, and reduced them almost to question the interference of Providence in the course of human affairs. Among our neighbours on the southern shore of the Channel, scepticism received an unfortunate extension at the time of the revolution; an extension to be attributed partly to the youth and unthinking character of many of the reformers, partly to the odium to which the Catholic clergy exposed themselves by their opposition to the new cause. During many years the success of a restless despot seemed to confirm the doubts of the intervention of a higher power, since it was not till the Continent had been overrun, that political justice resumed its course.

But if such impressions may be expected in a country where religion wears a form ill calculated to obtain the conviction of a reflecting mind, ought we to have expected in England a favourable reception to such a doctrine as that of our national wealth being augmented by war? Happily no such conclusions are suggested by the writings of those who have most successfully investigated the sources of national prosperity; by the labours of Turgot, Smith, or Say. If to describe the structure of the human frame; to explain the connexion and the subserviency of its various parts, has been declared equivalent to a hymn in praise of its divine Author, not less is that testimony due to the study of the causes of the success of productive industry. Researches into that subject, when prosecuted in the spirit of impartiality, tend more and more to establish the connexion between equity and prosperity, between fairness in principle and success in practice.

This connexion, we can safely assure our readers, is no philanthropic dream, but is practically recognized by the directors of our mercantile policy. The system of prohibition and high duties, so long in favour with our ancestors, is now renounced, and our Board of Trade has, during the last eight years, acted on the conviction that the increase of our wealth is, in a great measure, dependent on the increase of that of our neighbours. Further, if we pass in review our mercantile history during the war, and discriminate the gain and loss of particular classes, we shall find that the change of circumstances since the peace has, in general, been such as to constitute a fair retribution to those who had either benefited or suffered by fluctuation. Annuitants have been relieved from their long depression, and now find their income restored, or nearly restored, to its former value. Of our countrymen at present in a state of suffering, we may be permitted to remark that they belong in general to the classes whose gains were greatest during the war; a remark made without the slightest intention of weakening their claim to relief, since not humanity only, but the public interest (see the chapter on Agriculture, p. 142.) calls on us to prevent their farther depression. And we have adverted to their case merely to show the transient and unsubstantial nature of gains derived from a state of war; — the frightful recoil to be apprehended by those who imagine that in them they have found a source of permanent advantage.

The result, therefore, is, that the late war, so long accounted a source of national wealth, involved a sacrifice of property not inferior to the sacrifice of lives. To this double drain in our resources, what has been the grand counterpoise? Our progress in the arts of peace: the power of extracting a larger supply of subsistence from our soil; a larger revenue from our labour and capital. By what criterion are we enabled to compute the amount of the addition thus obtained? We know of none more satisfactory than a return of the numbers added to our population and supported by our resources; a subject replete with satisfactory conclusions, and which we have already discussed at considerable length. At present, without recurring to our arguments on that head, we shall merely advert to a very common, but a very erroneous notion, that " the rapid increase of our numbers in the present age is to be attributed to the war." Whatever may have been the case in regard to the middle classes, the wages of many of the lower orders, particularly those of the country labourer, bore, even when added to the poor-rate (see the chapter on Poor-rate, p. 203.), a smaller proportion to the expense of rearing a family than in peace. Now, as the lower orders form by far the most numerous portion of the nation, and the circumstances affecting them *are decisive of the general increase of our numbers,* we can by no means join in ascribing the surprising augmentation in the present age to the excitement arising from the war, although that opinion may have (Lord Liverpool's speech, March 1822) the sanction of ministerial authority. It has continued with equal rapidity since the peace, and our rulers may, we believe, trace it with confidence to causes of a cheering and permanent character; to the effect of vaccination, to the improvement in the lodging, cleanliness, and sobriety of the lower classes.

In thus dwelling on the evils of war, our object is not to join with the decided Oppositionists, in lamenting what cannot be recalled, or in affixing a general censure on a course of policy, which though reprehensible in some respects, admitted in many others of vindication from the conduct of our enemies; or of defence, from the limited foresight of human nature. Our purpose is strictly statistical, and our wish is merely to impress on the public a consideration of great importance to their future welfare, viz. that the injury to national prosperity resulting from war, however it may be palliated or postponed, is eventually of most serious magnitude, even when, in a military sense, the issue of the contest has proved triumphant.

We now proceed to a more enlivening theme, — to a survey of the present state of our productive industry, and of the prospect opened to us by a continuance of peace. To our reasoning on this head we shall endeavour to give a definite form by bringing it before the eye of the reader in the shape of arithmetical calculation. We begin our table with the year 1813, as the last in which our prices bore the stamp of a state of war. In comparing this with the present year, we keep in view two important facts.

1. The increase of our population, which, since 1813, is about 15 per cent.

2. The fall in the price of commodities, in other words the reduction of expence, which to most classes we compute at 25 and to some at 35 per cent.

An attention to these facts is indispensable to a correct estimate of our situation : we should otherwise fall into the common error of considering ourselves rich or poor, merely as prices happened to be high or low. The complexity of the following table will, we trust, disappear after an attentive examination.

ESTIMATE OF OUR TAXABLE INCOME. (Great Britain distinct from Ireland.)

	I.	II.	III.	IV.	V.	VI.
	Its computed amount in 1813. (See Property Tax returns for 1812 and 1815.)	Had individual incomes kept up as during the war, there would have been, in the income of the nation at large, an increase in proportion to that of our numbers (15 per cent.) The respective sums would then have been in 1823.	But the actual incomes (in 1823) of the respective classes appear from our table in p. 257. to be only.	On the other hand, from reduction in our taxes and in the price of provisions, £100 is now equal, in the power of purchase, to £125 in 1813; and, in some classes, to more; thus,	Consequently the sums in in column III. being in money of 1823, are equivalent to the following sums in money of 1813.	By comparing col. II. and col. V. we are enabled to calculate the Increase of income in certain classes since 1813; reckoned not by the amount of the money, but by its power of purchase. / Decrease of income in other classes since 1813, reckoned in the same manner;
Rent of Houses - - - -	16,000,000	18,500,000	17,000,000	£100 to 125	21,250,000	15 per cent.
Income from trade and professions -	30,000,000	34,700,000	22,000,000	100 to 125	27,500,000	— 20 per cent.
Wages in agriculture, manufacture, and every department of industry	90,000,000	110,000,000	90,000,000	100 to 135 (from the fall in provisions)	121,500,000	10 per cent.
Interest of money lent on private securities and on foreign stocks, estimated conjecturally - - -	15,000,000	20,000,000	20,000,000	100 to 125	25,000,000	9 per cent.
Tithe - - - - - - (In the following sums no addition is made to the income of 1815.)	5,000,000	5,800,000	4,000,000	100 to 125	5,000,000	— 14 per cent.
Rent of land - - - -	48,000,000	48,000,000	30,000,000	100 to 125	37,500,000	— above 20 per cent.
Farming income - - -	40,000,000	40,000,000	12,000,000	100 to 135 (farming charges having fallen greatly)	16,200,000	— 60 per cent.
Interest of our public funds - -	30,000,000	30,000,000	30,000,000	100 to 125	37,500,000	25 per cent.
Income of the army, navy, and civil servants of government; also, of contractors - - - -	40,000,000	reduced by peace to 16,000,000	15,000,000		18,750,000	{ between 50 & 60 per cent.
Total for Great Britain - -	319,000,000	323,000,000	240,000,000		310,200,000	
Ireland; conjectural amount of her taxable income - - -	35,000,000	40,000,000	25,000,000	100 to 135 (from the fall in provisions)	33,000,000	— 16 per cent.
	354,000,000	363,000,000	265,000,000		344,000,000	

The reader, who shall bestow a little time on studying this table, will not, we trust, be long in finding his labour repaid, and in making the satisfactory discovery that the decrease of our financial means since the peace is by no means so great as is commonly supposed.

Remarks on Col. II.—Interest of Money.— The surplus in the receipts of our monied men above their expenditure supplies, is, as is well known, an annual fund for investment, and as there has been of late no opportunity of making loans to our exchequer, this surplus has sought a vent in advances to private individuals, or to the French, American, and other foreign governments. We have accordingly made in our table a large addition to the estimated amount of interest arising since the peace from such investments.

Agriculturists.— Though the increase of number in this class since 1813 has been considerable, and has evidently been accompanied by a corresponding increase of produce, we have declined, for obvious reasons, to suppose it productive of increase of income.

Tithe.— Here the same objection does not altogether hold, tithe not having experienced either so great a rise in war or so great a decline since the peace.

Wages.— Under the head of wages, we have supposed between 200 and 300,000 men withdrawn at the peace from the militia, army, and navy, and have added the amount of their probable earnings, (6,000,000*l.*), to the head of wages.

A corresponding deduction is made under the head of income to individuals in the public service. The great diminution in this branch puts in a striking light the stagnation attendant on the transition from war to peace.

Ireland. — The *untaxed* income of Ireland rests (see Appendix p. 78.) on a very different calculation from her taxed income, and must, from the increase in the number of her peasantry, have received a very large augmentation since 1813.

Remarks on Col. IV. — *Reduction of Expence.* — We may, perhaps, be charged with making a somewhat too large allowance in this respect, the saving compared to 1813 being, in various situations, not yet carried to the extent of 25 per cent. Our answer is, that peace being evidently the policy of our government, there is a probability of reduction continuing, and of that which has not taken place in the present year, being accomplished in the next.

Farmers. — Amidst all the distress of this respectable part of the nation, it is some satisfaction to perceive the large reduction in their disburse for labour and other farming charges.

The Lower Orders. — These form so great a portion of the community, that we can hardly advert too often or too attentively to their situation. The transition from war to peace bore, doubtless, very heavy on particular classes, principally manufacturers, whose wages were very low at a time when provisions were by no means cheap. Since 1820, however, circumstances have altered greatly in their favour, the fall of provisions having rendered 22*s.* a week equivalent, in the power of purchase; to 30*s.* during the war.   If this fall was too great and too rapid, it is at least a satisfaction that the advantage of it should have accrued to the most necessitous part of the community.   Viewing this very numerous body collectively, we find their situation, whether in town or country, more comfortable at present than at almost any period within our recollection.

Remarks on the Table generally. — In comparing the amount of national revenue at different periods, it is fit to keep in view the increasing number of consumers, in other words, of individuals to be supported from that revenue.   This increase, including Ireland, amounts to nearly 3,000,000 for the ten years that have elapsed since 1813.   For this surprising addition to our numbers, allowance is made in Col. II., but as it may be thought from the estimate in Col. III., that our means are not adequate to the support of this new charge, we must remind the reader, that increased population happily brings with it the means of supporting itself, and that on comparing Cols. II. and V., he will discover that, even after making a deduction from the favourable part of our statement, our present means of affording wages, salaries, and income of different kinds, are not inferior to our means during the war, by more than 10 per cent.   Now a reduction of the income of the community to the extent of 10 per cent. would not, had it been equal and general, have proved disastrous : it would have necessitated a diminution of expense, and have given a general check to sanguine expectation, but could never have been the cause of severe distress.

But the transition unfortunately took place in a very unequal manner, for while in the case of the landholders, the decrease of income appears to be 20 per cent., and in that of farmers not less than 60 per cent., annuitants on the public funds have benefited or will soon benefit to an extent of 20 or 25 per cent.

In what order or succession did these reductions of income take place? First, in the army, the navy, and the classes, such as contractors and manufacturers, who derived their support from government: the agriculturists followed almost immediately, in consequence of the unchecked import of foreign corn during 1814. Trade and manufactures, though undiminished as far as regarded export, experienced, during several years, a great decrease at home, from the cessation of government purchases, and an overstock of hands from the discharge and non-enlistment of men for the army and militia. Among the liberal professions, the medical suffered a direct surcharge from an obvious cause: the same held in regard to the civil service of government, and if in the law and the church, the overstock has been less rapid, it has not been the less certain, so much does stagnation of demand in any of the great departments affect the community at large.

Our public Burdens; their comparative Pressure in War and Peace.—Since the peace, the numerical amount of our burdens has been considerably diminished, the repeal of the property-tax, along with the reduction of the duties on malt, salt, and leather, having formed (previously to the reduction of the assessed taxes) a diminution of nearly 20,000,000*l.* This sum, however, large as it is, has been balanced, or nearly balanced, by the rise in the value of money; the 65,000,000*l.* which we have paid annually since the peace, having formed an amount of equal value with the 80 or 85,000,000*l.* paid at the close of the war. There was thus no real reduction of our burdens until the present year, and, unfortunately, from the evils of transition, from the sudden diminution in the income of particular classes, our taxes have been found a burden of greater pressure since the peace, than during the war.

Effect on our Public Debt of the Rise in the Value of Money. — We come now to the circumstance in the series of our transitions, which, more than any other, has contributed to increase the burden of our taxes. To comprehend this fully, the reader should bear in mind, that government stands permanently in the capacity of a debtor; that its responsibility is represented not in land, houses, or what is technically termed real property, but in money; and that whatever raises the value of money, increases the pressure of its debt. During the long depreciation of money attendant on the war, the payment of 9 or 10,000,000*l.* of interest, at the Treasury, required no greater drain on the national resources, than the payment of 7 or 8,000,000*l.* previous to 1793. This fact, long known to our finance ministers, formed during a time the basis of very confident calculations : so long as high prices were kept up, so long did our leading men at the Treasury and in Parliament imagine, that the pressure of the debt contracted during the war, would be alleviated by the continued depreciation of money. At the peace, indeed, a degree of re-action or rise in the value of money was anticipated; but in the opinion of the public, as of government, that re-action was likely to be slight. Had such proved the case; had the price of corn been kept up both here and on the Continent, the evils of transition would have been comparatively slight, and our national burdens would have been less severely felt. Their pressure would have gradually decreased as our numbers augmented, and we might have considered the expence of the contest as in a great measure liquidated from two sources, — the extra profits of labour and capital which had supplied our war taxes, and the depreciation of that money debt, which represented the undischarged burden. But all such calculations were disappointed: reaction took place on a large scale; and without experiencing any direct increase of charge, the public were subjected to serious embarrassment from the general diminution of the sums paid for rent, salaries, wages, in short, for almost every thing except the income of annuitants.

Has this increase of burden been accompanied by any circumstances of alleviation? In private life we have for some time experienced relief from the reduction of our expenditure; but what is the situation of government? It feels the pressure on more than two-thirds of its disburse; the benefit on less than one-third. The former consist of interest of debt, military and naval pay, pensions, half-pay, salaries, and retirement allowances, all of a fixed amount in money, and all virtually increased as the price of commodities has fallen. On the other hand, a reduction of government charge from the fall of prices, was, till very lately, experienced only in the victualling of our navy, the purchase of stores, and in a portion of the miscellaneous services.

These discoveries may be said to constitute the

denouement of the mysterious financial drama that has been acting during the last thirty years. Our power of pecuniary contribution, so often and so loudly ascribed to generosity in the sacrifice of our wealth, may now be, in a great measure, traced to causes of a humbler character; to an increase of our productive industry, founded on loans, and to a great, but temporary rise of prices. Both of these remarkable features in our situation were expected to be permanent; but the rise of prices has disappeared, and to the extension of our productive industry, circumstances were long unfavourable. Add to this, that though from the time of the overthrow of Bonap. rte, the prospect of continued peace produced a radical change in our situation, our ministers were tardy in bringing forward any measure of finance founded on that change, or on the confidence with which we may anticipate an increase of our wealth and numbers. In fact, until the present year, we made little progress towards relief, unless we account as such a more correct knowledge of our situation; a discovery of certain errors; a perception of the transient nature of the aids on which we relied during the first years of peace.

———

Have our public men, since 1793, *understood our financial situation?* — After ascertaining the existence of such general misapprehension, it is impossible to avoid asking whether several important circumstances in our situation and prospects have not been unknown to our political guides. Were they aware during the war, that the extension of our productive industry was, in a great degree, artificial, and must decline with that government expenditure which called it forth? Looking to the amount of the interest of our public debt, of our pensions and other fixed payments, did they or did they not foresee that, on the cessation of this artificial stimulus, the natural course of circumstances would cause a rise in the value of money, and a consequent increase of pressure? To what degree do these considerations affect the reputation of Mr. Pitt, the leader in that course of policy, which, in a military sense, produced so brilliant a result,— in a financial, so much embarrassment? That Mr. Pitt was at first averse from the war with France, is apparent, from several circumstances, whether we refer to the declaration of respectable writers*, or to the undeniable fact, that a state of war was altogether contrary to his plans, for the reduction of our public burdens. That, after the campaign of 1794 had disclosed the weakness of our allies, and the strength of France, he lamented our involving ourselves in the contest, there seems little reason to doubt: but when the country was fairly engaged in it, and our resources were called into full activity, it accorded with his confident and persevering character, to maintain the struggle, in the hope of recovering the Netherlands so unfortunately lost. Hence a continuance of the contest, notwithstanding the defection of our allies and the financial difficulties of 1797; hence those war taxes, which no other minister would have ventured to propose, and certainly no other would have succeeded in

---

* Nichols' Recollections of George III. and J. Allan's Biographical Sketch of Fox, in Napier's Supplement to the Encyclopædia Britannica, page 361.

raising : hence also, our second attack on France by the coalition of 1799.

But the perseverance of Mr. Pitt was not blind persistency: on a renewed experience of the weakness of our allies, on a proof of the sufferings of the country from heavy taxation and deficient harvests, he felt the expediency of peace, retired from office to facilitate its conclusion, and gave it, when not responsible for its conditions, a sanction unequivocal and sincere. His ardour in 1803 for the recommencement of war, admits of a less satisfactory solution : it discovered much more the zeal of a combatant, than the discretion of a senator ; a disposition to sink the admonitory recollections of our late struggle in ardour for a new contest. He warned us once in Parliament of the magnitude of the expense, and of the necessity of preparing ourselves for sacrifices greater than before ; but his caution was general and cursory, unaccompanied by any private admonition to the inexperienced ministry of the day, or any advice to delay hostilities, until circumstances should give us an assurance of co-operation on the part of the great powers of the Continent. His last great measure, the attack on France by the coalition of 1805, was, doubtless, on the whole, injudicious, preponderant as France then was in military strength, the whole under the guidance of a single head. Still it may be added that it is by no means uncommon with men of ability to fall into the miscalculation made by Mr. Pitt on that occasion ; and to anticipate, as a matter of course, judicious conduct on the part of their coadjutors. Every impartial man must allow, that it would have been carrying mistrust to an extreme, to have apprehended the commission of faults so gross as those which led to the disasters of Ulm and Austerlitz. And those who are surprised that a man of talent should misplace his confidence, or should calculate on others acting with the discrimination natural to himself, will be at no loss to find similar examples in the conduct of the most eminent men of the age: in that of Lord Wellington, when he expected discretion from Blucher; and in that of Bonaparte, when he allowed the command of Spain to remain in the hands of Jourdan ; or when, at a subsequent date, he committed that of his main body at Waterloo, to Ney.

Since the distress that has followed the peace of 1814, it has been publicly said, that the embarrassment likely to ensue to our productive industry on the cessation of the war expenditure of government, had not escaped the foresight of Mr. Pitt. Such assertions are often made loosely and inaccurately ; but the one in question seems to rest on probable grounds. Mr. Pitt was no stranger to the limited produce of our revenue in peace; he had felt the financial difficulties of the first years of the contest, and the surprising relief afforded to the Treasury by the imposition of war taxes. He could thus hardly fail to be aware that the spring given to our national industry was, in a great measure, artificial ; still less could he be unconscious of the ultimately injurious operation of loans and taxes when carried to an extreme. Nor is it incompatible with such impressions, that he should for a time have overlooked the inferences which they seem so naturally to suggest, and have been hurried along by ardour in the contest, by an earnestness to obtain a present advantage at the hazard of a future burden. It is not when engaged in the bustle of business, that the mind is

capable of reposing on itself, of meditating, pa-
tiently and impartially, the result of favourite
measures. How few plans of remote operation,
of a nature that requires continued thought in the
combination or length of time in the execution,
originate with men in office! Add to this that the
great evils of our financial system, the depreciation
of our bank paper, the extreme pressure of taxation took place not only after Mr. Pitt's death,
but, in some measure, in consequence of a deviation from his principles. Never would he have
given his sanction to such a measure as our Orders
in council; or if, for the sake of argument, we
suppose him to have been led, by urgency or by
plausible argument, to their adoption, will any one
maintain that he would have been likely to persist
in so absurd a course during four years, until it,
in a manner, drove the Americans to the alternative of war—a war carried on between us and
our best customers—a war in which it was apparent that injury to our opponents must be almost
as pernicious to our national industry, as injury to
ourselves.

The responsibility of a great part of our existing burden, is thus transferred from Mr. Pitt to
his successors, of whose measures, in regard to
neutrals, from September, 1807, to May, 1812, it
would be difficult to give a satisfactory explanation.
They implied a total unconsciousness of the precarious state of our paper currency, and, in regard
to trade, either a disavowal of principles generally
admitted, or a readiness to infringe those principles for temporary purposes—purposes that could
have no decisive effect on the result of the grand
struggle with France. In 1812 began a different
æra: our Orders in council were withdrawn; peace

was repeatedly offered to the United States of America; and, at a subsequent date, no harsh treaty of commerce was imposed on France in the day of her adversity. Add to this, that since the peace, no attempt has been made to give a fallacious prop, by bounties or prohibitions, to any of our suffering interests. Admirable rules of conduct these, and yet in regard to our finances, we must repeat, that ministers have not been prompt in rendering the national resources instrumental to the national relief. Their fault appears to have lain, not as is usual with governments, in interfering with the course of productive industry, but either in deficient foresight in regard to the changes occurring in our situation, or in deficient vigour in acting on such changes. Take for example the rise in the value of money, a natural consequence of a return to a pacific system, and one which, with some temporary exceptions, has been regularly gaining ground since 1814. Would Mr. Pitt, had his life been prolonged, have delayed until the ninth year of peace a reduction of public salaries, an adaptation of government payments to the augmented value of the money in which these payments were made? Is it not more likely that he would have long since anticipated the result of the general change, and have given, in his own case, a decided example of what he would have exacted from others? Farther, is it probable that in peace he would have adhered blindly to the financial routine pursued during the war, without attempting some measure, founded on the circumstances that have predominated in our situation since 1814, — the reduced interest of money, and the prospect of long continued peace, in consequence of the conviction annually gaining ground that a state of war is as contrary to policy as to humanity, and, from our growing power, far less necessary for defence than when France was so preponderant?

If ministers are open to the charge of deficient vigour in finance, in what manner can the impartial reasoner characterize the conduct of their parliamentary opponents? On their part there existed no motive for reserve, in regard to public distress; no dread of disseminating alarm, by the proposition of change; yet the investigations of most of the Opposition members have been confined to insulated points, their objections to specific grants. Where, in the long list of those who opposed the war, did we find a speaker capable of giving the House or the country a distinct conception of the operation of our augmented expenditure; of the temporary nature of the activity caused by it during war; of the unfortunate re-action to be apprehended at a peace? Where, on the part of those who have combated the measures of ministers since the peace, do we find a comprehensive view of our national means, the suggestion of any measure of a new or of a general character, adapted to our present circumstances? To what shall we ascribe this deficiency of resource, this scanty measure of statistical knowledge on both sides of the House? To a cause to which we have owed no small share of our political disappointments in the present age—an education on the part of our representatives very little suited to their functions as men of business. This topic has a claim to our attentive examination, for by nothing has the situation of the public during the present age, been more materially affected.

Education of our public Men.—The course of study followed in this country, in the case of young men destined for public life, is remarkable as indicative of the tenacity with which established usages maintain their ground. Previous to the 17th century, the acquisition of Latin was indispensable to a polite education, no modern language being in these days a depository of elegant learning, or a received medium for the correspondence of either men of letters or diplomatists. It is thus that we are to account for the interchange of voluminous epistles in Latin, between the scholars of Italy, Germany, France, and England, as well as for the study of the classical languages by females of rank, as was exemplified in the case of Queen Elizabeth, of Lady Jane Grey, and of the daughters of Sir Thomas More. The colleges added in these days to our universities, were naturally confined to the branches of literature familiar to the founders ; and in no part of Europe has this limitation been more strictly maintained, or the changes suggested by modern discoveries been less adopted, than at Oxford and Cambridge. If academical chairs have been provided for chemistry, for moral or for natural philosophy, an adherence to the established usage of these seminaries has prevented their being generally attended, and continues to confine the labours of our youth to mathematical and classical pursuits, to which alone, are awarded honours at the public examinations.

The study of mathematics has obviously little connexion with the business of life, or with the intended profession of nine-tenths of those who pursue it. The evidence by which the inferences of the student are there guided, is of a nature altogether different from that which he will be called

on to weigh in his intercourse with the world, in
the transaction of business, in the discrimination of
character. On this we shall not enlarge, as it will,
of course, be readily admitted, and the defence of
the study made to rest on its " tendency to improve
the reasoning powers of youth :" but would it not,
we may ask, be practicable to attain equal improvement in that respect by directing their labours to subjects connected with their future
occupation? Taking for example young men intended for public life, would it not be preferable
to seek an exercise for their intellect in the history
of our country as related by Hume, or in the conclusions of political economy as exhibited in the
writings of Smith or Say? By history they would
be introduced to a knowledge of characters, such as
they are likely to meet on the stage of life ; while
political economy would lead them to the examination of subjects which they will be called on to
discuss, and which they will find as yet very imperfectly understood. In regard to impressions
of a higher kind, the tendency of these studies to
convey liberal views, to prove the connection between the justice of a government and the welfare of its subjects, between the course of public
events and the ordination of Providence, we have,
we trust, said enough in a preceding paragraph of
this chapter.

  Classical erudition, says an elegant writer*, is
by the custom of England more peculiarly called
learning ; and we admit that in education, its claim
to attention is powerful, even when we keep out of
view its fascinating appeals to the imagination, and

---

* Sir James Mackintosh on the character of Fox, in the
collection by Dr. Parr, under the name of Philopatris Varvi-
censis.

are content to contemplate it with a mere reference to utility. The record of instructive facts, the delineation of character, the illustration of the rules of composition, the exemplification of the finest precepts, all belong to the writers of Greece and Rome, and warn us to beware of neglecting to cultivate that grateful soil. Of this we are so fully satisfied, that our doubts are confined to the time requisite to acquire a knowledge of the critical niceties of the languages, and to the question whether we ought not, in most cases, to be satisfied with that progress which enables us to comprehend, with tolerable accuracy, the sense of a writer. And here, fortunately, the line of distinction seems to admit of being traced with considerable confidence. By the youth intended for an active pursuit, for the bar, the pulpit, or the senate, philological researches need hardly be carried further than is necessary to enable him to understand the meaning of an author, while a more minute and scrupulous investigation is incumbent on him who directs his labours to the instruction of others, or cultivates literature in retirement with all the advantage of the command of time. But why, it may be said, cannot the two be combined by persons intended for active professions? To do so would, we apprehend, be to underrate the sacrifice of time indispensable to the attainment of thorough knowledge, and to lose sight of the scrupulous care with which the eight or ten years, in general allowed for education, must be appropriated, if we mean to avoid the frequent error of misapplying our labour, of undertaking studies which we may be unable to follow up.

Conduct of public Affairs since 1793. — Let us proceed to make a brief application of these remarks to the statesmen of the present age ; to the men who guided our councils in the stormy period of the French revolution. How different, in all probability, would have been the course of their policy had their early impressions partaken more of the light to be derived from the study of recent periods of history, from an attentive observation of foreign countries. Had they possessed a more accurate knowledge of the national character of the French, of the degree in which the invidious distinction between the titled and untitled classes was kept up, of the circumstances which rendered a revolution as much the wish of the majority of the nation as it was in this country in 1688, our ministers would have known with how much qualification the declamations of Burke, and the assertions of the emigrants were to be received. In regard to this country, they would probably have discovered that the support of the middle and upper classes afforded a sufficient safeguard against the danger of innovation without resorting to the alternative of war. Or, supposing that after the loss of the Netherlands in 1792, and the alarm given to our sovereign and our nobility by the violence of the Jacobins, it became impossible to avoid an appeal to arms, how different, with the knowledge we have supposed in our political guides, would have been the conduct of the war? Had they been aware of the backward state of the countries, in particular Austria, on which we relied for military co-operation, of that blind adherence to old usage, that deference to family rank and court influence, which clogged the wheels of government and restrained the energy of the people, is it likely that our ministers would have counselled an offensive course against a nation emancipated from those fetters, and which conferred its appointments, whether civil or military, by very different rules ?

If from foreign affairs we turn to our interior situation, is it likely, we may ask, that, with a thorough knowledge of the principles of productive industry, our ministers would have been so deluded by appearances as to mistake a rise in the price of commodities for an increase of national wealth, or to imagine that war could, under any circumstances, be conducive to commercial prosperity ? Had they studied the lesson to be learned in the history of Holland, and, in some degree, in our own, (since intervals of stagnation have followed almost every war since the revolution,) our public men would have anticipated a reaction at a peace, and have carefully circumscribed their expenditure during the war. If we examine the discussions that have from time to time taken place on one very material question,—the state of our currency,—we shall find the speeches of our leading men indicate little more than an elementary knowledge of the subject. These discussions began in 1810, when if we could not resume cash payments, we might have desisted from our measures against neutral navigation ; but the degree to which the restraint imposed on that navigation affected the credit of our bank paper was unknown to parliament, and inadequately felt by the Cabinet. Nothing consequently was done ; and, when at a subsequent date, and under very different circumstances, we mean in 1819, parliament did interfere with the currency, the measure was ill-timed, and tended, if not to aggravate the evil, to mislead the public in regard to its cause.

After all these examples of error, does it seem necessary to add that the labours of our public men ought to be modelled on a new plan? To give a cursory attention to a multiplicity of topics, leads to a knowledge very little beyond that of first impressions: to obtain a satisfactory conviction, to place our opinions on a firm basis, it is indispensable to make a selection, to restrict the objects of enquiry, and to give a long continuance to our research and reflection on the prescribed themes. Looking round in private life, and extending our view to men of eminence generally, commercial as well as professional, what else than this limitation of object and perseverance in pursuit, do we find to form the basis of such characters, and to distinguish them from the credulous multitude, from those who listen with ready acquiescence to every plausible assertion? If the habits of our representatives are different, if they unfortunately betray the absence of such discrimination and perseverance, ought it to be matter of surprise, that delusion should have prevailed among them during so many years: that a temporary rise of prices and increase of activity, should have been mistaken for a permanent augmentation of national wealth; and that the unwelcome discoveries of late years, the *finale* of which is no less than a suspension of their incomes, should have come on them by surprise?

CHAP. X.

Value of Money.

SECTION I.

Fluctuation in the Value of Money or in the Price of Commodities.

THE fluctuation in prices consequent on the great political transitions of the age, has been already discussed in our second chapter : at present our object is to pursue the same inquiry on a more comprehensive plan, and to carry back our views to changes that have taken place in former ages. Changes of this nature rank among the most interesting subjects of inquiry in political economy. To the reader of history, a knowledge of them is indispensable to the formation of a correct estimate of the price of labour, of the public revenue, and of the comparative wealth of a nation at different periods ; while, in a practical view, an acquaintance with this subject is of very serious interest, as connected with the future value of bequests, leases, and time-contracts generally. The discussion naturally divides itself into the following heads : —

The tendency of prices to fluctuate.

The impracticability of foreseeing or preventing such fluctuation.

A plan for lessening its injurious operation.

Publications on the Fluctuation of Prices.—The documents for forming an estimate of these changes, have as yet been given to us scantily and imperfectly, the subject never having engaged the attention of government, and but lately that of any of our public bodies. In France, a country little remarked for statistical research, the attempts hitherto made to compare the rate of prices at different periods have been confined to a few literary men : in England, one of the earliest was that of Bishop Fleetwood, who collected prices of wheat during a number of years from the 13th to the 17th century, and reduced them to money of our present standard. His labours, published in 1707, formed the chief materials for the reasonings of Dr. Smith, whose life was not prolonged until the publication (in 1797) of a very valuable addition to such collections by Sir Frederick Eden, in his work on the " State of the Poor," the copious materials of which have been termed a *fons perennis* for succeeding inquirers.

In 1798 there appeared in the Transactions of the Royal Society, a tabular statement by Sir George Shuckburgh, which, from the clearness of its form (See Appendix), and the confidence of its deductions, obtained much more credit than it deserved, being far from correct, even in the fundamental points. In 1811, the late Arthur Young, alarmed at the impression made on the public by the Report of the Bullion Committee, and dreading a contraction of paper currency attended by a fall in the price of agricultural produce, entered into researches of great extent, both as to the past and current prices of commodities, and published the whole in a pamphlet, entitled " An Inquiry into the Progressive Value of Money in England."

This tract, however inaccurate in a theoretical sense, has a claim to attention, as well for the value of its materials, as for a correction of the mistakes of Sir George Shuckburgh. Since 1811, serious beyond example as has been the fluctuation of our prices, there has appeared no treatise of consequence on the subject until Mr. Tooke's valuable publication on "High and Low Prices since 1792."

Historical Sketch of the Fluctuation of Prices. — It is a prevalent notion that the money prices of commodities have been progressively rising since the Norman conquest, or even since the earlier period, when the luxury of Rome, and the revenue paid to it by tributary provinces, disappeared before its rude invaders from the north and east. To this opinion, however, there are several strong objections. The supply of gold and silver from the mines, was, during the middle ages, scanty and precarious; while the numbers of the society requiring the use of the precious metals, in other words, the population of the west and central part of Europe, were, in some degree, in a state of increase. Dr. Smith, reasoning on the price of commodities generally, from the price of corn, and founding his view of the latter on the collections of Bishop Fleetwood, assumes, that from the year 1200 to 1550, there was no considerable rise of prices; and that such rise did not begin till the reign of Elizabeth, the time when the American mines became productive on a large scale. The import from that quarter, small as it would appear in the present age, was sensibly felt at a time when silver was very little used in manufacture, and not largely in plate: its amount was, under such circumstances, almost wholly added to the circulating medium of Europe. This addition was considered by Dr. Smith the main cause of the rise of prices which continued until towards the year 1650, when, from circumstances on which we shall enlarge presently, prices ceased to rise, and became either stationary or declining. This state of things lasted until 1764, when, as is well known, a new æra commenced and continued until 1814.

Effect of a State of War. — Dr. Smith's view of the progressive value of money is admitted by Mr. Young, but neither of these writers has thought of tracing a correspondence between the fluctuations in the precious metals in the 16th and 17th centuries, and the political transactions of Europe. A state of war tends, as we have shown in a preceding chapter, greatly to advance prices, and the rise in the reign of Elizabeth may, in no inconsiderable degree, be ascribed to the increase of military establishments in that age, to our defensive attitude against Philip II., to the obstinate contest carried on between him and his insurgent subjects in the Netherlands, to the civil wars of France, and to the troubled state of Germany. On the other hand, after the treaty of Westphalia, the chief part of Europe enjoyed tranquillity, and the effect on trade and agriculture, of reduced armies and diminished taxes, is described by Sir W. Temple, in a manner that strikingly resembles the state of this country and the Continent since the late peace. This political change accounts for the decline of prices that prevailed after 1650, but the application of our theory is, it must be allowed, less clear after 1672, when war was renewed on a great scale, and continued, with comparatively little intermission, during forty years. Add to this, that there took place, during all that time, an import of specie from America, to an extent somewhat increased; viz. to the amount of three, four, or five millions, annually. In what manner, under the operation of this double cause of enhancement, are we to account for prices experiencing no great or permanent rise? Perhaps by the following considerations: —

1. An increased use of the precious metals, in plate, manufactures, and ornaments, in consequence of the general increase of wealth.

2. An augmented export of them to the eastern world, chiefly through the means of the Dutch East India Company.

3. The fact, that previous to 1672, the supply of agricultural produce in England, as in the northwest of Europe generally, had become somewhat more than equal to the consumption; an excess of which the effects are generally felt for a long series of years.

The peace of Utrecht was the commencement of a period of general tranquillity; government expenditure was reduced, labourers were restored to agriculture, and the decline of prices became general and progressive. In vain did our landholders look to the bounty on the export of corn, for a counteraction of the fall in the market: they exported largely, and received premiums on a liberal scale, but their abundant growth kept down the home market, and the excess of supply over consumption continued during half a century, terminating only in 1764. Nor is it at all probable that it would have ceased at that time, peace having been but lately concluded, had we not had a succession of indifferent seasons: these raised

prices, and the contest that ensued with our colonies, prevented their fall.

After 1783, the restoration of peace tended,
naturally, to reduce prices, but its effect was
retarded by several causes, in particular, the demand of hands for our manufactures, and the
occasional occurrence of indifferent seasons. After
1792, the progress of enhancement was accelerated
in an unexampled degree by the general state of
war consequent on the French revolution.   A rise
of prices progressive during twenty years, and
amounting at last to more than 60 per cent. above
those of 1792, overturned time-contracts throughout the kingdom, depressing annuitants while it
raised tenants on lease, with various other classes,
above their former station, — an elevation, unfortunately, of short duration, since they have been
made to descend from it with still more rapidity in
the years that have followed the peace.

Can such Fluctuations be foreseen or prevented? —
After this summary of facts in regard to the past,
the next and still more important point is to
ascertain how far such fluctuations are likely to
continue.   But here the most indefatigable inquirer will find the result uncertain, and be obliged
to admit, that in so complicated a question, all
that we can do with confidence, is to state the
arguments on either side.   Those in favour of the
rise of prices, are,

The contingency of war.

The probable increase of the produce of the
mines, from the application of steam-engines and
other improved machinery.

The farther substitution of bank paper for metallic currency; a substitution, which, in its ge-

neral (though not in its local) effect, operates like the increased productiveness of a mine. *

On the other hand, the arguments for the fall of prices are equally substantial ; viz.

The tendency of all improvements in productive industry, whether in agriculture, manufacture, mechanics, or navigation, to produce cheapness.

The increasing demand for the precious metals, from the increasing population of the civilized world.

As to England in particular, the tendency of a country where prices are higher than in the neighbouring states, to approximate (see p. 325), by commercial intercourse, to the standard of other countries.

Supply of Specie from the Mines. — The amount of specie extracted annually from American mines, was computed in 1760, at 6,000,000*l.* sterling : in the course of the succeeding twenty years, it had increased to fully 7,000,000*l.*, and some time after (Appendix to the Bullion Report of 1810) to 8,000,000*l.* In this, as in other respects, Mexico is by far the foremost of the Spanish colonies, the yearly produce of her mines being nearly five millions sterling, while that of the rest of Spanish America may be estimated at three millions more. Adding to these, somewhat less than a million sterling for Portuguese America, and somewhat more than another million for the mines of our own hemisphere, we make a total of nearly ten millions annually added to the stock of the precious

---

* Our mention of bank paper must always be understood as of bank notes payable in cash : a resort to non-convertible paper will, we take for granted, be henceforth excluded from our financial creed.

metals throughout the world. From this, however, is to be made, both at present and for some time back, a deduction on account of the political troubles of Spanish America : still the importation is on a large scale, and would speedily produce depreciation, were not the demands of the civilized world on the increase.

Consumption of Specie. — The demands for the produce of the mines, arise from various causes, of which the greatest, by far, is the annual consumption of it for plate, watches, gilding, and ornamental manufacture, generally. The amount of this admits of no satisfactory calculation, but is probably (Appendix, p. [89]) not far short of two-thirds of the total produce of the mines. Next comes the demand for coin : the currency of almost all the Continent of Europe is metallic, and an annual supply is requisite, partly to make good accidental loss or the effect of wear, partly to meet the increase of population. This, though not large, may, when joined to the annual export of specie to India and China, (to say little of losses arising from shipwreck or hoarding), account for the absorption of the remaining third of the produce of the mines. What then appears to be the general result ? That in ordinary times these various sources of demand are equal, or nearly equal, to the amount supplied from the mines ; but that for some years back (since 1818), they appear to have been more than equal, in consequence of the extra-demand for gold on the part of the banks of this country, Russia, and Austria, for the purpose of substituting a metallic for a paper currency.

Dr. Smith, in adverting to the future supply of specie from the mines, considered it an equal chance that old mines may become exhausted, as that new mines may be discovered, or the produce of the old increased. Without contesting the accuracy of this opinion in his age, it will hardly be doubted, that since the discovery of the powers of steam, the application of improved machinery to the existing mines, would be productive of a very considerable extension of produce ; but whether, or in what time, it will be carried so far as to lower materially the value of specie, it appears in vain to conjecture.

Circulation of Bank Paper. — Our countrymen, accustomed during more than half a century to the use of bank notes, have observed, with some surprise, that a currency so cheap, and apparently so easy of introduction, should, as yet, be hardly known on the Continent. The bank of France, though of undoubted stability, has found it practicable to establish branches in very few of the provincial towns : several, containing a population of 40,000 and upwards, are still without such branches; and there is not a private bank of circulation in the whole country. The causes are, the distrust excited by the recollection of the assignats, the want of confidence in government, the absence of commercial enterprise, as well as of the habits of care and arrangement, which are indispensable to success in a line of itself less profitable than is commonly imagined. Holland, with all her commercial improvements, has never adopted the banknote system, while in Austria, Russia, and Sweden, the paper circulated is a forced government currency, not convertible into cash.

The obstacles to the circulation of bank paper on the Continent, might perhaps have yielded to the effects of peace and augmented trade, but they have been strengthened of late years, by the increased facility of forgery. It would thus be vain to calculate on the extended use of bank paper, or on any effect likely to arise from it in regard to the value of the precious metals.

Supply of Agricultural Produce.—Though corn is so liable to fluctuation, as well from difference of seasons, as from the occurrence of peace or war, it is remarkable that a character of rise or fall when once stamped on a period, is found to prevail during a considerable time. Thus, the rise of price begun in the early part of the reign of Elizabeth, continued, with only occasional intermissions, to 1650, not far short of a hundred years. At that time began an æra of stationary, and, in some degree, of decreasing prices, which, with temporary suspensions during the indifferent seasons and expensive wars of the reigns of William and Anne, continued until 1764. From that year until 1814, we had no less than fifty years of brisk demand and high prices; while at present, as far as can be judged from appearances, either in England or on the Continent, we are entering on a period similar to that which followed 1650 or 1713, — a period when our growth being somewhat more than adequate to the demand, the market long continued heavy, and prices, in a great measure, stationary.

In what circumstances are we to look for the cause of a stagnation continuing during so long a period as half a century? In the investment of capital and labour in agriculture, to an extent productive of a surplus growth; and in the fact, that, as in the natural course of things, the producers increase in the same proportion as the consumers, the disproportion continues, year after year, until the occurrence of some great national change, such as a war, or the direction of an extra portion of labour to manufactures.

To return to the more immediate object of our enquiry — the effect of the cost of corn on prices generally. This effect is of the greatest importance, both as corn is the chief object of family consumption, and as it regulates, in a great measure, that other main constituent of prices, the rate of labour. Since 1814, and more particularly since 1819, the operation of the corn market has tended to reduce prices, by gradually extending to other articles the reduction that has taken place in agricultural produce. Nor does this tendency seem likely to alter : part of our taxes on agriculture are reduced ; the effect of the remainder is, as we have shewn in a preceding chapter, considerably over-rated ; and the charges of tillage bid fair to return to a standard little higher than that of 1792. Such is also the prospect in France and the Continent at large ; a state of peace reducing the cost of labour, and preventing, in consequence, any permanent rise of prices in the corn market.

Effect of Continental Prices on those of England. — In the case of two countries enjoying peace and the benefit of commercial intercourse, there is a perpetual tendency to equality of price. The reasons are obvious ; there exists a direct motive for emigrating from the dearer country, and for making in the cheaper, articles for importation, whether open or clandestine, into the dearer. In the latter, the rate of interest is generally lower, and affords a temptation to send out of it funded and other monied property. The operation of these causes, steady, though almost unseen, has been a main reason of the fall in our prices since 1814.

War ; Mode of its Operation.—Of the effect of war there can be no doubt; it enhances commodities in various ways : — First, by the addition of a tax to the price of an article; next by a general rise in labour from the demand for men for government service, whether in the field or in the preparation of clothing, arms, and other warlike stores; and, lastly, by the interruption of international intercourse, and the increased charge of transport. If in the 16th and 17th centuries these causes had a serious operation on prices, their effect was greatly increased by the adoption of the funding system, since which, the scale of military expenditure has been enlarged in every country of Europe.

What, in this respect, was the situation of France during the reign of Bonaparte ? His unsettled government and personal want of credit, discouraged loans, and diminished one great source of expenditure; nor was his power displayed with much effect in the imposition of additional taxes. But the demand of men for his service, was on a arge scale, and, without the operation of either paper-currency or war taxes, prices in France rose between 1792 and 1814, about 30 per cent. From this important fact we may form some idea of the effect of a new war on the price of commodities in England, without supposing a repetition of extreme measures, such as an exemption from cash payments, or the stoppage of neutral navigation. Even in a mitigated form, the effect of war on prices would be so decisive as to counteract, in the course of a few years, the operation of almost all the causes of reduction. On this, however, we forbear to dwell, because the advantages of peace are now better understood, and a recurrence to a state of hostility, to that state which subverts the calculations of the governor, as it destroys the happiness of the governed, will be less and less frequent, as sovereigns become aware that the field of combat presents only barren glories.

The arguments for the rise, as for the fall of prices, are thus of great weight, and no question, it is evident, can be more complicated, or present a longer catalogue of opposing causes. On the one hand, what a prospect of fall is held out by the application of improved machinery to the American mines, and the introduction of bank paper on the Continent of Europe! On the other, what a counterpoise from the prospect of increased population or the recurrence of a state of war! To attempt to strike a balance between these contending causes, to advance an opinion in regard to future probability, would be vain : all we can pronounce, is, that *fluctuation in the value of money cannot be prevented;* that it can hardly fail to recur on any great political transition ; and that a measure which should put an end to uncertainty in time contracts, would relieve us from a great national evil.

Injurious Effect of Fluctuation in the Value of Money.—Money, as Dr. Smith remarks, (Book I. Chap. V.) is, in buying and selling, an unexceptionable measure of value ; and in a contract from year to year, it is, in general, a safe measure ; but in a contract of long duration it is far otherwise. How great was the depreciation of money during the late wars; and notwithstanding the various disadvantages attendant on landed property, how general was the preference given to it in the case of a provision for a young family, for grand-children, or for any remote object. Is it not in the unfortunate tendency of money property to fluctuate, rather than in any distrust of the stability of the public funds, that we are to look for the cause of stock selling for 6, 7, or 8 years' purchase less than land? Then, as to land itself, and the mode of letting it, can we trace among the various objections to long leases any so powerful as the uncertainty of the value of money? Lastly, amidst all the difficulties in the question of a commutation for tithe, what operates so greatly as this uncertainty to prevent the church from acceding to a fixed income, from reducing to a determinate form those collections which, in their present unsettled state, leave open so wide a field for contention?

Situation of Annuitants.—We have already explained in our second chapter, that as to land and houses the fluctuations in price during the war, were, in a great measure, nominal; that it was, in general, money that changed, and commodities that maintained their value. This maintenance of value was exemplified in many other respects; in income derived from personal exertion, whether in the shape of wages, salaries, or professional fees; in each, the money received was increased in proportion, or nearly in proportion, to the decrease of its value, the whole exhibiting a tendency in the transactions of life, to find their level, and to counterbalance all artificial changes, whether arising from additional taxes, the non-convertibility of paper-currency, or the restriction of national intercourse. But "from the benefit of this tendency to equality, of this antidote to enhancement, the fixed annuitants are excluded;" they are unable to guard against a progressive decline of income during a war; and the recovery of income which may indirectly take place at a peace, will hardly prove an indemnity to them if it arise, as at present, from circumstances which bear hard on the solvency of other classes. Are we not, therefore, justified in inferring, that the case of the annuitant, as it stands at present, is unnatural, and at variance with the rules of equity; and may we not conclude that, by conferring on money income the stability attendant on income derived from labour or real property, we shall correct an essential defect in our institutions?

Money-property in the Kingdom — Magnitude of its Amount. — We proceed to calculate the amount of money-property in the kingdom, — the property that would be beneficially affected, or relieved from uncertainty of value, by the adoption of such a measure. In former ages, when the funding system was unknown, and loans of money from one individual to another were of very limited extent, land, houses, furniture, implements and clothing, comprised almost every description of property: they constituted " the moveables and immoveables" of our ancient statutes. But within the last century, there has arisen in the public funds, in canals, docks, and other undertakings, held in shares, as well as in private loans, (on mortgages and otherwise), a property *represented solely in money,* of which the aggregate approaches to two-fifths of the total wealth of the kingdom.

Thus, were we to compute the land, the houses,

the farming, the manufacturing, the mercantile stock of Great Britain and Ireland at 2,000,000,000*l.* (see Appendix, p. [82]), we should not be disposed to rate our public funds, the amount of loans existing between individuals, the value of shares in public works, in short, all property of which the value is directly affected by the rise or fall of money, at less than 1,200,000,000*l.* Though of this sum the greater part can hardly be called an addition to the national property, the whole is evidently individual property; and its amount is demonstrative of the magnitude of that income, which is most exposed to suffer by fluctuation of prices.

SECTION II.

Plan for lessening the Injury arising from the Fluctuation of Prices.

IF we proceed to analyze the use of money, whether for national or individual purposes, we shall find it resolve itself into " the power of purchase," or, in other words, into the power of procuring articles for consumption. It is consequently of much more importance in all contracts of duration to look to the *value* than to the numerical amount of a given sum. The expediency of this has long been felt, and the price of corn has been recommended as a standard of regulation in regard to leases and other time contracts. Such it, in some measure, may be in a country like France, where the majority of the lower orders are strangers to the use of foreign articles, such as groceries, and expend literally three-fourths of their wages on bread. The price of corn is farther of importance in that country in an indirect sense, from its influence on the price of labour, as manual labour is there made to perform much more in agriculture, and even in manufactures, than with us : the whole exemplifying the doctrine of Dr. Smith, who assumed labour as the measure of value, and corn as the measure of labour.

The case of France is that of the Continent at

large, and was that of our ancestors a century ago; our situation, however, is now materially altered, our consumption of corn having undergone a comparative reduction, while manual labour enters in a proportion far smaller than formerly into the cost of our manufactures.

That corn occupies a very different proportion in the expenditure of different classes, will be apparent from a short comparative table.

Heads of Expenditure. (See Appendix, p. [11].)	Family of a Cottager; Expence about £37 a Year. Proportions in 100.	Family of the middle Class, residing in a Provincial Town, Expence £370 a Year. Proportions in 100.
Provisions - - -	60	33
Clothing and Washing	20	18
House-rent - -	6½	10
Fuel and Light -	10	6
Other charges, namely, Wages, Assessed Taxes, Education, Medical Attendance, &c.	3½	33
	100	100

This sketch, brief as it is, puts in a very clear light the difference between the wants of the lower and those of the middle and upper classes. To the latter, corn is evidently ineligible as a standard of value. In a direct sense, it forms hardly a third of their expenditure, and though, on making allowance for its indirect operation, in particular for its effect on wages, we become more aware of its importance, it will hardly be denied, that in an age of such varied and refined expenditure, a standard of a more comprehensive character, ought if possible to be adopted. Now, the pro-

gress of statistics, and the multiplication of official
returns within the last half-century, have supplied
data which, in the time of Dr. Smith, were not accounted reducible to a definite form. Of this,
some idea may be formed from a table in the Appendix (p. [95]) comprising a list of articles of
general consumption, corn, butcher-meat, manufactures, tropical products, &c. and containing the
probable amount of money expended on each by
the public. This table is followed by explanatory
remarks, of which the object is to show that contracts for a series of years ought to be made with
a reference to the power of money in purchasing
the necessaries and comforts of life ; that after
fixing a given sum, say 100*l.* as the amount of an
annual salary, the payment in subsequent years
should be not necessarily 100*l.*, but either 95*l.*,
100*l.*, or 105*l.*, according to the varying power of
money in making purchases.

Being aware of the uncertainty of calculations,
when unsupported by official returns ; as well as
that to give to a table the authority requisite to
constitute it a regulator of the value of money,
must be a work of much time and labour, we
decline inserting our list in the text, and confine
ourselves to an enquiry in regard to the means of
obtaining the

*Documents for the Formation of a Table of Refer-
ence.* — As yet our official returns are scanty, or
rather the use made of them has been on a confined scale : enough, however, has been done
to show the practicability of obtaining the information we desire. Thus, in regard to corn,
the registers, both as to price and quantity,
are now on a more satisfactory footing than in

former years : of sugar, a similar record has long been kept, and there are also registers, which might easily be rendered more complete, of our woollen and linen manufactures. Of the consumption of all excised articles, estimates approaching to correctness may be formed from documents in possession of that Board ; while in regard to foreign commodities, the custom-house would supply similar results. Then, as to average prices, there are the Books of the Victualling Office, of the Commissariat department, and of public hospitals, such as Greenwich. The Board of Agriculture has at various times obtained information, not strictly official, but substantially correct, by sending circular letters to their correspondents throughout the kingdom ; a plan acted on to a great extent by the late Arthur Young, in 1811.

Returns of this nature, when obtained, might easily be reduced into the tabular form on the plan of the late Mr. Colquhoun, but with more selection and discrimination. Since the date of his calculations (1812), great changes have occurred in respect both to price and quantity, and to complete the collections with the accuracy requisite to form a document of authority would require an extent of labour beyond the means of an individual. A task of such length, and of such general utility, should be defrayed from a common fund, and government, if unwilling to give so direct a sanction to a new project, as would be implied by the appointment of persons for collecting and comparing materials, would, doubtless, on the demand of any respectable association, communicate from the public offices all returns applicable to the subject.

For the details of the table, and the calculations connected with it, we refer to the Appendix : at present we shall, for the sake of illustration, suppose it in operation, and bestow a few paragraphs on the effects that the adoption of such a measure would have on the great interests of the country.

In what, it may be asked, would the benefits of it consist? In ascertaining on grounds that would admit of no doubt or dispute, the power in purchase of any given sum in one year, compared to its power of purchase in another. And what would be the practical application of this knowledge? The correction of a long list of anomalies in regard to rents, salaries, wages, &c., arising out of unforeseen fluctuations in our currency. In the present undefined form of leases, annuities, and other time contracts, the 100*l.* of this year may, three years hence, be equivalent in power of purchase, either to 110*l.* or to 90*l.*, the former being probable, if peace continue, while the latter is a moderate estimate of the change that would follow the first year of a war. So much are the chances on the side of fluctuation, in the value of money, that it may almost be said, that, " in a contract of duration, an adherence to a fixed sum of money implies an acquiescence under a change of value." But a table exhibiting from year to year the power of money in purchase, would give to annuitants and other contracting parties, the means of maintaining an agreement, not in its letter only, but in its spirit ; of conferring on a specified sum a uniformity and permanency of value, by *changing the numerical amount in proportion to the change in its power of purchase.*

It does not follow from this, that a change of

numerical amount ought to be annual : it would, in general, be sufficient that it took place at periods of three, four, or five years, taking as the criterion the average value of money in purchases throughout the whole period.

Effect on the labouring Classes of the adoption of such a Standard.—The use of money to the country labourer is very simple, extending to little beyond the purchase of the articles mentioned in the preceding sketch of his annual expenditure. In the case of the inhabitants of towns, the proportion required for house-rent, fuel and clothing is somewhat larger, while that for provisions is somewhat smaller than in the family of the cottager. To both, the chief object of expence is corn, the average price of which is already ascertained periodically; but to render the table complete, our wish would be that the average of the other articles consumed by the labouring classes, such as beer, coarse clothing, fuel, were in like manner put on record. If to such returns were added a few plain tables of the average consumption of the lower class in various situations, one for an unmarried labourer, others for a labourer married, and having two, three, or four children, it would be an easy process to calculate how far a given sum of wages (for example 45*l.* annually) was more or less adequate than in former years to the supply of such wants. We should then possess completely the means of judging of the comparative comfort of the working classes; of making, in a manner satisfactory and conclusive, the calculations hitherto prepared with much labour, and an unavoidable share of error, by Sir F. Eden, Mr. Barton, and others.

How important would such a standard of reference have been throughout the last thirty years, a period of such frequent contention between the employer and the employed! During the war, workmen in towns were repeatedly obliged to combine for the purpose of raising their wages to the level of provisions, and in rural districts, where combination was impracticable, the poor-rate was called in to supply the deficiency. At present the case is reversed ; the employer, particularly when resident in a town, has found, and will long find it a matter of great difficulty to reduce wages to the standard justified by the fall of provisions.

What a scene of inequality is exhibited at present by the current payments of the metropolis! Wages, salaries, professional fees, are almost all on as high a scale as during the war, notwithstanding the diminution of the two great causes of rise,—the expence of living and the extra demand for labour. The persons, whether of high or low station, who are in receipt of the established allowances, if called on for an abatement, would naturally plead the uncertainty of provisions continuing at a reduced rate : and nothing, it is evident, will induce them willingly to assent to a reduction, except a guarantee against a recurrence of the grand evil — a rise of prices without a correspondent rise in wages. Such a guarantee we should hope to afford, not by an interference between the payer and receiver, but by an alternative offered to their voluntary adoption ; by putting it in their power, when making a time contract, to affix a permanent value to a money stipulation ; or to have access, when no such precaution was taken, to an equitable standard of reference.

What would be the probable effect of having this authenticated record of the price of commodities, this monitor to declare the rise or fall in the value of money? It could hardly fail to operate greatly in abridging altercations. At a time when a reduction of wages became expedient, it would relieve the inferior from the humiliation attendant on such a step ; and, in the case of a rise of prices, it would guide the employer to a fair advance of wages, the distributor of charitable aid to a fair apportionment of relief.

Effect of such a Measure on Agriculture. — In no department of our productive industry has our progress as a nation been less conspicuous than in tillage ; our superiority over our continental neigh-bours being in a great degree limited to our live-stock and our machinery. On computing the annual amount of property created in the kingdom, we find, after making a great deduction from the prices (moderate as they were, considering the state of markets at the time) assumed by Mr. Colquhoun, that the annual produce of the agriculture of Great Britain and Ireland still amounts to 120,000,000*l.* What a field is there here for the application of skill and judgment, and how great the call for both in the present situation of our agriculturists !

Leases. — It is not a little remarkable, that several of the counties, such as Norfolk and Northumber-land, in which our husbandry is most improved, are by no means our most fertile districts naturally. To what, then, are they indebted for their supe-riority? To a cause which Mr. Coke has repeatedly pressed on his brother land-holders, both in and out of parliament, —that there is *no good agricul-ture without leases.* In what other way can we ex-plain the high rents paid in a country in general so little favoured in soil and climate as Scotland? The objections of our landlords to long leases, are various, arising partly from the habits of their predecessors; partly from a reluctance to part with the command of their property for a number of years; but, more than all, from the uncertainty of the value of money. During the war this uncertainty was of very serious import: at present it is removed, as far as regards landlords, by the return to cash payments, and the difficulty now is to induce a solvent tenant to take a lease. To both parties, therefore, the fluctuation of our currency, even when metallic, is replete with anxiety.

Corn-rents. — Of late, the great fall of price has induced several of our principal land-holders to regulate their rents by the price of corn; a plan open to many objections, when varied from year to year, because, a season of high price may be, and generally is, a season of deficient produce. When calculated on the price of a series of years, this course is less exceptionable: in any form, however, it seems less eligible than the plan which (Appendix, p. [98]) we are desirous to propose, of combining the price of corn with that of other articles of consumption.

Tithe. — Referring to the remarks under this head in the Appendix, we shall at present merely observe, how great would be the benefit accruing from a regulating standard, applied to clerical income, and calculated, as far as regards permanency of value, to justify the church in commuting tithe for a money stipend. A change of that nature would, on the one hand, put an end to altercations unfortunately too frequent; while, on the other, it would prevent tithe from operating as an impediment to agricultural improvement. The great, and, at present, well-founded objection of the clergy to a permanent commutation of tithe, is a dread, not of the faith of parliament, but of the uncertain value of money : remove that apprehension, and you give them substantial motives to prefer a fixed sum, whether they look to the interest of themselves or their successors. In the Protestant church of Holland, they have an example of stipends paid during more than two centuries, by local magistrates or by government, without any derogation from the respectability of those who received them : and if in France the amount of clerical income be too small to be dwelt on when we are treating of a Protestant establishment, the regularity of its payment during twenty years, under circumstances of great financial embarrassment, is calculated to lessen one material ground of apprehension.

The commutation to which we allude does not, of course, imply any reduction of the existing income of the clerical body, nor a relinquishment of any security arising from the tenure by which they are at present invested with tithe. A change from an unfixed to a fixed money income, may evidently take place without interfering either with such security, or with the patronage of the church as at present established. It might be proposed as a temporary arrangement, to last only during the interval required to carry into effect a plan that has been more than once proposed, and which has lately received a kind of legislative recommendation — the purchase of land for the purpose of affording the church a revenue from rent instead of tithe. But on this we will not enlarge, our subject naturally confining us to the operation of the measure with a view to the relief of the agriculturists ; a view in which it would soon disclose satisfactory results.

Under our present system, the church is entitled to an increase of revenue *in proportion to the increase of produce ;* such, we may safely take for granted, would form no part of its demand under a different arrangement. All that its representatives would be likely to desire, would be an assurance that the contract should be maintained *bonâ fide*, that the sum once fixed should be made good, whatever be the fluctuations of our currency. And what would be the result to the agriculturists of tithe being thus limited ? That all, whether landlords or farmers, might extend their tillage as they chose, without being annually taxed in a portion of the produce. Our numbers are on the increase ; our production increases with them, and it is, above all, in a case of such increase, that the pressure of tithe is felt. An exemption from such pressure is most strongly called for by our situation, present and prospective ; and may we not add, that when viewed in connexion with the various circumstances stated in our chapter on Agriculture, it would render probable a result, on which, at present, it seems somewhat bold to speculate? we mean Mr. Tooke's idea of the practicability of our competing with foreigners in the export of corn, as was done by our countrymen previous to 1764.

Application of the proposed Plan to the Public Funds. — To offer any suggestion connected with the public funds is, we are aware, to tread on delicate ground, men in office being very properly backward to interfere, in even a slight degree, with the existing contract with the fund-holder. We shall, however, satisfy the most cautious, by premising that the acceptance of the plan should be

optional on the part of each stock-holder, although
we can have little doubt of the beneficial tendency
of a measure, the effect of which would be to en-
sure to the stock-holder and his posterity, the same
income, whether the country was at peace or war ;
whether its currency were sound or depreciated ;
whether the mines of gold and silver throughout
the world, became more or less productive. The
100*l.* of 1792, which in 1806 was equivalent to
80*l.*, and seven years after, to less than 70*l.*, would
thus remain 100*l.* throughout. The apprehensions
which at present not unfrequently lead to sales of
stock against the wish of the holders, would cease
or be materially diminished, and funded, like landed property, would be seldom disposed of, except
on particular occasions, such as when a division of
property became expedient on the demise of a tes-
tator, on legatees attaining majority, or on their
entering on mercantile business. In fact, after the
adoption of such a measure, the chief features of
distinction between land and stock, would be, that
while the one possessed the attraction of local influence, the other would have the more direct advantage of dispatch and certainty in regard to receipt of income.

The present is, we believe, the first proposition
of a measure for giving a permanent value to our
funded property. Our public men, or rather the
few among them who are accustomed to take comprehensive views of finance, have hitherto contemplated a very different course. Money, they saw,
was declining in value during half a century, and
funded property declined with it; a fall carefully
kept by them in the back ground, and consequently
in a great measure unknown to the public. Our
successive chancellors of the exchequer antici-

pated (see p. 300.) a continuance of this decline, and silently calculated on its producing a diminution in the pressure of our debt. But the re-action of the last eight years has greatly shaken this calculation : money has recovered, and along with that recovery, the pressure of our debt has greatly increased. It is time, therefore, to seek relief in a measure of a different character.

Its Effect on the Price of Stocks.—Nothing can be more different than a rise of stock caused by the adoption of a plan such as we propose, and a rise that might be consequent on the operation of a large sinking fund. The latter would be liable, as we shall show in our chapter on Finance, (p. 360.) to various objections : in particular, it would afford a strong inducement to sell out and to vest capital in other securities, probably in foreign stock. But a rise proceeding from a course such as we are anxious to recommend, would prove an inducement to keep capital in our funds, the value conferred by the measure being, in its nature, permanent and likely to increase.

Consequent Advantage to the Public.—This brings us to a question, which, under present circumstances, may very naturally be asked by our readers,—why confer additional value on the funds, at a time when they have risen so considerably in the scale of comparison with land, houses, and merchandize? Our answer is, that we contemplate no undue favour to the stock-holder ; we merely point out a measure, which, by benefiting him in the first instance, may give government a fair plea to demand from him a return calculated to afford relief to other classes of the community. To require such from the fund-holder without a consideration, would, of course, imply a sacrifice on his part, but the results which we anticipate from the proposed measure, will, if they be well founded, confer on him in one way as much as he may be called on to relinquish in the other. Thus, if it continue a favourite object with ministers to reduce the interest on the old four per cents., nothing is so likely to promote that measure, as conferring an additional value on funded property. And if it be said that such would be a return partial and inadequate to the advantage conferred, the discussion may be cut short by the general argument, that if the legislature improve materially the circumstances of the fund-holder, or of any great class in the community, there can be no great difficulty in rendering that prosperity conducive to the relief of the public at large.

All this may be admitted, but the plan, it will be said, can be adopted by the governments of other countries, and our stocks soon deprived of any relative superiority which it might confer. Our answer is, that the success of such a plan, and the extent of rise attendant on its adoption, will depend chiefly on the degree of confidence that each nation has in its government; a point in which we possess a great and undoubted superiority over the rest of Europe.

General Remarks.—We conclude this chapter by a few remarks on the general characteristics of the proposed plan. Does it, it may be asked, contain any thing compulsory or unfair, and in particular, does it imply the imposition of any burden on posterity? Our posterity will, in all probability, be in a far easier condition than ourselves, and would incur no loss from our conferring the character of permanent value on our dividends: on the contrary, they will (see p. 404.) be benefited by whatever shall be found conducive to the relief of the present generation. Our proposition may be considered an attempt to fill up a blank in the mode of regulating our productive industry, and to do it in a way not fanciful or artificial, but on the principles of unreserved freedom so strongly recommended by Dr. Smith and other eminent authorities. But the use to be made of it would be perfectly optional. It would be in itself merely a table of reference, and all contracts, whether relative to loans, leases, or bequests, might, at the will of the parties, be made payable, either according to the proposed standard, or, as at present, in money of undefined value.

Our preceding pages explain the operation of the proposed plan in respect to individuals. In regard to its result in a national sense, we may be allowed to anticipate that the removal of uncertainty from time contracts would contribute very effectually to the extension of our national industry. That industry and its results have been carried farther by us than by almost any of our neighbours, but they are still far from having reached a limit. Circumstances have of late become more favourable and the pressure of taxation less heavy ; but great exertions will still be requisite to carry our national income to an amount corresponding with our burdens; that is, to increase it so that the proportion of our taxation to our resources shall not be greater than in other countries.

How far, it may be asked, has the proposition brought forward in this chapter the sanction of precedent? That sanction, though it cannot be cited as of frequent occurrence, is not altogether wanting. The course now suggested, is analogous to the plan of corn rents lately adopted by several of our great proprietors, and which, for many years has been exemplified in the proceedings of the Court of Teinds, or tithe, in Scotland. The decisions of that court purport that clerical income shall be regulated by the price of corn in the public markets during a series of years. But were precedent wholly wanting, the rule, " that prospective engagements should be framed so as to maintain their *bonâ fide* value, whatever be the value of money," is so equitable, and apparently so easy of execution, that there seems no little difficulty in accounting for its not yet having found its way into practice. This has, we believe, been owing to two causes; the unfortunate neglect of political economy in the education of our public men; and the interest of government, the greatest of all debtors, to prevent the public from fixing its attention on the gradual depreciation of money that went on during the half century previous to the late peace.

CHAP. XI.

Our Finances.

WE now approach the end of our volume, and have arrived at the department which forms at present the chief object of public attention. In this, as in the former chapters, we shall begin by a statement of facts, a retrospect to past events, and after removing, or endeavouring to remove, several popular errors, we shall proceed to develope the measures apparently best adapted to our present situation, greatly altered, as it has been, by the events consequent on peace.

We propose dividing our discussion into the following heads : —

A historical sketch of finance operations ;

Our prospects in regard to trade and national income ;

The views of finance suggested by such prospects.

SECTION I.

Our National Debt.

A public debt in one form or other, has been, in almost every country, an appendage of established government. Its amount, however, seldom exceeded an anticipation of one or two years' revenue, until the adoption of the funding system, or plan of rendering public obligations transferable from hand to hand, gave governments a surprising facility in borrowing. This, like many other ingenious schemes, both in civil and military affairs, originated with the Italians, and was adopted early in Venice, Genoa, and Holland. In England, it was not introduced until our participation in the great struggle made by King William against the aggrandizement of Louis XIV.; but if we were somewhat late in following the example, in our ultimate progress we have far surpassed our neighbours. Our debt amounted,

At the peace of Ryswick	-	in	1697	to -	£21,500,000
of Utrecht	-	-	1713	-	54,000,000
of Aix la Chapelle	-		1748	-	78,000,000
of Paris	-	-	1763	-	134,000,000
of Versailles	-	-	1783	-	238,000,000
of Amiens	-	-	1802	-	452,000,000
of Paris	-	-	1815	nearly	700,000,000

To which, adding the debt of Ireland, somewhat
more than - - - - 100,000,000
_____

Total present debt about - 800,000,000
_____

These sums represent the total of our debt at each period, without the perplexing distinctions of funded and unfunded, redeemed and unredeemed. Though the figures express an amount, not of money but of stock, the difference at *peace prices* is not much more than nominal : thus, our present debt, were it practicable to pay it off at the market price, would require an amount in money, not greatly below the 800,000,000*l.* of stock. But as there is no more reason to anticipate the liquidation of the debt of this than of other countries, the more correct course, and that which conveys the more distinct idea of the extent of the burden, is to follow the French method of computing, not by the principal, but by the sum required to pay the interest; a sum which, since the reduction of the Five per cents., may be called, in round numbers, 30,000,000*l*.

Fluctuations in the Price of Stock. — By fluctuations in stock, we must be understood to mean changes proceeding, not from the rumours perpetually in circulation on the Stock Exchange, which are too absurd for notice, and operate only for a few days, but from causes of a more comprehensive and permanent character ; — the credit or discredit of government ; scarcity or abundance of capital ; the adequacy or inadequacy of our resources to our burdens. The extent of fluctuation, has, of course, been very great at different periods of our history. During the long peace that followed the treaty of Utrecht, and under the prudent administration of Walpole, stocks rose greatly, the three per cents. having attained par in 1732, and being, in 1739, the time when that minister was forced by popular clamour to declare war against Spain, at the very high rate of 107*l*. in cash for 100*l*. in stock. They continued high during several years of the war ; and it was not until the range of hostilities widened, and assumed a serious aspect, that their fall became great. The same may be said to have applied to the more successful contest begun in 1756, the three per cents continuing between 70*l*. and 80*l*., until 1760, when our loans, in consequence of the national ardour and the confident character of Lord Chatham, were carried to an amount at that time unprecedented. In the American war the fall was more serious : it was great from the time that France took part against us, and the public became aware of the inability of our ministers to conduct the contest with success.

Mr. Pitt's Administration. — It was in 1784 that Mr. Pitt succeeded to his financial charge, and found it during several years productive of great contention and embarrassment. Our prospects, however, gradually brightened, and ere the expiration of the ten years of peace that preceded the war of 1793, the nation had risen superior to its difficulties. This was the æra of the so-much applauded revival of the sinking fund. Partly by the effect of that measure, more by the general prosperity of the country, our 3 per cents were carried in 1792 to the high price of 97; a price from which they fell as soon as the public became aware that our government had determined to take part in the coalition against France. But as during the first two years of the war our expences were comparatively limited, the great decline did not take place until 1796, or rather 1797, when the 3 per cents. sunk to the unexampled low rate of 47. It was then that our minister felt the necessity of altering his financial plan, of lessening loans and augmenting taxes : he came forward accordingly with the bold proposition of raising a large proportion of the supplies within the year ; a course which, alarmed as the nation was at the aggrandizement of France, obtained general concurrence, and soon received a consolidated form by the imposition of the income or property-tax.

In consequence of this decided measure, and of the splendid success of our continental allies in 1799, our stocks revived, but they fell towards the close of the year, when the fickle Paul forsook the coalition, and Bonaparte, arriving from Egypt, gave new vigour to the resources of France. Large loans became again indispensable, and our funds continued comparatively low, until the signature of the preliminaries in October 1801. That event had a tendency to reinstate them, but the peace was too short and too doubtful to admit of any great rise.

War of 1803. —On the renewal of war in 1803, the 3 per cents. fell from 70 to 57, and during some time, the general dread of invasion kept them at a very low rate. War taxes, however, were cheerfully submitted to, and in the succeeding years (1805, 6, 7.), these potent auxiliaries enabled government to lessen the loans, and to raise the three per cents. to 60 and upwards. The same cause explains their continued high price in 1808, a year of commercial distress, and in 1809, a season of general over-trading. Nor was it till the multiplied bankruptcies of 1810, and the heavy drain of money for the peninsular war, that the fall became considerable. Large loans were now unavoidable, and stocks were lowered not only in 1812, a year of chequered fortune to our arms, but during part of 1813, when our prospects were equally cheering in Spain and Germany. At last the balance inclined to the favourable side : the victory of Leipsic, and the evident superiority of the allies, outweighed the demands of our Treasury, enormous as they had become.

From 1815 *to* 1822. — In the early part of 1815 the 3 per cents were fluctuating from 62 to 65, when the return of Bonaparte from Elba, produced a very sudden reduction. In the contest that ensued, government were unluckily obliged to contract for a loan early in June, and were thus deprived of the benefit of the rise which immediately followed the success of our arms. In 1816, peace was consolidated, but the price of commodities experienced a great fall, and much distress prevailing in both trade and agriculture, the funds recovered very slowly. In 1817, appearances improved, and in the early part of 1818 the 3 per cents. having risen above 80, our prospect became very encouraging. Unfortunately the rise was not of long duration : the mismanagement of the French loan, the over-trading in this country, the distress of the United States of America, all concurred to depress the funds. They continued low during the two years from the summer of 1819 to that of 1821, after which, they gradually improved so as to enable ministers to carry into effect an important and long contemplated operation. *

Reduction of the Five per Cents. — The five per cents. comprised a sum, which in round numbers we shall call 140,000,000*l.*, and which government were at any time at liberty to pay off, by giving 100*l.* in cash for 100*l.* in stock. How then, it may be asked, did it happen that the discharge was delayed so long after the peace ? Because the

* Average Prices of the 3 per Cent. Consols during the following years : —

1803	70, 57, 53.	1813	58, 57, 60, 61.
1804	55, 56, 58.	1814	64, 66, 64.
1805	56, 58, 60.	1815	65, after Mar. 58, 60.
1806	60, 62, 64.	1816	60, 62, 63.
1807	61, 62, 64.	1817	63, 70, 75, 83.
1808	62, 64, 66, 68.	1818	80, 82, 79.
1809	67, 68, 70.	1819	77, 74, 65, 70, 68.
1810	70, 71, 69, 66.	1820	68, 69, 70.
1811	65, 64, 63.	1821	69, 72, 75, 77.
1812	62, 61, 59, 58.	1822 (to Aug.)	76, 77, 78, 80.

discharge of so large a sum could take place only by the substitution of one security for another; and as the new fund to be created, would, in most of the years that have elapsed since the peace, have fetched an indifferent price, ministers were from time to time obliged to postpone the measure. In the early part of 1818, circumstances becoming favourable, a new stock bearing 3½ per cent. interest, and not reducible below that rate during ten years, was created evidently for the purpose of supplying the desired substitute. The project, however, failed, in consequence of the general fall of funded property, and there afterwards occurred no favourable opportunity until the beginning of the present year, when, as is well known, the reduction was very successfully accomplished.

There remains open to reduction a farther portion of our stock, viz. the old four per cents, which distinguished from the four per cents created in the present year, amount to about 70,000,000*l.* This sum is considerable, but in other respects the question of reduction stands on very doubtful grounds. The saving of a half per cent. in the interest would give only about 300,000*l.* clear, and it seems very doubtful at what period the course of circumstances will admit of even that diminution.

Our other Financial Measures. — The course contemplated by government at the close of the war, was to keep up an efficient sinking fund, and to continue during several years the property-tax on the reduced scale of 5 per cent. This plan fell to the ground on the rejection of that tax by the House of Commons on the 18th March, 1816; a rejection altogether unexpected by ministers, and which was afterwards declared by them to have been productive of great public injury. To this opinion though expressed deliberately, and long after the first impression of disappointment, we can by no means subscribe. Had the burden been inevitable, and had the question been merely a commutation of one payment for another, a property-tax might have been somewhat less oppressive than several of the existing imposts; but, under all the circumstances of the case, the rejection of the bill was, we are satisfied, productive of public good. Men in office, immersed in a routine of business, are often very imperfectly apprized of the circumstances of particular portions of the community. In the session immediately preceding, they had, by the magnitude of their grants, shown themselves unconscious of the extent of the loss attendant on the transition from war to peace; of the approaching fall of prices, the increasing pressure of taxation. To all this they were awakened by the loss of the bill, and taught, for the first time in twenty years, the necessity of negativing the importunate demands to which the holders of office are perpetually exposed. Besides, a property-tax, had it been imposed in 1816, would have been productive, distressing as was the time that followed, of loud complaint, perhaps of serious and general injury.

The next financial measure of importance took place in 1819, when ministers having called on parliament to give efficiency to the sinking fund, proposed and carried a measure little expected in the midst of peace,—the imposition of new taxes to the amount of 3,000,000*l.* These were imposed chiefly on malt, spirits, and tobacco, and paid with great reluctance during the interval of doubt and embarrassment which ensued. Of late, however, brighter prospects have opened, and a diminution of expenditure has been promoted by a concurrence of causes, — tranquillity among our lower orders; the reduction of the 5 per cents; and the transfer of a portion of our half-pay and pension list to the next generation. The consequence has been important and gratifying — a reduction of taxes in the last two years to the amount of 6,000,000*l.*

The Sinking Fund.

The idea of a Sinking Fund is of old date, having been conceived more than a century ago, by Sir R. Walpole, the only public man of his age who appears to have been conversant with finance. Its plan was simple, the fund being formed in the first instance of a small sum of surplus revenue, and augmented progressively by the interest of such part of the debt as was paid off by its operation. Here was no display of the wonders of compound interest, but the long peace that ensued favoured the reduction of debt, and the fund, though small, was progressively increasing. Such continued the course of circumstances until 1733, when the troubled aspect of the Continent, and the difficulty of imposing new taxes, necessitated an interference with some disposable resource, and the sinking fund was encroached on. A precedent once given, trespasses became frequent, and this fund, though never abolished, proved of so slender operation, that in the course of *half a century* it had not discharged above 15,000,000*l.* of our debt. At last, in 1786, the scheme was revived with augmented energy, aided on the one hand by Dr. Price's flattering calculations of the effect of compound interest, on the other by Mr. Pitt's declared determination to consider its funds inviolable. The new plan was in substance the same as that of Sir R. Walpole, but the reserve was invested with many additional safeguards, being committed to a special board of commissioners who were independent, not merely of the Treasury, but in some respects of Parliament.

It was at this time that the public first became familiar with the term " Consolidated Fund," which meant, however, nothing more than our taxes formed into an aggregate, out of which government pledged itself, whatever might be the proportion of our revenue to our expenditure, to pay a million annually to the new commissioners.

The sinking fund consisted consequently of

1. An annual million, to which were added :

2. The amount of government annuities as they successively expired ; and

3. The interest of such stock as was annually redeemed.

The measure now brought into operation, paid off the following sums :

In 1787	£ 662,750 Stock.		In 1790	£1,558,850 Stock.
1788	1,456,900		1791	1,587,500
1789	1,506,350		1792	1,507,110

These sums, small as they were, could hardly be considered *bonâ fide* reductions of the public debt, since the Spanish armament in 1790 necessitated an addition to our burdens of nearly half their amount. In an arithmetical sense, accordingly, the effect was inconsiderable ; in a political sense it was otherwise, as it excited the expectation of great subsequent deductions. To strengthen this expectation, and to remove an apprehension that a renewal of war, by necessitating new loans, might cast these annual liquidations into the shade, Mr.

Pitt obtained, in 1792, an act of parliament declaring that all future loans should carry in themselves the means of their progressive extinction, ministers, on contracting a loan, being pledged to " provide taxes, not only for the interest but for an addition to the sinking fund." This provision, whether in reality judicious or not, was very favourably received by the public, and had, in concurrence with the commercial prosperity of the year, the effect of producing a very considerable rise in the funds.

But this flattering prospect was forthwith overcast by our participation in the war against France, and the unparalleled magnitude of our expence. The sinking fund was maintained, and operated a large apparent reduction, but the result, in a definitive sense, was null, our debt being augmented by our annual loans in a far greater *ratio*. After all that we have been told of the operation of the sinking fund; after the pompous statements of hundreds of millions redeemed by it; after all the eloquent effusions in its praise by both sides of the House, the public will learn with some surprise, that since 1786, this fund has had a real operation during twelve years only, and that the *actual reduction* effected by it, has not averaged a single million a year! In this we are to be understood, as leaving the twenty-three years of war wholly out of the question, and confining our calculation to the six years preceding 1793, and the six years subsequent to 1815.

Compound Interest. — The surprising results ascribed in our time to compound interest will be cited by the future historian, as affording a striking example of the power of enthusiasm in the original calculator, and of the extent of credulity on the part of the public. In war, the sinking fund is supported by loans, and is it not apparent, that whatever may be the beneficial result of accumulation in the hands of the commissioners of the sinking fund, the loss to the public from the additional loans required by it must be in the same compound *ratio ?* We might even add, that in all cases of taxation, where the impost has not (and it very rarely has) the effect of inducing economy in the individual, the loss is to be reckoned by compound interest, since, had the money been left in the hands of the subject, the increase would have been in the compound form.

Without entering into any arithmetical statement, or even pressing the argument in an abstract form, we may safely make the general assertion, that the power of the sinking fund, whatever it may have been, has arisen " not from actual payments, but from its influence on the public mind;" — from its presenting a *possibility* of an ultimate repayment of the debt;—a possibility transformed into confident expectation by the ardour of the public and our natural inclination to believe what we wish.

Present State of the Sinking Fund. — Such was the state of our financial concerns until the beginning of 1822, when, by the double effect of reduction of expenditure and increase of revenue, an actual surplus was produced, and the sinking fund was likely to become efficient to the extent of 4 or 5,000,000*l.* a year. We seemed now on the eve of attaining the result so long represented as desirable by ministers ; the possession of an engine for raising the price of stocks, or, in other words, for reducing the rate of interest on private securities. In what manner, it may be asked, would the latter prove a consequence of the former ? In France, where the interest of the public debt does not form 10 per cent. of the income arising from property, and government securities do not command general confidence, the interest of money vested in land, houses, and trade, is not materially affected by the price of the public funds. Land continues to be bought with eagerness, though yielding only 3, $3\frac{1}{2}$, or 4 per cent. on the purchase money, at a time when the same capital would yield between 5 and 6 per cent. in the funds. In this country the case is otherwise. Our public dividends form a considerable proportion of the income arising from property; they are held by individuals in all parts of the country; and their value naturally influences that of other investments of capital. It follows that a rise in the price of stock, in other words, our obtaining less interest from purchasing in the funds, has a direct tendency to lower the interest on private securities, as has been exemplified by the general diminution of the interest on mortgages during the last and present year.

What, in a statistical sense, are the characteristics or accompaniments of a low rate of interest? It is indicative of abundant capital, and of a very advanced state of productive industry. It was this which formed the great feature in the situation of Holland during the chief part of the 17th and 18th centuries, and enabled her government to lower her dividends at a time (1654) when France and other states borrowed at very high interest. It was this which, under Sir R. Walpole, afforded the strongest proof of the revival of our financial credit, and which in 1749 enabled Mr. Pelham to effect a well-known and highly beneficial reduction. But, neither in these cases, or in any other of which history has preserved the record, did the fall of interest proceed from the *operation of a sinking fund.* It rested on a much broader basis : it was the natural consequence of confirmed peace ; of the diminished demand for capital ; of a fall, or tendency to fall, in the rate of interest on all securities whether public or private ; it was to a concurrence of these circumstances, much more than to any surplus in the revenue, that we attributed the fortunate accomplishment of that great operation, the reduction of the five per cents.

If our readers see with some surprise these deductions from the efficiency of a measure so much vaunted, they will be no less struck with the farther part of our argument ; viz., that a large sinking fund, or, to describe it in the most simple terms, a large surplus revenue applied to the redemption of stock, would be *productive of public injury.* By lowering unnaturally the rate of interest, it would send capital abroad, and operate as a fund to raise the stocks of France or America. This result is too obvious to have escaped the observation of either the Bank directors or ministers : in fact, the readiness with which ministers consented both in the last and present year to relinquish their surplus revenue by remitting taxes, seems to indicate a conviction, that a rise in the value of stock, produced artificially, would be replete with injury to the public. They cannot fail to be aware, that since the reduction of the 5 per cents., there remains no adequate motive for interfering with the current rate of interest, or for discovering a solicitude on the part of government, to raise the value of the funds more than of land, or any other description of property. If, in commercial affairs, ministers have, during the last ten years, evinced a prudent forbearance, and abstained from the inter-

vention so unfortunately exercised by their predecessors, is it likely that in finance they will follow
a different course? Our debt will hardly admit
of direct reduction: our hope of relief is in that
diminution of pressure which will follow the increase of our means;—the augmentation of national income;—a result most likely to be promoted,
by strict impartiality as to property, whether vested
in land or the public funds.

But, if such be the conviction of our rulers,
why, it may be asked, do they still cling to a name,
and hold forth the sinking fund to parliament and
the country, as an institution entitled to such
zealous support? Partly, we believe, from a wish
to retain a surplus of revenue at their disposal,
for the relief of suffering interests, or to facilitate
measures of evident utility, such as the commutation of tithe in Ireland: partly perhaps, from
a deficient acquaintance with the backwardness of
other countries, and a consequent diffidence in calculating the relative progress of our own. Our
*true sinking fund is to be sought in the more rapid
increase of our national income,* an increase that
rests on no visionary basis, but on our mines, our
navigation, our capital. Yet no speaker in parliament, whether ministerialist or oppositionist, appears to have as yet studied the comparative
prospects of England and her neighbours, or to be
sufficiently aware of the inferences which they
justify.

The admissions successively made by the supporters of the sinking fund (Appendix, p. [103].)
have removed part of the mystery which, by the aid
of such phrases as "inviolability of deposit" and
"operation of compound interest," had so long
encircled it. Our present Chancellor of the Exche-

quer has had the good sense to relinquish the nominal part of the sinking fund, and to describe the remainder merely as a surplus revenue appropriated to the redemption of stock. As such we request our readers to consider it, and to enable them to compute its amount without unravelling a long list of finance papers, we subjoin an

Estimate of our Annual Expenditure for 1823 and 1824.

Half pay and pensions for the Army, Navy, and Ordnance, about -	£ 4,800,000	
Of which advanced by the Bank, nearly -	2,000,000	
Remainder to be paid out of the current revenue - - -		2,800,000
Army, exclusive of half pay and pensions - - -		7,000,000
Navy - - - -		5,500,000
Ordnance - - - -		1,200,000
Miscellaneous - - - -		1,500,000
Civil list; pensions for Civil Services; Courts of Justice; civil Government of Scotland, and some lesser heads, all charged on the Consolidated Fund. - - - -		2,000,000
Amount of expenditure distinct from the interest of the debt - - - - - -		20,000,000
Interest of the public debt - - - -		30,000,000
Total -		£ 50,000,000

Such is our present expenditure; and our *bonâ fide* sinking fund can, of course, be nothing else than the surplus of our income above it: it will be found to amount to three, four or more millions, according to the productiveness of the revenue.

The next and equally important question is, whether a surplus when found to exist, " ought to be applied to the redemption of stock, or made a ground for the further remission of taxes." We subscribe, without hesitation, to the latter, not merely for the sake of relief to the public, but on the less-understood ground of the injurious consequences of interfering with the price of stocks. Against this, however, it may be urged, that men of the most opposite views in politics have concurred in eulogising the sinking fund—that Mr. Fox, was, in this respect, no less zealous than his great antagonist. Mr. Fox, it is well known, never made a study of finance, still less of political economy; his conclusions in these, as in many other respects, when well founded, owed their justness less to continued research or careful comparison, than to rectitude of feeling, to a manliness of character, which, in a question like the present, would prompt him to adopt without much investigation that course, which should place the burden on the shoulders of ourselves, instead of our posterity. Again, Mr. Pitt, when he introduced the sinking fund, was only in his twenty-seventh year, and could not, from the pressure of other avocations, have been able to study very closely the operation of a surplus revenue, applied to the purchase of stock. He was necessarily unacquainted with the statistical returns which we possess, and which shall be more fully noticed in the following pages. He had before him no example of a measure tending, by unnatural interference with the rate of interest, to send capital out of the country: still less could he foresee the rapid increase of our numbers, the surprising extension of our productive industry, and the consequent motives for pursuing a system, the reverse of that which maintains a sinking fund—we mean, bearing light on the present generation, and transferring a portion of taxation to their less burdened successors.

If these remarks are at all useful in correcting popular misapprehension, we shall hope somewhat of a similar result from the following paragraphs, ralating to the situation of different classes of stockholders.

Stockholders : Distinction between Permanent and Temporary Depositors. — Those of our countrymen who have travelled and paid attention to topics of this nature, must have remarked that in France, Germany, Spain, in short, in every country on the Continent, except Holland, the public funds are comparatively little resorted to as a deposit for private property. The governments of these countries have not as yet acquired the confidence attached to a representative assembly, and the inhabitants are little acquainted with the security conferred on property by public register, the power of transfer, the steady observance of good faith towards the public creditor. Continental lenders require the visible, and, as they account it, solid security of land and houses. Such, a century and a half ago, was the case throughout England generally, and such, in no small degree, was the case in the provincial part of the kingdom at the beginning of the late war. The general ardour of our countrymen in the contest, their confidence in government, and the comparatively high interest then given by the Treasury, led to the deposit in that ready absorbent, of sums of which the magnitude would have startled the caution of our forefathers. The result of the whole is, that funded property so insignificant in a former age, when compared to the general wealth of the kingdom, is now of an amount approaching to the value of our land, particularly if we estimate it not by capital, but (see p. 258.) by income.

Annuitants on our public funds, instead of being confined, as in the last age, to London, Bristol, and a few of our principal towns, are now found in every district, and in every variety of occupation. The great majority of them are permanent depositors, strangers to the manœuvres of the stock exchange, speculating neither on buying or selling, and attentive merely to the half-yearly receipt of their dividends. These persons consider the stocks as a fund permanently eligible for themselves and their families, confiding, on the one hand, in the good faith of Parliament, and aware, on the other, of the serious drawbacks attendant on property in land and houses, — the difficulty of collecting rents, the heavy charge attendant on transfers. The funds, they are aware, involve neither delays nor lawsuits, while, with a view to bequest, they admit of an easy and direct repartition. It is in results such as these, that we recognize all the advantage of established institutions, of the steady observance of good faith on the part of government. Viewed in a national sense, they render a people capable of efforts such as those which maintained the independence of Holland against the successive attacks of Spain, England, and France : — Viewed in regard to the individual, they offer a mode of investment almost as much superior to that of the circle of private connexion, as is afforded by Saving Banks, when compared with the precarious deposits to which the lower orders were formerly accustomed to trust their petty savings.

What proportion do these persons, the permanent depositors in our funds, bear to the body of stockholders at large? Not less, we believe, than *four-fifths of the whole*, whether we look to number or property. The temporary depositors, however, few as they are, fill a more conspicuous place in the public eye : it is they who bustle on the Stock Exchange, who confer with the Chancellor of the Exchequer, and who come conspicuously forward to bear a part in loan contracts. But these persons consider the funds merely as a transient property, a security in which, as in Exchequer bills or mercantile acceptances, they may vest a floating sum until the occurrence of a more eligible mode of appropriation. Their calculations as to the price of stocks go no farther than the month or the quarter which may elapse ere it suit them to withdraw their money, for the purpose, perhaps, of transferring it to the funds of the United States of America, France, or the lesser Continental powers. Merchants, it has long been said, are citizens of the world, but of all mercantile men, that is particularly the case with temporary stockholders, to whom London, Amsterdam, and Paris, present but one vast exchange. How different this from the permanent depositor who exhibits so many characteristics of the retired capitalist, of the inheritor of real property, preferring British security, even at a reduced interest, and not seeking to escape his portion of sacrifice, when satisfied that it is conducive to the general relief! These persons are much more interested in preserving than in acquiring ; their object is not a rise of price for the purpose of sale, but security in regard to their capital and strict punctuality in the payment of the interest.

This disposition has been strikingly exemplified in the late reduction of the five per cents., of which *not a fiftieth part was sent out of the country*, notwithstanding the great temptation offered by foreign funds. And if in the three per cents. the permanent depositors do not surpass the temporary in so great a proportion, they form, even in these, beyond all comparison, the majority.

With what view, it may be asked, do we enter into this discrimination of temporary and permanent depositors? Partly because it is little understood, but more for the purpose of showing the unimportance in a national sense, of the class who come forward as the representatives of the fundholders at large. It follows, that any measures that may be taken in regard to the funds, should be adapted to the unobtrusive, we may almost say, the silent majority of stockholders. Persons circumstanced as they are, can desire no aid at the expence of the community; no addition to the market price of stock, except such as shall naturally arise from the continuance of peace, the growing abundance of capital.—An artificial prop, such as the sinking fund, they will not hesitate to forego, when apprized, that in peace it is of injurious tendency, and should be considered only as an ingenious scheme by which the financier, in a season of difficulty, seeks to stimulate the avidity of capitalists, and to provide for the calls of the Treasury, without an extravagant sacrifice.

After these preliminary explanations and the removal from the mind of the reader of certain popular impressions, we shall proceed with advantage to our farther illustrations.

Comparative Taxation of this Country and France.

GREAT BRITAIN AND IRELAND.

Computed for 1823, *after deducting the taxes on salt, leather, and malt lately reduced : also a portion of the Assessed Taxes.*

Gross amount, inclusive of the expence of collection.

Assessed taxes - - -	£5,000,000
Customs - - - -	11,000,000
Excise - - - -	27,000,000
Stamps - - - -	6,800,000
Land-tax - - - -	1,200,000
Post-office (nett amount) - -	1,400,000
Crown lands - - -	200,000
All other government receipts - -	1,400,000
	£54,000,000
Tithe (including Ireland) - -	5,000,000
Poor-rate, after deducting the portion paid (see page 199.) in lieu of wages -	5,000,000
Total -	£64,000,000

being 25 per cent. on our national income
as computed in page 257.

FRANCE.

Gross amount, inclusive of expence of collection.

Foncier, or land and house tax - -	9,000,000
Mobilier a farther house tax; also the window tax and *patentes*, or tax on professions -	3,000,000
Customs - - - -	2,300,000
Excise, viz. duties on salt, tobacco, snuff, wine, spirits, beer, and some lesser articles, the whole comprised under the name of *droits réunis* - - - -	9,000,000
Stamps, viz. *enregistrement, domaine et timbre* -	6,000,000
Post-office (nett receipt) - - -	600,000
Sale of wood from the public forests - -	800,000
All other receipts and contingencies, including a large municipal revenue collected from *octrois* and other charges borne by the inhabitants of towns - - - -	6,300,000
	37,000,000

Equal, after adding a fifth for the greater value
of money, in France than in England, to - 45,000,000

This forms nearly 18 per cent. on the national
income of France, as computed in page 270.

In this table of comparative taxation, the chief
distinctive feature is the magnitude of our excise,
customs, and assessed taxes, the proportion of
which to the same taxes in France, is as forty to
twenty millions. This puts in a striking light the
greater ability to pay on the part of a commercial
community, of which so large a proportion are resident in towns, a circumstance conducive equally
to ease of collection on the part of government,
and to free consumption on that of the public.
Hence, the magnitude of our receipts on spirits,
beer, tea, sugar, wine, fruit; on certain articles of
dress, as silk; or on that which more immediately
marks a mercantile society, postage. It lessens, at
the same time, the weight of an argument, frequently brought against our taxation, but which
we are far from adopting in a literal sense, viz. that
when computed at so much a head, it amounts to
more than twice the average capitation of our
neighbours.

Corn Laws. — These laws may be termed an indirect impost on the public, payable to landholders
as an indemnity for the land-tax, tithe, and poor-
rate. They have in particular years formed an
addition to our payments greatly beyond the
amount expended by the landed interest for these
burdens; but at present the case is so different,
that our corn laws may, in some measure, be considered a dead letter. In our table accordingly we
have avoided noticing their operation, and have
preferred introducing the amount of the charges

which they are intended to counterbalance.   In France also there exist restrictions on the import of foreign corn, but they are of little consequence in a country where the growth is, in general, fully equal to the consumption, particularly as import becomes free whenever the average of wheat of home growth approaches to 50*s.* the Winchester quarter.

What, it may be asked, is the object of the preceding tables? To draw with distinctness and precision, that which is so often attempted in a loose and exaggerating manner, — a comparison between the burdens of this and other countries, our competitors in the sale of manufactures.   The Agricultural Committee of 1821 advanced an opinion (Report, p. 22.), that the taxation of other countries compared to their resources is as high as our own.   This conclusion our statement does not confirm, but it will probably be instrumental in modifying a very general impression of an opposite nature ; viz. that our burdens exceed those of our neighbours, to a degree which, in a manner, baffles all hope of approaching to an equality.   Far from joining in this discouraging view of our situation, we are inclined to augur very favourable results from a perseverance in the course of reduction lately adopted by ministers.

SECTION II.

Our Prospects in Commerce and Finance.

$P_{ROBABILITY}$ *of continued Peace.* — The events that have recently occurred on the Continent, unsatisfactory as they are to the friends of constitutional freedom, have had at least one good effect, that of putting beyond doubt the determination of our ministers to maintain peace. The debates of 29th and 30th April last, will be memorable for the declarations to that effect, made by Mr. Canning and Mr. Robinson, and confirmed by the votes of an overpowering majority. But this, we may be assured, was no new determination on the part of our rulers, the course of circumstances having long since shown to the reflecting part of our public men, that the only effectual remedy for the national embarrassment was to be sought in a steady adherence to a pacific system. It will be in the recollection of many of our readers, that the late Lord Londonderry, in his speech of 29th April (1822), dwelt strongly on the improbability of our being again called on to bear a part in war, on a scale at all similar to that of our late contest. Had the reserve of office permitted his lordship to express himself at large, he might, we believe, have given the most *conclusive* arguments for this opinion, avowing that the magnitude of our loss, by the war, was unperceived at the time it was incurred ; that ministers, had they comprehended its extent, would have followed a much

more cautious course, and that no consideration
should again prompt them to the once popular system of vigour.   Never, we may add, did a contest
close with more success in its main objects — the
change of government in France, and the restoration
of independence to Europe; while, as to territorial
acquisitions, it rested with us to retain or give back
whatever suited our policy.   Would it be easy to
imagine circumstances more calculated to heal the
wounds of protracted warfare, or to prevent that
distress in which we have, notwithstanding, been
so deeply involved?   After such dear-bought
experience, is it probable that our government
will be easily led to act an aggressive part ; or is
it not more likely, that its conduct will, in future,
be stamped with a prudence similar to that of a
Cecil or a Walpole, — to that which the unambi-
tious government of Holland has for ages studied to
exemplify?

How far is this pacific prospect confirmed by
the situation of foreign powers?   The United
States of America passed, in February 1821, an
Act for reducing to one half, an army which
already was far from numerous ; and the building
of ships of war, prosecuted only in compliance
with a temporary enthusiasm, is now also relaxed.
Next, as to our great European rival, France is no
longer to us the France of Louis XIV. or of Bonaparte: not only is her national power comparatively
very different, but the springs of court intrigue,
the hazard of secret influence on the executive
branch, are checked, as in this country, by the
freedom of parliamentary discussion.   If it be
urged, however, that though the nation be inclined
to peace, the cabinet may be misled by foreign
influence or ministerial prejudices, and that in the

varying scene of European politics, there may arise contingencies calculated to draw France into war, let it be remembered, that her internal situation affords the strongest motives for a return to peace. Her ministers cannot long be blind to her real situation, — to the fact, that her population is in a more divided state, the preservation of her present government less assured than was the case in England a century ago, when, the Hanoverian family being recently settled on the throne, it required a steady adherence to pacific policy to prevent a rupture, of which the result might have been, that the regal prize would have been fought for on British ground.

Causes of War that no longer exist. — On taking a retrospect of our history, we shall find that several of the most popular, as well as most substantial grounds of continental war, have ceased to exist. This country began to take an active part in foreign politics nearly a century and a half ago, a time when France was so preponderant, that during the reigns of William and Anne, continued exertion was necessary to preserve the independence of Europe. The wars of 1740 and 1756 owed their origin chiefly to peculiarities in the situation of Austria and Prussia. If these no longer furnish a probable ground of war, it is still less likely that we shall be involved in any contest for colonies such as that of 1775, or in an attempt to regulate the government of our neighbours, such as that which called Europe to arms in 1793. Those liberal views in politics, that conviction of the barren nature of military trophies, and of the substantial fruits of peace, which were so long confined to the philosophic reader of history, have at last reached our cabinet, and have influenced it since 1812, to a degree greater than is generally known. Neither the troubles of Greece or of Spain have, for a moment, shaken the pacific determination of our ministers. Add to this, that the restrictive laws, so long connected with our colonial system, have now ceased to fascinate our rulers, and will soon cease to fascinate our merchants. Our Board of Trade has expunged from our commercial code, the acts most offensive to foreigners : · it no longer listens to schemes of monopoly, or seeks to found our commercial prosperity otherwise than in concurrence with that of our neighbours. The discovery of the real sources of national wealth, has shown the folly of wasting lives and treasure for those colonial possessions, which, during the last century, in the reign of the mercantile theory, were accounted the chief basis of commercial prosperity. It is now above forty years since the United States of America were definitively separated from us, and since their situation has afforded a proof, that the benefit of mercantile intercourse may be retained in all its extent, without the care of governing, or the expence of defending these once-regretted provinces. Mexico, Peru, Chili, Brazil, the regions so much coveted by our forefathers, are now open to every flag, and never likely to become, on commercial grounds at least, a cause of war.

Is it necessary to add arguments to show the fallacy of expecting any national advantage from war ? If we cast our eyes on France, we find her, after considering herself, during many years, the mistress of the Continent, brought back, in 1814, to her ancient limits : if we look at home, we find our countrymen, after believing that our naval superiority, our conquests in the east and west, had brought us unparalleled wealth, have made the mortifying discovery that our burdens far exceed our acquisitions, and that the only substantial addition to our resources, arises from domestic improvement and augmentation of numbers; circumstances that had little or no connexion with a state of hostility. Frederic II. of Prussia afforded, perhaps, the most striking example of success arising from keeping up a large standing army, having acquired by it, in the first instance, Silesia, and eventually part of Poland : yet, whoever will calculate, on the one hand, the amount of his sacrifices, on the other, the natural progress of population and wealth during so long a period as his reign (forty-five years), will find that the increase of his power would have been fully equal, had he confined himself to the plain and direct course of remaining in peace and improving his hereditary dominions.

To follow up such a course, to surmount our financial difficulties, and to heal the wounds of Ireland, are, doubtless, the chief objects of government. When these grand points shall be attained, the magnitude of our resources will be so evident as to dispel all apprehension of attack, not only on this country, but on the independence of the Netherlands, the maintenance of which seems now to form the only sufficient ground for our interfering in a continental contest.

Our Prospect of increased Resources. — We have already expressed (p. 254.) a belief that if we can so conduct our affairs as to get over a few years of difficulty, our financial prospects would brighten beyond those of any other country. The more we examine our situation, the more we shall find ourselves enabled to trace its evils to transition, derangement, and other causes of a temporary character. Our recent experience has shown, that a season of peace will not always be a season of stagnation, and that an increase of population, producing consumers as well as producers, has no tendency to over-stock. The order of Providence evidently is, that the industrious should be at no loss for employment. And the old adage, that " England is England's best customer," will be exemplified with ample effect whenever the course of circumstances shall restore things to their level, and whenever the unnatural effect of war and taxation shall be removed.

In the belief of several of our countrymen, we have arrived at that point beyond which we can hardly expect to carry either our numbers or our wealth. Their apprehension, however, will be found to require no lengthened refutation, and is noticed here chiefly to satisfy those persons, necessarily numerous in a commercial country, who, immersed in their respective occupations, have little means of generalizing or of reasoning from the past to the future. The fact is, that our improvements, whether in agriculture, manufacture, or navigation, are at present no more arrived at a limit, no more threatened with obstacles to their farther progress, than they were a century ago. A negative impression of this nature was general thirty years since, yet no age has been so fertile in discovery, in invention, in increase of productive power; and happily no country possesses, in its resources, whether physical or political, greater means of continuing the career of advancement. Our capital and labour, of which so large a portion was long directed to military purposes, are now applied to objects of permanent utility. The two great anomalies of our inland situation, poor-rate and tithe, can hardly fail to yield to the intelligence of the age; and their removal would go far towards healing the wounds of the suffering portion of the community.

To bring our calculation to a point, — what annual sum may we consider as likely to be added to our national revenue, in a season of peace? This it is no easy matter to reduce to a specific form, but after establishing (p. 262.), the intimate connection between population and wealth, we may, we trust, on very safe grounds, as far as regards England and Scotland (leaving Ireland, at least the cottagers of Ireland, out of the question), assume the increase of numbers as the *ratio* of the increase of our taxable income. Such certainly may be taken for granted, when the reduction of our taxation shall have been carried somewhat farther, removing the chief part of the extra pressure on our national industry, and placing it, in regard to public burdens, more nearly on a level with that of our continental competitors.

We proceed to exhibit the result in the form of arithmetical computation. First, as to our numbers: — instead of requiring our readers to assent to the probability of an addition annually augmenting, we shall confine ourselves to that which is past and ascertained; viz. the individuals born in the early part of the century (1802, 3, 4.), who are now entering, year after year, on the age of productive labour. Next, as to the fruits of their labour, represented in the form of money, we have already (Appendix, p. 77.) calculated the annual addition to our national income from that source at 3,000,000*l.*, and as our taxation, even on a reduced scale, will be fully 20 per cent. on our income, the consequent addition to our revenue is above 600,000*l*. But here also we shall make a large abatement, and shall call the addition in question only 400,000*l*.

Computated Increase of National Income from the Progress of productive Industry and Population, assuming such Increase at 400,000*l. a-year.*

Years.	Annual Increase of the Produce of Taxes.	Years.	Annual Increase of the Produce of Taxes.
1823	£ 400,000	1837	£ 6,000,000
1824	800,000	1838	6,400,000
1825	1,200,000	1839	6,800,000
1826	1,600,000	1840	7,200,000
1827	2,000,000	1841	7,600,000
1828	2,400,000	1842	8,000,000
1829	2,800,000	1843	8,400,000
1830	3,200,000	1844	8,800,000
1831	3,600,000	1845	9,200,000
1832	4,000,000	1846	9,600,000
1833	4,400,000	1847	10,000,000
1834	4,800,000	1848	10,400,000
1835	5,200,000	1849	10,800,000
1836	5,600,000	1850	11,200,000

This increase supposes neither new taxes or improved circumstances on the part of those who pay them : if the latter merely escape deterioration, the increase of numbers, the acquisition of the additional labourers in the productive field, will, by the augmented consumption of taxed articles, make the computed addition to the revenue.

Diminution of public Expenditure. — If it ' be accounted somewhat confident to anticipate so regular an increase of national income from the mere augmentation of our numbers, we shall call in an auxiliary of another kind, — the effect of diminishing expenditure. Economy is evidently the wish of ministers, and the rising value of money bids fair to enable them to carry reduction considerably farther, without injury to the individuals reduced. What is, in this respect, the effect of the repeal of 6,000,000*l.* of taxes in the last two years? To lower prices ; to bring money more nearly to the value it bore in 1792; to render 95*l.* in the present year equivalent to 100*l.* two years ago. Much, it must be allowed, remains to be done ere the long list of charges, rent, wages, professional attendance, &c., which constitute domestic expenditure, can be brought to their due level ; but the course of circumstances cannot be resisted ; a continuance of peace must be followed by a reduction of these charges in correspondence with that which has already taken place in regard to provisions ; and when that is accomplished, a diminution of payment to the servants of the public may be effected without injury to the individuals reduced.

Comparison of our National Income at present, with its Amount a Century ago. — How far do these encouraging anticipations receive support from the evidence of the past, from a parallel between the England of the present age, and the England of the early part of last century, of the reign of George I.? Since that æra, the produce of our revenue has increased in the proportion of more than five to one; but we disclaim *in toto* this mode of computing our national wealth, and shall build our inferences on a surer foundation. Our population in the reign of George I. appears (see Preliminary Observations to the Population Return of 1821) to have been, including Ireland, about 9,000,000 ; at present it is 22,000,000, or more than double. But that is not all: when treating (Appendix, p. [75]) of the increase of national revenue, we enumerated among the indications of an improving society —

An increase in the proportion of persons deriving their income from property distinct from labour.

An increase in the comparative amount of town population.

A decrease in that of agriculturists, in consequence of the improvements in husbandry, supplying the requisite produce with less manual labour, and enabling the country to send a portion of its youth to follow manufacturing and mechanical pursuits in towns.

Without professing to define the amount of our national income a century ago, no one will doubt that the proportion of "persons living on income derived from property," has, in that period, greatly increased. Still less will they question the effect of improvement in agriculture, and the probability that in the reign of George I. above 40 persons in 100 were required to raise the national subsistence, which we now find to be produced (see Appendix, p. [72]) by 33 persons in 100. In estimating the whole of our national income, we should probably not exceed the mark by assuming it to be at present *three times* its amount in the time of George I., but as it is quite unnecessary to press our calculation to its extent, we shall consider it only to have doubled. The next question is, what prospect is before us for the ensuing age or century? How far useful discovery and invention may or may not be carried, we cannot venture to calculate, but in other points, there is, fortunately, less uncertainty. Can it be doubted that our public men are more enlightened than their predecessors a century ago; that our productive labourers, whether merchants, manufacturers, or farmers, are better provided with capital; that the public in general are more experienced; and the hope of long periods of peace established on a better foundation? — This reasoning will be put in a clearer light by a parallel of the resources of our country and those of her hereditary rival.

Comparison of the Resources of England and France. — The reader, on referring to a statistical return of very remote date, (Appendix, p. [75]) will find, that five centuries ago, the town-population of England was so insignificant that the number of places containing above 3,000 inhabitants, did not exceed eighteen. In these days, France took a decided lead in population, as in political power : and the subsequent accessions to her territory, by the incorporation of extensive provinces (Brittany, Dauphiné, Burgundy), rendered her for a long period an over-match for England. In an age of timid navigation, our ancestors could derive little advantage from their extent of coast, or from the richness of their coal mines, which are valuable only in as far as their bulky products, or the almost equally bulky manu- factures promoted by them, can be conveyed by water. A better prospect was opened by the im- provements that followed the æra of the reforma- tion, and the wise government of Elizabeth — the period from which we date, the effectual cultiva- tion of our national resources. Still our continental rival continued preponderant, and the revenue of Louis XIV. was computed at nearly three times that of Charles II. The alliance against France, cemented by the perseverance of William, and rendered victorious by the talents of Marlborough, relieved us from the dreaded overthrow of the political equilibrium; but even after our splendid successes, it continued a common opinion among foreigners as among ourselves, that the resources of the French were more solid, and that they would soon equal or surpass us in those arts which form the constituents of national wealth. But so different has been the result, that in no period of our history have we out-run so decidedly the competition of other countries. In the reign of George I., England, Scotland, and Ireland bore to France, in point of population, the proportion of only 45 to 100 (See Napier's Supplement, heads of " England and France "); nor was that of tax-able income much more considerable: at present, in point of numbers, we hold the proportion of 70 to 100, and in taxable income of 100 to 100.

Such has been our comparative progress during the last hundred years; but what, it may be asked, is our prospect for the future? This may be in part answered by observing the principal discove-ries of late date, and marking the connection that happily prevails between them and the physical advantages which belong to our country. Steam navigation, for instance, is evidently of greatest avail to the country which possesses coals, iron, and extent of coast. But even in branches totally different, such as the manufacture of silk, a branch in which we long despaired of success, we have of late years gained ground on our continental rivals: nor need we, since with the aid of Ireland we are assured of an adequate supply of agricultural pro-duce, apprehend the recurrence of a high price of labour, or the emigration of our master manufacturers.

We proceed to bring our statement to the test of arithmetical calculation, taking as our basis, the comparative increase of numbers in France and this country. To those who do not clearly understand in what manner increase of numbers conduces so directly to increase of national resources, we would recommend to leave out of the question the infantine part of society, and to confine their attention to those approaching to the age of twenty, the age of productive labour. Our population returns have, ever since 1801, exhibited an increase of $1\frac{1}{2}$ per cent. a year; these persons are now attaining maturity, and entering the field as new contributors to our national income, while in France the proportion of such new contributors is, and has been ever since 1801, not quite one per cent. annually. Assuming a similar proportion for the future, the inference is, that in France the augmentation of national income, reckoned at 10 per cent. in ten years, will be hardly - - - - £21,000,000
But in this country, the increase,
computed by the same rule, viz. the
ratio of the addition to population
(15 per cent. in ten years) will produce nearly - - - 30,000,000
The increase of numbers in this country takes place chiefly among mechanics, manufacturers, merchants, and others, whose exertion is directly conducive to increase of wealth; but in France, the increase of numbers is *as slow in towns as in rural districts ;* in consequence of which, the augmentation of property seems merely to keep pace with that of population. Hence, the tardy increase of

the public revenue, and the stationary condition
of the inhabitants, many of whom follow no other
occupation, and hold no higher rank in society
than their forefathers two centuries ago.

Were we inclined to continue the parallel, we
should find that even as to population, we shall probably overtake our ancient rival, ere another generation pass away. Meantime, those who know
that the issue of a military struggle depends not so
much on population as on disposable revenue, will
be satisfied that at present we should have no
cause to dread a contest, single-handed, with that
power against which our forefathers were obliged
to seek safety in continental alliances. Or, supposing that from any unforeseen cause, our maritime force should become less predominant, and
that a war between the two countries were to be
decided on shore, we should have no great reason
to dread the result, or to regard invasion with the
alarm which it excited during the last century.

This course of reasoning applies in a considerable degree to Russia, Austria, and other continental powers : in none is the degree of increase
in population, and certainly not in national wealth,
on a par with this country. We have, therefore,
little to dread from attack ; and as we shall assuredly not make our superiority a source of aggression, the conclusion is, that our situation presents
a solid hope of continued peace, and of all the
advantages arising from the undisturbed extension
of our productive industry.*

---

* Those among our readers who imagine that there is still
somewhat of over-confidence in the preceding reasoning, will
do well to consult the following sketch of " the public revenue" of the two countries, which is, we believe, sufficiently

accurate, and puts in a striking light the progress of this country
during the last two centuries.

Years.	Public Revenue.		England, after deducting for difference in the value of money.
	France.	England.	
1550	£1,500,000	£600,000	£600,000
1600	2,500,000	900,000	900,000
1660	4,000,000	1,200,000	1,200,,000
1700	8,000,000	4,000,000	4,000,000
1750	12,000,000	7,000,000	7,000,000
1790	22,000,000	16,000,000	13,000,000
1823	33,000,000	52,000,000	42,000,000

SECTION III.

Views of Finance suggested by our Situation and Prospects.

DIFFERENCE in the Nature of our Resources since the Peace.—The radical difference in the sources of our financial supplies, in peace and in war, is, as yet, very imperfectly understood by the public : it may, however, receive some illustration, from a reference to the measures adopted during our great contest. It was in 1797, in the fourth year of the war, that circumstances pointed out to Mr. Pitt, the necessity of a radical change in his financial plans —the substitution of war taxes for loans. The length to which the latter had been carried, exceeded the disposable funds of the monied interest; while, on the other hand, the increase of productive industry, the rise of wages, salaries, rents, all concurred to strengthen the hope of a liberal supply from taxation. Mr. Pitt seized the distinction with his usual promptitude, and erected on it a structure, the eventual magnitude of which, proved one of the wonders of the age. What concurrence of circumstances enabled him and his successors to carry taxation so far ? During the war, our capital and labour had ample employment : competition from abroad on the part of foreigners, or what might have proved far more formidable, our emigrating countrymen, was wholly out of the question. The transfer of English capital to the continent was prevented, as well by a dread of lawless conduct on the part of the French government, as by a more gratifying consideration, the profits realized at home. Since the peace, circumstances are entirely altered; the competition of foreigners is to be dreaded ; capital has been placed in foreign funds, and emigration, had not the price of provisions fallen among us, might have been carried to a ruinous length. The profit of stock, the wages of part of the lower classes, the emoluments of the higher, most incomes, in short, except those of the annuitant on the public funds, have undergone diminution, the whole pointing as much to the necessity of reducing taxation in peace, as our situation during war indicated the practicability of its increase.

How far is Taxation a Cause of Embarrassment? — What, it may be asked, have been the most prominent characteristics of our national embarrassment since 1814? A deficiency of employment, among part of the lower orders, and distress, from insufficiency of wages, at those intervals when provisions were high priced. In the middle classes, whether merchants, manufacturers, or agriculturists, the general ground of complaint has been an inadequacy of profit ; a disproportion of prices to the cost of production. The principal cause of these and other difficulties was, doubtless, as explained in the preceding chapters, the magnitude of the transition, the suspension of government expenditure, and the consequent over-stock of hands. That such would have been severely felt under a taxation as light as that of Switzerland or the United States of America, admits of no doubt ; but it never would have reached such an extent, or continued until the ninth year of peace, had not our public burdens, and consequently the expence of living, been higher than among our neighbours. Emigration and the export of capital would, in a different case, have been comparatively inconsiderable; and additional means of promoting productive industry would have been possessed at home.

Having no wish to press our arguments to an extreme, we disclaim, without hesitation, the aid of certain popular notions, such as that " a taxed commodity after passing through three or four different hands, is enhanced by 20 or 30 per cent. charged by the dealers for their advance on the tax." We know too well the slender profit of either wholesale or retail business, to give credit to such loose assertions; a dealer is in general satisfied with a charge of 2 or 3 per cent. on his advance, so that this argument, though not undeserving of attention, has no claim to a prominent rank in the objections to taxation. These will be found sufficiently serious without the aid of exaggeration: it can hardly be disputed that our high duties tend, to raise our prices above the currency of our neighbours, and we have the sanction of Dr. Smith for saying that " a rise in the money price of commodities, *when peculiar to a country*, tends to discourage more or less every department of industry carried on within it, enabling other nations to undersell it, not only in the foreign but in the home market;"— an opinion to which we subscribe in the words of its illustrious author, notwithstanding all the qualifications of it which we have read in the publications of the political economists of the day. To bring this question into a more definite form, we subjoin a table of the

Taxes which bear, more or less directly, on the comforts of life, or interfere, more or less directly, with the extension of productive industry.

Assessed Taxes since the late reduction	£4,500,000	Leather since the reduction in 1822	£300,000
Malt and Beer since the reduction in 1822	6,500,000	Foreign Wool -	300,000
		Cotton - -	500,000
Stamps - -	6,500,000	Paper - - -	400,000
Sugar - - -	3,000,000	Glass - -	400,000
Tea - - -	3,000,000	Candles and Tallow	400,000
Foreign Timber -	1,000,000	Bricks and Tiles	300,000
Coals carried coastways	900,000	Auction Duties -	240,000
		Hemp - -	200,000
		Starch - -	50,000
Soap - - -	900,000		

The whole forming a sum of nearly 30,000,000*l.**

To draw the line of distinction between the necessaries and superfluities of life, between the greater or less injury arising from taxation to productive labour, is a task of great nicety. There can, it is true, be little doubt that such imposts as those on leather, candles, green glass, bricks, tiles, soap, starch, coal, are direct burdens on industry; charges which must have many bad effects, such as

* To give the reader a complete view of our fiscal burdens, we subjoin the following, which are left out of the text, as

Taxes which appear to interfere less with our productive industry.

Post-office -	£1,400,000	Printed goods (home manufacture)	£570,000
Foreign spirits, chiefly brandy	2,300,000		
British spirits -	3,000,000	Foreign linens -	80,000
Licences for publicans, &c.	700,000	Foreign butter and cheese	100,000
Wine - -	1,600,000	Tallow - -	100,000
Tobacco and snuff (Excise)	2,400,000	Raisins and other fruits	400,000
Tobacco (Customs)	600,000	Barilla and other drugs	150,000
Coffee and cocoa	300,000		
Rum - -	200,000	Pepper - -	150,000
Silk, raw and thrown	500,000	Skins and furs -	50,000
East India piece goods	100,000	Mahogany -	50,000
		Various other duties	1,000,000

impairing personal comfort, raising the nominal rate of wages, or lessening our exports. On the other hand, it may happen that imposts, the least exceptionable in the view of individuals, may, on the ground of fiscal calculation, have the earliest claim to diminution. Thus, wine, spirituous liquors, and lace, appear fair objects of high taxation, but if the duty be so great as to hold forth to smugglers a premium such as enables them to prosecute their business in spite of all the vigilance of our cruisers, an abatement of duty may be found an indispensable alternative. In the case of sugar, the question of abatement stands on different grounds. In an article so acceptable to general taste, and so innocent in its effects, we are justified in expecting *a regular extension of sale, in proportion to the diminution of price.* This has been in a considerable degree exemplified at different intervals of depression in the market, and seems to authorize the inference, (and a very important one it is,) that a reduction of the duty would have the effect of extending the consumption, and of gratifying the lower orders without much injury to the revenue.

On these different claims to priority in the reduction of taxes we acknowledge our inability to decide. The records of the Treasury, doubtless, contain materials calculated to throw light on these intricate enquiries, although even with such an aid the result of reduction will, at times, be found to differ considerably from previous expectation. We decline accordingly to enter on this uncertain field, and confine ourselves to the general question of the pressure of taxation.

Examples of Injury from Taxation. — The unseen injury arising from taxation, its interference with the free course of manufacture, is much greater than is suspected by the public. To form a correct idea of this, would require an investigation into all the branches in which the activity and invention of individuals are repressed by the regulations of the excise. Of their effect in the case of distillers, some idea may be formed from the evidence given before the Sugar Distillery Committee in 1808. To advert to a very different case, we shall take an illustration familiar to those who transact business as underwriters, and who know the extent of the reduction produced by peace in the terms of insurance. To a war premium of 6, 8, or 10 per cent., a policy duty of one-fourth per cent. on the sum insured formed an addition of little consequence, but when premiums were lowered to 2 or 3 per cent., it was found a heavy proportional charge, and afforded an inducement to foreign merchants to effect their insurances at Hamburgh and other ports, where the duty is comparatively light. The consequence is, that the recent reduction of our policy duty has, in some degree, come too late.

Ship-owning, often a losing investment of capital during the war, has been doubly so since the peace, and can hardly prove otherwise, until by reducing the attendant charges, we shall enable our builders, our rope-makers, and others, to meet foreign competitors on equal terms. Navigation does not, like home trade, admit of controul by interior regulation: its scene of competition is the ocean, and success in it can be attained only by a clear superiority over foreigners. Countries possessing forests of timber in the vicinity of a navigable river, enjoy already one great advantage over our ship-builders: to increase that by an impost on the foreign timber used by our countrymen, is to place them on a footing of inferiority inadequately balanced by our extra duties on goods imported in foreign vessels. A reduction of the duty on foreign timber and hemp, seems an indispensable preliminary to our successful competition with foreign ship-builders, —a competition which would not then be hopeless, when we consider the superiority of our workmen, and the recent fall in the cost both of their maintenance, and of the conveyance of foreign materials to our shores.

It would be easy to multiply examples of pressure from taxation, but there can, we believe, be little doubt on several essential points, as

That it forms a main obstacle, to the general freedom of trade which government seem so desirous to introduce;

That on a considerable part of the public it bears harder now than during the war; and

That in general its pressure is greater in England than on the Continent.

After all the additional means conferred by our navigation, our extent of town-population, and our superior agriculture, the payment of 64,000,000*l.* a year, must bear harder on the national income of this country than that of 45,000,000*l.* (see p. 369. of this chapter) on that of France. On the Continent, the evils of transition from war to peace have not been altogether so serious; the failures among merchants and manufacturers have been less numerous; while among their agriculturists the decline of price, much as it is complained of, has been less ruinous than in this country.

How far would a Reduction of Taxation be productive of Relief? —We shall suppose, for the sake of giving our argument a definite form, that it is proposed to discuss the expediency of making a farther reduction of our taxes to the extent in all of 6,000,000*l.* Were that abatement directed *in toto* to some specific branches of industry, for example, those connected with the use of such articles as leather, coals, timber, there seems little doubt that, though like all other changes, it would for some time be productive of a derangement of work, the stock of employment eventually created would supply that which in years of distress was our principal *desideratum,* — a sufficient demand for labour. We shall take, however, the least favourable supposition, assuming that our public men are not agreed in regard to the farther taxes to be repealed, and that the 6,000,000*l.* of which we contemplate the reduction, must be abated in the form of a per centage on the revenue at large. What, it may be asked in the next place, would be the result of such abatement to the individual? A diminution of charge to the extent of two or three per cent. on his expenditure, — an object of no great consequence, it is true, to the land-holder, the retired capitalist, or any person out of business ; but one which in the hands of the merchant, the manufacturer, or the farmer, would form an engine of great efficiency. In the case of an individual out of business, the amount of annual disburse represents only the expenditure of himself and family ; in business, on the other hand, it comprizes wages, salaries, and other outlay to an amount frequently of three, four, or five times the house-keeping expence. That which in the one case would prove a saving of only 20*l.* a year might, and generally would amount in the other to 100*l.* Now persons in business form evidently the stay of a commercial country, the class whose prosperity is decisive of that of the community at large.

This will be apparent on our pursuing our reasoning a step farther, and examining the effect of a reduction on our means of maintaining a competition with foreigners. The consequence would be that our woollens, our cottons, our hardware, might be sent to foreign markets two or three per cent. cheaper than at present. To those who have a due sense of the smallness of mercantile profit, (Speech of Mr. Baring, 15th July 1822,) even this limited reduction will appear of great importance, enabling us to compete with our foreign rivals, the manufacturers of France, Germany, and the Netherlands. To these, since the inauspicious æra of our Orders in Council, we must add the inhabitants of the Northern States of the American Union, the return of the State of New York for 1821, exhibiting a value of 8 or 10,000,000*l.* sterling, (chiefly woollens and cottons,) manufactured among a population of little more than a million.

But our national industry is, it may be said, already amply productive, whether in agriculture or manufacture ; — the evil lies in a want, not of produce, but of vent, and our neighbours, whether Germans or Belgians, have long complained of the free admission of our fabrics. This, however, proves little more than that in certain branches foreigners are unable to compete with us, and that our rivalship, if continued, may induce them to give a different direction to a part of their labour and capital, manufacturing commodities of which we should probably become the purchasers, in consequence of changes that would follow the increased freedom of trade. A state of continued peace implies a reduced scale of profits, a limited return for capital, but not necessarily an overstock of merchandize or deficiency of employment. In harvest we generally have an opportunity of observing, that the supply of labourers is not superabundant, and since the beginning of last year, there has existed no over-stock but in agriculture. Even in a dull season the surcharge of hands is less great than is commonly supposed. To add a twentieth or even a thirtieth to the existing demand for labour, in other words to find employment for 100,000 individuals of the lower order, would, on most occasions, prove a change completely satisfactory.

If we proceed to make an analysis of the causes which determine the quantity of produce prepared among us, either by the loom or the plough, we shall find it to depend mainly on the " amount of capital and number of workmen in the country," points in which, of course, no legislative provision can effect any speedy change. It is a fact, that for a series of years the quantity prepared for a losing market is nearly as large as for a profitable one; so great is the power of habit, the necessity of following up an established trade or profession. This result, so different from the inferences of some political economists, is, doubtless, promoted by our poor-law system : it was exemplified on the part of our manufacturers amid the continued distresses of 1819 and 1820 ; and experiences at present a confirmation in the case of our farmers.

From all these facts what inference do we make, and what are we to consider the probable result of a reduction of taxation? *Not overstock in any branch of manufacture, but security from foreign competition?*

Objections answered.—Various arguments may, we are aware, be advanced as well by men in office as others, against any considerable change in our fiscal arrangements. Taxes repealed or modified, cannot, they will say, be re-imposed. Charges that have interwoven themselves with our habits ought not to be abruptly removed. To this we answer, that several of our taxes are such as ought never to have been imposed, indicating, as they do, the rudest state of financial science, and betraying an almost total unconsciousness of the check given by these burdens to productive industry. As to the question of re-imposition, we have, happily, good ground for dismissing the apprehension of retracing our steps ; but, supposing, for the sake of argument, that such were to become in some degree necessary, the new taxes would be of an altogether different nature. A property-tax to the extent of 2½, perhaps 5 per cent., would, doubtless, receive the sanction of parliament, in preference to a revival of such duties as those on malt, salt, leather, coals, or the house and window-tax.

Next, as to the evils apprehended from transition, — from that state of change, which, to a nation as to an individual, is always unprofitable and frequently pernicious. Evils of that nature, would, even on a diminution of our burdens, occur in a variety of modes not anticipated by the public, but their duration would necessarily be temporary, and their amount might be lessened by various arrangements, such, perhaps, as making our future reductions consist less in an absolute repeal of a few particular taxes than in a modification, a partial diminution of a number ; — a course which might, besides, have the effect of relieving government from much importunate solicitation.

Such are the arguments for a reduction of taxation. Inconsiderable as the proposed abatement may appear, no one can say how materially our productive industry may be promoted by it : but were immediate relief not to prove the consequence, we should have at least the satisfaction of entering on that path, which must eventually lead to a favourable issue. The modifications made last session in our navigation and corn laws have a title to general approbation, yet no one expects from them immediate relief, or regards them in other light than as an approximation to a better system. In like manner a diminution of taxes would bring us more nearly to a level with the rest of the civilized world, giving our manufacturers a fair chance in the field of competition, relieving our annuitants from the necessity of emigrating, and placing us nearer to that equality of prices which would admit of unrestricted trade, and establish our prosperity on a solid basis.

Plan of Finance pursued by M. Necker. — The financial concerns of France have been, in general, badly conducted, and taxation has, time immemorial, been a subject of complaint among a people whose national character is far from querulous. This was more particularly the case in the latter years of Louis XV., after winding up the arrears of the expensive and inglorious war concluded in 1763. The 18,000,000*l.* constituting, at that time, the clear produce of the taxes of France, were levied in so aukward and circuitous a mode as to cost 4 or 5,000,000*l.* in the collection, and a sum perhaps equally large in the injury arising from the obstructions which it caused to the free course of industry. Different provinces in France were subject, in these days, to different imposts ; the frontier lines were discriminated from each other by custom-houses like the boundaries of distinct kingdoms; the transit of merchandize was taxed ; the *douaniers* or custom-house officers multiplied beyond all due proportion.   At that time, as at present, the imposts on consumption were comparatively small, and a great part of the revenue arose from a land tax similar in its nature, but more unequal in its collection than the present *Foncier*.

M. Necker, the first real financier whom France had seen for a century, received his official appointment in 1776, and had hardly begun to introduce order into this chaotic mass, when, in 1778, the course of circumstances caused the French court to depart from its pacific policy. The humane character of Louis XVI., and the necessity of continued economy, were strong arguments for the preservation of peace, but the cause of the American colonists, when opposed to England, could not be otherwise than popular while the French had fresh in recollection, a war in which we had struck such fatal blows at their navy, and deprived them of so many Trans-Atlantic possessions. Louis and his ministers were thus obliged to yield to the public voice ; fleets were to be equipped, and considerable expence to be incurred.   M. Necker, on whom the task of providing the pecuniary supplies devolved, was aware of two things ; first, that at that time the imposition of fresh taxes would be wholly unadvisable ; and next, that eventually the resources of France would be more than equal to her burdens.   He conceived accordingly the plan of meeting the new demands by annual loans, for the interest of which, he made provision, not by taxes, but by the abolition or reduction of pensions, and of many unnecessary appendages of the court. At that time, as at present, France exhibited few sinecures of the first magnitude, but an endless list of unmerited grants, of supernumerary offices, of unauthorized appropriations of the public money. The confidence inspired by the personal respectability of the minister, and the prospect of great improvements in the fiscal administration of France, induced the monied interest on the continent to subscribe to the loans of M. Necker, without the guarantee of a parliament, or the allotment of specific funds for the payment of the interest. In this manner, he succeeded (Hennet on French Finance) in borrowing 15,000,000*l.* sterling, in three years, at moderate interest, and would, doubtless, have conducted the war to its close, without a single impost, had not circumstances led to his abrupt retirement from office in 1781.

Does this example supply any inference applicable to our present situation? If the amount borrowed by M. Necker, appear small, it was far from small when we consider the limited resources of France. Then, as at present, her towns were neither numerous nor large : the majority of her inhabitants were scattered over rural districts ; her manufacturers were adequate only to home consumption ; the increase of her population was slow. How different the present state and prospect of productive industry in this country, possessed as it is, of rich mines, extensive water communication, abundant capital, — the whole with a population rapid in its increase, and formed to habits of business. With such auxiliaries, is it going too far, to ask, whether we are not justified in looking to the future with the favourable expectation entertained by M. Necker, especially as in one material point

we may reason with a confidence greater than he
could feel, — we mean the hope of continued peace ?'

Nothing indeed can be more flattering than our
prospects, provided we are enabled to give relief to
the suffering part of the public. This, it is evident,
could be best accomplished by cancelling or reducing the more injurious of our fiscal burdens; and
we now proceed to enquire whether circumstances
justify our imitating the example of the French
minister, and substituting a small annual loan for
a portion of the taxes repealed. We say a portion,
because there seems little doubt, that the productiveness of the remaining imposts would be so much
increased, as to enable government, if they determined on borrowing £4,000,000 annually, to repeal
taxes to the extent of 5 or £6,000,000.

The Question of a small Annual Loan in lieu of Taxes.

State of the Monied Interest. — Amidst all the
losses and complaints of late years, the monied interest, that mixed body of bankers, retired merchants and capitalists, have, in a great measure,
escaped the general distress. Their situation has
exempted them from the fluctuations experienced
by many other classes ; by our agriculturists, our
manufacturers, our exporters of merchandize to
the West Indies and America. The monied interest comprises a number of old establishments,
who conduct their business more conformably to
rule and calculation than several other portions of
the mercantile community : they are strangers to
the hazard of credit, and the still greater hazard
of distant markets. The cloud, which, from the
depreciation of our currency, overhung them in

the latter years of the war, has disappeared, and
the late reduction of the rate of interest, considerable as it is, may be considered as innoxious to
them, their incomes having gained, or being likely
to gain, in value what they have lost in amount.
The fact is, that they have periodically at their
disposal, particularly after receipt of the public
dividends, a fund of ready money, which has
caused the rise in our stocks, so idly ascribed to a
sinking fund, and which has also afforded large
supplies to the exchequers of our neighbours.

Transmission of Capital to Foreign Countries. —
The interest of money is always highest in the least
advanced communities, and capital has consequently a tendency to move thither, not rapidly,
we allow, but progressively. It is thus that at present it begins to be withdrawn from England, exactly as in the 17th and 18th centuries it was withdrawn from Holland. Last year was remarkable
for the extent of such transfers, and by writers who
do not scruple to take an extra latitude in a popular argument, the imprudence with which these
advances were made, and the losses of which they
were productive, might be made the ground of
a vehement appeal in support of our plan of exchanging a part of our taxation for an annual loan.
We are desirous, however, to avoid all such appeals, and to state deliberately and impartially, the
arguments on either side. If, on the one hand, it
be asked " Why should we not render subservient
to a reduction of taxes that periodical surplus of
capital which has for some years been transferred
to foreigners?" the advocate of commercial freedom may say on the other, " You are not at
liberty to exercise any interference, or to divert

capital from the direction which it naturally takes: its transfer to foreign countries may be, for aught you know, the most profitable means of employing it in a national as in an individual sense. The capitalist who, living in England, draws a large income from the French or American funds, is enabled to make a larger expenditure, to be a more liberal contributor to the productive industry of his own country."

Between these contending opinions what course ought we to hold? The last mentioned argument would be excellent against any legal restraint which might exist, in the shape of a tax or otherwise, on the transmission of capital abroad; a restraint which would be quite as absurd as the lately repealed prohibition to export specie. Farther, were our burdens no greater than those of our neighbours, or were the doctrine of freedom of trade generally adopted, we should be inclined to look with a favourable eye on the most unreserved transmission of capital. But at present we are obliged to reason in a more narrow circle, and to calculate what peculiar aid we can oppose to peculiar pressure. Our situation is unfortunately anomalous; our taxation higher than that of any other country; and if, as we have reason to apprehend, its magnitude be such as to reduce the profit of stock, and in that manner to cause, or to be likely to cause, capital to leave us, the objection of the political economist, however true in the abstract, ceases to apply, or becomes in a manner, lost in the urgency of circumstances.

Though we are thus hardly called on to combat objections, it may be useful, in this day of theorizing, to remark that the application of general principles in regard to money transactions is found to require no slight share of the caution that has proved necessary in other departments — our corn trade, our navigation, our custom duties. To explain our meaning by example. In 1815, Mr. Robinson, at that time President of the Board of Trade, was as fully convinced as Mr. Horner, or any member of the House, of the radical impolicy of our corn laws ; but while he regretted that they should ever have been enacted, or that agriculturists should ever have relied on so unnatural a support, he felt that any change must be gradual, that the advantage from a return to sound principle would be remote, and the evils of transition immediate. The Agricultural Committee of 1821 acknowledged, in like manner, the benefit of free trade, but felt the inexpediency of its early adoption : while in regard to our navigation, the bills brought forward during the session of 1822, for repealing the obnoxious part of our statutes, experienced, as is well known, much opposition and curtailment from the same cause.

We must not, however, be understood as proposing any obstacles to the transmission of capital abroad, except that of giving an additional opening for its investment at home.

We are perfectly aware, that the principles of productive industry prescribe, in the words of Vauban, *que l'argent le mieux employé est celui que le roi laisse entre les mains de ses sujets* — that government should, if possible, avoid draining it from the pocket of the individual in the shape of either a loan or tax. Were it practicable to avoid both, we should be reluctant to urge, or even to listen to the project of an annual loan, however justified by our prospect of increasing wealth. The question, however, has no such scope, being unluckily confined to the alternative of taxing or borrowing ; and we appeal to those who have studied the nature of our resources, whether we cannot at present raise a given sum, for example £4,000,000, with less injury as a loan than as a tax.

Probability of Financial Relief. — We should on on account suggest a transfer of a portion of our burdens to the next generation, were it probable that their situation would partake of that embarrassment which, since 1814, has borne so heavily on us. But whether we look to the increasing caution of our rulers, the resources arising from improvements in our national industry, or the diminution of our burden by its repartition among augmenting numbers, we find reason to consider the prospects of our successors far superior to our own. And though the assertion may excite a smile, it is, notwithstanding, true, that to relieve ourselves from a portion of our taxes, is an effectual method of preventing loss to our posterity, inasmuch as the present pressure, if continued, would, by sending abroad the family of the annuitant, and, as we fear, the money of the capitalist, operate to curtail the fund destined to become in the hands of the next generation the basis of national wealth.

Would the proposed Loan affect the Rate of Interest ? — One of the chief features in the great transition from war to peace, was an increase of disposable capital, and considering the magnitude of this increase, we may well question, whether government ought not, several years ago, to have made a demand on the monied interest for a loan, rather than on the public for taxes.   If such would have been at that time a fit application to the national wound, there seems still less doubt of its being so at present. To take a few millions annually out of the money market would, doubtless, operate in some measure to retard the fall of interest, and the advantage slow, but sure, which follows that fall ; but that it would do so in a slight degree seems probable, whether we consider our present abundance, or our satisfactory prospects in regard to disposable capital. The dread of scarcity of currency from the resumption of cash payments has proved groundless; and there seems, assuredly, no reason to apprehend an early demand for money for the payment of corn imports, still less for subsidies or military charges on the continent.

The power of habit is in nothing more strongly exemplified than in the appropriation of the disposable funds of our monied men. Accustomed to a few simple securities, they have no idea of changing their investments, even under an alteration of circumstances. Our bankers and city capitalists confine themselves to stocks, exchequer bills, or mercantile acceptances, (all convertible into money at short notice,) and have no idea of investing money on mortgage, still less of adventuring in trade, or making a *permanent loan* to a mercantile house. They look more naturally to foreign stocks, particularly since business of that kind is transacted so largely on our own exchange. In what manner does this reasoning apply to the present question? It implies that government by giving a new opening to our capitalists in the form of a small annual loan, would withdraw comparatively little from the accommodation of our merchants and landed interest : the diminution, we believe, would hardly be felt, except in the demand for foreign stock.

Would it affect the Price of Stocks? — This question we shall answer first as it regards the public,
and next in respect to the stockholders. Since the
reduction of the five per cents, government appears
to have hardly any greater interest in keeping up
the funds than in maintaining the price of land,
merchandize, or any other description of national
property. The only direct advantage from a rise
in the funds, would be the power of reducing the
old four per cents, and the farther power of reducing the new four per cents, five or six years hence.
Any diminution of interest in the great mass of our
debt, the three per cents, is a very doubtful and
remote object : a result not likely to ensue, until
after a long continuance of peace, and a concurrence
of circumstances, which of themselves would materially improve our financial condition. But, whatever may be the probable time of the occurrence of
such a power, there can be no doubt that to endeavour to accelerate its arrival, in regard to either the
three or the four per cents, by *artificial means*, would
be highly impolitic. The reasons against such a
course are, even when briefly stated, (p. 360.) so
direct and substantial, as to render it incumbent on
every well-wisher to his country to dissuade it ; and
nothing prevents our enlarging on the evils that
would attend it, except a conviction that it can form
no part of the plans of the present Chancellor of the
Exchequer.

Next, as to the effect of a loan on the interest of
stockholders. Dividing these into the two classes
of temporary and permanent depositors, and considering the former as loan contractors, we shall soon
find that they may safely venture on such a loan
without the pledge of taxes. Four millions, borrowed at an interest of four per cent., would involve

an annual burden of 160,000*l.* which, if the plan of a sinking fund provision for each loan were retained, might be carried to 200,000*l.*, a sum not insignificant certainly, but not equal to *half* the addition that is annually making to our revenue by the increasing consumption of taxed articles. Was such security, we may be allowed to ask, ever offered on a war loan in the most brilliant days of our finance?

Lastly, as to permanent depositors and the probable price of stocks for a series of years. What have been the causes of the slow rise of stocks since the peace? The years 1814 and 1815 required heavy loans; 1815 was a season of general distress, but no sooner did our prosperity return in 1817, than stocks rose and continued high during 1818, when the mismanagement of the French loan, and, soon after, the effect of overtrading in this country, produced a fall. These causes, joined to the general disquietude during a trial (in 1820) of unfortunate notoriety, delayed the rise of stocks; and a farther delay took place from an apprehension in that and the succeeding year that the magnitude of the agricultural distress would necessitate a reduction of the public dividends. Since then, however, the circumstances of the public, and the amount of the revenue have both materially improved.

Two points will be readily admitted by the permanent depositor in our funds; first, that whatever conduces to the relief of the suffering classes has a tendency to raise stocks; and next, that a loan for the purpose of reducing taxes is altogether different in its operation on his property from a loan for the purpose of expenditure. By augmenting the value of money it *augments his income,* and affords him a substantial return for any delay of rise in the market price of stock, which may be attributable to the act of borrowing.

Limitation to borrowing. — Were the plan of an annual loan to be adopted, and found to answer, what limit, it may be asked, ought there to be to our borrowing ; at what time ought we to suspend our demand on our future resources? Our answer is — "at the time when our taxation shall have been brought to a level with that of France and other countries, our rivals in manufacture." If in these countries the public burdens form 18 or 20 per cent. of the national revenue, let the same be considered the limit of taxation in England ; the point below which we make no attempt to reduce it, satisfied with the superiority given to our productive labour by our physical advantages, — our mines, and our command of water communication.

Retrenchment. — Nor ought the adoption of the loan system, though productive of financial relief, by any means to lessen the demand on the part of the public for retrenchment : on the contrary, it would bring with it a direct motive for reduction, the effect of all abatement of taxation being to increase the value of money ; to add to the emoluments of the servants of the public. The allowance to Prince Leopold, for example, has been imperceptibly, but substantially increased from 50,000*l.* to 60,000*l.* by the fall in prices since passing the grant ; and if taxes are further reduced, it will, ere long, attain the value of 65,000*l.* It follows, that a reduction to a sum representing the value of 50,000*l.* at the date of the grant, might take place without injury to the Prince, and without deviating from the spirit of the act of parliament.

Have Loans, in time of Peace, been sanctioned by example? — As yet, only by that of the United

States and some continental powers who, seeking their supplies from alien capitalists, have no title to be held forth as an example to England. But, had Holland in former ages possessed that evidence of progressive increase of population and income, which at present happily belongs to our country, her course would probably have been that which we recommend, and without any departure from her habitual caution ; for if, in peace, wages, salaries, and profits are lower, and the power of present payment less, the labourers in the productive field are more numerous, the results of their exertion far more conducive to eventual prosperity. During the late war, our national income was large but of uncertain duration : at present, it is reduced in amount, but much improved in prospect. If, in the former case, it was politic in government to defray a large share of the current expence out of our passing gains, a different course is obviously suited to a state of peace.

The Annuity Bill. — These truths have at last been felt, and the proceedings of Parliament in the last and preceding session, have evinced a considerable change in the measures of ministers. Till then, whatever might be their merits in regard to foreign politics or commercial regulations, their financial arrangements were unsatisfactory to the attentive enquirer, discovering, apparently, little discrimination between a state of war and peace, in regard to the power of bearing taxes, and a very inadequate impression of the superiority of our progress to that of our neighbours. The measures adopted previously to last year, seemed to proceed from the suggestions of merely practical men — of men accustomed to estimate a financial proceeding by its effect on the Stock Exchange, on the mere monied interest, rather than on the productive industry of the country at large. At last was brought forward, unexpectedly, the plan for exchanging life-interests in half pay and pensions for long annuities; a plan, which, since the moment of its announcement, we have considered indicative of consequences considerably beyond the anticipation of the public. Its temporary failure, or, as we may now say, the delay of its success, was owing to the engagement being brought before the public on too extended a scale : the duration of the contract being such as naturally to startle men not then apprised of all the reasons which determine our rulers to adhere to a pacific course. But our confidence in it was unshaken, connected as it is with considerations on which we build the hope of farther and extensive relief. The adoption of such a measure confers a kind of official sanction on views such as those we have endeavoured to take, and shows that in the highest quarter there prevails a conviction of the promising nature of our prospects; an assurance that our only *desideratum* is present relief.

Of our suggestions in this, as in a previous chapter (p. 344.) it may, we trust, be said, that we propose to do nothing by surprise, by contrivance, or by plausible calculation; all may be gradual, voluntary, and open, where necessary, to recall. From circumstances beyond the power of foresight, a great pressure has fallen on the present generation : it is proposed to transfer a part of it to future years, but on a plan that will leave those on whom it may devolve, whether of the present or of the next age, far less burdened than we now find ourselves. How singular, that in all our distress since the peace, amid all the schemes for our relief, none of this nature should have been brought forward until the recent transfer of life interests into long annuities. Had our finances been administered by a statesman of the bold, inventive mind of Pitt, the increase of our population and the connection between it and the increase of taxable income, would, ere this, have been made the ground-work of some decisive measure. Let it not be objected that such was not his course during the period of his administration that passed in peace, and that the plan pursued for the support of our credit after the American war, was the imposition of additional taxes. At that time the increase of our numbers was less rapid, and for want of regular returns, was unperceived. The recent loss of our colonies forbade the expectation of a progressive extension of trade, and there were few examples in our history, of taxes repealed in the hope of stimulating productive industry. Mr. Pitt pursued, therefore, the only expedient within his knowledge, but had peace been preserved after 1792, there can be little doubt that the result of the favourable state to which circumstances had brought our finances, would have borne the stamp of his discriminating mind, and of the example given, under circumstances somewhat similar, by Sir R. Walpole: it would have been, not the support of the sinking fund, to an extent that would have afforded an inducement to send capital out of the country, but the repeal or reduction of the taxes which interfered most directly with productive industry, in conformity to the course recommended many years before by Dr. Smith.*

* Wealth of Nations, vol. iii.

The Period from 1784 *to* 1793. — To mention the name of Pitt, is to recall the attention of the financial inquirer to the time, unluckily too short, when the plans of that minister were undisturbed by the expenditure of war; we mean the interval from 1784 to 1793. No period of our history is, as far as regards our productive industry, entitled to an equal share of our attention. The circumstances of that interval of peace were in many respects similar to those of the present time. Beginning in financial embarrassment, our prospects gradually brightened, and our trade flourished without the aid, as in a period of war, of artificial causes: all was the legitimate result of the application of capital and industry to the improvement of our national advantages. Agriculture prospered without a rise of prices: the revenue increased without new taxes: labour was paid not largely but satisfactorily, and the addition to the poor-rate was very gradual. Let us not imagine that the period in question possessed peculiar advantages; or that the progress of our cotton manufacture, and the troubles of France, placed our countrymen in those days on commanding ground: they felt severely the pressure of taxation, and were not altogether exempt from the pernicious operation of corn-laws. With confidence, therefore, may we conclude, that could but a part of our present burdens be removed, we should follow the career of productive industry with equal or superior advantage.

CONCLUSION.

We have now brought our labour to a close, after endeavouring to exhibit a picture of our national situation, and enumerating its various advantages and drawbacks, in a manner which, whatever may be thought of the degree of ability, will hardly be arraigned on the score of partiality. Political allusions have been avoided as much as was at all practicable, in an inquiry in which statistical results were frequently affected by the decisions of the cabinet. If we have ventured on questions of great difficulty, and occasionally expressed opinions with a degree of confidence, it has proceeded from no other feeling than a consciousness of the advantage arising from command of time, and the opportunity of giving long-continued attention to a few select subjects.

Summary. — Our first chapter was appropriated to a much disputed question, the causes of the unexpected abundance of our financial resources during the war, and their still more unexpected deficiency since the peace. This was followed by an inquiry into the subject of " currency and exchange," which, uninviting and intricate as it is, could not with propriety be omitted in a work requiring such frequent reference to changes in the value of money. The state of agriculture claimed a longer chapter and more ample details, as well from sympathy for a very numerous and respectable class, as from the importance of the subject to the nation at large. The price of produce influencing so directly the price of labour, it became an object of great solicitude to arrive at an opinion as little doubtful as possible in regard to our prospect of the supply of corn both as to quantity and price. On that must, in all probability, depend a variety of future measures : the regulation of wages, salaries, and money incomes, generally ; the degree of equality in the means of competition between our manufacturers and those of the continent ; and the latitude which may consequently be taken by government in removing the restrictions on our commercial intercourse.

From these doubtful and anxious points we turned with satisfaction to the evidence of our progressive advance in agriculture, manufacture, and the useful arts generally, accompanied, as it is, by a large increase in our population. Augmentation of national power ; the prospect of continued peace ; the means of reducing taxes — are all consequences of our decided superiority to other nations in the progress of national improvement.

The examination, in a subsequent chapter, of the fluctuations in the value of gold and silver, was prompted by a double cause — the revolutions in the value of money during the last thirty years ; and the evident disproportion existing at present, particularly in the metropolis, between the rate of wages and the cost of the maintenance of the individual. A hope of being instrumental in correcting these anomalies led to researches of which the object is to give a permanent and uniform value to money contracts; to lessen the prevailing objection to leases ; to give facilities to the commutation of tithe; and finally, to show annuitants that it is possible for them to make an abatement in the numerical amount of money income without incurring a sacrifice.

In our concluding chapter we have conveyed our ideas in regard to the operation of a sinking fund; the comparative weight of English and French taxation; the growing nature of our resources; and the prospect of a farther and considerable reduction of our burdens.

It may appear somewhat singular to our readers that subjects of such general interest should not long ere this have been fully discussed; that questions of such importance to our welfare should not have been decisively answered. But in such researches the magnitude of the labour is found to exceed all previous calculation: the number of persons fitted for it by situation or habits is not great; and, immersed as they generally are in official or professional pursuits, a long period elapses in this, as in the province of general history, before an individual is enabled to bestow on such topics the time and attention they require.

———

Comprehensive as the preceding investigations may appear, there still remain for discussion several subjects of great interest.

Our Trade. — Of our commercial history during the last thirty years, we propose a sketch as circumstantial, and as carefully grounded on official documents as that which has been given of our Finances and our Agriculture. The fluctuations in our trade, the over-rating of our profits during the war, the distinction between real and nominal additions to property, are all subjects which require examination and perspicuous statement.

Emigration. — Though the recent improvement in the state of our productive industry has lessened the necessity of emigration, a disquisition into that subject would open views connected with the diffusion of civilization, not only in our colonies, but in many districts in Europe. The state of these is more backward than can well be conceived by the untravelled part of our countrymen. Though to send settlers to these neglected tracts would form no part of our policy, their improvement would be of interest to us, both as opening markets for our manufactures, and as proving to continental powers how much it is their policy to maintain peace, and to seek in the diffusion of civilization that increase of population and revenue which they have hitherto so fruitlessly attempted from conquest.

Public Retrenchment. — This question, much as it has been discussed, still stands in need of an exposition unconnected with party views, and founded on considerations strictly statistical, in particular the power of money in the purchase of commodities, and the extent of the change attendant on the transition from war to peace.

Finance. — On this head we have communicated in the present volume only a part of our materials : to arrange and condense the remainder might tend to give clearness to official statements, and to support the arguments for a farther reduction of our burdens.

Parallel between England and France. — We have exhibited a comparison of the charges on agriculture, and of the general taxation of the two countries: but there remains much to compare in regard to the state of trade and manufactures; of military and other public establishments; of education, science, and national usages.

Tithe and Poor-rate. — These subjects acquire an increased interest from the course of recent circumstances : — the improbability of any great or permanent rise in agricultural produce: the highly beneficial measure about to be carried into effect in Ireland; and the evident ability of our monied interest to afford relief to their landed brethren, whenever an eligible plan shall be brought forward by government. Of this plan the main features would, perhaps, be as to tithe, redemption at a moderate valuation; and as to poor-rate, the equalization of the burden throughout a parish or district, by assessing (see page 185,) the income of all instead of that of the farmer or householder only.

What is the present prospect in regard to the price of commodities generally? That a rise is very unlikely, and that in all probability no injury would accrue to the clergy from their accepting a money income in lieu of tithe for a few years, until, by the purchase of land or otherwise, arrangements should be made for a permanent commutation.

Our West India Colonies. — The attention of the public has lately been directed to two questions, — a reduction of the duty on East India sugar, and the gradual abolition of slavery in our West India colonies. The discussions in both have hitherto been conducted in a manner of which, to borrow the expression of a foreign historian, *la moderation n'est nullement le caractère.* Neither party has shown much solicitude to observe a medium, or to ascertain decisively a few fundamental points ; such as, whether the purchase of sugar in India at a low price is or is not practicable to a large extent; or, whether, in regard to the West Indies, it is not the interest of the planter to co-operate cordially in the accomplishment of the proposed change, after the principle of compensation shall be distinctly admitted.

These several topics it is our intention to discuss, in an additional volume, whenever circumstances shall afford the time requisite for such laborious researches.

APPENDIX.

APPENDIX

TO

CHAPTER II.

(Page 20.) *Expence of the late Wars, reckoning from the beginning of* 1793 *to the beginning of* 1816.

MONEY RAISED.

War of 1793.

Years.	By Taxes.	By Loans.	Total.
	£	£	£
1793	17,170,400	4,500,000	21,670,400
1794	17,308,811	11,000,000	28,308,811
1795	17,858,454	18,000,000	35,858,454
1796	18,737,760	25,500,000	44,237,760
1797	20,654,650	32,500,000	53,154,650
1798	30,202,915	17,000,000	47,202,915
1799	35,229,968	18,500,000	53,729,968
1800	33,896,464	20,500,000	54,396,464
1801	35,415,096	28,000,000	63,415,096
1802	37,240,213	25,000,000	62,240,213
	*263,714,731	200,500,000	464,214,731
Deduct sums for the service of Ireland - -		13,000,000	13,000,000
		187,500,000	451,214,731

* Dr. Hamilton on the National Debt, pp. 157, 269.

War of 1803.

Years.	By Taxes.	By Loans.	Total.
	£	£	£
1803	37,677,063	15,202,931	52,879,994
1804	45,359,442	20,104,221	65,463,663
1805	49,659,281	27,931,482	77,590,763
1806	53,304,254	20,486,155	73,790,409
1807	58,390,225	23,889,257	82,279,482
1808	61,538,207	20,476,765	82,014,972
1809	63,405,294	23,304,691	86,709,985
1810	66,681,366	22,428,788	89,110,154
1811	64,763,870	27,416,829	92,180,699
1812	63,169,854	40,251,684	103,421,538
1813	66,925,835	54,026,822	120,952,657
1814	69,684,192	47,159,697	116,843,889
1815	70,403,448	46,087,603	116,491,051
	770,962,331	388,766,925	1,159,729,256

Deduct the proportion of the above
raised for the service of Ireland -   - 46,612,106

1,113,117,150

NOTE. — See a very short but clear summary, entitled, " Statement
of the Revenue and Expenditure of Great Britain, in each year, from
1803 to 1814, by C. Stokes."

Summary. — Instead of dwelling on these complicated
statements, we invite the reader to fix his attention on the
following abstract in round numbers:

War of 1793.

Total money raised by loans and taxes, exclusive of the loans for the service of
Ireland, about   -   -   £ 450,000,000

Deduct the probable charge in Great Britain and Ireland, had peace been pre-
served, 18,000,000*l.* a-year.   -   180,000,000

Balance constituting the war expenditure - 270,000,000

War of 1803.

Total money raised, exclusive of the sums for the service of Ireland, about -	£1,113,000,000
The deduction for the probable expence of a peace establishment, may, after 1803, be called 22,000,000*l.* a-year, as well on account of our augmented population, as because in the table of the war of 1803, the charge of collecting the revenue is not deducted; say 22,000,000*l.* for 13 years - -	286,000,000
Balance constituting the war expenditure	827,000,000
Average war expenditure from 1793 to 1802, both inclusive - - -	27,000,000
Average war expenditure from 1803 to 1815, both inclusive - - -	63,500,000
Total charge of the two wars, exclusive of an ample allowance for a supposed peace establishment, nearly - -	1,100,000,000

Explanatory Remark. — This amount, adopted in the text, as representing the total of our war expenditure, may require some explanation. It is exclusive of the sums raised for the service of Ireland during the twenty-three years in question, whether by taxes in that country, or by loans in England; on the other hand, it comprizes a large sum appropriated in England not to the war, but to the reduction of the national debt. Still, as the amount of money thus applied did not materially exceed the sums raised for the service of Ireland, and as it forms no part of our object to aim at fractional accuracy, we may safely consider the sums thus left out as balancing each other, and assume the 1,100,000,000*l.* as a representation of our total war expenditure.

Addition to the Public Debt. — Though the expenditure of the war of 1803 exceeded that of the war of 1793, in the *ratio* of more than three to one, the addition made to our public debt was not at all in that proportion; the war of 1793 having added to it fully 200,000,000*l.*, that of

1803 about 260,000,000*l.* In the war of 1803, the far greater part of the expence was defrayed by the property-tax and other supplies raised within the year.

Such were the total sums raised for our war expenditure: but it is fit to recollect that they do not indicate with accuracy the extent of sacrifice connected with the war. There remain, as we shall see presently, considerations of great importance on either side of the account; such, on the one hand, as the loss arising from the transition to peace; on the other, the amount of supply derived from the extra profits attendant on a state of war.

(Page 25.) — *Explanation of the " official Value of Goods."* — The " official value of goods" means a computation of value formed with reference, not to the prices of the current year, but to a standard fixed so long ago as 1696, the time when * the office of Inspector-general of the Imports and Exports was established, and a Custom-house Ledger opened to record the weight, dimensions, and value of the merchandize that passed through the hands of the officers. One uniform rule is followed year after year in the valuation, some goods being estimated by weight, others by their dimensions; the whole without reference to the current or market price. This course has the advantage of exhibiting with strict accuracy any increase or decrease in the *quantity* of our exports.

Next, as to the *value* of these exports in the market. In 1798, there was imposed a duty of two per cent. on our exports, the value of which was taken, not by the official standard, but by the declaration of the exporting merchants. Such a declaration may be assumed as a representation of, or at least an approximation to, the current or market price of merchandize; there being, on the one hand, no reason to apprehend that merchants would pay a per centage on an amount beyond the market value; while, on the other, the liability to seizure afforded a security against under-valuation.

These two scales of valuation, we mean the official register and the current price, afford the means of solving a question of no slight importance, viz. the comparative value of merchandize in the present age and at the remote date of 1696. Some articles, in particular coffee,

* Chalmers' Historical View of the Domestic Economy of Great Britain and Ireland. 1812.

cottons, hardware, are cheaper than in the reign of King William ; but the great majority were, during the late war, so much dearer, that it was usual to calculate the real or market value at 50 per cent. above the official value. Since the peace the case is greatly altered, the market price of goods having, as we shall perceive from the following statement, been greatly reduced.

Comparison of Exports in War and in Peace.

I. Total Exports from Great Britain, comprising home produce and manufacture, as well as foreign and colonial goods, the whole according to the *official* value.

1814. - - £56,591,000	1818. - - £56,851,000
1815. - - 60,984,000	1819. - - 46,912,000
1816. - - 51,260,000	1820. - - 51,731,000
1817. - - 53,125,000	1821. - - 56,445,000

Annual average of the eight years of peace,
above - - - - - - £54,200,000
This is the average referred to in the text, p. 27.

We subjoin, in the next place, the *declared* value of our exports since the peace; in other words, their value according to the state of the markets in each year.

Exports from Great Britain, taking home produce and manufactures at the value declared by the merchants, and adding in the case of foreign or colonial goods 25 per cent. to the official value, an addition considerably less than that which was made in war.

1814. - - £73,489,000	1818. - - £64,263,000
1815. - - 74,372,000	1819. - - 52,031,000
1816. - - 61,138,000	1820. - - 52,982,000
1817. - - 58,032,000	1821. about 54,000,000

Annual average of the eight years of peace
from 1814 to 1821, both inclusive, mentioned in the text, p. 28. - - - £63,787,500

In either way, the value of our exports is greater since the peace than during the war.

II. For those who may wish to carry farther these calculations of our exports, and of their effect on our productive industry, we add a return of that part of our exports which is illustrative of the extent of our home trade.

War.   Exports of Home Produce and Manufacture from Great Britain, previous to and during the late wars.

	In Money of the particular year.	Supposed to be equivalent at the prices of 1792 to
Average of six years ending with 1792	£22,151,000	£22,151,000
Ditto - - - - - 1798	25,658,000	23,325,000
Ditto - - - - - 1804	36,817,000	30,681,000
Ditto - - - - - 1810	43,575,000	33,519,000

These sums are calculated by adding 50 per cent. to the official value, so that ample prices are allowed for the period of war.

Exports of Home Produce and Manufacture from Great Britain *since the peace*, according to the value declared by the exporting merchants.

Years.	Money of the particular year.	Supposed to be equivalent at the prices of 1792 to
1814	£47,851,453	£37,000,000
1815 - -	53,217,445	42,000,000
1816 - -	42,955,256	34,000,000
1817 - -	43,626,253	35,000,000
1818 - -	48,903,760	39,000,000
1819 - -	37,940,000	35,000,000
1820 - -	38,620,000	38,000,000
1821. about	40,000,000	40,000,000

The returns for these years of peace, when compared with years of war, sufficiently establish the *greater value of our exports since the peace.* They may appear at variance with a statement published in a work of very wide circulation, (Quarterly Review, No. LII., p. 534.) in which the exports of three years of war, 1811, 1812, 1813, are contrasted with three years of peace, 1819, 1820, 1821, and the amount of the former found to be considerably greater. This, however, is to be understood of foreign merchandize, and was owing to the extent of our transit trade during the years when neutrals had very little direct navigation, and were obliged to carry almost every article through the medium of this country. But a transit trade may be very large, without making any great addition to the productive powers of a country, and our object being to show the connexion between the amount of our exports and the degree of activity existing among our population, our tables are confined to returns of our home produce and manufactures.

The reduction to money of a uniform value (that of 1792) is expedient for a period in which money has varied so greatly: it removes a part of the exaggeration to which we habituated ourselves during the war, and simplifies the comparison with years of peace.

Decline in the Price of Goods.—We subjoin a farther extract illustrative of the general fall in the price of merchandize since 1818.

Exports from Great Britain, of Home Produce and Manufactures.

Years.	Official value.	The declared or market value.
1818 - -	£ 44,564,000	£ 48,904,000
1819 - -	35,634,000	37,940,000
1820 - -	40,240,000	38,620,000
1821, exclusive of our export to Ireland	40,195,000	35,826,000

Prices, as our readers may remember, began to fall very soon after the peace: yet in 1818 they were still from 10 to 12 per cent. above the official value. In 1819, a year of stagnant trade, the market value fell to within 7 per cent. of the official value, and since 1820 it has been below it. By this we are to understand, not that all merchandize is cheaper than in the reign of King William, when the standard of official value was formed; but that cottons and hardware, (in particular cottons) form so very large a proportion of our exports as to counterbalance the rise in woollens, leather, and other articles, which are still somewhat dearer than they were a century ago.—Returns such as these are of the highest interest to the political arithmetician.

Effect of Taxation.—Taxation is injurious chiefly in two ways: in an individual sense, when the parties assessed have not the means of indemnifying themselves; and in a national sense, when the magnitude of the burden is such as to reduce the profits of labour and capital materially below those of other countries. The former receives at present a distressing exemplification in the case of our agriculturists; the latter has long prevailed in the Dutch provinces, at least in the maritime provinces of Holland and Zealand, in which the charge of defence against the sea is superadded to heavy demands of a political nature. Such also has been, in a considerable degree, our own situation since the peace; that it was by no means so during the war, has, we trust, been satisfactorily shown in the text.

We consider, therefore, our taxes during the war in the light of circulation, without ascribing to them all the detrimental effects alleged by the majority of political economists, and still less the beneficial operation attributed to them by others. The latter opinion, singular as it may seem, is nearly a century old, and was supported by repeated references to the case of Holland before her decline. In this country it seemed to receive a striking confirmation from the stagnation that followed the peace, as the public did not take sufficiently into account how much the circulation of *borrowed* money had been the cause of the general activity during the war.

APPENDIX

TO

CHAPTER III.

Rise of Prices during the War.

Country Labourer.—Computation of the annual expence of the family of an agricultural labourer, supposed to consist of 5¾ persons; calculated chiefly from a table of the expence of 66 families of labourers, in different parts of England, collected by Sir F. Eden.

	In the year 1792.		In 1813.		In 1823.	
	£	s.	£	s.	£	s.
Bread, butcher meat, beer, and other provisions of home growth	16	0	32	0	17	0
Tea, sugar, and foreign articles	2	0	3	0	3	0
Rent	1	13	2	0	2	0
Fuel and candles	2	10	3	10	3	0
Clothes and washing	4	7	6	10	6	0
Contingencies	0	10	1	0	1	0
	£27	0	£48	0	£32	0

Town Mechanic.—Computed expence at different dates, of the family of a mechanic living in a provincial town, and supposed to consist, as in the case of the agriculturist, of 5¾ persons.

	In the year 1792.		In 1813.		In 1823.	
	£	s.	£	s.	£	s.
Bread, butcher meat, beer, and other provisions of home growth	20	0	38	0	21	0
Groceries and other provisions imported	4	10	7	0	6	0
Rent of cottage or rooms	2	10	4	0	4	0
Fuel and light	3	0	5	0	4	0
Clothes and washing	7	0	11	0	10	0
School fees, apothecary's bill, and other contingencies	5	0	8	0	7	0
	£42	0	£73	0	£52	0

The Middle Classes. — Comparative estimate of the expence in different years of house-keeping in a family of the middle class, supposed to reside in London.

	In the year 1792.		In 1813.		In 1823.	
	£	s.	£	s.	£	s.
House rent - - -	60	0	100	0	90	0
Assessed taxes and poor rate	18	0	47	0	40	0
Wages; two women servants	18	0	22	0	22	0
Clothes - - -	60	0	85	0	70	0
Boots and shoes - -	9	0	18	0	16	0
Wine, spirits and strong beer	16	0	35	0	30	0
Table beer - - -	7	0	11	0	9	0
Tea, sugar, and other groceries	22	0	38	0	35	0
Fuel - - -	24	0	35	0	30	0
Light, viz. candles and oil -	6	0	10	0	8	0
Washing - - -	16	0	25	0	22	0
Bread - - -	25	0	50	0	25	0
Butcher meat - - -	25	0	45	0	30	0
Milk, butter, fish, cheese -	50	0	85	0	70	0
Education - - -	14	0	22	0	20	0
Medical attendance - -	14	0	20	0	20	0
Furniture; annual repairs, and purchases - - -	14	0	24	0	20	0
Incidents, such as postage, stationery, charity, pocket disbursements - -	35	0	55	0	50	0
Expences of a less necessary character, such as excursion to the sea side, or the country - - -	30	0	50	0	40	0
Expence of company - -	35	0	60	0	50	0
Furniture; interest on the money invested in its purchase; also its insurance against fire	42	0	63	0	53	0
	£540	0	£900	0	£750	0

We are next to exhibit these charges in a more concise form, classing them under specific heads, and showing the per-centage, or proportion borne by each head ; thus:—

	Expence of the family of a country labourer. Parts in 100.	Expence of the town mechanic. Parts in 100.
Bread, butcher meat, beer, and other provisions of home growth or manufacture - -	55	42
Provisions, such as groceries, of foreign produce -	5	10
Clothes and washing -	20	19
Rent - - -	6½	8
Fuel and light - -	10	8
Contingencies - -	3½	13
	100	100

	A family of the middle class expending between 500 and 800*l.* a-year in London, or nearly 500 in a provincial town. Parts in 100.	A family of larger income, expending 1000*l.* and upwards. Parts in 100.
Bread, butcher meat, beer, and other provisions of home growth - - -	25	20
Provisions, such as groceries of foreign growth - -	8	5
Clothes and washing -	18	14½
House rent - -	10	10
Assessed taxes and poor rate -	7	4½
Fuel and light - -	6	3
Education, medical attendance, repairs, and occasional purchases of furniture -	8	13
Travelling, entertaining company, and other less necessary expences - - -	7	14
Servants' wages - - -	3	5½
Incidents - - -	8	10½
	100	100

In calculating these proportions, we have taken the results, not of any particular year, but of a number of years.

Comparative Comfort of the labouring Classes in War and Peace. — The expence of the labouring classes is, of course, confined to the necessaries of life, and the above summary shows clearly the greater proportion of their income that is appropriated to the purchase of food. Now as food rose during the war more than any other head of expence, it follows that the *ratio* of enhancement was greater in the case of the working classes, than in that of their superiors. On the part of the middle and upper ranks, 160*l.* or 170*l.* were required to make those purchases for which 100*l.* sufficed in 1792; but on the part of the lower orders 180*l.* were probably not more than adequate. It thus becomes a question whether, after all the rise that took place in wages, the condition of the labouring classes during the war was more comfortable than in 1792. That at present it is much better, will at once appear from an inspection of the preceding tables, for while wages have been but little lowered, provisions have fallen greatly, and the reduction of housekeeping since 1814, which to the middle classes has been only about 20 per cent., is nearly twice as much to their inferiors.

Rise in the Price of Corn. — Towards the close of the war the price of corn, butcher meat, and most articles of country produce, became double that of the year 1792, which, considering the proportion borne by provisions to our total consumption, might have justified our computing at 33 per cent., the addition thus made to our national expenditure. But as this extreme rise lasted only a few years, we have called it in the text 30 per cent.

Causes of this Rise in Corn. — These shall be fully explained in our chapter on agriculture: at present we state them very briefly; viz.

1. The rise in labour and other farming charges attendant on the war.

2. The occurrence of a series of bad or indifferent seasons, 1794, 1795, 1799, 1800, 1811.

These two causes raised the quarter of wheat from 50*s.* to 80*s.*, where, in all probability, it would have stopped, had not,

3. The depreciation of our currency after 1809 subjected our import of corn to an enhancement so great, as to carry our average from 80*s.* to 100*s.*

Are such Causes likely to be operative in future? — Interference with our currency is, in all probability, excluded from the creed of our rulers, and a rise in the price of labour seems out of the question in a season of peace. Of the remaining cause of enhancement, the occurrence of bad or indifferent seasons, nothing can be said, except that so long as peace shall continue, the degree of rise proceeding from it, will be greatly checked by the facility of import.

Enhancement of Labour. — The proportion of rise attributed in the text to "Labour," may appear somewhat below the mark, since the rate of wages and salaries was doubled, or nearly doubled, in the course of the war, while our table of housekeeping expenditure is found, on comparing the years 1792 and 1813, to exhibit a large addition under the different heads, (clothes, furniture, house-rent, &c.) affected by rise of labour. These considerations, however, are subject to material qualifications. They apply only to the upper classes, since our humbler countrymen perform service for themselves, and exclude wages from the list of their charges. Next, in regard to one very extensive department, agriculture, the rise proceeding from "Labour" is comprized in the 30 per cent. attributed, in our summary, to the enhancement arising from "Provisions." Add to this, in the third place, that in various manufactures, such as cotton and hardware, the additional cost proceeding from rise of wages, was balanced by improved methods of working, and by the application of machinery. On the whole, therefore, it seems that we may account an addition of 20 per cent. to our general expenditure, a fair representation of the rise of prices during the war, as far as such rise is attributable to enhancement of labour.

Paper Currency — its Depreciation. — It may occur to our readers, that in the summary of the causes of enhancement in the text, paper currency ought to have found a place along with taxation, rise of labour, &c. Allowance, however, is made for its operation in our estimate of the enhancement of corn, and of the other imported articles, cotton, wool, tobacco, the cost of which was so greatly increased towards the close of the war by the decline of our paper.

Annuitants on Mortgage. — After explaining in the text the loss sustained by such annuitants in one point of view, it is fit to add that in another, viz. keeping up the rate of interest, the effect of the war proved favourable to them. Had peace continned after 1792 their debtors, instead of continuing to pay them 5 per cent. interest, would have obtained loans at 4½ or 4 per cent., and would, doubtless, have availed themselves of the power of paying off or reducing the interest on their mortgages, in the manner so generally practised during the last and present year.

APPENDIX

TO

CHAPTER IV.

Our Currency and Exchanges.

ON *the Amount of Bank of England Notes in Circulation.*
—The circulation of money is generally considered under
two heads; that of the larger sums, which takes place between
wholesale dealers; and that of the smaller, which applies to
retail, the payment of wages, and other petty transactions.
Between wholesale dealers money circulates with rapidity:
bank notes, like coin, being wholly unproductive, any superfluous stock of them is exchanged as quickly as possible
for mercantile acceptances, the purchase of government
stock, or other securities readily convertible into cash.   In
London, the vicinity of bankers to each other, and the
power of receiving an immediate supply on a deposit of
securities, enable banking-houses (Bullion Report, p. 26.
and Evidence, p. 123.) to lessen greatly the amount kept by
them as a reserve or unproductive fund.   Add to this, that
whatever renders money abundant in the metropolis has a
speedy effect on the kingdom at large; so intimate is the
connexion between town and country, so extensive the correspondence (Evidence Bullion Report, pp. 123, 124, 125.)
of bill and money agents.   If we assume six weeks as the
medium term of bills discounted at the bank, and suppose
the money to change hands once in two days, the result is
that 100,000*l*. thus obtained will, in the course of the six
weeks that the bill remains uncalled for, circulate about
2,000,000*l*. of merchandize.   How great, then, must have
been the distress of trade in the latter months of 1796, and
the early part of 1797, when our circulating medium was
contracted by two or three millions : how seasonable the

relief afforded in the course of 1797, by the resumption of discounts on their former scale !

An increase of Bank of England notes is not conclusive proof of an increase of our circulating medium at large. — If our readers are reluctant to admit this, we must remind them of a point in which the public opinion was long equally positive, viz. that we received an annual sum of money from foreign countries, in payment of our profits or balance of trade. This was a favourite notion with our ancestors, and is still a prevalent impression among our practical men. The balance was even reduced to specific computation, the received mode of calculating it having been to deduct the amount of our imports from that of our exports, and assume that the difference must be profit, payable to us in hard cash : a comfortable doctrine certainly, and one which, had it been well founded, would have brought among us, in the course of the last century, a sum little short of 400,000,000*l.* sterling. This is mentioned merely as an example of the hazard of deducing an inference from appearances : in regard to the present question, the increase of Bank of England paper, the doubt arises from our having no power to discriminate how far such increase forms an addition to our circulation, or is merely a substitution of paper for coin sent abroad. Or, if the state of exchange be considered as affording, in some measure, an index in that respect, what means have we of ascertaining another material point ; viz. how far an extra issue of Bank of England notes may not be a substitution for a corresponding amount of country bank paper withdrawn from circulation ? This was, doubtless, the case in 1810 and 1811, a time when a number of country banks became either insolvent or discredited by the insolvency of their neighbours. Again, on the fall of prices in 1815 and 1816, there took place in our paper currency a reduction of several millions ; but as the Bank of England experienced no variation of consequence, the inference is, that its paper must have been substituted in various districts for the diminished circulation of the country banks. Finally, we have the authority of both the Bullion Report, (p. 26.) and of that of the Bank Committee of 1819, that no satisfactory conclusions are to be drawn from the amount of Bank of England paper in circulation : a declaration of great importance, since the increase of that circulation formed, all along, to the antagonists of the bank, the fundamental argument for the charge of over issue.

Fluctuations in the Circulation of Bank of England Notes.
—Were we to attempt calculation on a subject necessarily
conjectural, we mean how far additions to the circulation of
the Bank of England formed an increase of our currency,
or were merely a substitution for coin sent abroad, we
should begin by considering in the latter sense all notes of
1*l.* and 2*l.*, and confine our attention to the fluctuations in
notes of 5*l.* and upwards.   The addition made to the latter,
in the years 1797 and 1798, appears to have done little
more than replace the contraction caused by the general
embarrassment and distrust of the early years of the war.
In 1799, 1800, and 1801, there took place an increase of
nearly two millions, proceeding from several causes, particularly the export of coin, and the general rise in the price
of commodities.   From the end of 1802 to that of 1808
there was hardly any increase; a circumstance in a high
degree remarkable, when we consider the extension of our
productive industry, the farther rise of prices, and the continued exemption of the Bank from cash payments.   From
1809 to 1814 the case was altogether different, the circulation increasing four, five, six, and even seven millions
above its amount in the preceding period.   Of this the
causes were various ; first, the almost complete export of
our metallic currency ; next, the discredit of country banks
after the insolvencies of 1810 ; but, above all, the rise of
prices which, at this period of the war, was owing chiefly
to the depreciation of our bank paper.
   The next æra of fluctuation (1815 and 1816) was of a
very different character : it affected chiefly the country
banks, and was evidently a consequence of the general fall
of prices, multiplied failures, and stagnation of business.
The amount of this contraction has not been ascertained
with any accuracy ; but from the returns inserted towards
the close of the Report of the Bank Committee of 1819,
it seems to have exceeded 8,000,000*l.*; a sum which, large
as it was, appears to have been nearly counterpoised by the
re-extension of country-bank circulation on the rise of prices
in 1817 and 1818.
   Since the peace, what have been the causes affecting the
circulation of the Bank of England ? The substitution, on
a greater or less scale, of coin for paper ; the rise or fall of
prices ; and, what is closely connected with that rise or fall,
the credit or discredit of our provincial banks.

Circulation of Provincial Banks. — To ascertain the
amount of country-bank paper in circulation, would be an

object of great interest and importance; at present our means of calculating it are very inadequate, and must continue so while private banks are so numerous and on so small a scale. The Bank of England, placed above the hazard of discredit, declares openly its circulation : private bankers require, or conceive that they require, the aid of secrecy. This will, in all probability, continue until the arrival of the much-desired period, when the country at large shall be admitted to the advantage at present enjoyed by Scotland alone, we mean that of having an unlimited number of partners in country banks. The consequence would be, a stability beyond all doubt; and the accumulation in a limited number of great establishments (chartered banks) of that business which is at present broken into small, and frequently insecure fragments. (See the evidence of E. Gilchrist before the Bullion Committee, 1810. ; also Mr. Joplin's pamphlet on Country Banks.

The Exemption from Cash Payments. — To exempt banks from cash payments was a measure altogether new in the history of finance, and the necessity for it is to be sought in difficulties that were peculiar to ourselves. France, Austria, and most other countries, know no mode of carrying on war but by furnishing men and military stores; but after 1795, England, in a great measure, exchanged this plan for the payment of subsidies. Then as to an occasional demand for a very different purpose, the supply of corn, the lower classes in most countries of the Continent, on the occurrence of scarcity, have recourse to coarse substitutes, or, being immersed in a poverty of which we have no idea, often fall victims to unhealthy food, sometimes to absolute want; while, in a wealthy community like England, an export of the circulating medium is made the means of obtaining relief. Now, though the sums sent abroad are in either case less great than they appear, our subsidies being furnished, in a great degree, in stores, and our corn paid, in some measure, by manufactures, the drain takes place from a stream already sufficiently small for its channel ; for in no country is there more of circulating medium than is *indispensable for the transaction of business.* This is apparent from various circumstances; from the rapidity with which money is made to circulate from dealer to dealer ; also, from a recent and striking fact, the distress that occurred in France in the autumn of 1818, when, notwithstanding the enjoyment of peace and free trade, the abstraction of a part of the metallic currency led to the most distressing results; an immediate reduction of discounts, a general fall of prices, and a long list of bankruptcies.

From difficulties of this nature we were relieved by that decisive measure, the exemption of our banks from cash payments: after its adoption no scarcity of money was experienced in the years of our heaviest continental demands: its effect, in fact, was to remove present pressure by incurring the hazard of depreciation, and of a great ultimate addition to our debt.

The Time of its Operation.—A considerable time elapsed before the operation of the act was fairly tried. In 1797 and 1798, our financial affairs were prosperous; our continental exchanges were favourable; and the suspension of subsidies and corn imports would, without the exemption, have restored confidence in our money market: when concurrent with it and with a vigorous increase of taxation, they raised the funds and added largely to the command of money on the part of our merchants, our manufacturers, our agriculturists. It was not till the autumn of 1799, that the aid expected from the act was put fairly to the test: our allies required large payments; our deficient harvest necessitated a great import; and both were supplied without the pecuniary embarrassment experienced before the exemption. The means now adopted were, the export of our coin to the Continent, and the substitution of bank paper: the result a partial depreciation (between 3 and 5 per cent.) of bank notes relatively to coin.

In 1800, notwithstanding the continuance of continental demands both for subsidies and the purchase of corn, both government and the mercantile world still escaped pressure from scarcity of money, and thus got over an interval of greater pressure than any in the early years of the war. The experiment had not, indeed, been made with impunity: we had exhausted our coin, and could not have undergone such another trial without a great depreciation of our paper. This was, doubtless, felt by Mr Pitt, and may be ranked among his principal motives for resigning and advising peace; but the shock was not perceived by the public, and was evidently of a nature to be repaired in a season of tranquillity.

Increase of Discounts explained.—The Bullion Committee in their Report (p. 26.) animadverted emphatically on the great increase that had taken place in the amount of discounts by the Bank of England, between 1797 and 1810. This they ascribed to over issue, but they omitted to make allowance for the operation of several causes of a wholly different nature. Thus, after the Exemption Act, the notes of the Bank of England were made to replace the cash reserve of every banker in the kingdom, and supplies of these notes could be obtained only by discount. Hence, the adoption of a practice, which, in the last age, would have been deemed not a little extraordinary by the cautious veterans of Lombard Street,—that of London bankers opening, like merchants, accounts with the Bank of England; and, when in want of money, sending thither bills for discount, in preference to a sale of Exchequer bills or stock. If the reserve fund of all the country banks of the kingdom, previous to the Exemption Act, be calculated at 4,000,000*l.*, we need be at no loss to account for a very large addition to the demands for discount on the Bank of England.

The Rate of Interest. — Our last reference to facts, or, as the French express it, to *les choses positives,* regards the rate of interest which, notwithstanding the magnitude of our war expense, rose only one per cent. above its average rate in peace. This was certainly a very moderate difference, and owing, in a great measure, to the substitution of war taxes for loans; to our raising so large a portion of our supplies within the year. It was owing, also, in a very considerable degree, to the advantage arising to bankers, from the Exemption Act; an advantage founded, in the case of provincial banks, on the saving of their reserve or dead fund, and wholly distinct from a power to increase their issues *ad libitum.* Had the latter been practicable, would not so gainful a business have been followed more extensively, and would not interest soon have been reduced by an eager competition, from five to four per cent? *

The Exemption Act considered as an economising Expedient. —The use of bank paper is a refinement enabling a community to turn to account a large proportion, suppose the half, of a currency which would otherwise be wholly unproductive. The exemption from cash payments

---

* For further arguments on the limited power of banks, see a pamphlet entitled " Observations on the Depreciation of Money; " also a second pamphlet, entitled " Farther Observations; " both published in 1811, by Robert Wilson, Esq. Accountant, and one of the Directors of the Bank of Scotland.

is a farther refinement, enabling bankers to hold, at the disposal of their customers, the chief part of their reserve fund; which, for the sake of precision, we shall consider a fourth of the paper currency in the country. Now, to keep the reserve fund as low as is compatible with security, has long been the wish of our bankers, and the object of a variety of arrangements: of these, by far the most effectual is that by which they settle their daily balances against each other, amounting (Evidence to the Bullion Report, p. 151.) to the very large sum of 5,000,000*l.* daily, by an exchange of cheques, without having occasion to use more than a tenth of the sum in bank notes. Of the same nature, are certain facilities given at the Bank of England, in regard to the hour at which a banking house makes its payment for the day; as well as the employment of money agents or middle-men (Evidence, Bullion Report, p. 124.) in obtaining sums from one banker for another, at very short notice. These various modes of lessening the amount of a dead stock are both ingenious and legitimate, affording a striking proof of the advantages attendant on a great commercial community, on mutual confidence, and vicinity of position. A farther saving of this nature would have formed one of the leading features of Mr. Ricardo's " plan for an economical and secure currency." Now, the result, which, on a comparative small scale, was attained by these arrangements, was accomplished, *en grand,* by the Exemption Act; which, by one decisive provision, enabled bankers to dispense with the most expensive and anxious part of their business. So far as regarded circulation at home, its effect partook of the beneficial character of the economising expedients; its weak side was towards the Continent, and there accordingly was received the wound which proved the source of so much pain and disquietude after 1809.

Report of the Bullion Committee.—This document, the merits of which have been so differently estimated, may be read with interest even at present, when the subject has received so much additional elucidation, both from research and from events that have intervened. The passages in the Report which treat of the regulation of money and exchange, whatever, in short, can be termed an exposition of general principles, are remarkable for accuracy and clearness: those of a different character are to be found in the latter part (pp. 23, 24.), and are open to censure, chiefly as implying a belief that the Bank had the means of *in-*

creasing its issues at discretion, as if the public were wholly without the power of checking the circulation, a power so clearly illustrated by Mr. Bosanquet, in his " Practical Observations on the Report."

Of the extent of misconception conveyed by disseminating the opinion that " the rise of prices was owing chiefly to our bank paper," some idea may be formed from one simple fact. The total rise of prices between 1797 and 1810 was above 30 per cent.; and of that not more than 5 or 6 per cent. was *at that time* attributable to the non-convertibility of our paper. (See the Essay on *Money* in Napier's Supplement, p. 526.) In this, we refer to the declaration of an eminent bullionist, (Mr. M'Culloch,) and cite his authority in contradiction to that of the Bullion Committee itself.

Another serious error, or rather omission in the Report, is an inattention to the " effect on the exchange of our subsidies and corn purchases." An admission is, indeed, made (p. 16.) in general terms, of the effect of political and mercantile transactions; but the impression conveyed by it is lessened by other passages (p. 21, &c.) in which the effects in question are treated as slight, and the result of the stoppage of American intercourse with the Continent is wholly passed over.

That the authors of the Report had deferred for a season the formation of their conclusions on a subject so new and complex, had certainly been desirable; but there seems no ground for the suspicion of their being actuated by party feeling. Their labours give evidence of great research and solicitude for truth ; while the imperfections in their reasoning admit of explanation from circumstances similar to those to which we have alluded in the text; in particular, the fact, that so much of the information now before the public was either unknown or very imperfectly disclosed to them. Thus, a witness of evident ability, and in the habit of very extensive discount transactions, gave (p. 124.) the following evidence:

" Do you know, in point of fact, whether such transactions as you have now described, were in practice previous to the suspension of the cash payments of the Bank? — Yes ; they were.

" Do you know whether they were practised to a similar extent ? — No; they were not.

" In what proportion, compared with the present time ? — I cannot form any exact criterion.

" Can you state to the Committee, the cause of such dif-ference? — I believe it to be on account of the increase of country paper, and also Bank of England paper."

When a witness of such intelligence, in accounting for the augmentation of discounts, leaves out of consideration the effects of the increase of our population and productive industry from 1797 to 1810, we need hardly wonder that they should have escaped the attention of the Committee. In fact, the errors of the latter may be easily accounted for. The chief writer of the Report, however temperate, impartial, and likely to rise in reputation, had his life been prolonged, was a stranger to the practice of business; and could not, from his youth, have had much acquaintance with the state of our money transactions previous to 1797. Of his coadjutors, one was a banker, never remarkable for clearness or accuracy; another, a man of undoubted ability, but at that time new, as he has himself admitted *, to questions of this nature. Accordingly, in historical and commercial matter the Report is very defective; no notice is taken in it of the pecuniary embarrassments of 1795 and 1796, arising from the double drain of specie for subsidies and corn; nor is the recurrence of these causes in 1799 or 1809 adverted to, although it was to them that we owed the chief increase of our bank notes. Nothing would have contributed so much to obtain the conviction of the mercantile body, we may say of the public at large, as a course of reasoning supported by facts. Such an inquiry, conducted with the candour that marks the Report, and was so conspicuous in the general parliamentary conduct of Mr. Horner, would have led to several very important conclusions; — to an estimate of the share in depreciation to be ascribed in the first place to the expenditure then making in Spain; next, to the corn imports then in progress from the Continent; and, lastly, to the interruption of the trade of the United States. Had the effect of the last been proved to be considerable, the inquiry might perhaps have led to a most desirable measure — the repeal of our Orders in Council before the United States resorted to the alternative of war.

Questions at issue between the Opponents and Supporters of the Bullion Report. — The points most strongly contested between the opposite parties in the bullion question were

---

* Huskisson on the Depreciation of our Currency, 1810.

two; — first, the cause of the fall of our exchanges; and, next, the cause of the progressive enhancement of commodities. As to the former, the events of 1815 showed, beyond doubt, that the *primary* cause of fluctuations in the exchange was to be sought in continental transactions, however much the non-convertibility of our paper might affect the degree and duration of the fall. The second question is more complicated, and there is still no small difficulty in convincing the bullionists that the operation of our non-convertible paper was passive, and necessarily posterior to the rise of prices. They will not, however, refuse their attention to facts, or deny that a very general rise of prices took place prior to 1797; nor will they object to admit inferences from the case of the agriculturists, the class whose circumstances operate most directly on the circulation of country banks.

Connexion between the Circumstances of our Agriculturists and the Circulation of Country Banks. — The continued inadequacy of our growth of corn rendered the war a period of activity in regard to inclosures, drainages, and other agricultural improvements: prices were carried to 30, 50, and in the latter years of the war to 100 per cent. beyond those of peace, requiring thus twice the sum to purchase the same commodities. Wages rose progressively; the style of living of the farmers, and even of their labourers, was visibly improved. Observe the reverse of the picture as exhibited in 1815 and 1816: prices and wages had fallen surprisingly; inclosures, drainages, and other improvements, were discouraged; the style of house-keeping on the part of the farmers was lowered, and a far smaller sum of currency was found sufficient for their transactions. In 1817 the high prices of corn brought back activity in agricultural improvements, and (see the Report of the Bank Committee of 1819) a renewed increase of paper currency. During the last four years the picture has been for the fourth time reversed; prices have fallen greatly, and with them the circulation of bank paper.

Prices of Merchandize. — In regard to these also, a similar course of reasoning will be found to hold: the adoption of a paper currency tended, doubtless, to promote enhancement; but the primary causes of it are to be sought in the war demand, or (see Tooke and High and Low Prices) in unfavourable seasons and obstructions to mercantile intercourse. It is a fact that almost all articles experienced a fall at the peace *before the reduction of bank paper.*

The Power of Banks over-rated.—We thus consider our banks as following the course of circumstances, and as *taking no lead*, either in extending or contracting their issues. Those who think otherwise, and who regard our banks as both possessing and exercising the power of over-issue, are pledged to show how it happened that these potent associations did not thus act at a much earlier period. Why did our banks defer until 1809, that which they might have done in 1797, at all events in 1803? On referring to the Bullion Report we shall find (p. 25.) that this difficulty is noticed, but not explained; and that the Committee, in pointing out two periods of extended issue, at the distance of more than seven years from each other (1801 and 1809), were wholly unable to give reasons for the circulation remaining stationary during that long interval. Farther, if our banks possessed this lucrative power, why suspend its exercise at the peace of 1814, so long before the act for the resumption of cash payments?

Inefficacy of an Exemption from Cash Payments in Peace.—We proceed to address a few sentences in the same style to a very different class of persons; to those who, suffering under the depressed price of merchandize or agricultural produce, regret that the exemption from cash payments should not have been made a permanent part of our policy. These persons cannot be aware that in peace this exemption would be of very rare and limited operation: it was in existence during 1819 and 1820, yet our prices continued progressively falling; in other words, the value of money progressively rose. The exemption from cash payments was, then, in one point of view, unnecessary; in another, it was inoperative. That it was unnecessary, was shown by the ease with which discounts were obtained; that it was inoperative, appeared from our exchanges keeping at or above par. Yet so little is this understood, that in the various debates on the subject in the House of Commons (*e. g.* 9th April, 1821,) the majority of our parliamentary guides attribute the great fall in prices to the return to a metallic standard; as if a state of peace and a favourable harvest were of little account, and the power of keeping up prices were actually vested in our banks.

Is it not apparent that in peace, when our exchanges are brought down by only one great cause, an occasional necessity for importing corn, the exemption from cash payments would be available only in a year like 1817, when the deficiency of the preceding crop led to a sudden demand on our neighbours, and when the exemption from cash payments would enable us to send abroad several millions of our metallic currency?

Mr. Peel's Bill. — Those who ascribe our present embarrassments to Mr. Peel's Bill, and the resumption of cash-payments, would do well to consider that no legislative arrangement has the power of converting a banker into a capitalist. The object of the latter is to obtain interest for his money, without the trouble or hazard of active business; while a banker is necessarily a man of business, and seldom a man of large capital. His funds, arising chiefly from deposit, and being subject to sudden demands, must be vested in securities easily vendible, such as mercantile acceptances, exchequer bills, or government stock. Any deviation from this course, any advance of money made on land, houses, or property of doubtful sale, is at variance with the rules of his business, and never fails to be attended with embarrassment or loss.

Publications on the Subject of Exchange. — The present age has been fertile in essays on the principles of exchange, among which the most entitled to attention are; the remarks in the Bullion Report, (pp. 10, 11.); Mr. W. Blake's pamphlet, entitled " Observations on Exchange," published in 1810; and an essay by Mr. J. R. M'Culloch, under the head of " Exchange," in the Supplement to the Encyclopædia Britannica. The last claims our attention, not only as an able and comprehensive treatise, but as differing in its general tone from the arguments advanced in the text; a difference, however, which, on an attentive examination, will be found less considerable than it appears.

Correspondence between our reasoning and that of Mr. M'Culloch. — Mr. M., in maintaining (Essay on Exchange, p. 220.) that corn purchases or expenditure abroad have no *permanent* effect on the exchange, does not deny that their temporary effect is great. Such is also our doctrine, as exemplified in the tabular statement in the text: the fall in our exchange was not permanent at all till 1800, nor permanent, in a high degree, till 1809; and in both cases it became, after a certain time, nominal.

Farther, a fall in the computed exchange, when there is no exemption from cash payments, is recovered during the continuance of the pressure, but when such exemption subsists, *the currency loses its reinstating power*, and becoming depreciated, the exchange continues depressed until the re-action of causes, mercantile or political, restore the value of the currency. Of both we have had striking examples in the present age : the fall of our exchange in 1795 and 1796, was redressed in the end of 1796, and beginning of 1797, before the termination of our subsidy to Austria ; whereas the fall in 1800, and still more that in 1809, and continued, until the conclusion of peace entirely altered the nature of our connexion with the Continent.

Fluctuations in the Exchange in 1815. — We have dwelt in the text on the fluctuations of the exchange in 1815, viz. on its sudden fall on the renewal of continental hostilities, and its no less sudden rise on the prospect of their termination. Both are evidently accordant with the general admission in the Essay in question (p. 220.), of the great temporary effects of foreign demand. They require, therefore, no farther notice, except as to the extent of the fall in April and May, 1815, which (nearly 20 per cent.) was very great, open as the Continent then was to our exports.

But does not this extent of fall furnish a strong presumption in favour of another part of our reasoning on this intricate subject, viz. our mode of accounting for the great and continued depression of the exchange during the years 1811, 1812, and 1813? The demands on us from the Continent, say the bullionists, were not great in these years ; but admitting the correctness of Mr. M'Culloch's statement (Essay on Exchange, p. 222.), that our remittances to the Continent for corn and subsidies did not much exceed 2,000,000*l.* sterling, in each of these years, we consider even that sum sufficient to continue the depression, England being then wholly exhausted of the precious metals, the counterpoising effect of the American trade removed, and our exports to the Continent greatly cramped.

Reduction of Country-Bank Paper. — In regard to the diminution of country-bank paper, which took place in 1815 and 1816, we agree with Mr. M'Culloch as to the fact, and are not disposed to dissent from his estimate of the extent of the reduction : the difference lies in our considering this reduction as *posterior* to a fall of prices, exactly as we consider the augmented issue during the war and in 1817 as posterior to their rise.

Depreciation. — Lastly, as to the extent of depreciation arising from the Exemption Act. That the unfavourable balance of exchange from 1809 to 1814 was chiefly nominal, and that in regard to continental payments our bank paper was depreciated to the extent denoted by the course of exchange, we readily admit. But as the use of our bank paper was to circulate commodities at home, and as the rise of prices consequent on its continental depreciation was by no means immediate, we have, we conceive, made a fair allowance in taking the average of home depreciation at somewhat more than the half of the foreign; meaning, that if in Spain or Germany 125*l.* in notes were required in 1812, to pay for that which might have been purchased for 100*l.* in metallic currency, the proportion at home was probably 10 per cent. less; 115*l.* in notes purchasing what, without the exemption from cash payments, might have been had for 100*l.*

APPENDIX

TO

CHAPTER V.

Effect of increasing Population on the Price of Corn.—
The reasoning in the text enables us to correct a very material part of the Report of the Agricultural Committee.
The writers of that Report, in adverting (p. 11.) to the
chance of a future deficiency of harvest, advance an opinion
that the magnitude of our consumption, as compared with
that of former periods, must render the pressure of deficiency more severe, and the means of providing against it
more difficult.

" A harvest," they add, " which should be one-third
below an average in wheat, would bring on this country a
very different degree of suffering, and would require a very
different degree of exertion and sacrifice, to supply the
deficiency, from what would have been required under a
similar failure fifty years ago." But to this opinion of the
Committee we must oppose a recent and highly important
fact; viz. that though the harvest of 1816 was (Evidence of
Mr. Hodgson, p. 264.) a full third below the average of our
wheat-crop, yet the degree of public suffering was *less intense*
than would have been experienced under a similar failure
fifty years before. For this there are several reasons :—

1st. If the agricultural part of our countrymen increase
their numbers in proportion to the consumers; if the
amount of produce depend on the extent of labour and
capital applied to cultivation; and if a recourse to the inferior soils mentioned repeatedly in the Report (and in
Mr. Ricardo's well-known work on Political Economy and
Taxation) be far less necessary than an improved cultivation
of the better soils; we stand nearly in the situation of our
forefathers, and find the prospect of adequacy of supply
very little affected by the increase of our numbers; because

that increase brings with it the power of augmenting our labour, and, consequently, our produce.

2dly. If such be the case at home, the chance of relief from abroad is decidedly improved, since the extension of tillage in the course of the last and present age. The surface of corn country in Europe, we mean of country producing corn in sufficiency for export, was formerly far from large; comprising only Great Britain, Ireland, the North of France, and North of Germany, with part of Denmark and Poland. We have explained in the text (p. 149.) the similarity of temperature prevalent throughout this tract, which is almost all maritime, and presents no very material difference of latitude. Hence a deficiency of crop, whether arising from blight as in 1811, or from excess of rain as in 1809 and 1816, was more or less common to the whole. But in the last and present age, tillage has been extended in the interior of Poland, and on the shores of the Euxine; countries differing considerably from ours in climate, and not likely to be affected by the causes which create disappointment in the north-west of Europe. As yet, the produce in these countries is far from large, but the improvements now taking place in river navigation bid fair to facilitate the access to several fertile tracts hitherto in a manner excluded from communication with the sea. Add to this, that a similar prospect is presented by the increased cultivation of the United States of America. To expect a very extensive supply from either would, on account of the distance, be absurd; but in a year of scarcity, an import to the extent of only a week or a fortnight's consumption has a very sensible effect on our corn market.

It follows that the result, in the present age at least, is very different from the anticipation of the Committee. The progress of improvement, and the extension of communication between different countries, which are the accompaniments of augmented population, have a very beneficial effect on the supply of corn: they widen the range of purchase, enable one nation to come to the relief of another, and convert into the mitigated form of scarcity those failures of harvest, which, in remote ages, were followed by all the horrors of famine.

National Disadvantage of a high Price of Corn.—After all that we have urged on the vital importance to the country of the prosperity of agriculture, we may, without suspicion of under-rating that importance, subjoin a few remarks on a subject at present very seldom mentioned:—

the evils that would attend a price of corn materially higher than that of our neighbours; we mean a price between 70s. and 80s. a quarter, while that of France, the Netherlands, or Germany, was at 45s. or 50s. The war closed, in a political sense, with so much success, with so great an appearance of national triumph, as to blind us for a season to the evils of transition, and to the embarrassment consequent on high prices. The injurious effect of the latter was, indeed, shown in part by the emigration of half-pay officers, annuitants, and persons with large families, who drew their income from this country and expended it abroad, giving to our neighbours the stimulus arising from reproduction, and subjecting England to an injury of the kind so long inflicted on Ireland by her absentee proprietors. The amount thus drawn by emigrants and travellers has been, we believe, moderately computed, for some time, at 5,000,000l., at present at 4,000,000l. a year; but how much greater would have been the evil had a continuance of high prices induced master manufacturers, or their workmen, to seek an establishment on the Continent? Those of our countrymen, who have travelled since the peace, remark, and apparently with justice, that continental manufacturers are as yet far from formidable; but they fail to take into account the surprising change that might have been effected by a transfer of British capital and master workmen. With these potent aids the inhabitants of Normandy, the Netherlands, or the banks of the Rhine, would soon become dangerous rivals, for we ought steadily to keep in mind that our superiority, as a nation, *lies not in the individual, but in our establishments; in the operation of collective bodies:* as workmen, our neighbours would soon attain an equality, were they placed on a par with us in regard to machinery, and the division of employment. Their merchants have not, it is true, the capital necessary to give long credit to customers, such as the Americans; but that want would have been supplied by our exporters, who, whether they emigrated personally or not, would have made a point of purchasing goods in those towns or districts of the Continent, where they could have been most cheaply manufactured.

Would our government have possessed any means of counteracting the tide of emigration? None; if our corn-market had been kept at an exorbitant height, the tide would have flowed in various directions, according to the respective advantages of particular situations. One part of the Continent possesses mines of iron, another mines of coal, a third abounds in timber, while several tracts of coast approach to ours in the number and capacity of their sea-ports. Happily no part of the Continent could offer these advantages collectively, so that although inquiries were made and calculations formed by many of our speculative men, no emigration of consequence took place among our labour-ing classes, and the present prices of the necessaries of life among us seem to remove such unwelcome enterprizes to an indefinite date.

Subsistence of the lower Orders. — In reasoning on the means of supporting the lower orders, we have not laid stress on the effects of spade husbandry, of deep ploughing, or other agricultural experiments described in late publica-tions. Nor do we dwell on the practicability of subsisting an increased population by the more general use of pota-toes, although, in 1817, a case in point was established by the French government, who recommended in public orders the more general cultivation of that root; and, in regard to Ireland, it is a curious fact, that the export of corn has be-come large since the great increase of the population. Our object, however, is not to dwell on the means of reducing the expense of subsistence; it is merely to show that in-crease of population *has no necessary tendency to raise it.*

Uncertainty of speculative Opinions. — In treating of the prospects of our agriculturists, our wish is less to press a particular opinion, than to show the uncertainty of many of the allegations advanced of late years with so much con-fidence. After the revolutions we have witnessed in statis-tics as in politics, it would be idle to attempt predictions as to what is likely to be either the amount or the price of our produce. In this season of profound peace, agriculture occupies a very large share of the national capital and in-genuity; discoveries and inventions are successively occur-ring to modify established methods and alter received opi-nions. Take, for example, the subject on which so much was urged in parliament lately, — a high protecting duty. If during peace our growth continue adequate to our consumption, what will have been the use of these pro-tracted discussions, and where would be the advantage so confidently promised to our farmers from the protection in question? From these various considerations, ought we not to conclude, that the only safe course is to be guided, as far as circumstances at all permit, by general principles, expecting little from any deviation, however plausible, and calculating that in the price of our produce, as in other results, this country cannot long differ from the civilized world at large? This naturally leads to a brief notice of the

Arguments in favour of a free Trade in Corn. — Without any wish to discuss this question at length, we lay before our readers the opinion of several well-informed writers.

Extract from a pamphlet entitled " Observations on the Commerce of Grain, by Dugald Bannatyne, Esq., Secretary to the Chamber of Commerce of Glasgow," 1816.

" All great authorities" (says Mr. B., p.10.) " were in favour of a free trade in corn, until Mr. Malthus demanded the same protection for the home grower of corn, as for the home manufacturer of particular commodities: but these manufactures (such as lace and silk) are productive of no benefit to the public, being all carried on in contradiction to natural and inherent obstacles, while our labour and capital would find a more beneficial direction, if transferred to the woollen, cotton, hardware, or other branches; in which, particularly in the latter, we possess local and permanent advantages over our continental neighbours.

" It seems extraordinary, that we should be so much alive to the advantages we gain from the division of employment in the prosecution of our home industry, and not see the benefit to be obtained from the more extended division of employment in the case of nations; a division pointed out by the separate facilities for carrying them on, which, from climate, soil, or natural productions, different countries possess. By keeping up the price of corn, we oblige ourselves to labour in our manufactures at a great disadvantage, when compared with other nations."

Extract from a pamphlet, by Major (now Colonel) Torrens, published also in 1816, and entitled " Letter to Lord Liverpool on the State of Agriculture:" —

" To any persons who will either investigate first principles, or recur to the experience of countries which, like Holland, have given freedom to trade, it must be evident, that this natural state of things is greatly preferable to any artificial system which can be substituted in its stead. As we extend the area from which subsistence is drawn, the inequality in the productiveness of the seasons diminishes. Hence when, under a free intercourse, a deficient harvest required an unusual import, abundant harvests in some other country of the world would supply the deficiency by an extraordinary export. On the other hand, a succession of unusually abundant years could occasion no deep depression in our markets, because this extraordinary quantity of corn of home growth could not (as when abundant harvests occur in the case of a country forcing in average years an independent supply) much exceed the consumption of the season."

To these opinions we add that of Mr. M'Culloch, who has inserted an Essay on the Corn Laws, in the same work as his Essay on Exchange, viz. the Supplement to the Encyclopædia Britannica. After regretting that the corn trade was not definitively laid open in 1815, a time when, as at present, our prices were so low that our agriculture had, in a manner, felt all the evils of transition, and the public would have reaped the greatest advantage from a return to unrestricted freedom, Mr. M. adds,—

" When this happy event" (a free trade in corn) " shall have taken place, it will be no longer necessary to force nature. The capital and enterprise of the country will be turned into those departments of industry in which our physical situation, national character, or political institutions, fit us to excel. The corn of Poland, and the raw cotton of Carolina, will be exchanged for the wares of Birmingham and the muslins of Glasgow. The genuine commercial spirit, that which permanently secures the prosperity of nations, is altogether inconsistent with the dark and shallow policy of monopoly. The nations of the earth are like provinces of the same kingdom — a free and unfettered intercourse is alike productive of general and of local advantage."

Political economists are more accustomed to deal in general reasoning, than to analyse the circumstances of a case, or to go through the details necessary to the suggestion of a specific remedy. This blank we shall now endeavour to supply, and, by way of supplement to the preceding arguments, add a sketch of the preliminaries indispensable to freedom in our corn trade. By these we mean the exemption of our agriculturists from such burdens as press on them either exclusively, or in a greater degree than on the rest of the public. Thus:—

Computation of Poor Rate and Tithe. — Of the sums levied for rates in England and Wales, the average annual amount will probably be, ere long, reduced to—

Highway rate, county rate, church rate - £1,200,000
Law suits, removal of paupers, and expence
   of parish officers - - - - - 300,000
Maintenance and relief of the poor, after assuming a reduction from the present charge
   of somewhat more than 1,000,000*l.* - 4,500,000

In all - £6,000,000

Of this amount what part bears exclusively on agriculture? To calculate that we begin by excluding

1. The proportion that appears to be raised in
   towns, including smaller towns than those
   mentioned in the Poor-rate Report of
   1821, p. 13., and referring to the assessment
   of 1815, in which a distinction is made between the contribution of landholders and
   householders - - - - - £1,500,000
2. A large sum which in fact is but *nominally*
   paid by agriculturists, the wages of country
   labour being lower than they would be without the rates: this sum we estimate conjecturally, in war at 2,000,000*l.*; in peace at 1,000,000
Remainder, being the *actual* burden on agriculture arising from rates, supposing the whole
   on a reduced scale - - - - 3,500,000

Total (agreeing with the preceding) £6,000,000

Now, were all classes equal contributors to
   the rates, the quota of the land would be
   only a third, or 2,000,000*l.* making a deduction from the 3,500,000*l.* of - - £1,500,000
Next, as to *Tithe.*—Amount of tithe of England, Wales, and Ireland, computed at the
   reduced price of produce, but including tithe
   paid to laymen, about - 5,000,000*l.*
If tithe also were rendered a national burthen,
   the land ought to pay only a third (1,700,000*l.*)
   which would form a deduction from its present burden of 3,300,000
Total deduction that would then be made from
   the burdens on agriculture - - £4,800,000

It is a remarkable coincidence that this sum (4,800,000*l.*)

is little more than the excess of the burdens on British over those on French agriculture. See the text, p. 172.

As our allowance of 4,500,000*l*. for the poor may appear below the mark, we shall compare it with the rate as it stood before the late wars : —

In 1792 our poor-rate, exclusive of law expences, and of highway or county rate, amounted to about - - - - £2,000,000
Add an increase of 50 per cent. proportioned to the increase of population - 1,000,000
Remains to add, as a kind of allowance for the greater embarrassment of the present time, and for abuses introduced into the system 1,500,000

Total - £4,500,000

Tithe: Mode of computing its present Amount. — Our estimate in the preceding page is founded on the property tax returns for the year 1812, (Nos. 248. and 250. for 1814-15). Viewing the question historically, we find a very close connection between the increase of our population and the increase of our tithe. As there are no means of ascertaining the amount of our agricultural produce, our reference must be to the increase of consumers ; and though our population returns go no farther back than 1801, we may with tolerable certainty compute the total addition to have been nearly 50 per cent. on our numbers as they stood in 1792. In fact, were we possessed of a correct return of tithe for that year, we should calculate its present amount by merely adding 50 per cent. to such return ; for the prices of produce being now similar to those of 1792, the comparative estimate becomes narrowed to a calculation of quantity.

Rent of Land. — Can we with any confidence observe a similar rule when calculating the progressive increase of rent ? In that the connection between augmented produce and augmented payment is less apparent than in the case of tithe : yet it would be obviously vain to attempt a mode of computation, which may at first claim attention, we mean one founded on the extent of additional surface brought into tillage. In proof of this we have merely to consider that the 50 per cent. added to our produce in the last thirty years has been raised with an addition of probably less than fifteen per cent. to the number of acres under corn culture, and has been chiefly the fruit of the additional labour and improved methods applied to the surface previously under the plough. The extension of tillage over inferior soils is rather an index of augmented rent, than a basis for its calculation: the latter we should seek by preference in the new methods that have been discovered, the old that are improved, the consequent abridgment of labour, and the additional quantity of corn produced at the same expence; for the effect of all improvements, whether they ameliorate quality or augment quantity, is to cheapen production: they are otherwise not entitled to the name of improvements.

What, it may be asked, is the benefit to the nation from such improvements? The power of supporting an additional population on the same territorial surface. — And what is the advantage to the proprietors of that surface? An increase of rent which there are, it seems to us, various reasons for calculating in proportion to increase of population. Were the number of consumers stationary, the result of agricultural improvements would be a fall of market price: with an increase of consumers, the results are the maintenance of price and the rise of rent. If the surface which, a century ago, produced wheat for the support of two millions of inhabitants, be now sufficient to maintain twice the number, the price of wheat being the same, we shall probably deviate little from the truth in assuming that, in the natural course of things, *the rent also ought to be doubled;* and that any excess or deficiency in this proportion of increase is to be sought in causes temporary, peculiar, or in some cases, little more than apparent.

How far is this confirmed by historical evidence? It seems to have long been the case in France, a country where corn still sells for the price it bore a *century and a half ago,* and the agricultural history of which is more simple and regular than that of England, being unembarrassed by fluctuations in the value of the currency, or by insufficiency in the average growth for the average consumption. But even in England, the proportion between increase of population and rise of rent will be found to hold in a considerable degree. It might, perhaps, be traced, were our documents complete, during the long period from 1650 to 1792; in which the price of corn bore, with casual and temporary exceptions, a character of uniformity. Even in the present age, we should not despair of finding a confirmation of our rule, could we succeed in clearing our calculation of the temporary effect of bank paper and of seasons unusually adverse. Such an attempt might, some years ago, have been ridiculed; but at present the temporary part of the increase has disappeared, and left us with the prices of 1792, along with a discovery in regard to rent not a little at variance with the high-flown language of those who saw in the war a source of unparalleled wealth; — that the present rental of the United Kingdom is, as far as we can judge, little more than 50 per cent. above that of 1792, or 36,000,000*l.*, instead of 24,000,000*l.*, its supposed amount before our rupture with France.

This sober result, if it fall below the sanguine expectation of those who still cling to high prices, and still put faith in the efficacy of corn laws, leaves, on the other hand, a rise fair and legitimate. We have no argument to found on the principle of calculating the future rise of rent by the increase of our numbers, but it seems to be just towards both parties. Our landlords certainly would have no reason to complain of it; for it presents to them the cheering prospect of being not only permanent but progressive.

Use of Salt in Agriculture. — We cannot forbear adding a few words on a topic closely connected with the freedom of productive industry, we mean the *increased use of salt in agriculture.* If there be any accuracy in the arguments of the late Sir Thomas Bernard, and of several others who have written on the subject, how sensible must be the benefit to our farmers and graziers, now that government has given the means of so decided an extension to the use of salt, either as a manure or for feeding cattle. Our inland navigation will enable almost every district to profit by the relaxation; and the injury to the revenue in one sense will, we trust, soon be compensated by benefit in another, since the only solid basis of taxation is the extension of the national industry.

There is thus little or no doubt, that, were our farmers relieved from their extra burdens, they would be enabled to raise produce on as low terms as our continental neighbours, and might, ere long, allow the public to reap all the benefit arising from unrestricted freedom in the corn trade. For the present, however, we consider " unrestricted freedom" as wholly out of the question, and shall confine our speculations to the effect of relaxation; of a protecting duty on a reduced scale.

Comparative Burdens on British and Foreign Agriculture.
—Abstract of the Evidence before the Agricultural Committee (April and May, 1821) of Mr. Tooke, partner in a
mercantile house extensively connected with the Baltic: —

Mr. T., aware how greatly the untravelled part of our
countrymen overrate the cheapness of foreign countries,
laid before the Agricultural Committee (Evidence, p. 224.)
tables of the prices of wheat from 1814 to 1820, at Peters-
burgh, Riga, and Archangel; the result of which is, that
it could seldom, in these years of peace, have been delivered in an English port for less than from 50s. to 60s. a
quarter. At Odessa the price is occasionally very low, but
the freight to England is high; and the hazard of damage
on so long a voyage is such as to put that port almost out
of the question for the British market. And as to another
point, the amount of supply to be expected from the Continent at large, Mr. T. concurs with Mr. Jacob, (Evidence,
pp. 232. 260.) that it is in general overrated.

In regard to our own agriculture, Mr. T. differs materially from those who imagine that a continuance of the
present low prices would throw much land out of cultivation. As a fall in the price of corn necessarily reduces the
cost of production, he sees no great reason (pp. 232. 288.)
why we should not, as half a century ago, raise corn *as
cheaply, or almost as cheaply, as on the Continent,* particularly now that the agriculture of Ireland is relieved from
restraint.

Mr. T. is also the only witness who brings forward
(p. 288.) an argument which we have been at pains to
enforce in the text, viz. that an import limit, if high, would
induce extended cultivation, and prove injurious to our
farmers. We have his concurrence, likewise, in another
important point, in accounting (p. 344.) for the great fall
in the price of commodities since the peace, less by a recurrence to cash payments, than by the application of a
great addition of labour and capital to productive purposes.
Lastly, he is favourable to a protecting duty on corn, provided (Evidence, p. 297.) it be no greater than the direct
taxes that operate on our own production.

The opinion, that our corn is likely to be raised at a rate
(between 50s. and 60s. the quarter) nearly as cheap as on
the Continent, has a claim to particular attention; and we
proceed to enquire how far it is confirmed by a consideration of either our past or present circumstances.

Prices during last Century. —If in the history of our corn trade we go back sufficiently far to reach a period of profound peace, we shall find little reason to expect that in such a season our prices can be kept much above those of the Continent. Throughout the hundred years that elapsed between the accession of Charles II. and of George III., corn was as low, or nearly as low, in England as in France, the Netherlands, or other adjacent parts of the Continent. After 1764, the case was different; but of the 8s. or 10s. per quarter of additional price obtained in this country, the half may safely be ascribed to temporary causes; we mean the American war, the extension of our manufactures, and the general aversion to vest capital in farming, after the discouraging experience of the preceding age. But our taxation, it may be said, is greater, compared to that of continental countries, than it was in the last century, and France is now exempt from tithe; — important considerations certainly, but balanced by others of great weight on our side; by the fact that the tillage of Ireland is no longer in fetters, that our machinery and implements have received much more improvement, our inland navigation a much greater extension than that of our neighbours. The advantage of all these to agriculture can be appreciated by those only who have seen the wretched roads, the clumsy implements and vehicles of the Continent, or who have duly weighed the cheapness of our canal carriage; by which salt, manure, or bulky commodities generally, can, in many parts, be transported ten or fifteen miles at the insignificant charge of a shilling a ton.

Our present Prospect. — The arguments in favour of Mr. Tooke's opinion derived from our present situation are as follow : —

1. During the war, rents rose without care or exertion on the part of our landlords; at present land affords a rent of consequence only when cultivated with skill — the most substantial of all arguments for the diffusion of the improved husbandry.

2. The evils that now bear so hard on our agriculture are evils of transition; the degree of pressure will be materially different when farming charges shall have been reduced (as reduced they must be) in proportion to the market price of corn.

3. As to the comparative burdens on our agriculture and that of other countries, we have in the text taken France

as a fair specimen of the Continent generally: if in Poland
and Russia the burdens are less heavy than in France, husbandry, as an art, is far more backward, and the charge
of freight to England is heavier.   A reference to the passage (p. 168.) containing the comparison with France, will
much simplify the present statement, enabling us to leave
out of the question the advantage of cheaper labour on
the part of the French, and on ours of better machinery,
lower interest of money, a more advantageous size of farms,
&c.   After enumerating the respective burdens, we found
the difference confined to a portion of our excise duty on
malt, beer, and corn spirits; a difference which, when, as
at present, the corn laws are in a manner inoperative, left
a sum of 4 or 5,000,000*l.* to the disadvantage of our
countrymen.   This difference forms a charge of 7 or 8 per
cent. on the rental of our landlords, and the income of our
farmers taken collectively.

Competition of continental Agriculturists. — Supposing
that the effect of a protecting duty is merely to keep our
market from 6*s.* to 8*s.* a quarter above that of France, or
the Netherlands, would there be reason to apprehend that
English capital would find its way abroad, and be applied
to the extension of culture on the Continent, with a view to
import into this country?   To such a question our answer
three years ago might have been in the affirmative; but our
charges are now so much reduced, and the advantages of
Ireland in regard to cheap labour, command of water
communication, and fertility of soil, are found to approach
so nearly to those of the most favoured tracts of the Continent, that we much doubt whether any transfer of capital
would take place to the latter, particularly as, on referring
to the evidence annexed to the Agricultural Report, we
find (p. 364.) that the cost of raising a quarter of wheat in
Prussia or Poland, including the conveyance to Dantzic,
but exclusive of rent, is about 36*s.* the quarter, an expence
little greater than the cost of raising it (p. 335.) free of
rent, in East Lothian.

Next, as to the storing or warehousing of foreign corn,
with a view to import. — The interest of the money vested
in the purchase of corn forms so considerable a part of the
annual charge of keeping it in granary, that were our prices
to rise materially, it might enter into the views of our corn
merchants to purchase in remote countries, like the interior
of Poland or the south-west of Russia, where the average

price of wheat is not above 30*s.*, and in some years (Evidence, p. 364.), lower.   At present such a course is out of the question, the inland provinces in these countries being unprovided either with proper warehouses, or with the means of giving security to deposited property.   Were these defects supplied by the erection of suitable buildings in a town adjacent to a navigable river, and by the protection of a military guard, a large supply of corn might be warehoused in cheap years, and on the occurrence of a rise, sent to a market in this country or elsewhere.   The transport to Dantzic or Odessa, added to the freight from Dantzic to England, or from Odessa to the south of France, might be averaged at 20*s.* the quarter, carrying the total cost, when brought to market, to somewhat more than 50*s.*, exclusive of our protecting duty; a price which, if not high, is greatly above that which is assigned by vague rumour (see Mr. Curwen's speeches in the session of 1821,) to the Polish market.

The United States of America. — The great distance of that country from Europe has long led to the practice of shipping its produce in the form of flour, rather than of grain; thus accomplishing a saving in freight, and avoiding the shifting and heating to be apprehended in a long and tempestuous passage.   Among other recent discoveries, we are apprized (p. 437. *Revue Encyclopédique,* for August, 1821, printed at Paris,) of a method of preserving flour during several years in perfect condition, by means of air-tight casks; but whether the expence of this or other methods of the kind be not too great for the chance of profit, remains to be ascertained.

Compared to these, what means are possessed by our own agriculturists in regard to keeping corn in the granary, and making the plenty of one season conducive to the supply of the next?   They have the command of better buildings; they pay a lower interest on capital; and are exempt, in a great measure, from the charge of conveyance to market: their chief disadvantage lies in the prime cost of their produce.

Improvements in Husbandry. — Those who are inclined to subscribe to the efficacy of some lately-promulgated methods of penetrating more deeply into the soil, whether by the plough or spade, may consider the Continent likely to benefit more largely from them in consequence of its cheaper labour, its greater agricultural population. But

in any improvement arising from such a process, this country can hardly fail to share equally, superior as we are in
horses, ploughs, and iron-work generally; while, in regard
to labour, Ireland is as cheaply and abundantly supplied
as any part of the Continent.

Probable Amount of Import. — A low rate of duty on
foreign corn would doubtless prevent any considerable rise
in our market; but it by no means follows that our tillage
would be materially circumscribed, or that the amount of our
import would be large. Of barley, our growth is in general
equal to our consumption : a considerable import takes place
only in particular years, and after seasons unfavourable to
this kind of grain, such as the summers of 1816 and 1817.
In oats the case has hitherto been different, our growth being
habitually below our consumption, and large imports being
required both from Ireland and the Continent: the amount
has varied, of course, in different years, but has not for a
long time averaged so little as half a million of quarters
from either. In future our import of oats, at least in
peace, is likely to be confined to Ireland. Of beans, pease,
and rye, our growth is in general adequate, and our imports insignificant: in regard to wheat, our imports, formerly on so large a scale, are at present suspended; nor
are they likely to be renewed during peace, except on the
accidental occurrence of an indifferent season.

What appears to be the average growth of corn of all
kinds in Great Britain and Ireland? According to Mr.
Colquhoun, it seems in 1812 to have been, including the
corn used as seed, about 40,000,000 of quarters, to which
may be added for increase in the period that has intervened
about 20 per cent., or 8,000,000 of quarters. In reasoning
on years to come, with the prospect of a progressive increase, we shall not greatly err in taking our growth at an
average of nearly 50,000,000 of quarters, of corn of all
kinds. Then, as to import — now that we are in the enjoyment of peace, and possess so ample a command of capital
and labour, we may calculate our average demand for
foreign corn at a very moderate amount. It must necessarily vary greatly, according to the seasons; but the average of a series of years of peace will perhaps not exceed a
million of quarters of grain of all kinds, or 2 per cent. on
the total of our annual growth.

" All undue protection to agriculture," says Mr. Ricardo
in his pamphlet on Agriculture, (p. 81.) " should be

gradually withdrawn. The policy which we ought, at this moment of distress to adopt, is to give the monopoly of the home market to the British grower till corn reaches 70*s.* per quarter. When it has reached 70*s.*, a duty of 20*s.* per quarter on the importation of wheat, and other grain in proportion, might be imposed.

" I should further propose, that the duty of 20*s.* should every year be reduced one shilling, until it reached ten shillings. A duty of ten shillings per quarter, on importation, to which I wish to approach, is, I am sure, rather too high as a countervailing duty for the peculiar taxes which are imposed on the corn grower, over and above those which are imposed on the other classes of production in the country; but I would rather err on the side of a liberal allowance than of a scanty one."

Ought a Protecting Duty to be suspended in a dear Season? — However adverse in general to high prices, we are by no means inclined to give this question an affirmative answer. The temperature which causes a partial failure in England being likely to prevail throughout the north-west of Europe, can hardly fail to raise the corn market in the Netherlands, the Danish dominions, and the north of Germany, in the same manner, though not in an equal degree, as in this country. Prices may thus be brought, by a natural course, to the limit at which the protecting duty ceases: if not, a suspension of it would be impolitic, as well from the general inexpediency of tampering with an established law, as for another reason, viz. that a rise of price does not (Evidence, p. 36.) in a year of deficiency form an equivalent to a farmer for short quantity; he can be indemnified only by the continuance of the advanced price during the succeeding year. To that he is fairly entitled: to deprive him of it by a suspension of the protecting duty, would be to cast on tillage a discouragement similar to what it has experienced from unlimited import under the corn law of 1815.

But in what manner, it may be asked, should we then lessen to the poor the pressure of a dear season? By charitable contributions; which, when limited to an interval of real want, have few or none of the bad consequences of an established poor-rate. And in what way are the public indemnified for taking this burden on themselves instead of suspending the protecting duty? By the moderate rate at which that duty is fixed.

To these observations we subjoin the opinion of a writer who differs in many points from the political economists of the school of Smith : —

Observations of Mr. S. Gray on the Corn Trade. — Mr. G. has given, in the papers added in 1819 to his work entitled " The Happiness of States," an opinion (pp. 34, 35.) on the corn trade, similar in most points to that of the Agricultural Committee of 1821.   He always considered our late corn law as likely to make importation affect the home price suddenly or violently ; while a protecting duty would make it flow in a gentle stream, tending to keep prices fair, and inducing the foreign cultivator to look to England as a market, on certain conditions ; according to which he would regulate his purchase of our colonial goods and manufactures.   This opinion proceeds from a writer by no means inclined to regard low prices as a public advantage, but who considers (Happiness of States, p. 665.) fluctuating gains as highly pernicious, tending to raise rents and labour extravagantly, and to produce a premature change in the style of living.   The true interest of the farmer is in a steady price, tending to rise gradually with the national improvement, and proportioned consequently to the prices of other commodities.

Tenants on Lease, and Debtors on Mortgage. — The case of a tenant on lease, on the occurrence of a rapid fall of prices, is peculiarly hard ; the evil overtakes him in all its extent, while the relief is but partial, the grand charge of rent remaining unadapted to the altered state of things. He must in the first instance lay his account with a sacrifice of part of his capital, with refunding the gains arising from the previous depreciation of money.   This, it must be confessed, is but fair, since the profit arising during the war from depreciation was reaped chiefly by the tenant. But after a certain period of suffering, a liberal landlord will consider what is due to equity, and what in many cases, where the covenants of the lease are not drawn in the anticipation of such a change, is necessary to prevent injury to his land.

Debtors on mortgage are, in like manner, heavy sufferers, their means of payment generally diminishing as the value of their money debt increases.   They have, however, in one respect a substantial ground of hope ; the prospect of reducing their interest to 4½, and some time hence to 4 per cent.

Interference by Courts of Justice.—During the half century from 1764 to 1814, the change in the value of money was all on the opposite side, commodities tending to a rise: gradual, and almost imperceptible during thirty years, it was after 1794 so regularly progressive, that in the course of twenty years 160*l.* became equivalent to only 100*l.* of 1794. During the latter years of the war, annuitants, and the landlords who had granted long leases, received hardly two-thirds of the original value; yet no appeal on the ground of depreciated currency was brought before parliament or our courts of justice. Any attempt of that kind in parliament would have been resisted by government, partly from an aversion to interfere with private contracts; more from a solicitude to prevent the public attention being fixed on the depreciation then going on in the greatest of all debts, that of the nation.

Since 1814 we have had a reaction, and of so rapid a nature, that in trade 100*l.* are equal to 130*l.* at the close of the war; in farming to much more. How, it may be asked, does this sudden change affect the question of judicial interference? In equity, there can be little doubt that all engagements ought to continue payable in money of the value at which they were contracted : the objections to interference arise, therefore, from considerations of expediency; from a dread of exciting litigation among individuals, and a still greater dread of shaking indirectly the credit of our funds, open as are the exchequers of other countries to our capitalists. Some time hence it may, perhaps, be found practicable to combine two very nice points — a farther reduction of our burdens with the preservation of the dividends at their present value. But on this we cannot now enter; and any intervention on the part of our courts of justice seems at present out of the question. It could be seriously expected only in the case of our corn trade being thrown open, and the continuance of low prices being thus put beyond all doubt. In any event, it would probably not go beyond the suspension of legal process for a given period of years, against a debtor who should have paid or tendered in money the chief part (perhaps three-fourths) of his previously contracted debt: a sacrifice apparently large on the part of creditors, but which, in very many cases, may be unavoidable without such intervention, since a continuance of low prices would involve the majority of agricultural debtors in insolvency.

Dr. Smith on Agricultural Improvers.—In the Wealth of Nations (Book V. Chapter II.) Dr. Smith discusses the expediency of inducing landlords to cultivate for their own account a portion of their lands, with a view to the discovery and diffusion of improvements in husbandry. He remarks, in another part, that men of mercantile habits frequently become successful agriculturists, being more accustomed than the hereditary farmer to calculate eventual advantages, and to hazard an outlay for a remote return. Had his life been prolonged, he would have seen, during the war, an ample addition to the list of gentlemen farmers, and have had occasion, since the peace, to qualify very materially his favourable opinion of agricultural undertakings when in the hands of men of other professions. In his time the practical farmers were comparatively poor and uneducated; the hope of improvement in husbandry seemed to rest in the occasional adoption of a country life by men of different habits. Had the case been otherwise, and had our northern and eastern counties possessed half a century ago a tenantry equal to the present, Dr. Smith would probably have taken a different view of the subject, recommending that agriculture, like other pursuits, should be confined to those who had made it their business for life, and accounting for the success of gentlemen farmers during the twelve or thirteen years previous to the publication of his book (1776) by a cause unforeseen, and, in some measure, accidental,—we mean the progressive rise of the price of corn.

Value of Land during last Century.—In treating historically of the value of land, Mr. Arthur Young, in his "Inquiry into the Progressive Value of Money," 1812, expresses an opinion, that about the year 1770, estates sold at thirty-two years' purchase; a rate higher, compared to the rent, than they bore during the preceding forty years. The reason, doubtless, was, that during that long period we had not an interval of peace of sufficient length to reduce the interest of money. Next, as to rents, it is a remarkable fact, that from the beginning of last century until towards 1770, they had experienced hardly any rise. "A neighbour of mine in Suffolk," says Mr. Young, (Inquiry, p. 102.) "who inherited a considerable landed property, informed me, that in various conversations which he had, between thirty and forty years ago, (between 1770 and 1780) with a relation far advanced in years, and from whom much of that property was derived, that much surprise was expressed at the rise of rents, which then began to take place. Through the long period of his relation's experience, no rise was ever thought of; and lease after lease, in long succession, was signed, without a word passing on the question of rent: that was an object considered as fixed ; and grandfather, father, and son, succeeded without a thought of any rise: in many cases landlords were much more apprehensive of losing a tenant at the old rent, than having the smallest conception of raising it to a new one."

Comparative Price of Wheat on the Continent, and in England, previous to the French Revolution.

Official Return of the price of Wheat at the Rosoy, or Paris Market, by the Septier of 240lbs. French.

	livres	s.	d.
Average of the 10 years preceding 1776 -	28	7	9
Average of the 10 years preceding 1786 -	22	4	7
The year 1786 - - -	20	12	6
1787 - - -	22	2	6
1788 - - -	24	0	0
Average per septier, during the 23 years preceding 1789 - - -	24	18	2

Reducing this to English measure and money, the exchange being then twenty-four livres for the pound sterling, the result is an average for these twenty-three years, per Winchester quarter, of 38s. 6d. sterling.

At Dantzic the average price of wheat in the twenty years from 1770 to 1789, both inclusive, after adding 7s. per quarter for freight and charge to England, was (Evidence, Agricultural Report, p. 366.) about 41s.

But in England, the annual returns of purchase at Eton market, during the same period, give an average of 49s. : the whole computed by the Winchester quarter.

This difference was not a little remarkable at a time when our taxation was hardly greater than that of our neighbours. Arising, in the first instance, from bad seasons, it owed its continuance partly to our corn law ; more to the extension of our manufactures, and to our war with our American colonies while the continent of Europe remained in peace.

Average Prices of Grain in England in the year 1822, *taken
from the Official Return.*

Wheat	-	43s.	3d.	Rye	-	20s.	3d.
Barley	-	21s.	3d.	Beans	-	23s.	9d.
Oats	-	17s.	7d.	Pease	-	25s.	7d.

Export and Import of Corn.

(From the Agricultural Report of June, 1821.)

Quarters.

Exporting period. — In the seventy-six years
between 1697 and 1773, the amount of our
export of corn of all kinds above our import was   -   -   -   - 30,968,000

Importing period. — During the forty-two years
from 1773 to 1815, the amount of our import
above our export was about   -   - 24,630,000

Ireland. — The import of corn of all kinds
from Ireland to Great Britain, in the thirty-
two years prior to 1806, was only   -   - 7,534,000

But after the act of 1806 had rendered such
import free, it amounted in fifteen years (to
1821) to   -   -   -   - 12,304,000

REMARKS

ON

The Agricultural Report of 1821.

No public document was ever more eagerly expected, or
more generally perused, than the Agricultural Report of
1821. How far, it may be asked, did it fulfil the public
expectation ? On the ground of impartiality and liberality
of view, no reasonable disappointment could have been
experienced, but the composition of the Report was by no
means of equal merit with its substance. We do not
allude to a deficiency of those graces of style which custom
does not require in a parliamentary paper, and which
would probably be misplaced there, but to a want of that

brevity and arrangement which in any composition are indispensable to a distinct conception of the language of business. The Report begins without any sketch or outline of its objects, and terminates with a very limited summary of its conclusions. The consequence has been that many have read, while few have understood it; for he who aims at understanding it thoroughly, or at viewing it in its *ensemble*, must go over the whole, not as a reader, but as an analyzer; forming an arrangement for himself, frequently altering the succession of the arguments, and collecting them under general heads.

The object of the Committee was, to express ourselves in official language, " to consider the various petitions complaining of the depressed state of our agriculture, to inquire into the allegations of the petitioners, and to report their observations thereupon." In pursuance of this authority, they examined a number of witnesses, and composed the Report partly from the evidence, but, in a far greater proportion, from their own views and conclusions on the corn-trade, considered as a general question. The whole may be said to embrace the following topics.

Admission of the distress of the Agriculturists ; Attempt to ascertain its course, and to define its extent ; Reference to former periods of distress.

Principles of our corn-trade : Historical retrospect : its prosperous state from 1773 *to* 1814, *a period comparatively exempt from legislative interference. Various disadvantages of our present corn-law ; Modifications suggested, particularly a moderate fixed duty on foreign corn.*

Examination of the petitions of the Agriculturists with regard to taxes ; of the high duty (40s. *per quarter*) *which they propose on foreign wheat ; and, lastly, their objections to the unlimited warehousing of foreign corn.*

Such are the topics discussed in this long and interesting Report: the principal inferences from the reasoning are,

That the bounty-system, whatever might be its early operation, was accompanied by a torpid state of agriculture for the half century previous to 1773 :

That one cause of the prosperity of our agriculture from 1773 to 1814, was its comparative exemption from legislative interference.

That the high import-limit established in 1815 tended in some degree to excess of home-growth.

The advice of the Committee was to return, by cautious

steps, to an unrestricted state of intercourse; reducing our import limit; and substituting a duty of such an amount as should afford protection to the present cultivators of our inferior soils, but holding out no encouragement for the farther appropriation of these ungrateful occupancies. After this return to sound principle, the Committee hope that our increasing population, and the general improvement of circumstances attendant on confirmed peace, will relieve the distress of our agriculturists: but they anticipate no relief from such measures as the proposed high duty (40s. per quarter) on foreign wheat, or from a restriction on the warehousing of foreign corn in our sea-ports. The former would lead to an excess of home-growth; and the latter would merely transfer the deposits of the corn-merchants from our warehouses to those of Holland, Flanders, and other parts of the Continent which are convenient for shipping it to London.

To the general spirit of the Report we subscribe, in common with all who acknowledge the principles of free trade, and who lament that our legislature deviated from them so materially in the case of our corn-laws. Next as to the language, the manner of expressing an opinion is a consideration of great nicety in an official report; in which, far different from the unauthorized publication of an individual, confidence of tone may lead to serious results. In the present case, it was of great importance to avoid all assertions which might be construed into interference between landlord and tenant; into a discouragement of the continuance of tillage at its present extent; or, finally, into a protection of the consumer at the expence of the agriculturist. Against all this the Committee carefully guarded; enjoining nothing with respect to a point so delicate as the adjustment of wages or rent to the reduced price of corn, but leaving the change to the natural operation of circumstances. In like manner, with regard to our import-limit for foreign corn, while a modification of its amount and the introduction of a fixed duty were suggested, no confident calculation or authoritative prescription were given as to the rate of either. In short, the Report was calculated to awaken the landed interest to the folly of the late system; and to the injurious tendency of those interferences, to which, formerly in the shape of bounty, and lately in that of discouragement to import, they have clung.

If, on the whole, however, we think thus favourably of the Report of the Agricultural Committee, we are by no means blind to its defects; — to the omission of several topics, and to the imperfect illustration of others.

We have already noticed in the text (p. 158.)

The omission by the Committee of the grand argument, that the cost of raising corn has a tendency to fall with the fall of the market; and we have mentioned (App. p. [29]).

Our dissent from the opinion of the Committee, that increase of population augmented the difficulty of providing subsistence. In fact, the chief defect of the Report arises from the belief that the cultivation of an additional surface becomes necessary in proportion to the increase of our numbers. So much do the Committee appear to have taken this for granted, that they addressed very few questions to the witnesses on the practicability of augmenting crops by bestowing additional labour on the same soil. We, on the other hand, account the effect of labour in augmenting produce so great, the connection between the hands which raise and the mouths which consume, so direct, that in an attempt to calculate the relative productiveness of different countries, we should be guided chiefly by the returns of population. Almost every part of Europe raises subsistence enough for its inhabitants, with the exception of the maritime tracts of the Dutch provinces, or rather of the single province of Holland, which happens to have both an unusually large population, and a soil less adapted to tillage than pasture.

The Committee have allowed this theory to influence their reasoning in several points, such as (Report, p. 10.) the question of a remunerating price; the extent (p. 11.) of our probable suffering after a deficient harvest; the argument (p. 24.) against a high protecting duty. It may, in short, be said, that the effect of this impression is almost as perceptible in their labours, as was in those of the Bullion Committee the notion that the bank possessed the power of keeping an undue quantity of paper in circulation. — These drawbacks on the merit of the Report are neither few nor inconsiderable: they do not, however, prevent us from ranking it among the most important and instructive documents of the kind that have appeared for many years.

Corn-Law of 1815. — The Committee very properly stigmatised the corn-law of 1815 as adverse to the connection which it is our interest to keep up with the Continent, for the purpose of meeting our occasional deficiencies. Far from inducing our capitalists to purchase foreign corn, when it was cheap and abundant, that law discouraged all intercourse with our neighbours, except in years which, in consequence of the similarity of latitude and climate, were likely to be seasons of dearth with them as with us. The foreigner was thus prevented from buying our manufactures, at least from reckoning with any confidence on his means of payment. Hence the advantage of the Act of the present year, which, imperfect as it is, opens a prospect of eventual intercourse with our neighbours, and of lessening the extremes of rise and fall in our market.

Corn Law of 1822, *ordered to be printed* 20*th June.*

Abstract. — The Corn-Law of 1815 permitted import free of duty, whenever our own corn, as returned by the averages, was at or above

	Per Quarter.		Per Quarter.
Wheat - - -	80s.	Barley - - -	40s.
Rye, Pease, and Beans	53s.	Oats - - -	26s.

When our currency was below these prices, the import was prohibited.

The present Act repeals that of 1815, and permits the import for home consumption of foreign corn, whenever our own corn shall be at or above

Wheat - - -	70s.	Barley - - -'	35s.
Rye, Pease, and Beans	46s.	Oats - - -	25s.

subject to certain duties, the amount of which is regulated not by these prices, but by the following table:

SCHEDULE (A.)

	Wheat.	Rye, Pease, and Beans.	Barley, Bear or Bigg.	Oats.
If the average of British Corn be under, per Quarter - -	80s. - -	53s. - -	40s. - -	28s.
High Duty - -	- 12s.	- - 8s.	- - 6s.	- - 4s.
If at or above, per Quarter - - -	80s. - -	53s. - -	40s. - -	28s.
But under, - do. -	85s. - -	56s. - -	42s. 6d. -	30s.
First Low Duty -	- - 5s.	- 3s. 6d.	- 2s. 6d.	- - 2s.
If at or above, per Quarter - -	85s. - -	55s. - -	42s. 6d. -	30s.
Second Low Duty -	- - 1s.	- 8d.	- - 6d.	- - 4d.

Colonial Corn. — Corn from Quebec, or our other North American Colonies, is admitted to consumption in this country whenever our own averages are at or above

Wheat - - - 59s.	Barley - - - 30s.
Rye, Pease, and Beans 39s.	Oats - - - 20s.

At the following duties :

SCHEDULE (B.)

	Wheat.	Rye, Pease, and Beans.	Barley, Bear or Bigg	Oats.
If British Corn be under, per Quarter - -	67s. . -	44s. - -	33s. - -	22s. 6d.
High Duty - -	- - 12s.	- - 8s.	- - 6s.	- - 4s.
If at or above, per Quarter - - -	67s. - -	44s. - -	33s. - -	22s. 6d.
But under, per Quarter	71s. - -	46s. - -	35s. 6d. -	24s.
First Low Duty - -	- - 5s.	- 3s. 6d.	- 2s. 6d.	- - 2s.
If at or above, per Quarter - - -	71s. - -	46s. - -	35s. - -	24s.
Second Low Duty -	- - 1s.	- - 8d.	- - 8d.	- - 4d.

Additional Duty for the first three Months after Admission to Sale for Home Consumption. — To prevent an abrupt import, or lowering of the market, it has been judged advise-able to impose by the present act an additional duty on

Wheat - - - 5s. 0d.	Barley - - - 2s. 6d.
Rye, Pease, and Beans 3s. 6d.	Oats - - - 2s. 0d.

On all corn, colonial as well as foreign, payable *in addition* to those in the Schedules, during the first three months of admission to home consumption, whether the corn be taken from the warehouse or from on board of ship.

Corn in Warehouse. — Foreign or colonial corn at present in warehouse may be taken out and sold for home consumption, as soon as our averages shall be at or above the preceding rates respectively, of 70s. for foreign, 59s. for colonial wheat, &c., but subject to the highest duty in the Schedules A. and B. And

Corn at present in warehouse may be admitted to home consumption in conformity with the Act of 1815, that is free of duty, whenever our averages rise to the rates fixed in that Act, viz.

Wheat - - - 80s.	Barley - - - 40s.
Rye, Pease, and Beans 53s.	Oats - - - 26s.

Flour, whether of wheat or oats, is subject to duties proportioned to the above-mentioned duties on grain. In this respect also our North American colonies have a preference, which to them is a point of considerable importance, since the shipments on the opposite shore of the Atlantic take place more frequently in the shape of flour than of grain.

Flour made from wheat,

	Per cwt.		Per cwt.
The high duty -	3s. 3d.	Additional during the	
First low duty -	1s. 7d.	first three months	1s. 7d.
		Second low duty	0s. 4d.

Oatmeal per boll:

	Per cwt.		Per cwt.
High duty - -	4s. 10d.	Additional for first	
First low duty -	2s. 2d.	three months -	2s. 2d.
		Second low duty -	0s. 6d.

Additional labour bestowed on Tillage since 1814. — To our arguments in the text on this head it is objected in a respectable quarter, (Farmer's Magazine, published at Edinburgh, November 1822,) that the years since the peace have been in general a period of discouragement to farmers, and that the " amount of labour applied to tillage is more likely to have been reduced than augmented." To this, however, we cannot assent, and must observe in answer,

1. That several years since the peace, in particular 1817, 1818, and 1819, were years either of high price, or of favourable expectation on the part of our farmers, who at that time experienced no inadequacy of means for the payment of labour.

2. That throughout England, the produce of which forms fully three-fourths of the corn brought to market in the United Kingdom, farmers frequently employ labourers at a loss, to avoid an increase of poor-rate. Declarations to this effect are found in various parts of the Evidence before the Agricultural Committee of 1821, where also, we find that it is not unusual for landlords in England to pay a portion of the farming charges, on condition of the tenant keeping up the productiveness of the land, by applying lime, manure, &c.

3. A powerful circumstance of the same tendency is the difficulty of withdrawing labour and capital from tillage; a truth so strongly urged by Mr. Cleghorn, in his lately

published " Essay on the Causes of the Depression of Agriculture," (pp. 51, 52,) and proved by the experience of half a century (from 1714 to 1764,) during which the quantity produced was kept up, although prices continued very low.

4. Population returns 1811 and 1821. These, it is true, appear to favour the opinion that the number of labourers engaged in agriculture has not kept pace with the increase of consumers; for while the latter were augmented in the course of the ten years in question 15 per cent., the former appear to have increased hardly 10 per cent. It is, however, to be remembered, that

5. The distinction in the Population returns is made, not by individuals, but by families, and that the discharges from the army and militia, or rather, the suspension of drain by enlistment, by leaving the able-bodied at home, gives greater efficiency to the *same number of families.* Also, that

6. From the progress of improvement in husbandry the same number of labourers raise a considerably larger share of produce than they did ten or twelve years ago.

APPENDIX

TO

CHAPTER VI.

─────────

On Poor Rate.

(From the Reports on the Poor Laws in 1817 and 1821.)

Table of the Amount expended at different dates on the Poor of England and Wales, making the year close at Easter, and adding the corresponding average Price of the Bushel of Wheat.— These sums are distinct from church, county, or highway rates.

		Price of Wheat per Bushel.	
	£	s.	d.
1748-49-50 - - - average	689,971	4	5
1776 - - - - - —	1,521,732	6	9
1783-84-85 - - - —	1,912,241	7	7
1803 - - - - - —	4,077,891	8	1
1813-14-15 - - - —	6,129,844	12	8
1816-17-18 - - - —	6,844,290	10	0
1819-20 - - - - —	7,430,627	9	6
1821 - - - - - —	6,947,660	7	10

Amount of Expenditure in each Tenth Year since the middle of last Century, together with the Price of Wheat.

Years.	Expenditure.	Wheat per Bushel.	
	£	s.	d.
1750	713,000	4	2
1760	965,000	4	10
1770	1,306,000	6	5
1780	1,774,000	5	1ſ
1790	2,567,000	6	4
1800	3,861,000	10	2
1810	5,407,000	12	4

The following are given in successive Years.

Expended on the Maintenance of the Poor.

			Wheat per Bushel.	
		£	s.	d.
Year ending 25th March,	1813	6,656,105	16	8
" " " "	1814	6,294,584	12	3
" " " "	1815	5,418,846	8	10
" " " "	1816	5,724,507	7	9
" " " "	1817	6,918,247	10	11
" " " "	1818	7,890,148	11	3
" " " "	1819	7,531,651	10	4
" " " "	1820	7,329,594	8	8
" " " "	1821	6,947,666	7	10

London, Westminster, and Southwark.

EXPENDITURE.	Year ending Easter, 1813.	Easter, 1814.	25th March, 1815.
	£	£	£
Number of poor relieved permanently in work-houses -	13,389	13,373	12,341
Out of work-houses, without reckoning the children - -	12,654	13,762	13,341
Parishioners relieved occasionally either in or out of work-houses - - - -	40,993	69,332	70,322
Total -	67,036	96,467	96,004

Highway, Church, and County rate. — These minor charges form collectively somewhat more than a fifth of the large sum which passes currently under the name of poor-rate. Are they, it may be asked, likely to experience a reduction corresponding to that of the fund applied to the relief of the poor? As the chief constituent of charge in these lesser rates is the price of labour, it is evident that at the reduced wages of the present day, a smaller sum will suffice for an equal extent of work : on the other hand, it is very probable that from a sense of the necessity of providing employment for the lower orders, and of the advantage of carrying farther the improvement of our roads, a considerable extension may be given to such undertakings ; none, it is evident, can be more advantageous to the public, if conducted with judgment and economy.

Report of 15th July 1822, *on the Poor-rate Returns.* — This, the latest labour of the Committee on the management of the poor, puts in a striking light both the difference of plan followed in different parts of the kingdom, and our imperfect acquaintance with the system as a whole. There continues, says the Report, an evident connexion between the rise or fall of the price of wheat, and the rise or fall of expenditure for the poor ; the total decrease in the latter since 1818 being 22 per cent. The appointment of select vestries and assistant overseers goes on in different parts of the kingdom, but more slowly than might have been expected after the recommendation of the Poor-law Committee of 1817. But the present mode of keeping parish accounts presents a very imperfect check on the expenditure, and ought, in the opinion of the Committee, to be rendered much more specific. All charges either for law, or for such purposes as building or repairing workhouses, ought to be discriminated from the great head of " money expended for the relief and maintenance of the poor : " — while in regard to the latter the return ought to be very explicit, when aid is afforded according to the number of children, or, in particular cases, to able-bodied persons.

APPENDIX

TO

CHAPTER VII.

On Population.

Eᴍᴘʟᴏʏᴍᴇɴᴛ: _its Subdivision as Society advances._ — We follow up the reasoning in the text (page 213.) by a few familiar illustrations, for several of which we are indebted to Mr. Gray's Remarks on Population. — In a primitive state of society, like that of England in the days of the Britons and Anglo-Saxons, or like that of the interior of Norway in the present day, we find the inhabitants distributed into detached cottages or petty hamlets, each family being obliged to provide almost every thing for itself. To cultivate a lot of ground is, in such a state of things, indispensable; since no employment, not even those of first necessity, such as the business of the baker, the tailor, or the mason, would occupy the whole of their time, or prove adequate to their support. Each household is therefore obliged to build, to bake, to brew, to make and to mend for itself; how awkwardly and how imperfectly it is needless to say. To rear a family is to them, whatever the imagination of poets may figure of these days of supposed enjoyment, a task of greater difficulty than in this iron age of rents and taxes. Let us beware of forming our ideas of the condition of our ancestors from the ease of acquiring subsistence in countries such as the Cape of Good Hope, Upper Canada, or the United States of America. These enjoy all the advantages of colonies; they profit by the capital, the activity, the knowledge of Europe, exhibiting the application of the skill and formed habits of the old world to the improvement of vast tracts of unoccupied land. They exemplify, in short, almost all the circum-

stances which, in ancient days, led to the rapid growth of
the Grecian colonies in Italy and Asia Minor.

To revert to the characteristics of a primitive state of
society. In the course of ages the hamlet becomes a village, and as its population increases, a separation of employment gradually takes place; a process which goes on in an
augmented *ratio* as the village becomes a small town, a
large town, and eventually a city. How far is this subdivision carried in the case of a population of between 1500
and 3000? The more common species of labour, such as
that of the builder, the baker, the butcher, the tailor, the
shoemaker, are separated; but in other lines the division
is not complete, the shopkeeper is a linen and a woollen-
draper, a grocer, a druggist, a stationer; the doctor is
apothecary, surgeon, physician; the lawyer unites the functions of conveyancer, land-steward, and general agent. This
mixture undergoes a decomposition as the inhabitants increase from 5 to 10,000; and in a population of from 10 to
15,000, the various classes, whether of mechanics or dealers,
are tolerably subdivided, at least in our country; for in
France and most parts of the Continent, the subdivision,
even in large towns, is far less complete.

Subdivision of Employment in great Cities. — To mark this
subdivision in all its extent, the observer must repair to the
French, or rather to the English capital, where the mercantile, the manufacturing, the mechanical professions, all assume the most simple form. A London banker, different
from his provincial brethren, issues no notes, and keeps no
interest account with his customers: a merchant confines
his connexions to a few foreign sea-ports, perhaps to a particular colony or town; and the name of general merchant,
though not yet disused, is hardly applicable even to our
greatest houses. But it is in the mechanical arts that the
subdivision of employment takes a form the most familiar
and most intelligible to ordinary observation. In London
the class of shoemakers is divided, says Mr. Gray, into
makers of shoes for men, shoes for women, shoes for children: also into boot-cutters, boot-closers, boot-makers.
Even tailors, though to the public each appears to do the
whole of his business, are divided among themselves into
makers of coats, waistcoats, breeches, gaiters. In other
lines an equally minute repartition takes place: and as to
the ornamental or elegant arts, such as those of jeweller,
painter, engraver, nothing would be more easy than to ex-

hibit a long list of professions limited to large towns, and wholly unknown in a thinly-peopled district.

Effect of this Subdivision. — What, it may be asked, is the practical result of this minute subdivision, this nice distinction of employment? By fixing the attention of the workman on a single part of his business, it renders him surprisingly correct and expeditious : his performance gains equally in quality and in dispatch. This is the result of a mechanical dexterity, acquired without any particular effort of the mind; for we must by no means infer that the quickness characteristic of the inhabitants of a large town, that promptitude which distinguishes the Londoner and the Parisian from the hesitation and circumlocution of the countryman, is the consequence of any innate superiority : those who walk in a crowd must adopt the step of others, and advance with the rapidity of the moving mass. The attainments of these persons, meaning such attainments as they possess accurately and thoroughly, are often confined to a few branches ; but these are the objects of their profession or business ; and the result is, that their work proceeds straight forward, very little time being lost by them in planning, altering, or correcting.

Proportion borne by different Classes in our National Income. — In consequence of our insular position, our canals, and our mines, the proportion of our national income, derived from manufacture and trade, is greater than in most other countries. The following table is taken, as far as regards its plan, from a publication by Mr. Gray ; but it is subjected to several modifications, arising in one respect from the late population return, in another from the fall in the price of commodities. It is founded partly on conjecture, partly on official documents.

Great Britain distinct from Ireland.	Proportion of the income of the class to the national income at large.
Agriculturists and all engaged in the supply of subsistence, whether farmers, labourers or dealers - - - -	30 per cent.
Manufacturers and all persons occupied in making clothing, hardware, and other articles for home consumption - -	20 do.
Mechanics, masons, and all engaged in supplying houses with furniture - -	10 do.
The professional classes, viz. lawyers, clergy, medical men, artists and teachers, to whom is added a very numerous, though not an affluent class, that of domestic servants -	17 do.
The army, the navy, the civil servants of government, the annuitants drawing an income from our dividends; all, in short, who are paid through the medium of taxes	20 do.
The classes receiving parish support and other charitable aid - - -	3 do.
Total -	100

The proportion allotted to the agricultural classes has unfortunately not been earned by them in the depression that has prevailed since 1820; but the case must ere long alter; and in a table intended to be referred to for years, it is fit to keep temporary irregularities out of sight.

In Ireland the distribution of productive industry is very different from that of England: were it added to our estimate, there would be a great augmentation of the agricultural proportion.

Population; its different Degrees of Increase.

In a primitive stage of society the rate of increase is, doubtless, very slow, since no advantage arising from the boundless command of territory, can counterbalance the anti-population habits of the hunter state. This is sufficiently exemplified among the North American Indians, and proves that in the early peopled regions of Asia, the increase, even with the aid of a fine climate, could not

have been considerable until the adoption of pastoral habits; nor great, until these gave way to the agricultural
state, in which the augmentation of subsistence concurs
so directly with health of occupation to augment our
numbers.

The Mercantile or Manufacturing Stage.—The last stage
in the progress of society may be termed the mercantile;
the stage in which a large proportion of the inhabitants of
a country are assembled in sea-ports and manufacturing
towns. Manufactures and trade are by many accounted
adverse to population, the former leading to sedentary
habits, the latter occasionally prompting a resort to dangerous climates. These, we admit, are serious objections;
but, on the other hand, the commercial state is favourable
to early marriage, as will be readily allowed by all who
have resided in an agricultural country like France, and
marked how slowly population increases amidst the penury, the ignorance, and unenterprising habits of the
tenants of the soil. Add to this, that many of the irregularities of the manufacturing state have arisen, not from
permanent causes, but from the fluctuation of wages inci-
dent to a state of war, or from the insalubrity of antiquated
and ill-planned structures. Evils such as these are in a
state of progressive cure from various causes, and from
none more than that distribution of population throughout
provincial towns which canal communication so directly
promotes, by enabling a particular place to confine itself
to a particular manufacture, instead of accumulating, as on
the Continent, a multitude of workmen in a crowded and
overgrown city. Paris and Vienna are, far more than
London, the centre of manufacture for their respective
countries; for France, Germany, and the Netherlands,
united, do not exhibit provincial towns to be compared
to Manchester, Glasgow, Birmingham, Leeds, Sheffield.
These, and other places of the kind in England, while
exempt, in a great measure, from the drawbacks of a metropolis, in regard to health and expence, possess advantages nearly equal, in access to markets and division of
employment. The district of Birmingham in particular,
inhabited as it is by several hundred thousand persons,
affords a striking proof that a numerous population may
prosecute manufacture without crowding themselves into
narrow streets or lanes.

Effect of the Enlargement of Farms. — Increase of population is conducive to increase of employment in many respects, in which, at first, we should hardly suppose it to exert such an influence. Thus the common notion of small farms being conducive to increase of numbers, is far from correct; it being, in the first place, impracticable in these petty occupancies to do justice to the productive powers of the soil, while farms of larger size (from 300 to 500 acres) have many advantages, admitting of the application of machinery and the beneficial employment of capital. In the next place, it is a remarkable fact, that while the quantity of subsistence disposable for the market is augmented beyond comparison, the number of persons supported on the spot is (as we find from the population returns of counties so highly cultivated as Norfolk and East Lothian) greater than it was in the age of small farms.

Effect of Machinery on the Condition of the working Classes. — The effect of mechanical improvement in adding to the income of a community admits of no doubt, its result being to afford a commodity frequently of better quality, and always at a cheaper rate. To be satisfied of the latter, we have merely to compare the prices of either our cottons or hardware of the present day with those of similar articles made by us thirty years ago, or with those made at present on the Continent, where machinery is as yet but partially adopted. But what, it will be asked, is the effect of machinery on the income and comfort of the workman? At first injurious, bringing with it the evils of transition, which are very serious in a time marked, like that which followed the peace of 1814, by a great reduction in the demand for hands for the public service. To take an instance familiar to those of our countrymen who have resided in France: in that country coal is very little used, and the general fuel, whether in town or country, is wood: the trees, after being felled, are cut into short but thick blocks, carted into the towns, sold in the public markets, and broken up by men who make a business of it, but whose labour, aided only by the wedge and saw, is tedious and fatiguing, adding nearly ten per cent. to the cost of the article. To break these solid blocks by machinery would cause a considerable saving of both time and expence, but in the present stagnation of the demand for labour, it would be harsh, and indeed unsafe to resort to such an alternative, without providing for the thousands who would thus be deprived of employment.

Such, in a greater or less degree, is the case in almost every transition of importance. Eventually, however, the hardship is overcome, and the use of machinery becomes productive of great additional comfort to the lower orders. To prove that its beneficial effects are general, it is not enough to cite the prosperity of a few manufacturing districts, as the success of these may be accompanied by distress in other parts; the prosperity of Lancashire may cause embarrassment in Saxony, Flanders, or the banks of the Rhine. The advantage, then, arising from the use of machinery, rests on a broader basis; on that law in productive industry which makes every *real* reduction of cost an addition to individual income, or, what is the same thing, to the comforts procured by that income. The benefit of such reduction is enjoyed by the public at large : the evil, on the other hand, is partial, being confined to the manufacturer. He, however, is benefited in his capacity of consumer, and experiences relief from his distress as soon as it is found practicable to transfer to a new branch a portion of the capital and industry hitherto employed on his own. Such transfers are, it is true, tasks of great time and difficulty : we have felt them to be so in our own country, while in others less advanced, they can hardly be accomplished in the lifetime of a generation.

Increase of Population in the present Age. — The recent increase of our numbers, so greatly beyond that of any former age, is ascribed by many persons to the excitement attendant on the war, and to the encouragement it afforded to early marriage in the case of so many classes, the agricultural, the manufacturing, the mercantile. This, however, applied chiefly to the mechanical; all, in short, except the fixed annuitants, the middle classes : among the lower the advantage in wages was balanced, or nearly balanced, by the rise of provisions. We must also put in the opposite scale the serious injury to population arising from war, as well by the loss of lives in the field and in tropical climates, as by the removal from home of many who would otherwise have become fathers of families. When to this we add, that since the peace the *ratio of increase is not less great than during the war*, we are led to attribute the augmentation of our numbers to causes more permanent and satisfactory; to the preservation of the lives of children by vaccination; to the better lodging, the greater cleanliness and sobriety of our lower classes. This result, already exemplified in the return of deaths inserted in a subsequent page, will, we believe, be found to rest on a broad basis, whenever our official documents shall become more ample.

Similar causes prevail, though in a less degree, on the Continent: in France the increase of population, formerly so slow as hardly to yield an addition of 30 per cent. in a century, may now be computed at somewhat more than twice that proportion. In that country sobriety was always prevalent; but the abolition of monasteries, the improvement of medical practice, the ameliorated condition of the peasantry, are all peculiar to the present age. In Germany the degree of increase is probably not very different from that of France. Of Russia we have as yet no accurate returns: Spain, Italy, and the south of Europe generally, are also on the increase, but in a *ratio*, which, when we consider the general indolence and poverty of the lower orders, is, doubtless, slower than that of France. And in the countries subject to the Turks, the frequency of the plague, and all the pernicious effects of bad government, are likely still to counteract the natural tendency of population to increase.

Marriages. — The proportion of marriages to that of our population does not appear to have increased during the late wars :

From 1780 to 1789, marriages, compared to the whole population, were as 1 in 117

1790 to 1799 -   -   -   - 1 in 119½

1800 to 1809 -   -   -   - 1 in 119½

(*Barton on the Labouring Classes.*)

We shall be more successful in searching for an explanation of the rapid increase of our numbers in other causes: none can be more gratifying than the decrease of mortality in consequence partly of the introduction of vaccination, but partly too of the greater sobriety and comfort of the poor.

Progressive Decrease of Deaths in Great Britain.

From 1785 to 1789 -   -   - 1 in 436

1790 to 1794 -   -   - 1 in 447

1795 to 1799 -   -   - 1 in 465

1800 to 1804 -   -   - 1 in 474

(*Barton, ut supra.*)

To Mr. Rickman, Clerk-Assistant of the House of Commons, who has prepared the successive Population Abstracts of 1801, 1811, 1821,) I am indebted for much useful information, in particular for

A Comparative View of the Area and Productive Power of the several Counties of England and Wales.

COUNTIES ACCORDING TO THEIR AREA.

Counties.	Square Statute Miles.	Counties.	Square Statute Miles.
1. York - -	5,961	30. Surrey - -	758
2. Lincoln - -	2,748	31. Berks - -	756
3. Devon - -	2,579	32. Oxford - -	752
4. Norfolk - -	2,092	33. Bucks - -	740
5. Northumberland	1,871	34. Worcester -	729
6. Lancaster -	1,831	35. Hertford -	528
7. Somerset - -	1,642	36. Monmouth -	498
8. Hampshire - -	1,628	37. Bedford - -	468
9. Kent - - -	1,537	38. Huntingdon -	370
10. Essex - -	1,532	39. Middlesex - -	282
11. Suffolk - -	1,512	40. Rutland - -	149
12. Cumberland -	1,478		
13. Sussex - -	1,463	England -	50,535
14. Wilts - -	1,379		
15. Salop - -	1,341		
16. Cornwall - -	1,327	1. Carmarthen -	974
17. Gloucester - -	1,256	2. Montgomery -	839
18. Stafford - -	1,148	3. Glamorgan - -	792
19. Durham - -	1,061	4. Brecon - -	754
20. Chester - -	1,052	5. Cardigan - -	675
21. Derby - -	1,026	6. Merioneth - -	663
22. Northampton -	1,017	7. Denbigh - -	635
23. Dorset - -	1,005	8. Pembroke - -	610
24. Warwick - -	902	9. Carnarvon - -	544
25. Hereford - -	860	10. Radnor - -	426
26. Cambridge - -	858	11. Anglesey - -	271
27. Nottingham -	837	12. Flint - - -	244
28. Leicester - -	804		
29. Westmorland -	763	Wales -	7,425
		Total -	57,960

Scotland and Ireland are nearly equal to each other in area, and together are equal to or somewhat larger than England and Wales. The Assessed Rental of Scotland in 1811 was £3,899,364.

COUNTIES ACCORDING TO THEIR PRODUCTIVE POWER.

Rent and Tithe paid in each County in 1810, per square Mile of 640 Acres.

Merioneth	-	-	£137	Cambridge	-	-	£571
Brecon			154	Huntingdon	-		574
Cardigan			173	Hereford	-		585
Carnarvon	.		192	Lincoln			594
Montgomery			198	Salop	-	-	-	610
Radnor	-		229	Berks	-		611
Carmarthen			244	Bedford	-		619
Glamorgan	-		284	Derby			624
Pembroke	-		284	Kent	-		651
Anglesey	-		288	Wilts	-		652
Westmorland			299	Nottingham	-		659
Durham	-		300	Gloucester	-		680
Cumberland	-		327	Cheshire	-		684
Denbigh	-		331	Essex	-		692
Hampshire	-		435	Rutland	-		692
Monmouth	.		436	Stafford	-		693
Sussex	-		445	Northampton			702
Cornwall	-		470	Oxford	-		709
Norfolk	-		509	Bucks	-		713
Devon	-		516	Lancaster	-		718
Northumberland	-		520	Hertford	-		734
Flint	-	-	536	Warwick	-		744
Suffolk	-		537	Worcester	-		772
Dorset	-		538	Somerset	-		876
York	-	-	541	Leicester	-		891
Surrey	-		550	Middlesex	-	-	1,325

The area of the counties was measured on Arrowsmith's last map (date 1815—1816), which was formed on the trigonometrical survey. The process of squaring and computing the miles, as well as of estimating the parts of miles on the borders of each county, having been performed with much care and labour, the inacccuracies are few and inconsiderable.

Annual Value of Land by the square mile of 640 *statute acres.* — This is computed from the " rent and tithe collectively," and the average of England and Wales in 1811 was 17s. 2d. per acre : the counties which take the lead are Leicester and Somerset, and the chief cause of superiority is the extent of good pasture ground, which, of course, yields a return at little expence.

The Rental is taken from the Property-tax return for the year ending April, 1811, (see p. 66. of the Property-tax Accounts, printed 26 Feb. 1813.) The fall of rent on the one hand, and extension of culture on the other, probably render this return, though comparatively of old date, a tolerably accurate representation of the present rental of the kingdom.

One method of computing the productiveness of land under tillage is to " take for each county the number of families employed in husbandry, and to divide by it the amount of rent and tithe." The result may be said to exhibit the " average net produce of the labour and capital of each family thus engaged," and indicates, we believe with tolerable accuracy, the progress of the improved husbandry. For England and Wales the average, in 1811, was 41*l.* per family of agriculturists. The proportion was by no means greatest in the counties adjacent to the metropolis ; for while in Hertfordshire and Surrey it varied from 30*l.* to 40*l.* per family of agriculturists, in Lincoln and Durham it exceeded 50*l.*, and in Northumberland went considerably beyond that amount. A return of this nature, made after rents assume a settled form, would be a very interesting document, particularly if combined with a similar return from Scotland, where tithe and poor-rate happily form so slight a deduction from the income of the landlord.

Rank of our different Counties in point of Density of Population.

1 Middlesex	19 Berks	37 Denbigh
2 Lancaster	20 Norfolk	38 Dorset
3 Surrey	21 Oxford	39 Glamorgan
4 York, W. Rid.	22 Bedford	40 Hereford
5 Kent	23 Flint	41 Pembroke
6 Warwick	24 Buckingham	42 Caernarvon
7 Gloucester	25 Hertford	43 Monmouth
8 Nottingham	26 Wilts	44 Northumberl.
9 Chester	27 Southampton	45 York, N. Rid.
10 Worcester	28 Cambridge	46 Lincoln
11 Durham	29 Anglesea	47 Cumberland
12 Somerset	30 Huntingdon	48 Caermarthen
13 Suffolk	31 Stafford	49 Montgomery
14 Derby	32 Salop	50 Cardigan
15 Cornwall	33 Devon	51 Westmoreland
16 Leicester	34 Sussex	52 Merioneth
17 Northampton	35 Rutland	53 Radnor
18 Essex	36 York, E. Rid.	54 Brecon

CENSUS OF 1821.

England, Scotland and Wales ; Increase of the Population since 1811, exhibited by Counties.

Counties.	Increase per cent. from 1811 to 1821.	Counties.	Increase per cent. from 1811 to 1821.	Counties.	Increase per cent. from 1811 to 1821.
Peebles -	1	York, E. Rid-		Durham - -	17
Sutherland -	1	ing - -	14	Linlithgow -	17
Perth - -	3	Aberdeen -	15	Somerset -	17
Forfar - -	6	Bute - -	15	Banff - -	18
Kincardine -	6	Derby - -	15	Gloucester -	18
Salop - -	6	Devon - -	15	Norfolk - -	18
Kinross - -	7	Essex - -	15	Bedford - -	19
Berwick - -	8	Inverness -	15	Chester - -	19
Nairn - -	9	Kirkcudbright	15	Cornwall - -	19
Clackmannan	10	Montgomery -	15	Denbigh - -	19
Merioneth -	10	Northampton -	15	Lincoln - -	19
Hereford -	10	Nottingham -	15	Glamorgan -	20
Radnor - -	10	Orkney and		Middlesex -	20
Roxburgh -	10	Shetland -	15	Warwick -	20
Elgin - -	11	Hampshire -	15	York, N. Rid-	
Argyle - -	12	Wilts - -	15	ing - -	20
Berks - -	12	Worcester -	15	Cambridge -	21
Stirling - -	12	Brecon - -	16	Renfrew -	21
Westmorland	12	Dorset - -	16	Anglesea -	22
Dumbarton -	13	Flint - -	16	Ayr - -	22
Dumfries -	13	Hertford -	16	Pembroke -	22
Fife - -	13	Huntingdon -	16	Surrey - -	23
Haddington -	13	Leicester -	16	Sussex - -	23
Ross and Cro-		Monmouth -	16	York, W. Rid-	
marty - -	13	Northumber-		ing - -	23
Oxford - -	13	land - -	16	Wigton - -	24
Rutland - -	13	Stafford - -	16	Lanark - -	27
Selkirk - -	13	Suffolk - -	16	Lancaster -	27
Buckingham -	14	Cumberland -	17	Caithness -	29
Cardigan - -	14	Carmarthen -	17	Edinburgh -	29
Kent - -	14	Carnarvon -	17		

The *ratio* of most frequent occurrence is 15 per cent., or an average between 13 and 17 per cent.   In several counties the augmentation is to be ascribed to the increase of the principal towns ; thus the increase of Middlesex is the increase of London, Surrey of Southwark, Warwickshire of Birmingham, Lanarkshire of Glasgow, and Lancashire of Manchester, Liverpool, Preston, &c.   In the remote county of Caithness, the increase is owing to the extension of the herring fishery ; while the almost stationary condition of the adjoining county of Sutherland is owing to the emigration of cottagers, and the conversion of their petty occupancies into pasture ground.

England and Wales: Progressive Increase of our Population.

Its amount in 1801	-	-	-	9,343,578
Ditto	1811	-	-	10,791,115
Ditto	1821	-	-	11,977,663

Progressive Increase in the Ten Principal Towns of England.

	Year 1801.	Year 1811.	Year 1821.
London - - -	900,000	1,050,000	1,225,964
Manchester - -	81,020	98,573	133,788
Liverpool - -	77,653	94,376	118,972
Birmingham - -	73,670	85,753	106,722
Bristol - - -	63,645	76,433	87,779
Leeds - - -	53,062	62,534	83,796
Plymouth - -	43,454	56,060	61,212
Portsmouth - -	32,166	40,567	45,648
Norwich - - -	36,832	37,256	50,288
Newcastle-on-Tyne -	28,365	37,587	46,948

Scotland. — Here the *ratio* of increase in the towns, particularly Edinburgh and Glasgow, has been equally great.

Ireland. — The returns previous to 1811 were too imperfect to afford the means of calculating the progressive increase of population, nor have those of 1821 as yet been given to the public in a satisfactory form: the general result is, that the population of all Ireland amounts in round numbers to - - - - - - 7,000,000

That of the principal towns,

Dublin	-	-	-	-	186,276
Cork	-	-	-	-	100,535
Limerick	-	-	-	-	66,042

Great Britain: Return of 1821.

Distribution into Classes.	Families.	Proportions to the whole population in parts of 100.
Employed chiefly in agriculture	978,656	33
Do. in trade, manufactures, mechanical employment, &c. -	1,350,293	46
In all other situations - -	612,488	21
		100

Proportion of Agricultural Population. — This varies greatly, according to the particular county. In a highly manufacturing county, such as Lancashire, it is not half the average of 33 in 100; in Yorkshire, which in the West Riding is manufacturing, and in other parts agricultural, the return approaches to the average, but is still somewhat below it; while in Sussex, Essex, Suffolk, where there are so few manufactures, it greatly exceeds it, being above 50 in 100; in Cambridgeshire, Bedfordshire, and Herefordshire, the proportion is the largest of all, being above 60 in 100.

Comparison of the Population Returns of 1811 and 1821.

	England.	Wales.	Scotland.	Totals.	Increase per cent.
Families chiefly employed in agriculture, 1811	697,353	72,846	125,799	895,998	
1821	773,732	74,225	130,699	978,656	$9\frac{1}{4}$
Do. in trade, manufactures, and mechanical employment - 1811	923,588	36,044	169,417	1,129,049	
1821	1,118,295	41,680	190,264	1,350,239	$19\frac{1}{2}$
In all other situations, 1811	391,450	20,866	106,852	519,168	
1821	454,690	30,801	126,997	612,488	18

The most important reflection suggested by these returns, is the great superiority of increase in our town population over that of the agriculturists. This is remarkable on two accounts; first, as indicating a rapid increase of productive power, and next as peculiar to our island; the augmentation in France and the Continent generally being no greater in town than in the country.

Wales. — Here agricultural employment predominates. Among persons out of business there appears a remarkable increase; the consequence, probably, of Wales being found a comparatively cheap residence by half-pay officers and other annuitants.

Indications of an Increase of National Wealth, taken from Population Returns.— These are,

1. An increase in the proportion of persons who are independent of labour; we mean of those who derive their income from property, whether land, houses, or money lent.

2. A greater comparative increase of town population.

3. It follows that under such circumstances agriculturists will increase in a *ratio* inferior to that of the other classes: still the augmentation of produce may, and probably will, keep pace with the augmentation of the consumers, the improvements in husbandry and the increased use of machinery (such as threshing mills) contributing greatly to lessen the manual labour employed in raising corn.

Census of 1377. — As a matter of historical curiosity, we subjoin the population of the principal towns of England in the year 1377, when an enumeration was made on account of a poll-tax:

London - - - 35,000	Colchester - - -	4,500
York - - - - 11,000	Canterbury - - -	4,000
Bristol - - - 9,000	Beverley - - -	4,000
Plymouth - - - 7,000	Newcastle-on-Tyne	4,000
Coventry - - - 7,000	Oxford - - -	3,500
Norwich - - - 6,000	Bury, Suffolk - -	3,500
Lincoln - - - 5,000	Gloucester ⎰ Each ⎱	
Sarum, Wiltshire 5,000	Leicester ⎰ somewhat ⎱ 3,000	
Lynn - - - - 5,000	Shrewsbury ⎰ more than ⎱	

In that remote age the total population of England was 2,300,000; but the proportion of town population was far smaller than at present, since the number of towns containing above 3000 inhabitants was only 18.

APPENDIX

TO

CHAPTER VIII.

National Revenue and Capital.

*I*s our *annual Consumption equal to our annual Production?*—
In adverting to this subject, our limits prevent our enlarging on the distinction between productive and unproductive
consumption, as explained by M. Say and Mr. Mill, or
the much greater latitude given to the term productive by
Mr. Gray. We have, in fact, room for little more than
answering the plain practical question, " What part of our
national income appears to be saved or invested, so as to
form a permanent addition to the national property ?"

The part of our income thus appropriated will be found
very small, if considered in the limited sense of investments
in money securities, such as the funds or mortgage, transactions of that nature being confined in a great measure
to annuitants, or rather to the comparatively small portion
of them that are opulent. If to these we add the investments in the form of money in the part of all other classes,
including the saving banks of the lower orders, we shall
probably find for the kingdom at large, an annual appropriation of 9 or 10,000,000*l.*, the interest of which, at the present reduced rate, affords an addition of only 3 or 400,000*l.*
to our national income.

But if we take in a more liberal sense the difference between the revenue and expenditure of the nation, if we
consider as saving or as increase of our stock, all that is
laid out on the improvement of land, the building or repair of houses, the increase of furniture, and if to these we
add interest of money saved, we shall find on the whole, an

addition to our national capital of 50 or 60,000,000, making an increase in our taxable income of nearly 3,000,000*l*. a-year, and rendering it probable that the 260,000,000*l*. of this year will in 1824 become 263,000,000*l*.; in 1825 266,000,000*l*., &c. This result will be confirmed, if we take as a criterion the increase of our population, confining our estimate to those who annually attain the age of twenty, the age of efficient labour, and whose number we calculate as follows:

In 1802 the population of Great Britain and Ireland was about 16,000,000, the annual increase by births over deaths, 1½ per cent. or 240,000. The individuals then born, whether male or female, have now attained the age of useful labour, and must be considered as bearing the same share as the rest of the population, in augmenting the national income. In what manner ought the result of their exertions to be calculated? Our national income, taken in the largest sense, is (see p. 256) 350,000,000*l*. a-year, and the average contribution to it, reckoned per head of population, is nearly 17*l*. Estimated in that proportion, the addition from our new cultivators of the field of national industry would be little short of 4,000,000*l*. a year; but we prefer the safer course, and reckon as a *bonâ fide* addition to our resources only that income which is subject to taxes. Now, on dividing the *taxable* income of the nation by the number of our population, the result is about 12*l*. a head as the product of each individual, and the quota of our new contributors, reckoned by that scale, approaches to the 3,000,000*l*. mentioned above.

This will be found a fair and moderate estimate of the annual addition to our national income. If it be objected, that a deduction ought to be made from our assumed number of 240,000, on account of the deaths occurring ere our new contributors attain the age of labour, we answer that that is amply balanced by the following considerations:

1. The growing increase of our numbers, which, following the scale of our population returns for 1803, 4, &c. will be next year 244,000; the year after 250,000, and seven years hence, 270,000.

2. The fact that our new labourers living chiefly in towns where wages are higher than in the country, their contributions might fairly be estimated at somewhat more than 12*l*. a head.

3. Particularly as that sum forms the average contri-

bution of our population including *all ages*, whereas the 240,000 on whom we calculate have attained the age of labour.

A Table of annual Consumption substituted for a Table of Production. — Since all, or nearly all, that is produced, is consumed in one form or other, whether productively or otherwise, and since the taxes of this country are imposed chiefly on consumption, it will be more suitable to our reasoning to exhibit the amount in the form of consumption.

National Expenditure or Consumption of Great Britain and Ireland for 1823.

Expended on the produce of the soil for the food of man, or for purposes of manufacture	£120,000,000
On the produce of the mines	10,000,000
On manufactures for home consumption	70,000,000
On houses built or repaired; on furniture; and on improvement of land on whatever is termed in law real property	30,000,000
On all goods imported, whether for consumption, such as tea, sugar, coffee; or for manufacture, as wool, hemp, iron	70,000,000
On all commodities or products not comprized in the preceding	50,000,000
Total consumption	£350,000,000

Correspondence of this Sketch with the Calculation of other Writers.

Mr. S. Gray, in his addition to the Happiness of States, (p.636.) computes the total expenditure or consumption of the population of Great Britain in 1818 at £280,000,000
To which, if we add for Ireland   70,000,000

The result is as above   -   £350,000,000

Mr. Colquhoun's table of property annually created, will be found to differ in a few particulars only from our sketch of consumption.   We leave out in the latter

The produce raised for the food of horses, cattle, and the lesser animals ; also

The amount of manufactures exported; while in lieu of of the latter, and of some other heads in Mr. C.'s table, we insert the value of our imports.

Our next inquiry relates to a topic of considerable intricacy.

Proportion of National Expenditure exempt from Taxation. — In France and other countries of limited trade, the governments are obliged to impose their taxes chiefly on production, exacting from the landlord and farmer a payment equivalent in general to 20 per cent. of their incomes. With us the form of impost is different : the direct taxes since the peace are not considerable, but those on comsumption have long been, and still are so multiplied, that many persons imagine that hardly any portion of our expenditure escapes the visitation, direct or indirect, of the exchequer. In various cases, however, the transit from production to consumption is too direct to admit of assessment, particularly in regard to the lower orders. The oats, the potatoes, the kitchen vegetables reared by the cottager for his family, or by the farmer for his labourers, though all comprised in our estimate of national consumption, are subject to very slight demands on the score of taxation.

Case of Ireland. — This is strikingly exemplified in the sister island, where the taxed expenditure, limited as it is to the disburse of the gentry, the merchants, professional men, and the comparatively small portion of the lower classes residing in towns, cannot with confidence be computed at more than 25,000,000*l*. But a population of 7,000,000, supposing their average rate of subsistence not to exceed that of the English cottagers, as calculated by Sir F. Eden, (between 6 and 7*l*. a head,) could not exist without an annual produce of nearly 50,000,000*l*.; and if in forming a calculation for Ireland, we make allowance for the better circumstances of her town population, and for the comparative comfort of her linen manufacturers, we may, perhaps without exaggeration, carry the total property created in that island to 70,000,000*l*. a year, which is in the proportion of nearly 3 to 1 to the sum we have assumed as representing her taxable income.

That the supposed amount of the latter cannot be much above 25,000,000*l*. is unfortunately too clear from the state of the revenue, the amount of which, before making any deduction for collection, hardly exceeds 5,000,000*l*., or 20 per cent. on 25,000,000*l.*, although levied of late years on nearly the same scale of duties as in England, where taxation, distinct from poor rate, exceeds 20 per cent. of the national income.   How, it may be asked, does it happen that the two countries differ so greatly in the proportion of their taxed and untaxed consumption?   Because three-fourths of the population of Ireland are cottagers, whose consumption eludes the visit of the tax-gatherer, their clothing being of home manufacture, their food the patatoes of the neighbouring field, their fuel the turf of the common bog.   One generation thus succeeds to the poverty of another; and in the eye of the political arithmetician, Ireland is rich only in recruits.

France. — This country bears a considerable resemblance to Ireland in the density as in the poverty of her agriculturists; their total consumption (exclusive of the food of horses and cattle) is not over-rated at 180,000,000*l.*, but as in the rural districts of France the excise duties are very light, taxation in these districts is in a manner confined to the 45,000,000*l.* of rent and farmer's income returned as subject to *foncier.*   The assessment under that head, heavy as it is, would not, if calculated on the *produce* of agriculture, exceed 5 or 6 per cent.; yet to increase the amount of this tax is a matter of great difficulty, and the contribution of French agriculturists to their government takes place much more in men than in money.   Thus in 1793, when the cause of the revolution was highly popular, and the greatest efforts were necessary to repel invasion, the demand of the government was directed not to pecuniary aid, but to levies.   And after the discredit of the *Assignats,* the finances of France owed, in a great measure, their support to the resources of the Netherlands.

Such is the state of taxation in regard to agriculturists; the next question respects the situation of manufacturers. Among them the proportion of expenditure subject to taxation may at first appear large, the majority of the workmen residing in towns; however, a great part of them are indigent, and though the wages of the unmarried are expended in a great measure on taxed articles, such as beer, spirits, and tobacco, those of women, children, or the fathers of families, are more strictly confined to the purchase of the necessaries of life.

Lastly, in regard to the expenditure of merchants, professional men and traders, foreign commerce, transacted as it is in sea-ports, and by persons in the command of capital, creates, for the limited number employed by it, a great consumption of taxed articles. Of professional income the appropriation, from the respectable station of the individuals, is similar, but inland traffic comprises many persons of a very humble rank, mechanics, labourers, and others, of whose consumption a considerable part is but slightly productive to the exchequer.

It would, we believe, answer no useful purpose to enter on a more minute distinction of the expenditure of particular classes. Speaking generally, we may assume that about 25 per cent. of our national expenditure seems exempt from taxation, and that if the whole be computed at 350,000,000*l.*, the taxable part may, agreeably to the table in the text, be put down at somewhat more than 260,000,000*l.*

We may perhaps throw some light on this intricate topic by adding a few sentences containing the amount of national income in several of our great departments, with some remarks on its appropriation.

Income from the Produce of the Soil, 120,000,000*l.* — Of this very large sum, the portion constituting the income of the landlord and of the higher class of farmers, is evidently expended in articles subject to taxation; in regard to the smaller farmers or labourers the case is otherwise, their principal consumption of taxed articles being confined to malt liquor.

Produce of the Mines, 10,000,000*l.* — Here similar remarks apply in regard to the rent of the proprietor, the salary of the superintendant, or the wages of the workmen. As to the raw material, a considerable duty is raised from coal, but this charge is avoided on all that is not carried coastways, or in a particular direction by canal.

Manufactures for home Consumption, 70,000,000*l.* — The expenditure on taxed articles in this case arises from the income of master manufacturers, the salaries of clerks, and the wages of the less indigent workmen. The same may be said to apply to the expenditure (computed at 30,000,000*l.*) on buildings, furniture, and agricultural improvements.

Income from Trade, Professions, and all other Sources, 100,000,000*l.* — Under this very comprehensive head, the expenditure more particularly subject to taxation consists of the profit of merchants and bankers; of the income of professional men; salaries of clerks; income of shop-keepers; wages of ship-builders, seamen, &c.

National Capital.— Calculations of national capital are not, perhaps, of great importance in a direct sense, since taxation has seldom been imposed with reference to the amount of capital. A table of this nature is, however, of interest when viewed in connexion with a return of our national income, and rendered subservient to establishing the accuracy of the latter; this will, we believe, be the effect of the subjoined sketch.

The fall of prices attendant on a state of peace is, from causes which shall be explained presently, productive of much less diminution in regard to our capital than our income; and Mr. Colquhoun's calculation having been made on an estimate extremely moderate for a state of war, the difference between the present year and the year 1812, as calculated by him, is not considerable. Our table for the present year is consequently little more than a re-statement of his results, with a few modifications.

Calculation of National Property.

Great Britain and Ireland.	Computation for 1812, nearly in the form adopted by Mr. Colquhoun.	A similar computation for 1823.
Land under cultivation, whether in pasture, tillage, or gardens -	£1,280,000,000	£1,200,000,000
Farming capital, whether vested in implements of husbandry and farming stock, or in corn and other produce - - - -	228,000,000	200,000,000
Dwelling houses, warehouses, and manufactories - - - -	400,000,000	400,000,000
Manufactured goods in progress or ready for sale, whether in manufactories, warehouses, or shops: also foreign merchandize on hand - - - - -	160,000,000	140,000,000
British shipping of every description - - - - -	27,000,000	20,000,000
Here it seems fit to make an addition to Mr. Colquhoun's statements on account of		
Mercantile and manufacturing capital not specified by him, viz. money in hand; advances to correspondents abroad; manufacturing machinery; tools and implements of mechanics - - -	130,000,000	130,000,000
This carries to nearly300,000,000*l.* our mercantile and manufacturing capital employed in current business, and exclusive of whatever capital our merchants may have in fixed property, such as the funds, land or houses.		
Such are the great heads of our national property; the lesser as given by Mr. Colquhoun, are		
Mines and minerals - - -	75,000,000	65,000,000
Canals, tolls, and timber - -	50,000,000	45,000,000
Total - - -	£2,350,000,000	£2,200,000,000

This table is to be understood as representing private property, and exclusive of

1. All public property, such as military stores, churches, hospitals; also of

2. Such private property as is unproductive; viz. waste lands, furniture, or wearing apparel; and, finally, of

3. Whatever is expressive of a debt from one part of the community to another, such as the stocks, mortgages, or mercantile acceptances.

How, it may now be asked, does it happen that the decrease of our national property since the peace is so much less than is commonly supposed? The reasons are —

Land, as a property, is worth in peace from thirty-two to thirty-five years' purchase; in war, only twenty-seven or twenty-eight years' purchase; so that though on our rental we reckon a fall of fully 30 per cent., the principal has not sunk above 15 or 20 per cent.

Farming capital experiences at present a depression of value far beyond the reduction in our table; but its amount in 1812 was, we believe, under-rated by Mr. Colquhoun, while, in point of quantity, whether of implements, cattle, or corn on hand, it has increased probably 20 per cent. since that year.

As to buildings, whether warehouses, manufactories, or dwellings, the surprising increase in the number appears fully to have balanced the decrease of rent, particularly as such decrease appears to have been much smaller in this kind of property than in land.

In our manufactured and foreign goods on hand the fall of price, great as it has been, is nearly equalled by the increase of quantity. In our shipping the case is otherwise, and we have accordingly made a large deduction.

Such is the comparative amount of our national property in 1812 and 1822, when represented in money of the respective years. But were the calculation for both made in money of equal value, the balance would be in favour of the present year; we mean, that the valuations for the present year, if made in the money of 1812, would not be short of 2,500,000,000*l.*

Were we to take a retrospective view of the value of our national property since 1792, we should, in the absence of satisfactory returns for the earlier years, estimate it at *two-thirds* of the present amount.

Public Burdens in the present Year (1823). — Particulars
of the 64,000,000*l.* assumed in the text, p. 269.

Taxes, gross amount, including both the
  charge of collecting and the repayments
  in the form of drawbacks, discounts, and
  allowances   -   -   -   -   - £58,000,000

Deduct, not the charge of collection, but the
  repayments, which form in fact no part of
  our burdens   -   -   -   -   -   4,000,000

                Remain - -   54,000,000

    This is after a full deduction for the dimi-
nution in the duties on malt, salt, leather;
also in the assessed taxes.

Add for tithe, including Ireland *   -   -   5,000,000
Poor-rate, after deducting such portion as belongs properly to wages (see text, p. 201.)   5,000,000

                In all   - £64,000,000

This amount, reduced to money of 1792 in
  the proportion of nearly 130*l.* to 100*l.*,
  gives the sum expressed in the text, viz. £50,000,000
    Or, compared to our national income,
    a proportion of 25 to 100.

    * Tithe. All our tables include the tithe paid to lay impropriators.

APPENDIX

TO

CHAPTER X.

═══════

On Fluctuation of Prices.

(From Mr. Arthur Young's Inquiry into the Value of
Money, 1812.)

Abstract of part of Sir G. Shuckburgh's Table.

The Prices of the Year 1550 are taken for the Integer; viz. 100.

Years.	Wheat.	Twelve Miscellaneous Articles, viz. an Ox, Cow, Poultry, &c.	Butcher Meat.	Day Labour.	Mean of all.
1550	100	100	100	100	100
1600	—	—	—	—	144
1650	—	239	—	—	188
1675	246	—	166	118	210
1700	—	—	—	—	238
1720	—	434	—	—	257
1740	197	492	266	250	287
1760	203	—	400	275	342
1780	—	—	—	—	427
1790	—	752	—	—	496
1795	426	—	511	436	531
1800	—	—	—	—	562

This table presents a very great rise in prices, but the
grounds of calculation are far from accurate. Butcher
meat is put on a par with wheat, although with the mass of

the population it does not form a fifth part of the consumption. Each of the twelve miscellaneous articles, whether poultry or cattle, are considered of equal importance, and manufactures of every sort are omitted. There are, besides, a number of inaccuracies in the authorities from which the table is compiled.

Comparison of the 17*th and* 18*th Centuries.* — Bishop Fleetwood, whose inquiries, in regard to the particular period to which he confined them, were very accurate; and Dr. Henry, the author of the History of England, both exhibit results very different from Sir George Shuckburgh. From these Mr. Young attempted an estimate on the following plan.

	17th Century.			18th Century.			Rise per Cent.
	£	s.	d.	£	s.	d.	
Wheat - - -	1	18	2	1	18	7	Par.
Barley and oats - -	1	9	5½	2	0	0½	33
Butcher meat, butter, cheese, or whatever is the produce of grass land - - -	0	1	9	0	2	3	28½
Labour - - -	0	0	10¾	0	1	3	46¼
Wool - - -	1	9	1½	0	17	8¼	39½ fall.
Iron - - -	0	0	1½	0	0	1¾	16½ rise.
Coals - - -	1	5	10½	1	16	0	39¼

Repeating wheat five times, on account of its importance, barley and oats twice, the produce of grass land four times, labour five times, and reckoning wool, coals, and iron, each but once, while iron is considered the representative of all manufactures, the rise from the prices of one century to those of the other will amount to no more than 22½ per cent.; or only the tenth part of the rise stated by Sir George Shuckburgh.

Manufactures. — Under the important head of metals, and particularly of iron, Mr. Y. found that the rise for several centuries had been inconsiderable, the improvements in the process of preparing them sufficing, in a great measure, to counterbalance the enhancement of labour. But the great argument against Sir G. Shuckburgh's alle-

gation of general depreciation is to be found in the price of
manufactures, in the production of which, far more than
in agriculture, free scope is given to the application of all
the auxiliaries called forth by the progress of society; we
mean increase of capital, division of labour, and aid from
machinery.   The following short list is taken from the
books of Greenwich Hospital.

Average of the Years from			Shoes.		Stockings.		Hats.		Proportions in twenty, when taken collectively.
			s. d.		s. d.		s. d.		
1729 to 1765	-	-	3	11	1	7	2	2¾	14½
1770 to 1785	-	-	3	10	1	5½	2	3½	14
1770 to 1800	-	-	4	7½	1	5¾	2	4	15¾
1790 to 1800	-	-	4	6½	1	6	2	4	15½
1805 to 1810	-	-	5	5	2	2	3	0	20

These are articles of subordinate importance; but the
fact is, that in almost all manufactured commodities, we are
supplied cheaper than our ancestors, and that a rise, when
it has taken place, is to be ascribed either to a tax on the
raw commodity, or to some cause which may be termed
particular or incidental.   In regard to the *quality* of our
manufactures, we must speak with more hesitation, and can
hardly decide whether the balance be in favour of the present or of a former age; for if our fabrics are now much
more neat and convenient, they are in a considerable degree less durable.

Horses and Cattle.—In these the improvement in point
of quality admits of no doubt.   In comparing the present
price of sheep and oxen with those of a century ago, a great
part of the difference is to be ascribed to the inferior size of
the animal, at a time when the art of grazing was not understood; the same will be found to hold in regard to horses,
and at a later date than is commonly imagined.   The only
quarter affording authentic information in regard to the
price of horses is the War Office, from the records of which
Mr. Young extracted the following averages.

Years.				Price.		
				£	s.	d.
1766 and 1767	-	-	-	21	0	0
From 1768 to 1792, both inclusive			-	23	2	0
1793 to 1802	-	-	-	26	5	0
1803 to 1812	-	-	-	26	5	0

The rise of price in this period of forty-six years was much less than might have been supposed from the rate paid by individuals. But the War Office, looking chiefly to strength and the power of standing fatigue, bought, throughout the whole period, horses of nearly equal value. Private purchasers were not so easily satisfied; and of the higher prices so generally paid by them, a considerable part is to be ascribed to a size and beauty in the animal which half a century before was comparatively rare.

Sketch of the progressive Rise of Prices since the Thirteenth Century, taking 20 *for the Integer or highest Sum, and exhibiting the other Parts by their proportion to it.* (*Abstracted from a Table of Arthur Young.*)

Periods.	Wheat.	Beef and Pork, from the Books of the Victualling Office.	Labour.	Manufactures at Greenwich Hospital.	Population.	Trade, calculated from our Exports.
13th Century -	$5\frac{1}{2}$	—	$3\frac{1}{2}$	—	—	—
14th ditto - -	$6\frac{1}{4}$	—	$4\frac{3}{4}$	—	—	—
15th ditto - -	3	—	$5\frac{1}{2}$	—	—	—
16th ditto - -	6	—	$5\frac{1}{2}$	—	—	—
17th ditto - -	$9\frac{1}{4}$	—	8	—	—	—
18th ditto - -	$9\frac{1}{4}$	—	$12\frac{1}{2}$	—	—	—
66 years from 1701 to 1766 - -	$7\frac{3}{4}$	$7\frac{1}{4}$	10	$14\frac{1}{2}$	11	$5\frac{1}{3}$
23 ditto from 1767 to 1789 - -	11	11	$12\frac{1}{2}$	14	$13\frac{1}{2}$	$8\frac{1}{4}$
34 ditto from 1767 to 1800 - -	12	$12\frac{1}{3}$	14	$15\frac{3}{4}$	$15\frac{3}{4}$	11
14 ditto from 1790 to 1803 - -	13	17	$16\frac{3}{4}$	$15\frac{1}{2}$	$18\frac{3}{4}$	$15\frac{1}{2}$
7 ditto from 1804 to 1810 - -	20	20	20	20	20	20

*Annual Consumption of Gold and Silver for Plate, orna-
mental Manufacture, and Furniture.* — Calculations of this
nature have hitherto been founded on returns from towns
which, like Geneva, were remarkable for the manufacture
of watches, or like Paris and Birmingham, for gilding,
trinkets, and other ornamental fabrics. At present, however, we are inclined to draw our inferences from a wider
field, from a calculation of the probable amount of individual income founded on the public burdens of this and
other countries. If we refer to our property-tax returns
during the war, and make allowance, on the one hand, for
the reduction of income, on the other, for the increase of
numbers that have since taken place, we shall find reason
to estimate the number of

Families in England, Scotland, and Wales, pos-
    sessing 200*l.* a year and upwards, at - - - 100,000
And taking our island as representing, in point
    of such incomes, a fourth of the civilized world,
    we add for the latter, that is, for the rest of
    Europe and the United States of America - 300,000

                                   Together - - - 400,000

Families whose incomes are between
    60*l.* and 200*l.* a year amount in
    Great Britain to nearly - - -   400,000
Add for the rest of Europe and the
    United States of America - - 1,200,000

                                 Together - - - - 1,600,000

Now a consumption on the part of the former
    class at the conjectural average of 10*l.* a
    family annually, would give - - - - £4,000,000
The same for the second class at the rate of
    somewhat less than 2*l.* per family - - - 3,000,000
Add for the consumption of the lower orders
    in watches, ear-rings, buckles, &c. - - - 1,000,000

                              Total - - - - £8,000,000

These large sums include loss by accident and
    wear ; but, as a considerable amount of old
    plate or old manufacture is annually melted
    and wrought up, we deduct as *not forming
    a demand on the mines* - - - - - - 2,000,000

Remainder, being the conjectural amount of
   specie from the mines annually required for
   plate and ornamental manufacture or furniture -   -   -   -   -   - £6,000,000

Comparative Expence of France and England. — Notwithstanding our great intercourse with the Continent of
late years, the public are not yet in possession of a correct
comparison of the expence of living in France and England.
Nothing is more vague and unsatisfactory than the notices
on this subject in books of travels, proceeding, as they generally do, from persons who have little idea of comprehensive calculation, and who allow themselves to dwell with
undue emphasis on a few particular points in which France
happens to differ materially from England. Such persons
seldom make allowance for a countervailing tendency in
other items of the account. The proper mode is to frame
a general table, including not only provisions, house-rent,
fuel, wages, but manufactures, and professional charges.
After ascertaining these material points, there will remain
to be made a distinction between different periods : thus,
during the war, particularly in the latter years, the difference
between the two countries was very great, 100*l.* in France
being equivalent to 140*l.* or 150*l.* in England. Since the
peace, this difference has progressively decreased, the fall
of prices in France, though not inconsiderable, being much
inferior to that which has taken place in England. A comparison made in 1819 would have exhibited 100*l.* in France
as equal to fully 130*l.* in England; at present (1823) it
would not exceed the proportion of 100*l.* to 120*l.*

After attending to these preliminaries, the progress of
comparison becomes less difficult, and, by balancing one
point against another, is made to assume, at last, a clear
and simple form. Thus, as to the respective capitals, Paris
being inferior in water communication incurs a greater
enhancement than London in the conveyance of bulky
commodities, such as corn, coal, wood; while, in respect to
number of consumers, the cause of enhancement is considerably less, the population of the French metropolis being
less than two-thirds of that of ours. These causes may be
said to neutralize each other; and the inferences are, —

First, that Paris is as much dearer than the provincial
part of France, as London is dearer than the provincial part
of England.

Secondly, that the proportion mentioned above as constituting the difference with England, viz. 30 per cent. in 1819, and 20 per cent. at present, is applicable to the two countries throughout, provided we confine our parallel to places similarly circumstanced, comparing Paris with London, and Touraine or Lower Normandy, each about 150 miles from Paris, with Shropshire, Derbyshire, or other counties, at a similar distance from London.

Another point to which travellers are seldom sufficiently attentive is, that the degree of difference between one province and another, and even between one country on the Continent and another, is much smaller than it at first appears. Take, for example, the north and south of France, countries very different in climate, produce, and habits. At first the south appears much cheaper, affording in abundance wine, fruit, and other articles, for which we are made to pay so extravagantly in England; but these, on a closer examination, are found to be counterbalanced by the price of corn always higher there than in the northern districts of France. Again, the lower wages of labour, in a backward province like Brittany, make a very slight difference ultimately, when we take into account the inferiority of the labourers. Similar remarks are applicable to Germany, Italy, Switzerland: in none of these countries are the amount of taxation, the interest of money, the state of husbandry, or any of the main constituents of price so materially different as to cause any great difference in the expence of living. Accordingly, after all the assertions and exaggerations of travellers, the distinctions on the Continent are little more than

1. That provincial towns are considerably less expensive than capitals.

2. That by living in a petty town, or in the country, a farther reduction of expence may be accomplished, but with a greater sacrifice of comfort, a greater removal from business and society, than is implied by a country residence in England.

3. That in consequence of the want of water communication, the price of bulky commodities, such as corn or wood, varies more in the provinces of the Continent than in the counties of England; still the difference is less great than is often asserted, (Edinburgh Review, Vol. LXIV. p. 362.) land carriage on the Continent being moderate in consequence of the insignificance of tolls and turnpike dues.

4. That taking France as the representative of the Continent at large in point of expence, the difference with

England, great during the war, (particularly from 1809 to
1814), is at present not more than 20 per cent.; any disburse beyond that proportion being attributable, not to
difference of prices, but to additional comfort or luxury on
our side.

To what degree did a difference of prices exist between
France and England prior to the French Revolution?
Our materials for such a comparison are far from complete:
the tables collected by the late Arthur Young in 1789 indicate a considerable inferiority of price, but the articles
quoted are chiefly agricultural; and had manufactures
been included, the general result would have been less unfavourable to England. If we revert to a prior date, such
as the middle of the last century, we shall find reason to
consider the two countries nearly on a par. At that time
England was not much more heavily taxed than France,
nor were our manufactures or corn dearer, for both were
articles of export. The result accordingly is, that prior to
1760 the only material distinction between the two countries consisted in the style of living; the proportion of
English population in towns being even then considerably
greater, and the inhabitants consequently requiring comforts little known or thought of in the provincial part of
France.

Mr. M'Culloch, in his " Essay on reducing the Interest
on our National Debt," published in 1816, maintains, in
contradiction to common opinion, that the rise in the price
of corn on the Continent during the last half century has,
on the whole, been inconsiderable. He goes into the question at great length, treating in succession of France, Spain,
Italy, and the countries on the Baltic, and adducing several
cogent arguments in opposition to those who maintain,
that there took place on the Continent a rise of prices
nearly correspondent to the rise in this country. His conclusions are, that in France there was *no rise* in the price
of corn: that in Italy the rise was a consequence of the extension given to the freedom of trade; and that the partial
advance which he admits to have taken place in Russia
and Poland was a necessary result of the degree of improvement introduced in the present age into these very
backward countries. To this statement we have merely
to offer the qualifications naturally arising from a state of
war. In the long period from 1793 to 1814 every state on
the Continent was either engaged in hostilities, or obliged
to increase its taxes and military establishment. In all these

was felt a portion of the activity or excitement so conspicuous in England during the war, followed in all by a stagnation similar, though not equal in degree, to that which we have experienced since the peace. The consequence was, that prices rose during one period and fell in the other; but to ascertain the extent of change is a matter of great difficulty, there being few official returns in any part of the Continent, and the question being somewhat perplexed by the circulation of government paper so general during the war. On the whole, however, there took place, in family expenditure, calculated on a comprehensive plan, and including along with corn and butcher meat, wages, house-rent, fuel, &c. a rise of from 25 to 30 per cent. on the prices of 1792; a rise which has, in a great measure, disappeared in the continued reduction since the peace.

In forming conclusions on the price of corn, allowance ought evidently to be made for particular causes operating in particular countries: — thus, in France, the abolition of tithe, and the sale of the church lands, promoted tillage to a degree which nearly counteracted the rise of labour attendant on the war.

Annual Expence of the family of an Agricultural Labourer, supposed to consist of 5⅓ persons ; being an average of the expence of 65 families of labourers, in different parts of England, collected by Sir F. Eden, in 1796.

	£	s.	d.
Provisions (as dear then as in 1823) - -	£27	1	8
Rent - - - - - - -	1	13	3
Fuel and candles - - - - -	2	10	7
Clothes and washing - - - -	4	18	0
Contingencies - - - - - -	0	10	10
	£36	14	4

The same table, adapted to the present time by an addition of 25 per cent. to the respective heads of expence, with the exception of provisions.

	£	s.	d.
Provisions - - - - - -	£27	1	8
Rent - - - - - - -	2	1	7
Fuel and candles - - - - -	3	3	3
Clothes and light - - - - -	6	2	6
Contingencies - - - - - -	0	13	7
	£39	2	7

Table comprising articles of general consumption, to each of which is affixed the probable amount of money expended on on it by the public, referred to in the text, p. 333.

Articles.	Quantity consumed.	Average price.	Expended by the public on each article.
Produce of the Soil.	Qrs.	*s.*	£
Wheat - - - - -	12,000,000	50	50,000,000
Barley (used chiefly in the brewery and distillery) - -	7,200,000	25	9,000,000
Oats (the portion appropriated to human food) - - -	10,000,000	20	10,000,000
Butcher meat and animal food generally - -	—	—	35,000,000
Manufactures.			
The following sums representing the value, *exclusive of exports*, are, of course, considerably below the total of the value annually prepared - -	—	—	—
Woollens - - -	—	—	22,000,000
Cottons, (the exports exceed 20,000,000*l.*) - - -	—	—	20,000,000
Linen - - - -	—	—	15,000,000
Silk - - - - -	—	—	8,000,000
Leather - - -	—	—	15,000,000
Hardware - - -	—	—	9,000,000
Foreign Articles, such as			
Sugar - - -	—	—	9,000,000
Tea - - - - -	—	—	8,000,000
Various other articles of sufficient importance to be specified, and the amount of which it would probably be practicable to ascertain from official documents -	—	—	100,000,000
A multiplicity of articles of less importance, which being in a great measure superfluities, and dependent for their consumption on the taste of individuals, require to be noticed no farther than by assigning to them collectively their proportion to the aggregate: this proportion we shall at present suppose to be about 17 per cent., or - -	—	—	60,000,000
Total annual consumption - -	—	—	350,000,000

Such is, or rather would be when completed, a table of our annual consumption at the present time. In framing or correcting such a table, we have evidently to consider two main points ; the quantities consumed, and the price. As to quantity, a variation can take place only with increase of population or change of habits, and any alteration of that kind must be so gradual, that we run very little hazard in assuming a similarity of amount during a given period, which, for the sake of precision, we shall suppose to be five years. As to price, the case is different; the produce of the soil may, from casualty in the season, rise 10 or 20 per cent., while our manufactures may experience a fall. The result, as far as founded on prices, must therefore undergo some change annually : for the sake of illustration we shall suppose in one year a change differing in different articles, but ending in an average rise of 5 per cent. : thus, —

Articles.	Quantity consumed.	Average price.	Expended by the public on each article.
Produce of the soil computed on the same quantities ; but with an addition of 10 *per cent. to the prices.*	Qrs.	*s.*	£
Wheat - - -	12,000,000	55	33,000,000
Barley - -	7,200,000	27	9,000,000
Oats - - -	10,000,000	22	11,000,000
Butcher meat and animal food enhanced in the same proportion - - -	—	—	38,500,000
Manufactures ; here we suppose a decrease of 5 per cent. : thus,			
Woollens - - -	—	—	19,000,000
Cottons - - -	—	—	11,400,000
Linen - - -	—	—	14,250,000
Silk - - -	—	—	7,600,000
Leather - - -	—	—	14,250,000
Hardware - -	—	—	8,500,000
Foreign articles.			
Sugar the same - -	—	—	9,000,000
Tea the same - -	—	—	8,000,000
In the other component parts of the table the fluctuations are supposed to change the amount of 170,000,000*l.* to -	—	—	181,100,000
Total -			367,500,000

The final change supposed in this statement is that 105*l.* are required to effect the purchases for which 100*l.* sufficed in the preceding year. We proceed next to the

Apportionment of the respective Articles in the former Table.

Articles consumed.	Expenditure on each Article.	Proportion of the expenditure on each article to the total expenditure of the public, calculated in parts of 100.
	£	
Wheat - - - -	30,000,000	8.57
Barley - - -	9,000,000	2.57
Oats - - - -	10,000,000	2.85
Butcher meat and all animal food - -	35,000,000	10.
Woollens - - - -	20,000,000	5.71
Linen - - - -	15,000,000	4.28
Leather - - - -	15,000,000	4.28
Cottons - - -	12,000,000	3.42
Silk - - - -	8,000,000	2.28
Hardware - - - -	9,000,000	2.57
Sugar - - - -	9,000,000	2.57
Tea - - - -	8,000,000	2.28
All other heads of national consumption	170,000,000	48.62
Total -	350,000,000	100

To those who apprehend complexity in such calculations, we would observe, that the details would rest with persons employed for the purpose; and that the public would require to know only the result, which, as in the present returns of the averages of sugar and corn, might be communicated in a few sentences.

Ought a Table of National Consumption to comprise the smaller Heads of Expenditure? — To calculate the smaller items of expenditure would be a task of great difficulty, and, as far as we can judge, of little utility, since it is easy to make an allowance for the proportion omitted. Besides, we ought to introduce into the table no sum of which the accuracy is not ascertained with considerable confidence from official documents, and of which the importance is not such as to reward the labour of enquiry and comparison. Were the articles enumerated to form only 50 per cent. of the total national consumption, the result, supposing them to be articles of general use, would afford a very fair scale for comparing the prices of different years. A table complete in all its parts would, doubtless, be preferable; but as the heads of our public offices, like our individual enquirers, are as yet in only an early stage of statistical research, a considerable time must elapse ere their materials acquire a finished form.

In the case of the lower orders, a knowledge of the cost of a few great heads of expenditure, such as corn, coarse clothing, beer, fuel, would be found sufficient. There ought evidently to be a material difference in the plan of a table for them and of one for their superiors, a consideration which leads us to another query in this interesting but somewhat intricate discussion.

How far are particular Tables required for particular Classes? — A scale formed on the table in the text is adapted to very many persons in the middle and upper classes, —to the receivers of annuities, whether from the public funds or mortgages, —the landlord who depends on his rent, — the clerk who depends on his salary. But in regard to several of the classes currently termed productive, the question is different, as will appear from a reference to a specific case, such as that of

Farmers on Lease. — The situation of the farmer on lease, though materially affected by the value of money in purchases generally, depends still more on the price of the produce he raises ;—of corn, if his occupancy be chiefly under the plough ; of butcher meat, butter, cheese, if it be chiefly grass land.   Leases ought thus to be drawn with a reference to the market price of produce, computed on the average of a series of years.   Or, if a regulator of a more comprehensive character be desired, the price of the produce might be combined with a table of the price of commodities generally, (Appendix, p. [95]) taking the latter as the basis ; but modifying its result by repeating the price of corn or of butcher meat a certain number of times, so as to give due weight to these main constituents of the income of the lessee.

The average rate of labour, an object of the first importance in farming, might, in like manner, be added to the table, and repeated several times.

Mines. — In an undertaking of this nature, the profit evidently depends on two points : the market price of the articles produced (whether coal, iron, tin, or copper) ; and the average rate of the labour by means of which it is rendered saleable.   There are thus two ways of stipulating the conditional amount of the rent : by a table confined to the rate of labour and the price of the article produced ; or by a table of the price of commodities generally, (as in p. [95]) with such repetitions of the rate of labour, or price of the article produced, as the contracting parties might think expedient.

Tithe. — The case of tithe is different from that of rent. It is evidently more convenient to clergymen that the price of commodities generally should be the standard, tnan the price of agricultural produce. The latter determines, it is true, the ability of the payers of tithe; but as the payers are many, and the receivers comparatively few, as that which to the latter forms the whole of income is to the former only a portion of their disburse, the circumstances of the clergy have a claim to prior consideration : that is, without showing the slightest partiality to either party, equity suggests that the regulation of clerical income should be made with a view to the value of money in the purchase of commodities generally, and not exclusively in the purchase of corn, which can form hardly a fifth of their expenditure.

It would be no difficult task to suggest farther modifications for different lines of business; but to enter into detail seems wholly unnecessary, since every thing in the proposed plan is voluntary, and may be adopted or omitted as may suit the interest, or imagined interest, of the contracting parties. We shall, therefore, take leave of the question, after answering, by anticipation, a few objections, as follows : —

1. *Need there be any apprehension of a combination to produce undue returns of prices for the purpose of affecting the standard of particular contracts ?* — Attempts of that nature are very little to be dreaded in so extensive a country as this : they could be effectual only if undertaken throughout the whole kingdom, and persevered in during a series of years; a course which would suppose a command of capital, and a degree of concealment, wholly at variance with probability.

2. *Would a measure of this nature be likely to affect the sale price of other property, in particular of lands and houses ?* — The majority of fund-holders are, as we shall explain subsequently, permanent depositors; strangers to the manœuvres of the Stock Exchange, and almost as little inclined as our landholders to engage in speculative sales and purchases. But there is another class, persons retiring from business, succeeding to property, or having, from any other cause, funds of which they are desirous to make the investment. To these persons stock would, by the measure in contemplation, be rendered more eligible as a permanent

deposit, and the motives for purchasing landed property would in some degree be lessened. But the complaint of the country gentlemen does not regard inadequacy of sale price: instead of the 26 or 27 years' purchase to which they were accustomed during the war, land will now sell for 34 or 35 years' purchase: their *desideratum* is an assured income, — relief from present pressure; and such, to a certain extent, would be the result of the proposed measure.

3. It may be objected to our table, that " it does not comprise any heads of expenditure, except those represented by commodities;" while a considerable part of the disburse of the middle classes (not less than a third), is of another description, as appears from the concluding line in the following sketch:

	Proportions in 100 of each head of expence.
Provisions	33
Clothing and washing	18
Fuel and light	6
House rent	10
Other charges, namely, wages, assessed taxes, education, medical attendance, &c.	33
	100

To the objection that might be founded on a statement like this, our answer would be, that the money paid for wages, education, professional aid, &c. is ultimately expended on commodities; and were the case otherwise, there seems no necessity that a scale should comprise *all* the items of expenditure.

Extract of a Letter to the Author from a respectable Farmer in Hampshire, dated June 1. 1823.

" During the low prices of last autumn, I was led to consider of the plan suggested in your book for regulating the wages of my labourers, by a reference to the price of their subsistence, in other words, to the market price of corn. This plan met, at first, with considerable opposition, but the equity of it became, in the course of a few weeks, so apparent, as to remove all objections. My rule was to take the rate of wages (7s. a week) currently given in my neighbourhood, to explain to how much wheat this was equivalent, and to pay my people in wheat or in money, at their option. They soon preferred the former, to the extent of their consumption, and took in money only what they required for their lesser purchases. On taking an average of their weekly receipts, during the winter, and reckoning them in wheat, on the plan adopted by Mr. Barton, and stated in your book, (in the chapter on Poor Laws), I find it to have been about 80 pints of wheat, which forms a kind of medium of the wages of the country labourer, computed in wheat for the last seventy years.

" This was found sufficient for the maintenance of the families of my labourers, which averaged five persons: viz. the man, his wife and three children. During the whole winter none of my labourers, who were from 16 to 18 in number, had recourse to the parish.

" My inference is that 80 pints of wheat, or its value in money, would form a fair permanent rate of wages for the country labourers throughout all that part of England in which wheat is the usual food of the country people."

On high and low Prices since 1792. *By Thomas Tooke, Esq. Part I.*—It was after writing our chapter on the Rise of Prices during the War, that Mr. Tooke's Treatise fell into our hands. This First Part relates chiefly to the effect of the currency, and Mr. T. maintains that the bullionists over-rate greatly the effect on prices of the substitution of bank paper for coin; while their opponents are almost equally erroneous in refusing to admit a partial enhancement (about 20 per cent. in the latter years of the war) arising from that cause. He is not disposed to allow that the war had so great or general an effect on prices as has been supposed : the rise of corn he attributes chiefly to an extra-proportion of indifferent seasons ; and after recapitulating the events affecting other commodities of consequence, such as cotton, sugar or wool, his inference is, that the fluctuation in the price of each depended less on any general cause than on circumstances of *demand and supply peculiar to the particular article.* He steers a middle course throughout, and concludes (p. 201.) by reminding the bullionists of the remarkable fact, that money was less abundant during the bank restriction than at present, when prices are so much lower; while, on the other hand, he assures the agriculturists that as the fall of prices since 1819 may be explained by favourable seasons, they may safely forbear their complaints against Mr. Peel's Bill.

This publication is valuable as a collection of materials, as a specimen of reasoning founded on specific documents, instead of the *mania* for generalizing, so common in the present age.

APPENDIX

TO

CHAPTER XI.

On Finance.

S_{INKING} *Fund.* — On this subject a few explanatory paragraphs may be acceptable to those of our readers who are not initiated in the mysteries of the Treasury or Stock Exchange.

The Supplies constituting our Sinking Fund. — The complex form of our budget, and the appearance of inviolability given to the sinking fund, may induce persons in common life to imagine that that fund derived part of its income from taxes vested in the commissioners, and managed by them without reference to the rest of the revenue. The appropriation, however, never went so far: the income of the sinking fund, paid to the commissioners at the bank, arose chiefly from —

1st. The 1,000,000*l.* (increased in 1792 to 1,200,000*l.*) annually payable out of the general revenue.

2d. The dividends of redeemed stock, which, standing in the name of the Sinking Fund Commissioners, were considered as entitled to interest at the quarterly payments at the Bank, in the same manner as the rest of the public debt.

3d. The surplus interest provided on contracting each loan since 1793. This provision, adopted by Mr. Pitt on the suggestion of Dr. Price, will be understood by supposing that the loan for a particular year is 10,000,000*l.*, at 5 per cent., for which stock given in the 5 per cents. at par involves an annual charge of 500,000*l.* Now the plan was, to provide taxes yielding, not 500,000*l.*, but 600,000*l.*

a year, the 100,000*l.* forming a fund for the gradual extinction of the principal — a purpose which in the case in question would be accomplished in 37 years.

The merits or demerits of this plan of surplus interest are now only matters of historical curiosity, the season of loans being past, or at least suspended. The question, however, is not merely arithmetical ; it is in a great measure similar to that of the expediency or inexpediency of war taxes ; and if the war was a season of large profits, it was evidently politic to make it bear as large a portion as possible of our burdens. It is in a consideration of this nature, and not in the imaginary advantage of compound interest, that we are to seek for a justification of the measure of providing a surplus revenue ; we mean for a counterpoise to the sacrifice with which it may easily be shewn to have been attended.

The nominal Sinking Fund. — Our sinking fund exhibited until the late change a surplus, which, for illustration, we shall call 17,000,000*l.*, and the revenue at the same time a deficiency which we shall term 12,000,000*l.* It was for some time a question whether the better plan was to leave the 17,000,000*l.* to operate in weekly purchases for the redemption of stock, and supply the revenue deficiency by a loan, or to adopt the more simple course of receiving from the sinking fund the 12,000,000*l.*, and confining the redemption purchases of the commissioners to 5,000,000*l.* This gave rise to considerable discussion after 1815, the former plan being maintained by the converts to the doctrine of compound interest, the believers in the arithmetical wonders of Dr. Price. But in 1819 ministers consented to adopt the latter course, and found in it (see Ricardo on the Funding System, in Napier's Supplement to the Encyclopædia Britannica,) a degree of advantage which may be said to have given the first blow to the complex plan of paying with one hand, while we borrowed with the other.

The topic was again brought under discussion in the session of 1822, in the debates on the plan for converting our half-pay and pensions into long annuities. On that occasion Mr. Vansittart, unwilling to part with the semblance after he had relinquished the substance of the sinking fund, urged for a time the expediency of making the requisite loans from the public, but was at last persuaded to follow the direct course, and to admit of the loans being made from the portion of revenue at his disposal. This plan has been confirmed by Mr. Robinson; so that the sinking fund is now divested of its complexity, and brought back to a form from which, as far as we can judge, it ought never to have been made to deviate, — that of the balance of current revenue applied to the redemption of stock.

Comparison of our present Burdens with those of 1792.

Amount of taxation, tithe, and poor-rate, in Great Britain and Ireland in 1792 -	£22,000,000
The increase of our population since then (nearly 50 per cent.) enables us, without additional pressure on the individual, to bear a farther burden of - - -	11,000,000
Continental countries, our competitors in productive industry, having, in general, increased their burdens in a ratio somewhat greater than their population, we are justified (see Chap. IX. p. 280.) in regarding a corresponding increase on our part as not detrimental to our foreign trade. We add, on this account, a sum of -	5,000,000
The money in which taxes were paid in 1792 being, when compared with our present currency, as 100 to 130 in value, we make a corresponding insertion of - -	10,000,000
on the ground that, to that extent, the excess of our present taxation over that of 1792, *is nominal.*	
Amount of burden which can be borne by us at present, without greater disadvantage, in comparison with other countries, than we experienced in 1792 - - -	£48,000,000

Our actual burdens are (see App. p. [84]) 64,000,000*l.* We have here assumed the increase of population as the measure of the increase of national wealth, arising from our various improvements in agriculture, manufacture, navigation, &c. This proportion will be deemed considerably below the mark by the majority of those who write or think on such subjects, whether it be the convert to Mr.

Gray's doctrine, (p. 236.) that in the progress of society individual income increases in a *larger ratio* than population, or the practical observer, who founds his calculation on the surprising improvements in agriculture, manufacture, and productive industry generally, during the last thirty years. These arguments rest, doubtless, on a very substantial basis, and nothing but the unfortunate fluctuations in individual property, attendant on our rapid transitions, would have prevented us from inserting a larger sum (probably 16 or 18,000,000, instead of 11,000,000*l*.) as the measure of the increase of national wealth, arising from our improvements.

The Malt Tax.—The hopes of the agriculturists were at one time excited by the expected repeal of a large share of the duty on malt; but, while we sympathize with their sufferings and anxiously desire a diminution of their tithe and poor-rate, we cannot help expressing a doubt of the expediency of any great reduction of taxation on an article already so much cheapened by the fall of the materials. Sudden changes are to be avoided; malt liquor comes only in some respects under the description of a necessary of life; and the extended cultivation of barley that might have been prompted by a reduction of duty, would probably have prevented any material rise in the price.

Prices of Commodities a Century ago. Text, p. 379.—In comparing our present national income with that of the last century, we have assumed the power of money in the purchase of commodities as less at present by 30 per cent. than in the reign of George I., or in any period of last century prior to 1792. This allowance is ample when we take into account that prices have fallen since 1820, and that the prospect of war, at least of such a war as would be productive of general enhancement, seems very remote. On this interesting topic we have given a short table in page [7] of the Appendix. Those who dissent from this opinion, and who imagine money to have been formerly of much greater value, will do well to recollect that many manufactures are now cheaper than in that age, and that *corn is very little dearer.* The chief difference, in fact, is in professional fees, salaries, and wages, all raised during the war, and not yet brought to a level like the price of produce, manufactures, or whatever is regulated at an open market.

Then as to the charges of house-keeping in a comprehensive sense, the difference between the present time and
a century ago, resolves itself chiefly into a difference in the
style of living; not unlike the existing difference between
France and England, in which, though the prices of a
number of articles are on a par, the total outlay is less
in France, in consequence of the plainer habits of the
country.

*Historical Parallel of the Revenue of England and France
in* p. 385. *of the Text.*—These sums exhibit the *net* produce
of the taxes, after deducting the expence of collecting ; and
the latter years of the column of England include Scotland
and Ireland.

Backward State of France.

Extract of a letter from Mr. S. Gray to Monsieur J. B. Say,
  printed in 1817 in the Appendix to the volume, entitled
  " All Classes productive."

  " In a visit which I made to your country last year, I
confess I did not find such striking or brilliant results.
Travelling partly with a view to ascertain how far the doctrines, which I had deduced from the facts around me in
our island, as well as from information, agreed with the
facts found in so populous a state as France, I scrutinized
as narrowly as I could the circumstances of the population.
Considering the extension of buildings, and an improvement
in their style, which show the increase of population combined with the concomitant increase of wealth, as the surest
symptoms of a thriving country, I paid particular attention
to your towns and villages in these points, and am sorry to
say, I saw no progress whatever. I have no recollection
of any strictly additional buildings : the only new buildings
which I perceived were in some villages that had been partly
destroyed in the conflicts with the invading armies. In
truth, though we also are suffering from an unusual stagnation, I found, at my return, more new houses going on
in the petty suburb of London, Camden Town, and its
neighbourhood, than I had seen in the whole of my route
through France. Every town and every village seemed
stationary. I own, however, I found much of what I expected, on my principles, from a state so long well peopled.
There was an appearance of wealth, though, in general, it
is true, but of little capital. Your soil is almost universally
under cultivation, but, with some exceptions, in a very inferior style. Your people are generally employed and busy,

yet not very effectively. Though the population of France be to that of England only as about 150 to 230 per square mile, France seems to be at a still more considerable rate behind our island in capital, and the results of active capital. In several statistical points we have got the start of a full century before you."

THE END.